Get the eBook FREE!

(PDF, ePub, Kindle, and liveBook all included)

We believe that once you buy a book from us, you should be able to read it in any format we have available. To get electronic versions of this book at no additional cost to you, purchase and then register this book at the Manning website.

Go to https://www.manning.com/freebook and follow the instructions to complete your pBook registration.

That's it!
Thanks from Manning!

React in Depth

MORTEN BARKLUND

MANNING
SHELTER ISLAND

For online information and ordering of this and other Manning books, please visit
www.manning.com. The publisher offers discounts on this book when ordered in quantity.
For more information, please contact

    Special Sales Department
    Manning Publications Co.
    20 Baldwin Road
    PO Box 761
    Shelter Island, NY 11964
    Email: orders@manning.com

Manning Publications Co.
20 Baldwin Road
PO Box 761
Shelter Island, NY 11964

Development editor: Frances Lefkowitz
Review editor: Kishor Rit
Production editor: Kathy Rossland
Copy editor: Keir Simpson
Proofreader: Katie Tennant
Technical proofreader: Ninoslav Čerkez
Typesetter and cover designer: Marija Tudor

ISBN 9781633437340
Printed in the United States of America

Dedicated to my extraordinary ground crew: my wife and son.
"Behind every great pilot is a great ground crew."
—Unknown

brief contents

contents

preface

Welcome aboard, ace! You're here because you're the best of the best, destined to ascend to the next level of web development mastery. This book isn't just any textbook; it's a dynamic teaching tool packed with practical knowledge and seasoned insights, specifically designed to propel you into the elite ranks of programmers.

I penned this book driven by the same rush a pilot feels when soaring above the clouds at Mach speeds—fueled by a passion for React and a desire to share the strategies that have given me an edge in the digital arena. My transformation began when React revolutionized the way I approached web development, with its modular design and robust features making a profound impact.

Why React? In the high-stakes world of web technologies, React distinguishes itself with its elegant solutions to complex problems. This book goes beyond the surface, diving into sophisticated component patterns and state management with hooks, all delivered through a lens heavily influenced by real-world applications and my personal coding adventures.

As technology surges forward, staying current is crucial. This guide not only covers the fundamentals but also arms you with the latest maneuvers in React, preparing you for the innovations on the horizon, including the cutting-edge features of React 19.

Prepare for a high-flying journey through the React ecosystem. Each chapter is crafted to challenge you, enhance your skills, and inspire your problem-solving strategies. This book is your wingman in the pursuit of excellence in React development, offering battle-tested insights and strategies ready for deployment.

As you progress, consider this book to be your React Top Gun Flight School, in which every lesson sharpens your skills for the ultimate test. The final chapters are not just projects; they are your exams, challenging you to apply everything you've learned to prove yourself as an ace React developer. Success here means not just understanding React but also mastering it, ready to tackle the real-world challenges that await.

Throttle up, pilot. It's time to take to the skies and show what you're made of!

acknowledgments

In the high-stakes world of book publishing, as in an elite flight squadron, every team member plays a pivotal role. I extend my deepest gratitude to my squadron at the publishing house, without whom this mission would not have been a success.

Leading the charge as my development editor, Colonel Frances Lefkowitz was instrumental in navigating this journey. Her strategic insights and steadfast dedication helped sharpen and refine every section of this manuscript, ensuring that my maneuvers were both bold and precise.

Captain Andy Waldron, my acquisitions editor, believed in the vision of this mission from the outset. His guidance through the complex airspace of publishing was invaluable, helping me chart a course that stayed true to my ambitious objectives.

Technical proofreader Ninoslav Čerkez, call sign Eagle Eye, was the vigilant guardian of my technical accuracy. His meticulous attention to detail ensured that the code sequences were not only effective but also flawless, maintaining the integrity of the high-caliber content.

Copy editor Keir Simpson, the linguistic wizard of the squadron, expertly navigated the storm of excessive adverbs that once cluttered my manuscript. With precision and a keen eye, Keir surgically removed unnecessary embellishments, streamlining the text for clarity and punch. His skill in refining my language ensured that every sentence flew straight and true, delivering maximum impact with elegance and efficiency. Thank you, Keir, for keeping my narrative as agile and powerful as a fighter jet.

To the entire ground crew—the production team and the fearless reviewers who dared to challenge and push me further—I owe a debt of gratitude. Your hard work, dedication, and expert navigation were indispensable. You are the unsung heroes of this project; each of you played a crucial role in the seamless execution of our mission.

To all the reviewers—Adam Wan, Amarjit Bhandal, Bernard Fuentes, Brandon Friar, Chris Kardell, Habib Akinwale, Jaehyun Yeom, Jeremy Chen, John McCormack, José Alberto Reyes Quevedo, Karthikeyarajan Rajendran, Keith Kim, Laud Bentil, Lin Zhang, Matthias Cavigelli, Mladen Djuric, Nicolantonio Vignola, Paul Mcilwaine, Richard Vaughan, Rodney Weis, Sankaranarayanan Murugan, Sonja Krause-Harder, and Theo Despoudis—thank you, your suggestions helped make this book better.

Thank you all for your commitment and tireless efforts. Like a meticulously maintained and expertly piloted aircraft, this book could not have soared without you. Together, we've achieved something extraordinary. Let's fly high, knowing that we've equipped countless developers with the knowledge to rule the skies of React development.

about this book

This book is designed to help you master React by providing a mix of foundational knowledge and advanced techniques. It includes a variety of practical examples and exercises that will help you apply what you learn directly to real-world scenarios. Whether you are looking to deepen your understanding of React or expand your development skills, this book will provide the resources and guidance necessary to enhance your proficiency.

Who should read this book

This book is designed for web developers of all kinds. Whether you're working on the frontend or the backend or as a fullstack developer, if you're looking to deepen your expertise in creating both interactive web applications and static sites with modern generators, this book is for you. Ideal readers are already familiar with the fundamentals of React, including JSX, functional components, state management, event handling, and form processing. A solid grasp of HTML, CSS, JavaScript, command-line tools, Git, GitHub, npm, and browser developer tools is also strongly encouraged.

How this book is organized: A road map

This book contains 14 chapters, each building on advanced React concepts and exploring technologies in the React ecosystem. The initial six chapters delve into general advanced React techniques and concepts:

- Chapter 1, "Developer's guide to the React ecosystem," offers a comprehensive overview of the tools and libraries that complement React, helping you navigate and integrate them into your projects effectively.

- Chapter 2, "Advanced component patterns," explores complex patterns for structuring React components, enhancing their reusability and scalability.
- Chapter 3, "Optimizing React performance," focuses on strategies and techniques to boost the efficiency and speed of your React applications.
- Chapter 4, "Better code maintenance with developer tooling," discusses advanced tools that support maintaining and scaling large React codebases.
- Chapter 5, "TypeScript: Next-level JavaScript," shows how TypeScript integrates with React, enhancing type safety and component robustness.
- Chapter 6, "Mastering TypeScript with React," goes deeper into using TypeScript's advanced features to write cleaner, more maintainable React code.

The following five chapters are more specialized, focusing on technologies that enhance React development but are also part of the broader JavaScript ecosystem:

- Chapter 7, "CSS in JavaScript," discusses how CSS-in-JS libraries, such as styled-components, can streamline styling in React applications.
- Chapter 8, "Data management in React," covers advanced state management techniques that help you manage complex data flows in large applications.
- Chapter 9, "Remote data and reactive caching," explores strategies for managing remote data fetching and caching to optimize performance and user experience.
- Chapter 10, "Unit-testing React," provides insights into best practices for testing React components and applications, ensuring reliability and stability.
- Chapter 11, "React website frameworks," examines frameworks such as Next.js and Remix, which extend React's capabilities for server-side rendering and static site generation.

The book concludes with three practical projects that challenge you to apply your accumulated knowledge:

- Chapter 12, "Project: Build an expense tracker with Remix," guides you through the process of creating a complex application, reinforcing your skills with React and Remix.
- Chapter 13, "Project: Create a React UI library," involves developing a set of reusable UI components, demonstrating effective design patterns and practices.
- Chapter 14, "Project: Develop a word game in React," allows you to use React's capabilities for interactive web applications, focusing on state management and UI updates.

Although this book assumes familiarity with the basics of React, it is structured to enhance your understanding of advanced topics, which you can explore in sequence or in an order based on your specific development needs. The final project chapters serve as a comprehensive application of the advanced concepts discussed in the book, providing practical experience and a deeper understanding of React's potential.

About the code

This book contains many examples of source code, both in numbered listings and inline with normal text. In both cases, source code is formatted in a `fixed-width font like this` to separate it from ordinary text.

In many cases, the original source code has been reformatted; we've added line breaks and reworked indentation to accommodate the available page space in the book. In rare cases, even this was not enough, and listings include line-continuation markers (➥). Code annotations accompany many of the listings, highlighting important concepts.

You can get executable snippets of code from the liveBook (online) version of this book at https://livebook.manning.com/book/react-in-depth. The complete code for the examples in the book is available for download from the Manning website at https://www.manning.com/books/react-in-depth and from GitHub at https://github .com/React-in-Depth/react-in-depth. Additionally, you can interact with all examples directly in the browser by visiting https://www.reactindepth.dev/browse.

liveBook discussion forum

Purchase of *React in Depth* includes free access to liveBook, Manning's online reading platform. Using liveBook's exclusive discussion features, you can attach comments to the book globally or to specific sections or paragraphs. It's a snap to make notes for yourself, ask and answer technical questions, and receive help from the author and other users. To access the forum, go to https://livebook.manning.com/book/react-in-depth/discussion. You can also learn more about Manning's forums and the rules of conduct at https://livebook.manning.com/discussion.

Manning's commitment to our readers is to provide a venue where meaningful dialogue between individual readers and between readers and the author can take place. It is not a commitment to any specific amount of participation on the part of the author, whose contribution to the forum remains voluntary (and unpaid). We suggest that you try asking the author some challenging questions lest his interest stray! The forum and the archives of previous discussions will be accessible on the publisher's website as long as the book is in print.

Software requirements

To use and run the examples and projects in this book, you need only three things:

- A command-line environment with a recent version of Node.js and npm installed
- A text editor
- Source code from the repository

That's it! Now let me show you how to set up your command-line environment and select a text editor so you'll be ready for the first exercises in chapter 2.

Command-line environment with Node.js and npm

First, you want to check whether you already have compatible versions of Node.js and npm installed. You need at least Node.js version 12 to use the examples in this book:

- *Windows*
  - Open the command prompt or PowerShell by pressing Windows key+R and typing `cmd` or `powershell` in the Run dialog box.
  - Type `node -v` in the command prompt, and press Enter. If you have Node.js installed, it displays the version number.
- *Mac and Unix-like systems*
  - Open the Terminal app.
  - Type `node -v` in the terminal, and press Return or Enter. If you have Node.js installed, it displays the version number.

If you do not have Node.js installed or if your version is older than 12, please go to https://nodejs.org/en/download, download the proper package for your operating system, and follow the installation instructions. If you're a power user of your operating system, feel free to use any other package manager to install Node.js as long as you get at least version 12.

Text editor

It is likely that you already possess a text editor or have experience using one, given your familiarity with React, which is crucial for making the most of this book. In case you don't have a text editor installed, here are some widely used options that are compatible with most platforms:

- *Sublime Text*—https://www.sublimetext.com/download (free trial)
- *Brackets*—https://brackets.io (open source and free)
- *Visual Studio Code*—https://code.visualstudio.com (free)

Source code

To get started with the examples in this book, you need to set up the source code on your local machine. You can either clone the repository or download a zip file containing all the necessary files. To clone the repository, open your command-line interface, and then execute the following command:

```
git clone https://github.com/React-in-Depth/react-in-depth.git
```

This command copies all the project files from GitHub to your local machine.

If you prefer not to use Git, you can download the entire source code as a zip file from https://www.reactindepth.dev/browse. After the download, extract the files to a directory of your choice.

Next, navigate to the root directory of the project in your command-line interface and run

```
npm install
```

This command installs all dependencies required for the entire monorepo, allowing you to run any example or project in the book.

To run an individual example, use the command

```
npm run dev -w chXX/YYY
```

Replace chXX/YYY with the directory name that corresponds to the chapter and example you want to explore. This command configures Vite to build and serve the specific example.

For the content in chapters 11 and 12 that uses Next.js or Remix instead of Vite, follow the instructions provided in those chapters to set up and execute the examples. These instructions will guide you through using the framework's commands and settings to get the examples running.

By setting up the project as described, you will be equipped to dive into the examples and start experimenting with the advanced React techniques discussed throughout the book.

about the author

 **MORTEN BARKLUND** holds a Master of Science degree in Computer Science and boasts more than two decades of experience in frontend web development. Currently, he is a staff engineer at Corti, a pioneering medical AI startup. Beyond his day job, Morten is deeply involved in the tech community, hosting a local TypeScript meetup, speaking at various conferences, and teaching workshops. This book is Morten's third publication, reflecting his dedication to sharing knowledge and fostering the development of fellow web professionals through practical insights and expert guidance.

about the cover illustration

The figure on the cover of *React in Depth* is "Femme Chingulaise" ("Chingulaise woman"), by Claude Louis Desrais (1787), taken from the Miriam and Ira D. Wallach Division of Art, Prints and Photographs: Picture Collection, New York Public Library.

In those days, it was easy to identify where people lived and what their trade or station in life was by their dress alone. Manning celebrates the inventiveness and initiative of the computer business with book covers based on the rich diversity of regional culture centuries ago, brought back to life by pictures from collections such as this one.

Developer's guide to the React Ecosystem

This chapter covers

- Understanding the concept of React mastery
- Navigating the React ecosystem
- Introducing the React technology stack
- Creating a proper React stack

Greetings, and welcome to *React in Depth*, an essential travel companion for developers who are ready to deepen their expertise and keep pace with the dynamic React community. As you embark on this developmental odyssey, remember that mastering React is more than understanding the basics; it's also about embracing a universe of advanced methodologies, best practices, and evolving tools.

In this inaugural chapter, we chart the territory ahead. I'll introduce the concept of React mastery and guide you through the expansive React ecosystem. You'll learn about the essential components that make up the React technology stack and get a glimpse of how these elements interact to form effective solutions.

Although this chapter sets the stage for understanding, the rest of the book will take you on a deeper dive into selecting and crafting the right technologies and libraries for your projects. By blending theoretical knowledge with practical insights, I aim to equip you with the foundational understanding necessary to navigate the complex landscape of modern web development as a proficient React developer.

1.1 Navigating the React mastery journey

This book assumes that you have a solid understanding of React and are comfortable building simple applications. To explain in very simple terms, you have progressed from A to B in figure 1.1, and this book will take you from B to C. As you can see in the figure, you have a lot more to learn in this segment of the journey.

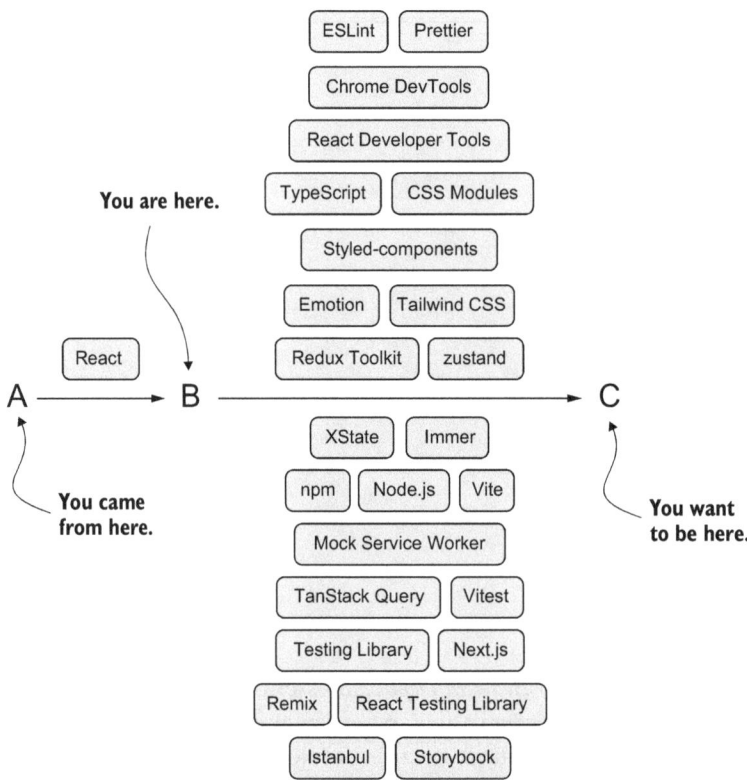

Figure 1.1   You knew how to write static websites using HTML, CSS, and JavaScript. And then you "just" had to learn React to get to your current level. Now you have to learn ESLint, Prettier, Chrome DevTools, React Developer Tools, TypeScript, CSS Modules, styled-components, Emotion, Tailwind CSS, Redux Toolkit, Zustand, XState, Immer, npm, Node.js, Vite, Mock Service Worker, TanStack Query, Vitest, Testing Library, Next.JS, Remix, React Testing Library, Storybook, and Istanbul. That doesn't sound too daunting, does it?

When you arrive at point B, you're probably capable of getting a good job as a junior or midlevel React developer and might even be able to make it to the senior level from there. But to kick-start your advancement and navigate your way forward quicker, let me introduce you to what I call React mastery.

React mastery is more than just writing code that works. It involves understanding best practices, designing applications for scalability and maintainability, and working effectively in a team environment. It requires a deep understanding of React and its ecosystem, as well as knowledge of the latest tools and techniques for building modern web applications.

At its core, React mastery is about building applications that are easy to understand, easy to maintain, and easy to extend, which means writing clean, modular code that can be easily tested and refactored. It means designing applications that can scale to meet the needs of a growing user base without sacrificing performance or stability. It means working collaboratively with other developers to build applications that meet the needs of stakeholders and users alike.

To become a React master, you need to have a solid understanding of React's core concepts and be comfortable working with a wide range of libraries and tools. You should be familiar with common design patterns and architectural principles, and you should be able to apply them to real-world problems. You should also be able to work effectively in a team environment, using version-control systems and agile development methodologies.

This book will teach you all these things. When you've finished it, you will be equipped to build, maintain, and collaborate on high-quality, scalable React applications for organizations of all sizes in all domains.

This opening chapter will dive a bit deeper into the *raison d'être* of this book: why I believe this book needs to exist and why you need to read it. Then we will explore the concepts of the *ecosystem* and *technology stack*—two topics that are very important when it comes to architecting React applications. We'll devote most of this chapter to discussing the ecosystem, how to navigate it, how to apply it, and how to understand any new technology that will inevitably spring to life even after this book has been set in stone (or paper, probably; I don't think we'll publish it on stone tablets).

In the rest of this book, we will explore the key concepts and tools that you need to become a React master. We will cover topics such as tooling, strong typing, data management, remote data access, unit testing, and website frameworks. We will also provide practical examples and real-world simulations to help you apply these concepts in your own work. So let's dive in and get on the road to React mastery!

1.2 Why a book on React mastery?

The truth is, many resources are available for learning React, from great books and online tutorials to official documentation. But few of these resources cover the practical aspects of building large-scale applications with React.

React in Depth is designed to fill this gap by providing a comprehensive guide. Whether you are a frontend developer looking to improve your React skills or a full-stack developer building complex applications, this book has something to offer.

Figure 1.2 shows the crucial knowledge areas that create a well-rounded React developer. What's unique about this book is that it addresses all these areas.

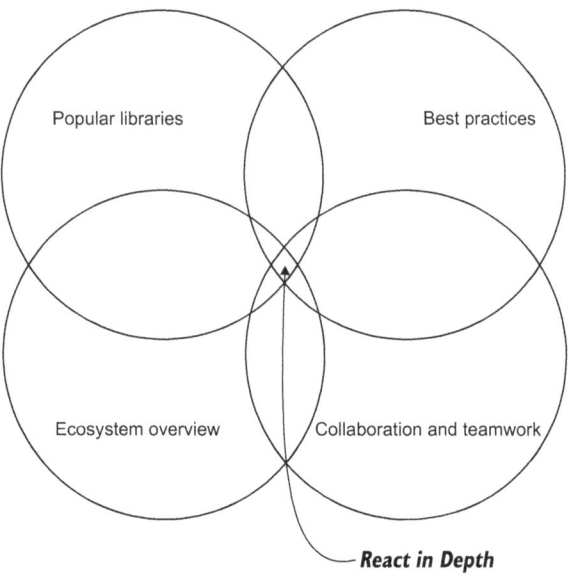

One of the key goals of this book is to help you become a more efficient and effective React developer. We will cover a range of topics that are essential for building high-quality React applications, from data management to testing to website frameworks. By mastering these topics, you will be able to build applications that are more scalable, maintainable, and robust.

Another goal of this book is to provide practical guidance for working in a team environ-

Figure 1.2   This book fits right in the intersection of popular libraries, best practices, ecosystem overview, and collaboration and teamwork.

ment. Building large-scale React applications requires collaboration with other developers, designers, and stakeholders. We will cover best practices for coding guidelines and developer tooling often used on large teams, as well as introduce TypeScript, a new flavor of JavaScript that's used by more and more teams.

Finally, this book aims to provide a road map for ongoing learning and professional development. The React ecosystem is constantly evolving, with new tools and techniques emerging all the time. I will provide guidance on staying up to date with the latest developments in React and improving your skills over time. Whether you are just starting with React at an advanced level or are already an experienced developer, this book will help you take your skills to the next level.

1.3   How does this book teach React mastery?

The scope of this book is broad, covering a range of topics related to React development, including libraries commonly used with React, data management, remote data, unit testing, and website frameworks. I'll cover each of these topics in detail, giving you the knowledge and skills you need to tackle real-world projects.

The focus of this book is on practical, hands-on development. Although I'll provide some background and theory on each topic, my main goal is to help you learn by doing. Each chapter includes a series of examples, and the book concludes with three complex projects that allow you to apply what you've learned and build your own React applications from scratch.

Throughout the book, I'll also emphasize best practices and common pitfalls to avoid. I want you to come away with not just a deeper understanding of React but also with the ability to build high-quality, maintainable applications that can stand up to the demands of real-world development. You can see your journey ahead in figure 1.3.

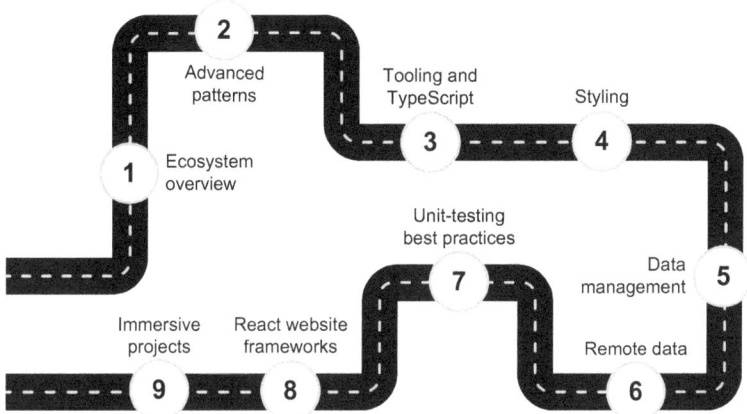

Figure 1.3 **Your journey to React mastery starts with the first step. These steps represent nine realms of React that will be covered in this book, with one or two chapters dedicated to each.**

Overall, this book is designed to help you become a master in the field of React development, equipped with the skills and knowledge you need to tackle any project with confidence.

1.4 *The React ecosystem*

The React ecosystem is a vast collection of libraries and tools built around the React library. As the popularity of React has grown, so has the number of tools and libraries that developers can use to enhance their workflows and improve the performance and functionality of their React applications.

One of the most significant advantages of using React is the sheer number of libraries available for it. These libraries cover a wide range of use cases, from data management and routing to animation and testing. Many of these libraries have become essential parts of the React developer's toolkit, and understanding how they work and how to use them effectively is a critical part of modern-day React development.

In this book, we will explore many of the most popular and useful libraries and tools in the React ecosystem. The book covers libraries for everything from styling to state management.

It's worth noting that not all libraries in the React ecosystem are created equal, and not all of them are necessary for every project. For those reasons, we will focus on the most commonly used libraries and tools, providing guidance on how to evaluate and choose the right libraries for your specific project needs.

By the end of this book, you will have a solid understanding of the React ecosystem and the libraries and tools available within it. You will be able to confidently choose the right libraries for your projects, and you will have the skills and knowledge necessary to build complex, high-performance React applications.

1.4.1   What's in the ecosystem?

To give you an idea of the enormity of the current React ecosystem, take a look at figure 1.4, which lists more than 150 tools and libraries currently being used with React.

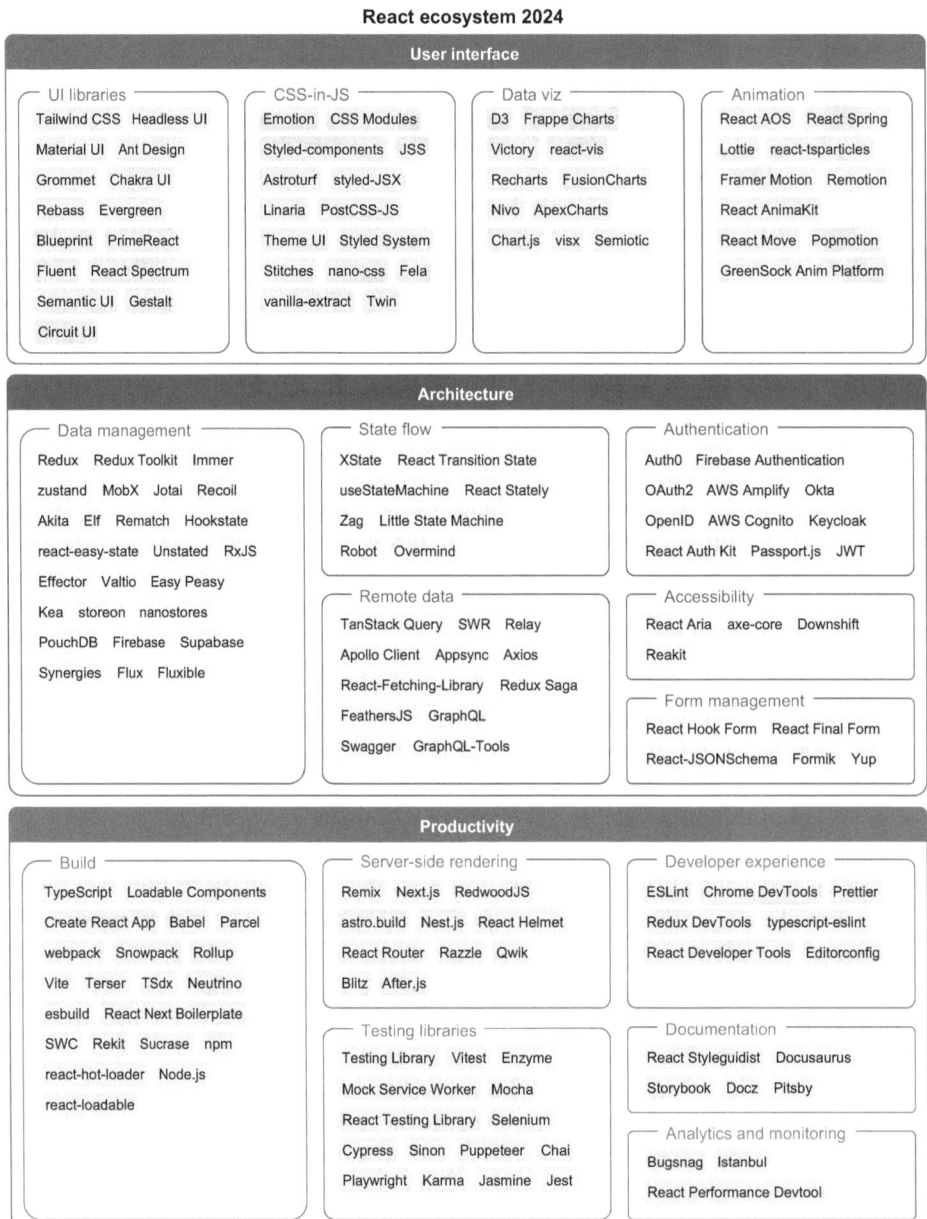

Figure 1.4   The React ecosystem is split into three main groups (UI, architecture, and productivity) and comprises hundreds of technologies, tools, and libraries. If you found the amount of technologies displayed in figure 1.1 daunting, this figure might break you.

The tools are sorted into three main groups, depending on what they do and where they are used:

- *User interface*—Includes things like UI libraries and animation tools
- *Architecture*—Includes data management tools, authentication libraries, and many others
- *Productivity*—Covers build tools, testing libraries, and more

The React ecosystem is fairly complex, with many tools, libraries, and technologies involved. Not all the technologies are specific to React, but many are. In this book, we'll at least partially cover the technologies highlighted in figure 1.5. I chose these technologies because they're popular and stable, representing either the diversity or flexibility within their categories. We'll get into more detail about how the technologies are located within their categories in each chapter.

You'll notice in figure 1.5 that most of the focus is on the productivity group because these tools are the most essential and also the most diverse. As an example, you can use any UI library from the UI library category to achieve the same result, but not all build tools are the same; neither are they interchangeable.

A lot of technologies are connected to an existing brand. This connection happens when some company decides to open up its internal tools or libraries to the public by open sourcing them. This situation is fairly common. Adobe appears three times in figure 1.4, for example, because React Spectrum is a UI library, React Aria is an accessibility toolbox, and React Stately is a state flow library. All three are contained with the overall React Spectrum architecture, and all are created, maintained, and (mostly) controlled by Adobe. In the same way, you can find libraries created by Airbnb, Facebook, Microsoft, Amazon, Google, Twitter, Palantir, IBM, Hewlett-Packard, Pinterest, and quite a few others. The following sections discuss each group and list all the technologies included in figure 1.4.

USER INTERFACE

This group is related to visual elements used in React applications. These elements are ready-to-use component collections (UI libraries), tools to help you write CSS in your React components more easily (CSS-in-JS), libraries to display complex data in beautiful ways using charts or interactive diagrams (data visualization), and packages to help you create animations and transitions (animation and effects):

- *UI libraries*—Tailwind CSS, Material UI, Ant Design, Chakra UI, Blueprint, Fluent, Semantic UI, Circuit UI, Headless UI, Grommet, Evergreen, Rebass, PrimeReact, React Spectrum, and Gestalt
- *CSS-in-JS*—Emotion, CSS Modules, styled-components, JSS, styled-JSX, Linaria, PostCSS-JS, Theme UI, Styled System, Stitches, vanilla-extract, Twin, nano-css, Fela, and Astroturf
- *Data visualization*—D3, Victory, Recharts, Nivo, Chart.js, Semiotic, Frappe Charts, react-vis, FusionCharts, ApexCharts, and visx

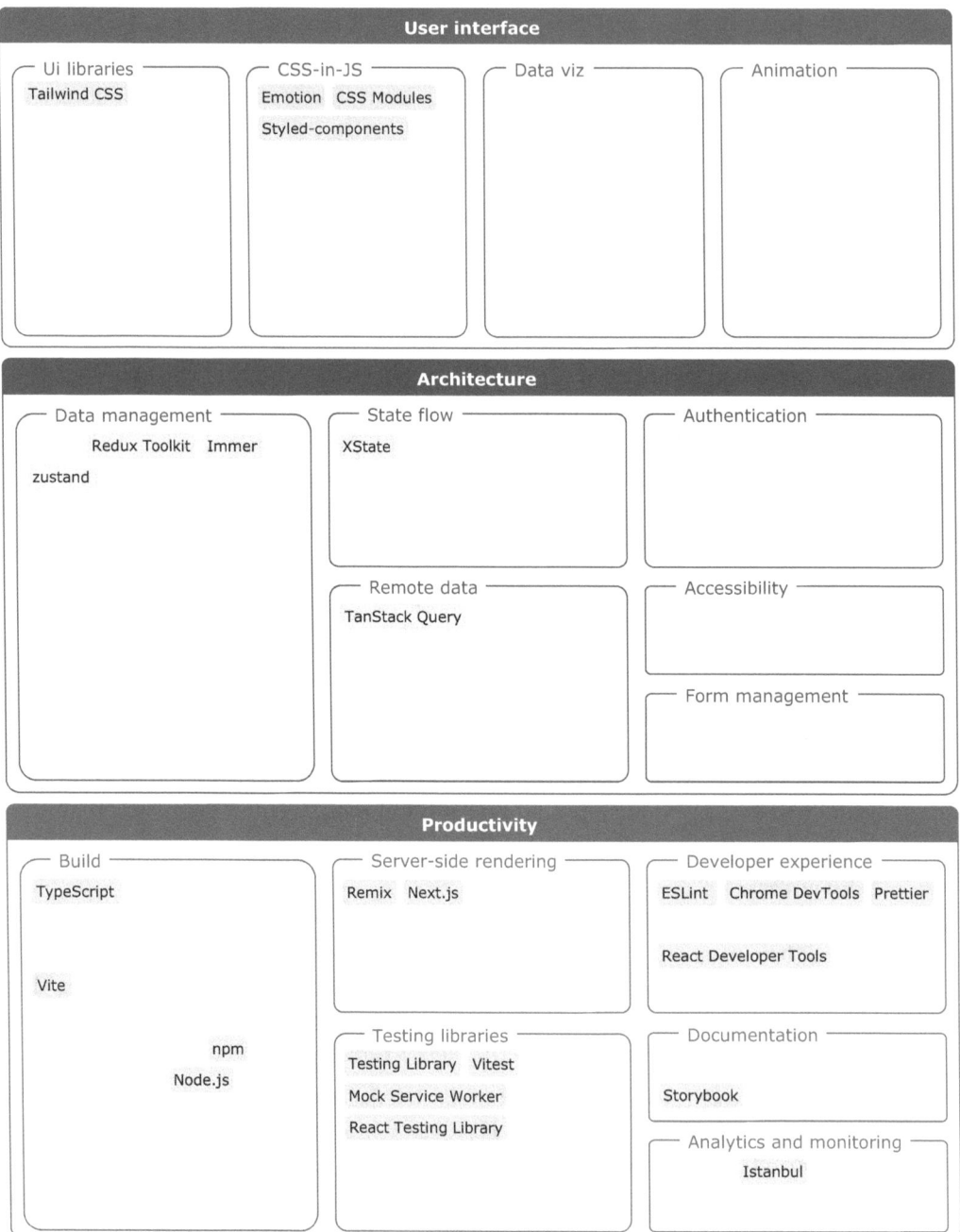

Figure 1.5   The React ecosystem with all the technologies not covered in this book removed. As you can see, this book aims for breadth, not depth, so it covers a bit of everything, with most of the focus on the productivity group.

- *Animation and effects*—React Spring, Framer Motion, Remotion, React Move, GreenSock Animation Platform, Popmotion, React AOS, react-tsparticles, Lottie, and React AnimaKit

ARCHITECTURE

The architecture group contains mostly technologies related to the overall structure of your application or complex parts within the application. These logic-based packages help with managing data, controlling the flow of the application, working with remote data, managing complex forms, handling authentication and authorization, or ensuring accessibility and inclusivity:

- *Data management*—Redux (and RTK), zustand, Immer, MobX, Jotai, Recoil, Akita, Elf, Rematch, Hookstate, react-easy-state, Unstated, RxJS, Effector, Valtio, Easy Peasy, Kea, storeon, nanostores, PouchDB, Firebase, Supabase, Synergies, Flux, and Fluxible
- *State flow*—XState, Robot, React Stately, Overmind, useStateMachine, Zag, Little State Machine, and React Transition State
- *Remote data*—TanStack Query, SWR, Relay, Apollo Client, React-Fetching-Library, Redux Saga, Appsync, Axios, GraphQL, FeathersJS, Swagger, and GraphQL-Tools
- *Authentication and authorization*—JWT, Firebase Authentication, OAuth2, AWS Amplify, Auth0, Okta, Passport.js, OpenID, AWS Cognito, Keycloak, and React Auth Kit
- *Accessibility*—React Aria, axe-core, Reakit, and Downshift
- *Form management*—Formik, Yup, React Hook Form, React Final Form, and React-JSONSchema

PRODUCTIVITY

This final group is not directly included in the actual application; it's related to creating, working with, or validating the application. The group includes libraries that create the basic setup and bundling, run React on the server, ensure a smooth developer experience across even large teams, test applications automatically, analyze and monitor application health, and document the application both internally and externally:

- *Build and bundle*—TypeScript, Create React App, webpack, Vite, esbuild, SWC, react-hot-loader, rcact-loadable, Loadable Components, Babel, Parcel, Snowpack, Rollup, Terser, TSdx, Neutrino, React Next Boilerplate, Rekit, Sucrase, npm, and Node.js
- *Server-side rendering*—Remix, Next.js, Redwood.JS, astro.build, Nest.js, React Helmet, React Router, Razzle, Qwik, Blitz, and After.js
- *Testing libraries*—Testing Library, Jest, Mock Service Worker, React Testing Library, Vitest, Enzyme, Mocha, Chai, Cypress, Sinon, Puppeteer, Playwright, Karma, Jasmine, and Selenium
- *Developer experience*—ESLint, Chrome DevTools, Prettier, Redux DevTools, React Developer Tools, typescript-eslint, and Editorconfig

- *Analytics and monitoring*—Istanbul, React Performance Devtool, and Bugsnag
- *Documentation*—Storybook, Docz, Styleguidist, Docusaurus, and Pitsby

1.4.2 Navigating the ecosystem

Remember that you don't need to know every single item in the ecosystem. Nobody does, not even me. But it's a very good idea to know about all the categories and their purposes and to know at least a few technologies within each category.

You will never need something from every category on every project. But when you do come across that new project that happens to need something special, it's a big help to at least have an idea about the landscape in advance.

It's also a good idea to be able to use the ecosystem in figure 1.4 in reverse. When a new technology arises (which is bound to happen a few seconds after this book has been printed and then every week going forward), you should be able to look at the new piece of tech, quickly determine what it does, and mentally place it in the ecosystem diagram.

Another good thing to keep in mind is that technologies within a single category aren't necessarily equivalent alternatives. Often, the technologies are used together and augment one another. Some projects might use several technologies within a given category. You might use Jest, React Testing Library, Puppeteer, and Karma in a single project, and all of them are in the testing category.

At other times, the technologies and libraries are direct competitors. It wouldn't make sense to include both Material UI and Ant Design, for example, as they are two completely different and mostly overlapping UI libraries that for the most part have the same responsibility in an application. Then again, on a large project, you might have different libraries used in different parts; those libraries might not work together directly, but at least they don't collide too terribly when they're used separately.

The manner in which libraries group together or function separately is also a critical aspect to consider when evaluating new technologies. A new technology might replace an existing item, such as zustand replacing Redux in the data management category (if you want to use zustand instead of Redux). But it might be a new augmentation to the existing libraries, such as Immer, that can be used with zustand or Redux (or many other data management libraries), as it's a tool used within data management to write simpler immutable code, not the entire data management itself.

1.5 The technology stack

The technologies used in a given project are often referred to as the *technology stack*, *solution stack*, or *stack* for that project. It's a common term that you might even find listed directly in a job posting or on a startup's website.

We'll cover where the concept of stacks comes from, as well as the contents of the Frontend React stack, how to quickly understand a stack as you join an existing project, and how to create your own stack for a new application.

One interesting side note: *Technology stack* is the concept from which the term *fullstack* originates. A *fullstack developer* is someone who works on the entire technology stack, from frontend to backend, in a given project.

1.5.1 Why do we talk about a tech stack?

In the realm of software development, the technology stack serves as a blueprint, guiding the construction of robust and efficient applications. This comprehensive outline details the combination of technologies, frameworks, and tools that form the foundation of a software project. Although it's commonly employed in various domains, frontend development in particular benefits from a well-defined technology stack description to streamline collaboration, ensure consistency, and maximize productivity.

The creation of a technology stack involves carefully selecting the frontend technologies that best align with project requirements and goals. This task may include choosing a JavaScript framework like React, Angular, or Vue.js alongside supporting libraries, build tools, and testing frameworks. By documenting these choices clearly and concisely, development teams can communicate their technological preferences effectively and facilitate seamless collaboration among team members.

A technology stack serves as a reference point for stakeholders in frontend development projects. It provides valuable insights into the tools and technologies employed, enabling effective project planning, resource allocation, and decision-making. For project managers, designers, developers, and quality assurance (QA) teams, a shared understanding of the technology stack description fosters a cohesive and efficient development process.

For frontend development, a technology stack holds particular significance. It outlines the essential components required for UI creation, data management, state handling, routing, and more. This description encapsulates the frontend ecosystem, encompassing frontend frameworks, UI libraries, data management solutions, build tools, and other specialized technologies. By defining the frontend technology stack, developers can ensure consistency, scalability, and maintainability throughout the project's life cycle.

It's crucial to acknowledge that the technology stack description is not static; it's an evolving blueprint. This goes double for frontend projects, as the ecosystem advances at a much faster pace than most backend technology landscapes. As a frontend project progresses and matures, new requirements emerge, and technological advancements become available. Consequently, the technology stack needs to adapt to accommodate these changes. This dynamic nature reflects the agility required in modern frontend development. Teams must remain flexible, continuously evaluating and adjusting their technology stack to embrace innovation and ensure that their frontend product remains competitive and aligned with evolving user needs. In this way, the technology stack becomes a living document that grows and evolves alongside the frontend project it supports, empowering developers to harness the latest tools and techniques to deliver exceptional user experiences.

1.5.2 Viewing the anatomy of a React stack

You'll often see React stacks boiled down to these five core layers (also illustrated in figure 1.6):

- Foundation layer (build tools, bundler, TypeScript, and so on)
- Data layer (data management and state flow)
- API layer (fetching libraries)
- UI layer (UI libraries and CSS-in-JS libraries)
- Testing layer (unit, integration, and end-to-end-testing)

Optional parts of the React stack include information about developer experience tools and various utility libraries that are large enough to warrant their own mention.

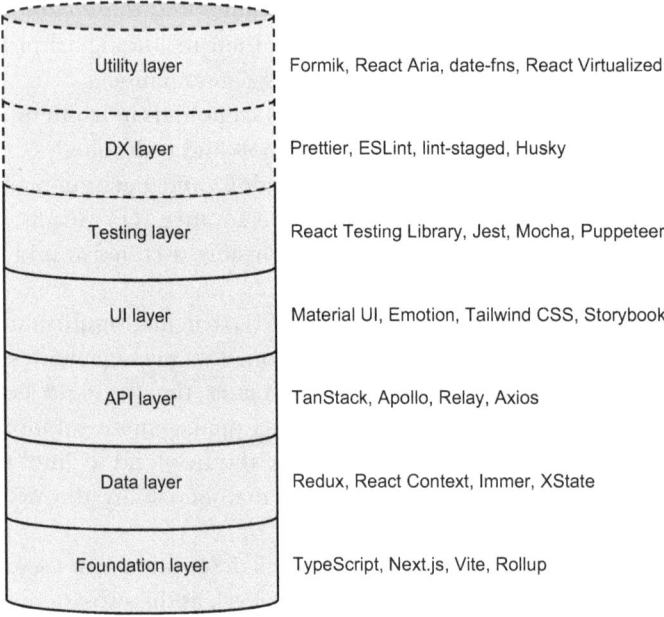

Figure 1.6   The overall layers of a React application, with several examples of each. Note the dashed lines around the top two layers, which are the most likely ones to be left out.

Note that each layer in the stack as described here may include more than one technology. When you're describing the data layer, for example, you might have zustand, Immer, and XState in the mix in different parts of an application. And the foundation layer in particular will often include many different technologies.

The level of detail you go into when describing a stack is up to you. The more detail, the denser the information is to your audience. If you want to give a high-level overview in a job listing, for example, saying "Next.js and TypeScript with Redux and Material UI" might be just fine. But if you're introducing said new hire to the entire application, you'd want to add a lot more detail to get them to understand the system.

If you're using a fullstack React setup with server-side rendering (SSR), you might also include information about the database layer and development operations (colloquially known as *DevOps*) items as the bottom-most layers in the graphic. Figure 1.7 illustrates this stack. We'll look at some example stacks later in this section, where we'll get more specific.

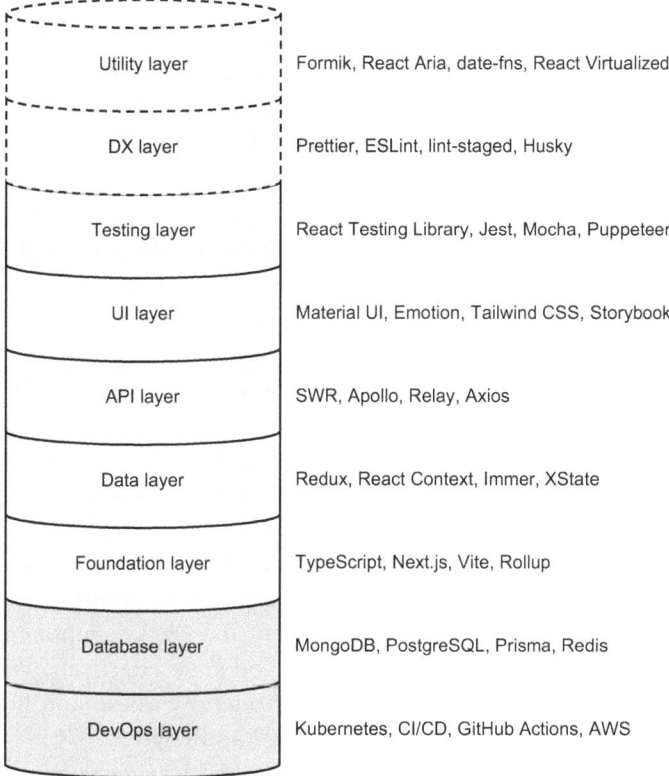

Utility layer	Formik, React Aria, date-fns, React Virtualized
DX layer	Prettier, ESLint, lint-staged, Husky
Testing layer	React Testing Library, Jest, Mocha, Puppeteer
UI layer	Material UI, Emotion, Tailwind CSS, Storybook
API layer	SWR, Apollo, Relay, Axios
Data layer	Redux, React Context, Immer, XState
Foundation layer	TypeScript, Next.js, Vite, Rollup
Database layer	MongoDB, PostgreSQL, Prisma, Redis
DevOps layer	Kubernetes, CI/CD, GitHub Actions, AWS

Figure 1.7   We've added two new layers in darker gray at the bottom of the stack for SSR setup: the database layer and the DevOps layer. Note that we're not restricting the database layer to actual databases but to anything that functions *in that realm*. The DevOps layer includes anything from hosting to deployment pipeline tools.

1.5.3   *Joining a project*

A well-defined technology stack serves as a guiding light for onboarding new team members, especially in the realm of frontend development. When a new developer joins the team, they are often confronted with a codebase that may seem complex and unfamiliar. In such situations, the technology stack acts as a compass, providing clear direction and an overview of the tools, frameworks, and libraries that power the project. New hires can use this document to orient themselves quickly, understanding the key components they'll be working with and how those components fit into the broader development ecosystem.

The technology stack also plays a crucial role in streamlining the learning curve for new team members. By offering insights into the chosen technologies and their purposes, it accelerates the process of getting familiar with the codebase. New developers can refer to this outline to gain an understanding of the frontend framework in use, the styling methodology employed, the data management solutions implemented, and more. This foundational knowledge allows them to dive into the codebase with greater confidence, knowing where to focus their efforts and how various components interact. In essence, the technology stack becomes an essential tool for reducing the time it takes for new hires to contribute effectively to the project.

As a new hire stepping into a team with a well-defined technology stack, a strategic approach to onboarding can significantly expedite your assimilation into the project. Don't dive headfirst into the codebase; rather, begin by studying the technologies mentioned in the stack. Familiarize yourself with each technology, especially if you already have experience with related technologies. If you're well versed in Redux but the project uses zustand, understanding that zustand serves as a Redux alternative gives you a head start. Instead of delving into zustand within the context of the specific codebase, you can focus on grasping the nuances of zustand itself, comparing its approach to that of Redux. This proactive knowledge-building approach empowers you to adapt swiftly to the technology stack in use.

Additionally, exploring the documentation, tutorials, and resources related to the technologies before diving into the codebase can be immensely beneficial. These external resources offer valuable insights and best practices for working with the chosen technologies. By gaining a solid understanding of the stack components independently, you enhance your ability to navigate the codebase effectively. When you eventually delve into the code, you'll find it easier to identify where and how these technologies are implemented, thanks to your existing knowledge.

Moreover, this proactive approach allows you to be a quick learner when it comes to new technologies introduced within the project. When you encounter unfamiliar stack elements, you can draw on your foundational knowledge to grasp their purpose and utility. This knowledge enables you to adapt swiftly to changes or enhancements made to the stack as the project progresses. In essence, by preparing yourself with a strong foundation in the stack technologies, you position yourself as an agile learner who can readily explore and adapt to new tools and frameworks introduced in the project.

It's essential to prepare strategically for rapid learning and efficient onboarding in a project with a well-defined technology stack. To help you get started, here's a practical to-do list that can significantly enhance your readiness:

- *Review stack components*—Begin by thoroughly reviewing the technology stack components mentioned in the stack; understand their roles and how they interact.

- *Review related technologies*—If you have experience with technologies related to those in the stack, such as Redux or MobX in the context of zustand, take time to refresh your knowledge.
- *Explore documentation*—Explore the official documentation and tutorials for the stack technologies. Familiarize yourself with their core concepts and use patterns.
- *Check online resources*—Seek online resources, blogs, or video tutorials that provide insights into best practices and common challenges related to the stack.
- *Seek external learning*—If certain stack elements are new to you, consider completing online courses or tutorials that focus specifically on those technologies.
- *Create practice projects*—Experiment with small practice projects using the stack components independently. Create a simple app with React and zustand, for example, to gain hands-on experience.
- *Study coding standards*—Study any coding standards and practices mentioned in the technology stack to align your coding approach with the team's expectations.
- *Have peer discussions*—Engage in discussions with your peers within the team to gather insights into how the stack is used in the project. Seek clarification on any queries or doubts you may have.
- *Bookmark documentation*—Organize and bookmark relevant sections of the stack documentation for quick reference during your initial work on the project.
- *Seek mentorship*—Don't hesitate to reach out to experienced team members for guidance and mentorship as you prepare to dive into the codebase.

By systematically tackling this to-do list, you'll enter the project well prepared to use your knowledge of the technology stack, making the process of familiarizing yourself with the codebase smoother and more efficient.

1.5.4 Creating a stack from scratch

Choosing the right stack for a React project can be challenging, as many options are available in the ecosystem. In this section, we'll discuss some of the factors to consider when choosing stack components by looking at some example scenarios and suggesting specific technologies for them.

The most important decision is the foundation layer of your application. This decision is the hardest to change at a later stage in development but of course still doable then, so don't get too stuck on it. Building on said foundation, you expand with technologies that solve your particular pain points in the easiest way possible.

One crucial balancing act rests at the center of creating a stack for a new project: familiarity matters, but new technologies surpass existing ones. If your team knows TanStack, it doesn't matter if some other data-fetching library might technically be a better fit for a given new project. Your team will work a lot faster in a library they're familiar with than in a completely new one. On the other hand, if you don't challenge yourself, you'll never evolve, and as technologies go stale or become outdated, you'll never learn about the new and simpler/better/faster tools replacing them.

Dancing on this balancing beam is at the center of the role of the team architect who's creating the technology stack. Where should we stick with what we know, and when should we challenge ourselves? These decisions don't exist just at the birth of a new project; they pop up continuously. Sometimes, you have to replace a given technology in your stack with a new one despite the growing pains it will inevitably introduce, simply because you have to keep up with the times. Let's go through some scenarios and see how we can solve them with a good choice of technologies.

SCENARIO: A MEDIUM-SIZE E-COMMERCE PLATFORM

You're tasked with revamping a medium-size e-commerce platform to improve performance, scalability, and user experience. For this kind of project, you want a stack that's proved itself time and time again, and you want to move fast and build things quickly. One good choice for a project like this one would be what we might call *The Popular Stack*:

- Next.js as the foundation
- RTK as the data management library
- TanStack as the data-fetching library
- Material UI with MUI as the styling library

The Popular Stack offers the familiarity of Next.js for server-side rendering, TanStack for efficient data fetching, RTK for state management, and Material UI for a polished UI. This stack provides the tools needed to enhance the platform's speed and user interface, ensuring an excellent shopping experience.

SCENARIO: A PERSONAL PORTFOLIO WEBSITE

You're a solo developer looking to create a personal portfolio website that showcases your skills and projects. For this kind of project, you're free to play around, but you also want to use the latest and greatest tools out there, both to show off your skills and to stay ahead of the competition. The stack for such a project will always be changing with the times, but one possible candidate is what we'll call *The Indie Stack*:

- Vite at the foundation
- Zustand as the data management library
- Tailwind CSS as the styling library

The Indie Stack is perfect for this scenario. Vite offers rapid development with blazing-fast bundling, zustand simplifies state management, and Tailwind CSS allows for quick and attractive styling. This stack empowers you to showcase your work efficiently and aesthetically.

SCENARIO: MAINTAINING A LEGACY ENTERPRISE DASHBOARD

Your team is responsible for maintaining a legacy enterprise dashboard built using older technologies. The stack for such a project was determined a long time ago, and you just have to play along. Refactoring this to a new stack is nigh on impossible as the project is huge. For now, you're stuck with *The Old School Stack*:

- Create React App (CRA) as the foundation
- Redux as the data management library
- Axios as the data-fetching library
- CSS Modules as the styling library

The Old School Stack, with CRA for stability, Axios for data fetching, Redux for state management, and CSS Modules for maintainable styling, is still a good choice. It ensures compatibility with existing code while leaving an open door for gradual modernization.

SCENARIO: A FINANCIAL SERVICES WEB APPLICATION

You're developing a comprehensive web application for a financial services company. For this scenario, you want something that's trustworthy, secure, and scalable and that won't ruffle any feathers in senior management. You can't go wrong with *The Enterprise Stack*:

- Pure React plus TypeScript as the foundation
- Apollo as the data-fetching and management library
- Styled-components as the styling library

The Enterprise Stack, combining React with TypeScript for strong typing, Apollo for managing complex data fetching and storage, and styled-components for consistent and maintainable styling, ensures robustness and scalability for handling financial transactions securely.

SCENARIO: RAPID PROTOTYPING OF A COLLABORATIVE TASK MANAGEMENT TOOL

Your startup is building a collaborative task management tool, and you need to prototype the core features quickly to attract potential investors and users. For this task, you want something that has a lot of magic built in and can very easily scale up and move fast. You don't mind if the design looks a bit derivative, as speed and features—and making early investors satisfied with the progress—are more important than a unique user interface. You should check out *The Prototype Stack*:

- Remix as the foundation
- Supabase as the backend
- Stale-While-Revalidate (SWR) as the data-fetching library
- Ant Design as the styling library

The Prototype Stack, featuring Remix for fast server rendering, Supabase for rapid backend development, SWR for scalable data fetching, and Ant Design for a polished, feature-rich UI, allows you to create a functional prototype swiftly, demonstrating the product's potential to stakeholders.

Summary

- This book addresses the gaps in practical, large-scale React application development, covering essential topics for improved skills, teamwork, and continuous learning in the evolving React ecosystem.

- This book offers comprehensive scope, hands-on focus, and emphasis on best practices to teach advanced React development, guiding readers through nine realms of React to become confident, skilled professionals.
- The React ecosystem is extensive, comprising various libraries and tools for enhancing React applications' performance and functionality.
- This book explores popular libraries and tools in the React ecosystem, emphasizing practical, hands-on development and best practices.
- Readers will gain a comprehensive understanding of the React ecosystem, allowing them to select the right tools for their projects and build high-quality React applications.
- A technology stack (also known as a *solution stack* or simply *stack*) is central to software development, guiding the selection of technologies, frameworks, and tools for a project.
- A well-defined technology stack enhances collaboration, reduces onboarding time for new team members, and provides a blueprint for efficient project development, with specific layers that encompass foundational elements, data management, API use, UI components, and testing.
- The choice of a React stack components depends on project requirements and familiarity with the technologies, with options ranging from established stacks like The Popular Stack for e-commerce platforms to innovative stacks like The Indie Stack for personal portfolio websites, each tailored to specific project goals and constraints.

Advanced
component patterns

This chapter covers

- Providing global state with the Provider pattern
- Managing complex component structures with the Composite pattern
- Creating clean components with the Summary pattern

The construction world, with projects ranging from sky-touching skyscrapers to peaceful neighborhood homes, adheres to a universal set of principles. In both architecture and construction, regardless of project size, there is a steadfast commitment to core engineering principles, which include designing load-bearing structures, selecting appropriate materials, and ensuring overall stability and safety.

In the digital realm, React development is committed to its own set of construction principles. Although the outer aesthetics and specific materials may differ, the underlying architectural principles remain constant.

Within React, as in software design in general, these principles are embodied in design patterns. This chapter will take an in-depth look at three foundational patterns used in modern React applications:

- Provider
- Composite
- Summary

Much like the blueprints and load-bearing structures in physical construction, these patterns, shown in figure 2.1, provide the framework for building stable and scalable React projects.

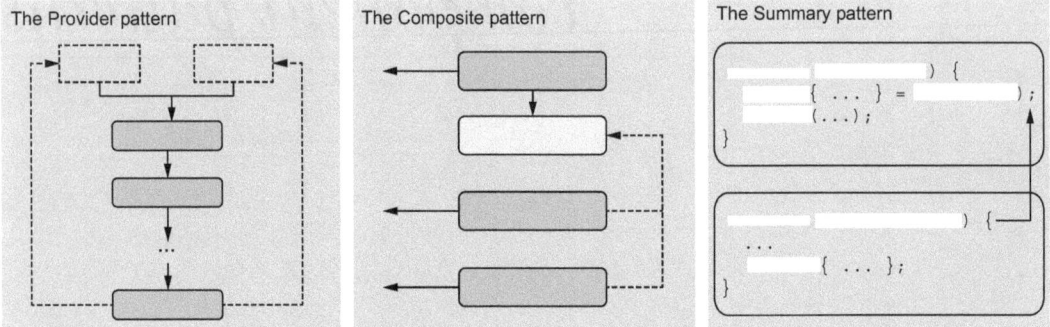

Figure 2.1   The three design patterns that we'll take a closer look at in this chapter, illustrated as though they're construction blueprints. I'll go over each illustration in detail in the appropriate section.

Consider figure 2.1 to be a metaphorical construction diagram that introduces these crucial patterns. Throughout this chapter, we will explore how these patterns enable you to construct resilient React applications that are capable of withstanding various challenges.

Just as architects and builders across the globe rely on consistent physical and engineering principles, React developers use patterns to create a diverse array of interactive experiences. By adhering to these foundational strategies, you can build React applications that are as varied and innovative as the world's architectural wonders. So gear up with your hard hat and tools and embark on a journey through the intricate construction site of React's advanced component patterns, where solidity and stability guide us to create robust digital structures.

> **NOTE**   The source code for the examples in this chapter is available at https://reactlikea.pro/ch02.

2.1   *The Provider pattern*

In this section, we delve into the Provider pattern, building on your existing knowledge of React context. We'll explore how to use the Provider pattern to manage multiple related values, such as state values and their corresponding setters. This approach (figure 2.2) represents a significant advancement beyond basic use of React context, offering enhanced flexibility and efficiency in state management.

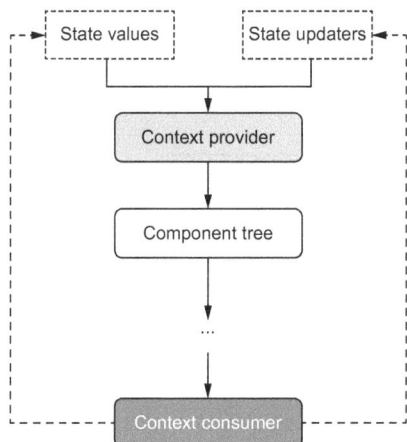

Figure 2.2 This illustration highlights the initial step of using the Provider pattern to handle multiple related values. It shows a basic context setup wherein the provider (light gray background) encapsulates both state values and updaters (dashed boxes), providing a comprehensive view of how we extend the conventional use of React context. The context consumer (dark gray background) can be at any depth inside the component tree below the consumer but can still easily access the values and updaters provided by the context (dashed arrows).

Our exploration is structured to facilitate hands-on discovery through the following stages:

- *Context with multiple values*—Starting with a straightforward example, we'll see how to wrap a child component in a provider that handles multiple related state values and setters. This foundational step showcases the basic extension of React context beyond singular data points.
- *Dedicated component for context management*—Next, we evolve our approach by creating a dedicated component for the provider. This refinement addresses the intricacies of managing multiple state aspects and illustrates a more structured and maintainable way to handle complex contexts.
- *Selectability for performance optimization*—Finally, we introduce selectability to our Provider pattern. This advanced technique focuses on minimizing re-renders, especially for components with stable content. It demonstrates how selective data flow can significantly enhance the performance of your React applications.

By the end of this section, you will not only have deepened your understanding of React context but also gained practical skills by implementing the Provider pattern for complex state management. This journey from basic implementation to sophisticated techniques will empower you to optimize your React applications, ensuring that they are both performant and maintainable.

2.1.1 Inventing a provider

A common approach is to use a context as a delivery mechanism for stateful values *and* setters. Suppose that we have a website with dark mode and light mode and a button in the header that can toggle between the two modes. All relevant components look at the current state and change their design depending on this state value.

We want to put two things in the state: a value that tells us whether we are in dark mode (`isDarkMode`) and a function that allows a button to toggle between the two modes (`toggleDarkMode`). We can put these two values in a single object and stuff that object into the context as the value. Figure 2.3 shows this system, which we'll implement in listing 2.1.

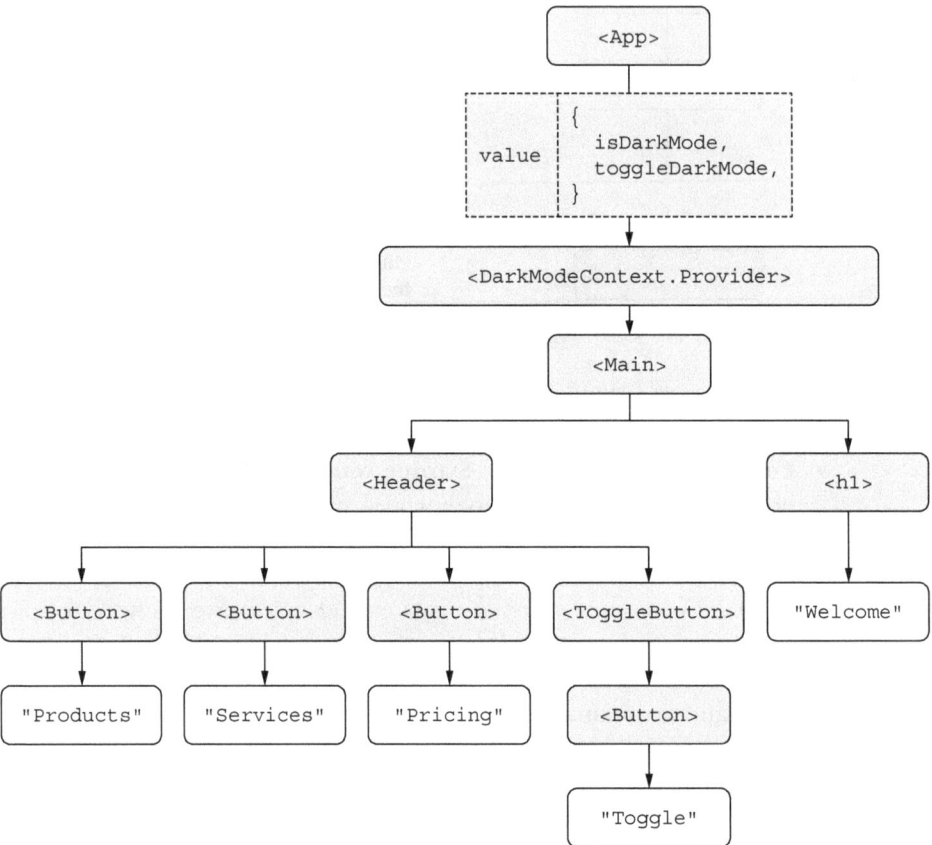

Figure 2.3   A document tree sketch of our website with a dark mode/light mode toggle. Note how we pass in an object to the context provider (dashed box), which we can deconstruct and use wherever we need either of the two values in the components below the provider in the document tree.

Listing 2.1   Dark mode with context

```
import { useContext, useState, createContext, memo } from "react";
const DarkModeContext = createContext({});
function Button({ children, ...rest }) {
  const { isDarkMode } =
    useContext(DarkModeContext);
  const style = {
    backgroundColor: isDarkMode ? "#333" : "#CCC",
    border: "1px solid",
    color: "inherit",
  };
```

This time, we initialize our context with an empty object. We always have a context at the root of the application, so the default values will never be used.

In these two locations, we use only the isDarkMode flag from the context.

```
    return (
      <button style={style} {...rest}>
        {children}
      </button>
    );
}
function ToggleButton() {
    const { toggleDarkMode } = useContext(DarkModeContext);
    return <Button onClick={toggleDarkMode}>Toggle mode</Button>;
}
const Header = memo(function Header() {
    const style = {
        padding: "10px 5px",
        borderBottom: "1px solid",
        marginBottom: "10px",
        display: "flex",
        gap: "5px",
        justifyContent: "flex-end",
    };
    return (
      <header style={style}>
        <Button>Products</Button>
        <Button>Services</Button>
        <Button>Pricing</Button>
        <ToggleButton />
      </header>
    );
});
const Main = memo(function Main() {
    const { isDarkMode } =
      useContext(DarkModeContext);
    const style = {
        color: isDarkMode ? "white" : "black",
        backgroundColor: isDarkMode ? "black" : "white",
        margin: "-8px",
        minHeight: "100vh",
        boxSizing: "border-box",
    };
    return (
      <main style={style}>
        <Header />
        <h1>Welcome to our business site!</h1>
      </main>
    );
});
export default function App() {
    const [isDarkMode, setDarkMode] =
      useState(false);
    const toggleDarkMode =
      () => setDarkMode((v) => !v);
    const contextValue = {
      isDarkMode,
      toggleDarkMode
    };
    return (
```

In the toggle button, we use only the toggleDarkMode function from the context.

We memoize the main component.

In these two locations, we use only the isDarkMode flag from the context.

In the main application component, we define the two values that go into our context.

We put these two values together in a single object.

```
        <DarkModeContext.Provider
          value={contextValue}                      We use this single object as the
        >                                            value for our context provider.
          <Main />
        </DarkModeContext.Provider>
    );
}
```

Example: dark-mode

This example is in the `ch02/dark-mode` folder. You can use that example by running this command in the source folder:

```
$ npm run dev -w ch02/dark-mode
```

Alternatively, you can go to this website to browse the code, see the example in action in your browser, or download the source code as a zip file: https://reactlikea .pro/ch02-dark-mode. You can observe this website in figure 2.4.

NOTE   In React 19, context providers are created in JSX by typing `<MyContext value={...}>` rather than `<MyContext.Provider value={...}>`. Furthermore, contexts can be consumed by using the `use()` function rather than the `useContext()` hook. The new `use()` function is not a regular hook and does not have to obey hook rules, so it can be used conditionally, but it doesn't give you any additional capability—only a different API. Creating and using contexts are otherwise the same in React 19 except for these slight syntax simplifications. I will be using the old syntax throughout this book.

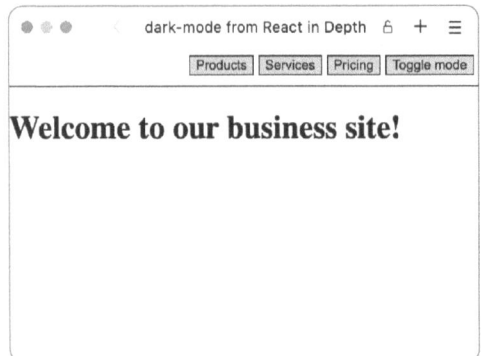 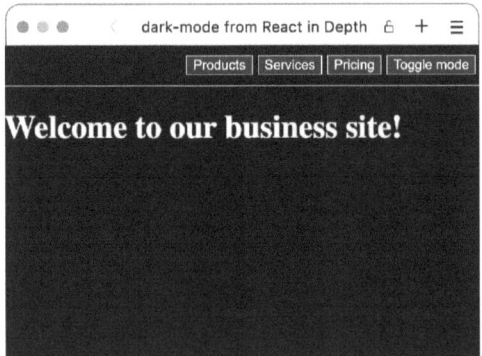

Figure 2.4   Our website in both light mode and dark mode. Both examples look pretty decent and even somewhat chic!

The important things to note here are how we give this context two different properties in the definition of the `<App />` component in listing 2.1 and how we memoize the first components inside the context provider in the definition of `<Main />`. This memoization is very important because our main `App` component will re-render every time the context changes, which is every time the dark mode flag toggles (because the state updates). We don't want all the other components to re-render just because the context does, however. In this instance, the `Main` component consumes the context, so it will re-render every time the context updates, but the `Header` does not consume the context, so it should not re-render. With our use of memoization, it doesn't, which is perfect.

We don't have to stop there. We can put a whole bunch of properties and functions in the context value.

2.1.2 *Creating a dedicated provider component*

The previous version of the dark mode application in listing 2.1 is fully functional, but we can do a bit better. The main application component is a bit crowded with the state value, toggle function, and context provider, so let's clean it up. Instead of this code,

```
function App() {
  const [isDarkMode, setDarkMode] = useState(false);
  const toggleDarkMode = () => setDarkMode((v) => !v);
  const contextValue = { isDarkMode, toggleDarkMode };
  return (
    <DarkModeContext.Provider value={contextValue}>
      <Main />
    </DarkModeContext.Provider>
  );
}
```

suppose that we have this code:

```
function App() {
  return (
    <DarkModeProvider>
      <Main />
    </DarkModeProvider>
  );
}
```

First, the second component is much more elegant. We remove the logic about what goes inside the actual context from the main application, but we also get one additional benefit: this new `<App />` component is not stateful, so it never re-renders. Because it never re-renders, it never causes `<Main />` to re-render.

Before, `<App />` was stateful and caused re-renders of the `Main` component, so we had to wrap that component in `memo()` to avoid unnecessary re-renders, but we don't have to anymore. One additional optimization we can make is to simplify these calls:

```
const ... = useContext(DarkModeContext);
```

We can create a custom hook that returns the context contents, so this line becomes

```
const ... = useDarkMode();
```

With both changes, we get the result in the following listing.

Listing 2.2   Dark mode with a dedicated provider

```
import { useContext, useState, createContext, memo } from "react";
const DarkModeContext = createContext({});
function Button({ children, ...rest }) {
  const { isDarkMode } = useDarkMode();
  ...
}
function ToggleButton() {
  const { toggleDarkMode } = useDarkMode();

  return <Button onClick={toggleDarkMode}>Toggle mode</Button>;
}
const Header = memo(function Header() {
  ...
});
function Main() {
  const { isDarkMode } = useDarkMode();
  ...
}
function DarkModeProvider({ children }) {
  const [isDarkMode, setDarkMode] = useState(false);
  const toggleDarkMode = () => setDarkMode((v) => !v);
  const contextValue = { isDarkMode, toggleDarkMode };
  return (
    <DarkModeContext.Provider value={contextValue}>
      {children}
    </DarkModeContext.Provider>
  );
}
function useDarkMode() {
  return useContext(DarkModeContext);
}
export default function App() {
  return (
    <DarkModeProvider>
      <Main />
    </DarkModeProvider>
  );
}
```

Uses the custom hook to access the context contents

Defines the main component without memoization

Creates a new dedicated provider component that wraps its children in the context provider

Creates a new custom hook to access the provided context

Returns a much more elegant JSX in the root app component

Example: dark-mode-dedicated

This example is in the `ch02/dark-mode-dedicated` folder. You can use that example by running this command in the source folder:

```
$ npm run dev -w ch02/dark-mode-dedicated
```

Alternatively, you can go to this website to browse the code, see the example in action in your browser, or download the source code as a zip file: https://reactlikea .pro/ch02-dark-mode-dedicated.

2.1.3   Avoiding rendering everything

The context provider in the preceding example has a minor suboptimal problem: *all* components consuming a specific context will re-render when *any* value inside that context changes. This situation occurs because now our context is a complex object with multiple properties, but React doesn't care; it sees only that the context value changes, so every component using that context will be re-rendered.

Our toggle component never needs to re-render, however, because it uses a function that can be memoized to be completely stable. The reason is that the `toggleDarkMode` function does not depend on the current value of the context. Unfortunately, we cannot tell React to re-render only a specific component when specific properties of a context update. At least, we cannot do that *yet*. That capability was expected to come with React 19 beta but didn't make it; it's hopefully coming in a future update.

If we want to avoid re-rendering every context consumer unnecessarily, we need to use an external library. One such library, called `use-context-selector`, allows us to not use an entire context every time. Instead, we can specify the specific attribute of the context that we are interested in (we select the relevant property—hence, the `selector` part of the name). Then React will re-render our component only when that specific property changes.

To use the `use-context-selector` package correctly, we also need to create our context with this package. We cannot use the regular context as created by `create-Context` in the React package; we have to use the `createContext` function provided by the `use-context-selector` package. The custom hook for accessing the context takes a `selector` function, like so:

```
function useDarkMode(selector) {
  return useContextSelector(DarkModeContext, selector);
}
```

We pass this new argument, `selector`, straight to the `useContextSelector` hook. This custom hook still makes sense, as it removes the need to reference the context every time. Let's implement this updated and more optimized version of our dark mode–toggling website in the following listing.

Listing 2.3   Dark mode with context selector

```
import { useState, useCallback, memo } from "react";
import {
  createContext,
  useContextSelector,
} from "use-context-selector";
const DarkModeContext = createContext({});
function Button({ children, ...rest }) {
  const isDarkMode =
    useDarkMode((ctx) => ctx.isDarkMode);
  ...
}
function ToggleButton() {
```

We have changed only a few things this time around. First, we imported two functions from the use-context-selector package.

Whenever we need a value from the context, we use the new useDarkMode hook, which now takes a selector.

```
    const toggle = useDarkMode((ctx) => ctx.toggle);   ◁─────
    return <Button onClick={toggle}>Toggle mode</Button>;
}
const Header = memo(function Header() {
    ...
});
function Main() {
  const isDarkMode =
    useDarkMode((ctx) => ctx.isDarkMode);   ◁─────
    ...
}
function DarkModeProvider({ children }) {
    const [isDarkMode, setDarkMode] = useState(false);
    const toggle =
      useCallback(() => setDarkMode((v) => !v), []);
    const contextValue = { isDarkMode, toggle };   ◁─
    return (
      <DarkModeContext.Provider value={contextValue}>
        {children}
      </DarkModeContext.Provider>
    );
}
function useDarkMode(selector) {
    return useContextSelector(
    DarkModeContext,
    selector
);
}
export default function App() {
  return (
    <DarkModeProvider>
      <Main />
    </DarkModeProvider>
  );
}
```

Whenever we need a value from the context, we use the new useDarkMode hook, which now takes a selector.

To avoid re-renders, we memoize our toggle function by using useCallback.

We create and initialize the context value the same as before from the two parts.

In the useDarkMode hook, we need to pass the selector argument to that new useContextSelector hook from the third-party package.

Example: dark-mode-selector

This example is in the `ch02/dark-mode-selector` folder. You can use that example by running this command in the source folder:

```
$ npm run dev -w ch02/dark-mode-selector
```

Alternatively, you can go to this website to browse the code, see the example in action in your browser, or download the source code as a zip file: https://reactlikea .pro/ch02-dark-mode-selector.

The result is the same website we had before with the same functionality, but now the `ToggleButton` never re-renders because it uses only a stable value from the context. Because the context never updates, there's no need to re-render the component. The two components listening for the `isDarkMode` flag inside the context will still re-render every time the flag updates because we select that exact property in the `useDarkMode` hooks in those two components.

This approach might seem like an overoptimization at this point because we're talking about whether a single component updates a few extra times or not. In a large application with many contexts, however, these extra updates add up quickly! So if you are using contexts to share common functionality throughout your application, you should be using `useContextSelector` rather than the normal `useContext` hook—unless React implements the selection logic as part of the normal `useContext` hook by the time you read this book.

2.1.4 Creating beautifully typed selectable contexts with the recontextual tool

In the previous examples, we used only JavaScript, not TypeScript. I'll talk a lot more about TypeScript in chapters 5 and 6 and in later chapters. For now, I'll say only that some of these patterns are quite tricky to type in an elegant way.

To make selectable contexts easier to type, I created a small package, `recontextual`, that wraps `use-context-selector` and provides a simple way to create well-typed selectable contexts with minimal typing effort. Without getting into too much detail, let's see how the dark mode application looks in TypeScript, using the new library in the following listing.

> **Listing 2.4 Dark mode with a typed selector**

```
import {
  useState,
  useCallback,
  memo,
  PropsWithChildren,
  ComponentPropsWithoutRef,
} from "react";
import recontextual from "recontextual";     ⟵ Imports the recontextual hook
                                               generator from the package
interface DarkModeContext {
  isDarkMode: boolean;                        Defines the interface for
  toggle: () => void;                         the context contents
}
const [Provider, useDarkMode] =
  recontextual<DarkModeContext>();            Calls the package function and
function Button({                             destructs a provider and a selector
  children,                                   hook from the response
  ...rest
}: PropsWithChildren<ComponentPropsWithoutRef<"button">>) {
  const isDarkMode =
    useDarkMode((ctx) => ctx.isDarkMode);
  ...                                              Calls the selector hook as
}                                                  before, but we don't define
function ToggleButton() {                          it ourselves this time; the
  const toggle = useDarkMode((ctx) => ctx.toggle);  package does that job for us.
  return <Button onClick={toggle}>Toggle mode</Button>;
}
const Header = memo(function Header() {
  ...
});
```

```
function Main() {
  const isDarkMode =
    useDarkMode((ctx) => ctx.isDarkMode);
  ...
}
function DarkModeProvider({ children }: PropsWithChildren) {
  const [isDarkMode, setDarkMode] = useState(false);
  const toggle = useCallback(() => setDarkMode((v) => !v), []);
  const contextValue = { isDarkMode, toggle };
  return <Provider value={contextValue}>{children} </Provider>;
}
export default function App() {
  return (
    <DarkModeProvider>
      <Main />
    </DarkModeProvider>
  );
}
```

Calls the selector hook as before, but we don't define it ourselves this time; the package does that job for us.

Provides the context in the usual way, using the Provider variable returned from the package

> **Example: dark-mode-typed**
>
> This example is in the ch02/dark-mode-typed folder. You can use that example by running this command in the source folder:
>
> ```
> $ npm run dev -w ch02/dark-mode-typed
> ```
>
> Alternatively, you can go to this website to browse the code, see the example in action in your browser, or download the source code as a zip file: https://reactlikea .pro/ch02-dark-mode-typed.

Some of this code may seem a bit complex if TypeScript is new to you. Don't worry. I cover all the details, such as interfaces and strict typing, in chapters 5 and 6.

2.1.5   *How useful is the Provider pattern?*

The Provider pattern seems to be a minor pattern that may be smart to use for some functionality, but it is a lot more. You can use this single pattern throughout even a large application as the single way to distribute and organize data and functionality in your entire application.

Your application can have dozens of contexts on many layers working on top of one another, providing global and local functionality to parts or all of your application. You can have your user authorization with the current user information, as well as methods to log in and log out in one context; you can have your application data in a second context, and you can, have data controlling the UI in a third context.

If it's used correctly, this pattern is the single most powerful one in your React quiver because it can apply to almost every application. You'll see this pattern used in several future chapters as we create more complex applications. The Provider pattern is extremely generic and versatile enough to apply to any situation, yet customizable for many constructions.

Some people might argue that instead of using React context with `useContext-Selector` to manage complex state throughout your application, it is better to use an established tool such as `redux-toolkit`. Truth be told, `redux-toolkit` uses this same functionality under the hood to provide its magic, so you're getting the same performance with either method. I will discuss other pros and cons of using context versus `redux-toolkit` (and other state management solutions) in chapter 7.

2.2 The Composite pattern

In this section, we delve into the realm of composite components in React, uncovering how they enable the creation of scalable and maintainable user interfaces. You can see a high-level overview of the Composite pattern in figure 2.5.

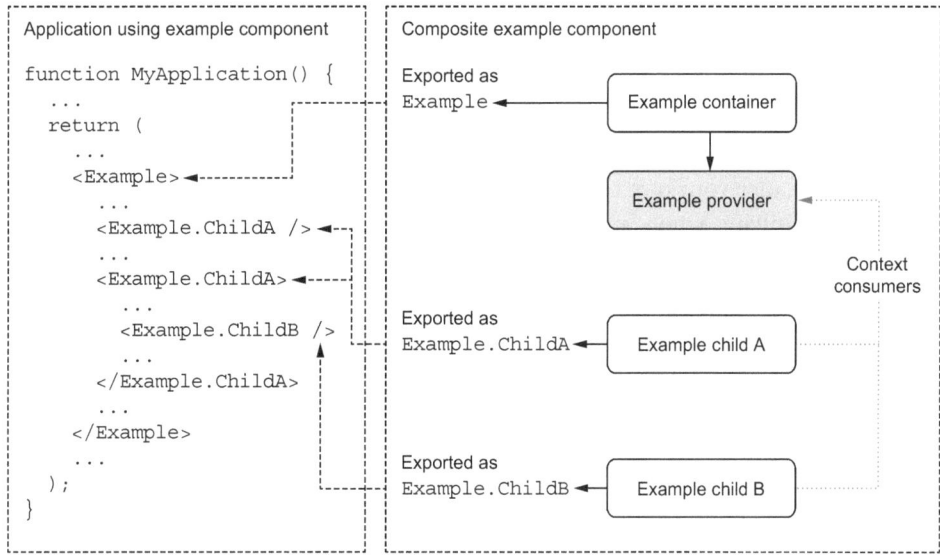

Figure 2.5   A high-level overview of the Composite pattern. From the outside, the components are used as if namespaced by the root of the composite component (dashed arrows), but on the inside, they're regular components, communicating via one or more contexts (dotted arrows).

As a key case study, we will examine the evolution of a radio group component. This example will demonstrate the journey from a single component to a composite structure, highlighting the challenges and benefits at each stage. The radio group, starting as a simple UI element and growing in complexity, serves as an ideal illustration of the need for and application of composite components. The following list details the steps we'll go through as we explore the benefits and use cases of this pattern:

- *Simple beginnings with single components*—Initially, the radio group is implemented as a single component, showcasing the simplicity and directness of this approach. Here, the example illustrates the initial ease of development but also sets the stage for potential challenges as complexity increases.

- *The challenges of increasing complexity*—As we add features and requirements to our radio group, the limitations of the single-component approach become apparent. This phase demonstrates how a once-simple component can become cumbersome, leading to a bloated, difficult-to-maintain codebase.
- *The ideal (clean, modular JSX with composite components)*—With the complexities of the radio group established, we explore a modular composite structure. This approach breaks the radio group into smaller, focused components, demonstrating how it leads to cleaner, more readable code that's easier to maintain.
- *Implementation of composite components*—Finally, we delve into the practical implementation of composite components, using the radio group as our guide. This implementation details how to manage state, props, and context effectively within a composite structure, ensuring that each component remains focused and maintainable. The radio group's transformation exemplifies the benefits of this approach in a real-world scenario.

By the conclusion of this section, you'll have gained a comprehensive understanding of composite components in React and will be equipped with the knowledge to refactor and enhance your own applications. The radio group example will serve as a blueprint for identifying when and how to transition from single to composite components, enhancing both your application's scalability and your development efficiency.

2.2.1 *The simple beginnings*

You've been tasked with building a breakfast-ordering web application for a restaurant. Customers can order in advance to get their food faster.

There's a chance that this project will evolve, but you've been given no hints about the future, so you don't need to try to anticipate anything. For now, build the minimal application that will meet the current needs. You can see the required output in figure 2.6.

This application is fairly straightforward. We can build it without any custom components by using plain HTML, but that would not teach us anything about React. Let's create a component to generate a list of related radio buttons where we pass in an array of options to be displayed.

Figure 2.6   The desired output of the initial breakfast-ordering form

THE MAIN APPLICATION

This application should be trivial for you to implement. My suggestion is a main application that looks like the following listing.

> **Listing 2.5 The main app for a simple list of radio groups (excerpt)**

```
import { useState } from "react";
import { RadioGroup } from "./RadioGroup";
export default function App() {
  const [data, setData] = useState({
    meal: "",
    bread: "",
    side: "",
    beverage: "",
  });
  const onChange = (name) => (value) =>
    setData({ ...data, [name]: value });
  return (
    <main>
      <h1>Breakfast order form</h1>
      <h2>Meal</h2>
      <RadioGroup
        name="meal"
        options={[
          "Small: $5.99",        Passes the radio group options
          "Medium: $7.99",       as a simple array of strings
          "Large: $9.99",
        ]}
        onChange={onChange("meal")}
      />
      <h2>Bread</h2>
      ...
    </main>
  );
}
```

THE RADIOGROUP COMPONENT

The implementation of this `RadioGroup` component could look like the following listing.

> **Listing 2.6 The `RadioGroup` component with a simple interface**

```
import { useState } from "react";
export function RadioGroup({ name, options, onChange }) {
  const [selectedValue, setSelectedValue] = useState("");
  const handleChange = (e) => {
    setSelectedValue(e.target.value);
    if (onChange) {
      onChange(e.target.value);
    }
  };
  return (
```

```
<div
  style={{
    display: "flex",
    flexDirection: "column",
    alignItems: "flex-start",
  }}
>
  {options.map((option) => (
    <label key={option}>
      <input
        type="radio"
        name={name}
        value={option}
        checked={selectedValue === option}
        onChange={handleChange}
      />
      {option}
    </label>
  ))}
</div>
);
}
```

> **Creates a controlled input managed by local state**

> **Example: radio-simple**
>
> This example is in the `ch02/radio-simple` folder. You can use that example by run-ning this command in the source folder:
>
> ```
> $ npm run dev -w ch02/radio-simple
> ```
>
> Alternatively, you can go to this website to browse the code, see the example in action in your browser, or download the source code as a zip file: https://reactlikea .pro/ch02-radio-simple.

NOTE React 19 comes with a new syntax for handling forms by using the `<form action>` property and async action functions. In the context of this example, the new form action function works the same way as a submit han-dler except that uncontrolled forms are a bit easier to manage. In this exam-ple, we have a controlled form, so we would gain nothing by upgrading to React 19 and using a form action.

2.2.2   *Complexity increases*

The simple version was good. The simple version was bliss. Alas, the world never stays simple. Following in the footprints of the Second Law of Thermodynamics, we might as well define a Second Law of Software Development: *complexity always increases.*

The client loved the breakfast-ordering system but wanted a few changes—a little bit here and there. You can see what the client came up with in figure 2.7.

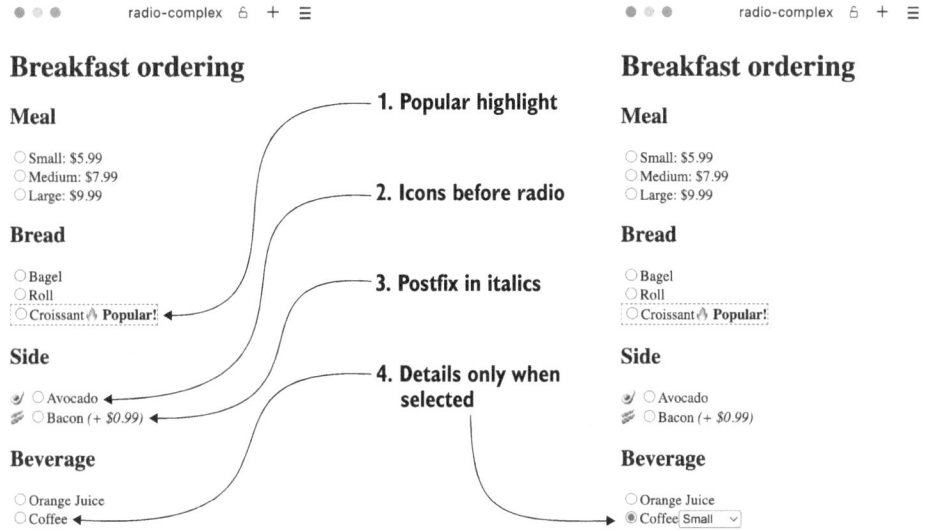

Figure 2.7   The new interface designed by the client. Notice that in the screenshot on right, the coffee beverage is selected. When a selection is made, additional details can be displayed next to the label.

For now, let's not overthink things; we'll expand the existing approach. We still pass in an options array, but now we're going to need more variables per option, so we'll pass in objects with various properties:

```
{
  label: "Bacon",
  value: "bacon",
  isPopular: true,
  icon: "🥓",
  postfix: "(+ $0.99)",
  details: <span>Details</span>,
}
```

Sets the label to be displayed as the main text after the radio button

Sets the value to be used as the value of the input element

Marks the option as popular (can be omitted)

Sets an optional postfix (can be omitted)

Sets an optional icon (can be omitted)

Adds optional display details if selected (can be omitted)

With that change, the main app file becomes a lot longer but is still relatively straightforward. However, notice that the file is a lot more like regular JavaScript and a lot less JSX now. Most of the component contents are defined in arrays before the JSX is created and returned, as shown in the following listing.

Listing 2.7   Passing option objects to radio groups (excerpt)

```
import { useState } from "react";
import { RadioGroup } from "./RadioGroup";
export default function App() {
  const [data, setData] = useState({
    meal: "",
    bread: "",
```

```
      side: "",
      beverage: "",
  });
  const onChange = (name) => (value) =>
    setData({ ...data, [name]: value });
  const meals = [                                          ◄┐
    { value: "small", label: "Small: $5.99" },
    { value: "medium", label: "Medium: $7.99" },
    { value: "large", label: "Large: $9.99" },
  ];
  const breads = [                                         ◄┤
    { value: "bagel", label: "Bagel" },
    { value: "roll", label: "Roll" },
    { value: "croissant", label: "Croissant", isPopular: true },  ◄┤
  ];
  const sides = [                                          ◄┤
    { value: "avocado", label: "Avocado", icon: "🥑" },
    { value: "bacon", label: "Bacon", icon: "🥓" },
  ];
  const beverages = [                                      ◄┘
    { value: "orangejuice", label: "Orange Juice" },
    {
      value: "coffee",
      label: "Coffee",
      details: (
        <select name="coffee_size">
          <option>Small</option>
          <option>Medium</option>
          <option>Large</option>
        </select>
      ),
    },
  ];
  return (
    ...
  );
}
```

Defines the four options arrays, where most of the information in this component lies

Adds a details property to the coffee option defined with JSX, which is added inside the options array for beverages

Now the implementation of the radio group has to deal with many more details for each option, and it becomes a bit messy, but it's tolerable, as you can see in the following listing.

Listing 2.8 A radio group with more complex objects

```
import { useState } from "react";
export function RadioGroup({ name, options, onChange }) {
  const [selectedValue, setSelectedValue] = useState("");
  const handleChange = (e) => {
    setSelectedValue(e.target.value);
    if (onChange) {
      onChange(e.target.value);
    }
  };
  return (
```

```
<div
  style={{
    display: "flex",
    flexDirection: "column",
    alignItems: "flex-start",
  }}
>
  {options.map((option, index) => (
    <label
      key={index}
      style={option.isPopular
        ? { border: "1px dashed red" }
        : undefined
      }
    >
      {option.icon && <span>{option.icon} </span>}
      <input
        type="radio"
        name={name}
        value={option.value}
        checked={selectedValue === option.value}
        onChange={handleChange}
      />
      {option.label}
      {option.postfix && <em> {option.postfix}</em>}
      {selectedValue === option.value && option.details}
      {option.isPopular
        ? <strong>🏆 Popular! </strong>
        : null}
    </label>
  ))}
</div>
);
}
```

Handles the new icon property → `{option.icon && <span>{option.icon} </span>}`

Handles the new isPopular property

Handles the new postfix property → `{option.postfix && <em> {option.postfix}</em>}`

Handles the new details property → `{selectedValue === option.value && option.details}`

Example: radio-complex

This example is in the `ch02/radio-complex` folder. You can use that example by running this command in the source folder:

```
$ npm run dev -w ch02/radio-complex
```

Alternatively, you can go to this website to browse the code, see the example in action in your browser, or download the source code as a zip file: https://reactlikea .pro/ch02-radio-complex.

Summarizing this new code, we find ourselves navigating a landscape that's rich in features yet teetering on the edge of complexity. Each option, now a small universe of properties and conditions, brings its unique flair to the RadioGroup. The once-straightforward component has evolved into a more dynamic entity that's capable of handling icons, popularity indicators, additional charges, and even conditional details.

Although the component handles this increased complexity, it's performing a balancing act. The simplicity of JSX is replaced by the richness of JavaScript logic, where most of the component's character is defined outside the realm of JSX, in the preparatory phase of defining options. This shift from a JSX-dominant structure to a JavaScript-heavy approach illustrates a key aspect of React's flexibility but also underscores the need for careful design choices. As developers, we must constantly weigh the benefits of feature richness against the clarity and maintainability of our code.

In essence, this phase of our journey with the `RadioGroup` component is a microcosm of software development at large. It reflects the constant push and pull between simplicity and complexity, between adding features and maintaining clarity. As we tread further, the need for a more structured approach—one that can handle this complexity gracefully—becomes increasingly apparent. This situation is where composite components, waiting patiently in the wings, come into play, ready to introduce a new paradigm for constructing our React components.

2.2.3   *The ideal JSX*

What if instead of defining options in JavaScript as an array, we pass in child components for each option to the radio group and then deal with all the complexity of an option inside those components? Then we get back to the ideal of dealing with structure, data, and content in JSX rather than in JavaScript, as we normally do in React. Ideally, we could define the bread group like so:

```
<RadioGroup name="bread" onChange= {onChange("bread")}>      ◄──────────────
  <RadioGroup.Option value="bagel">
    Bagel
  </RadioGroup.Option>
  <RadioGroup.Option value="roll">
    Roll
  </RadioGroup.Option>
  <RadioGroup.Option value="croissant" isPopular>       ◄──┐
    Croissant
  </RadioGroup.Option>
</RadioGroup>
```

The options are defined using the subcomponent RadioGroup.Option.

The radio group itself now takes only two properties.

Now we can add extra properties for each option as properties of a component rather than an object.

The following listing shows how the entire app would look in this structure.

Listing 2.9   The ideal JSX for the breakfast-ordering component

```
import { useState } from "react";
import { RadioGroup } from "./radiogroup";
export default function App() {
  const [data, setData] = useState({
    meal: "",
    bread: "",
    side: "",
    beverage: "",
  });
  const onChange = (name) => (value) =>
    setData({ ...data, [name]: value });
  return (
    <main>
      <h1>Breakfast ordering</h1>
```

```
    <h2>Meal</h2>
    <RadioGroup name="meal" onChange={onChange("meal")}>
      <RadioGroup.Option value="small">
        Small: $5.99
      </RadioGroup.Option>
      <RadioGroup.Option value="medium">
        Medium: $7.99
      </RadioGroup.Option>
      <RadioGroup.Option value="large">
        Large: $9.99
      </RadioGroup.Option>
    </RadioGroup>
    <h2>Bread</h2>
    <RadioGroup name="bread" onChange={onChange("bread")}>
      <RadioGroup.Option value="bagel">Bagel</RadioGroup.Option>
      <RadioGroup.Option value="roll">Roll</RadioGroup.Option>
      <RadioGroup.Option
        value="croissant"
        isPopular            ◁┐ Sets the isPopular property
        >                      │ directly on the relevant option
        Croissant
      </RadioGroup.Option>
    </RadioGroup>
    <h2>Side</h2>
    <RadioGroup name="side" onChange={onChange("side")}>
      <RadioGroup.Option icon="🐀" value="avocado">  ◁──  Adds an icon to an
        Avocado                                           option to be displayed
      </RadioGroup.Option>                                before the radio input
      <RadioGroup.Option icon="🥓" value="bacon">
        Bacon <em>(+ $0.99)</em>  ◁──  Defines a label postfix directly as a
      </RadioGroup.Option>             child of the option component without
    </RadioGroup>                      the need for an extra property
    <h2>Beverage</h2>
    <RadioGroup name="beverage" onChange={onChange("beverage")}>
      <RadioGroup.Option value="orangejuice">
        Orange Juice
      </RadioGroup.Option>
      <RadioGroup.Option value="coffee">
        Coffee
        <RadioGroup.Details>  ◁──  Specifies the details element, visible only when
          <select name="coffee_size">   the corresponding option is selected; uses
            <option>Small</option>      another component exposed by the radio group
            <option>Medium</option>
            <option>Large</option>
          </select>
        </RadioGroup.Details>
      </RadioGroup.Option>
    </RadioGroup>
  </main>
  );
}
```

This notion of having subcomponents as part of a larger component is the key to the Composite pattern. A radio group is defined not by one component but by two or three components, depending on how complex the group is.

2.2.4   *Implementation with composite components*

You might be thinking about how you'd implement this example. Two things should be clear: we need to pass information from the radio group to each option, and we need to pass information from an option to a potential details component inside it.

We have a couple of ways to perform these tasks, but the simplest solution is to use a React context for each information channel. You can see the required information flow in figure 2.8.

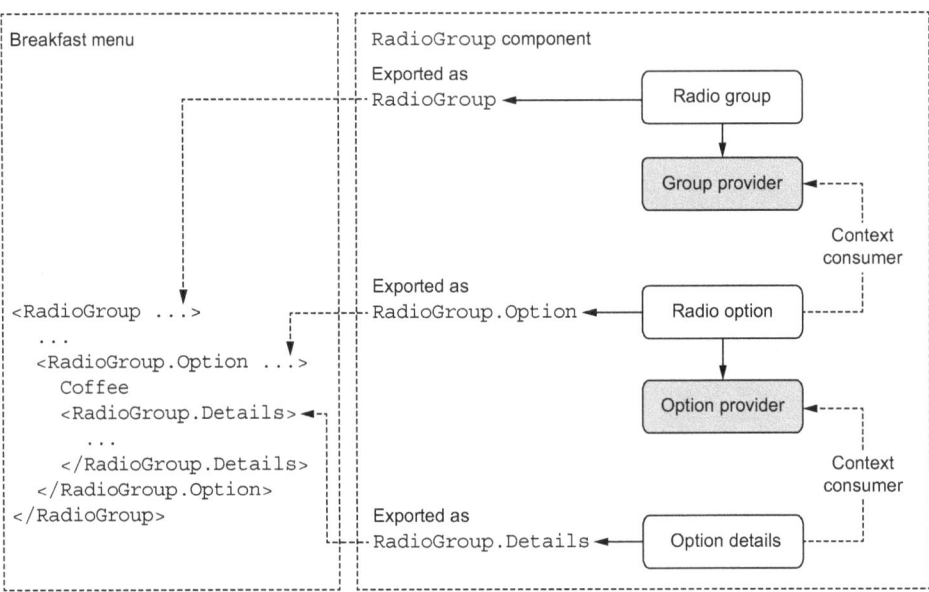

Figure 2.8   We need to pass information from a radio group to an option, including the input name, the currently selected value, and the callback to invoke when the option is selected, which happens through the group provider. We also need to pass some information from the option to the details element, if present—namely, whether it is selected. That happens through the option provider.

Now we're going to implement this iteration of the application in four different files. One file simply defines the contexts to be used by the other three files, which are the individual components. The structure looks like this:

```
/src
  /radiogroup
    contexts.js
    Details.jsx
    index.js
    Option.jsx
    RadioGroup.jsx
  App.jsx
```

We also have `index.js` there, but it simply reexports the main `RadioGroup` component, so the `index.js` file is trivial. Let's start with the contexts in the following listing.

Listing 2.10   Defining the required contexts

```
import { createContext } from "react";
export const RadioGroupContext = createContext();
export const RadioOptionContext = createContext();
```

This file is trivial. We'll use the `RadioGroupContext` to pass information from a radio group to its options and a `RadioOptionContext` to pass information from an option to a potential details element. Next up is the equally trivial `Details` component.

Listing 2.11   The `Details` component

```
import { useContext } from "react";
import { RadioOptionContext } from "./contexts";
export function Details({ children }) {
  const isSelected = useContext(RadioOptionContext);
  return isSelected ? children : null;
}
```

The component simply displays its children if—and only if—its parent radio option is selected. Next is the radio `Option` component, and things get a bit more complex, but this component is still manageable.

Listing 2.12   The `Option` component

```
                                              Accepts the four properties required
                                               to handle all the variants we need
import { useContext } from "react";
import { RadioGroupContext, RadioOptionContext } from "./contexts";
export function Option(
  { value, icon, isPopular, children }                  ⟵
) {
  const { name, selectedValue, onChange } =    Reads some important values
    useContext(RadioGroupContext);             from the parent radio group
  const isSelected = selectedValue === value;
  return (
    <label style={isPopular ? { border: "1px dashed red" } : null}>
      {icon}
      <input
        type="radio"
        value={value}
        name={name}
        checked={isSelected}
        onChange={() => onChange(value)}
      />
      <RadioOptionContext.Provider value={isSelected}>   Wraps the children in
        {children}                                       a context to allow
      </RadioOptionContext.Provider>                     anything in there to
      {isPopular ? <strong>🔥 Popular!</strong> : null}  figure out whether the
    </label>                                             option is selected
  );
}
```

Finally, we have the main `RadioGroup` component. This component is a lot simpler now because it doesn't have any options; it mostly accepts and passes through the children it receives.

Listing 2.13   The `RadioGroup` component and its composites

```
import { useState } from "react";
import { RadioGroupContext } from "./contexts";
import { Option } from "./Option";
import { Details } from "./Details";
export function RadioGroup({ children, name, onChange }) {
  const [selectedValue, setSelectedValue] = useState("");
  const handleChange = (value) => {
    setSelectedValue(value);
    if (onChange) {
      onChange(value);
    }
  };
  const contextValue = {
    name,
    selectedValue,
    onChange: handleChange,
  };
  return (
    <div
      style={{
        display: "flex",
        flexDirection: "column",
        alignItems: "flex-start",
      }}
    >
      <RadioGroupContext.Provider
        value={contextValue}                    Wraps the children in
      >                                          the proper context
        {children}
      </RadioGroupContext.Provider>
    </div>
  );
}                                      Reexports the constituent components as
RadioGroup.Option = Option;            properties of the main component, so we need
RadioGroup.Details = Details;          only a single import to use the radio group
```

Example: radio-composite

This example is in the `ch02/radio-composite` folder. You can use that example by running this command in the source folder:

```
$ npm run dev -w ch02/radio-composite
```

Alternatively, you can go to this website to browse the code, see the example in action in your browser, or download the source code as a zip file: https://reactlikea .pro/ch02-radio-composite.

With this code, we have all the components defined, and individually, they're a lot simpler than in the previous complex example, in which a single component handled all the responsibilities. The beauty of the Composite pattern is that it allows for a harmonious symphony of distinct functionalities, each encapsulated in its own component yet all working together seamlessly. This modular approach not only makes the codebase more intuitive and manageable but also enhances its extendability. With each component handling a specific aspect of the radio group's behavior, we've moved from a monolithic, rigid structure to a flexible, scalable architecture.

In this new paradigm, the `RadioGroup` acts as the conductor, orchestrating the flow of data and events through contexts, while each `Option` and `Details` component plays its part with focused responsibility. The `RadioGroupContext` elegantly manages the shared state and behavior among the options, ensuring a cohesive user experience. The `RadioOptionContext`, on the other hand, provides a direct communication channel to the `Details` component, allowing for dynamic content rendering based on the selection state.

The result is a `RadioGroup` component that is not only functionally rich but also a pleasure to work with and extend. It's a testament to the power of breaking complex interfaces into smaller, more manageable pieces, each with a clear purpose. This approach not only simplifies development and maintenance but also opens the door to more creative and complex UI designs while keeping the codebase clean and approachable. The journey from clutter and confusion to clarity and elegance showcases the transformative power of the Composite pattern in React development.

2.2.5 *How useful is the Composite pattern?*

The Composite pattern may initially appear to be a mere structural convenience for organizing components, but its utility in React development runs much deeper. This pattern is not just a tool for creating cleaner code; it's also a fundamental strategy for building scalable and maintainable applications. In a large-scale application, the Composite pattern can be the key to managing complex component hierarchies, allowing for a modular and flexible architecture.

Imagine your application as a collection of interrelated components, each serving a specific purpose. With the Composite pattern, you can construct intricate UIs by combining these components in various configurations, each component acting as a building block. A complex form could be composed of various input components, validation messages, and control buttons, each defined separately but all working together as a cohesive unit.

Some developers might prefer using direct parent–child relationships or other state management techniques for organizing component structures. But the Composite pattern offers a level of abstraction and flexibility that these methods often lack. By decoupling child components from their parent, the Composite pattern allows for greater reuse and easier modification of individual components.

This pattern excels when UI components need to be reused and recombined in various ways, making it an invaluable asset in your React toolkit. Understanding when and how to employ the Composite pattern effectively is crucial for any React developer who aims to build sophisticated, robust web applications.

2.3   *The Summary pattern*

All right, let's dive into our third and last React design pattern: Summary. Don't let its simple appearance fool you; this pattern is a game changer. It makes React components sleek and efficient, especially the part above the JSX return. Think of the Summary pattern as a neat trick for tidying your code by packing logic into custom hooks. Using this pattern is like giving your components a makeover for a more streamlined, sophisticated look. As a bonus, your fellow devs will thank you for making collaboration a breeze.

Now comes the fun part. We're going to walk through two examples that show off how handy the Summary pattern is. First, we'll see how a single custom hook can do wonders in simplifying a component, making it easy like Sunday morning. This example shows how one well-crafted hook can make your component look and function better.

Next, we'll jump into a trickier scenario in which two or three custom hooks come into play. The Summary pattern shows its true colors in handling complex situations with style. Splitting the logic into multiple hooks not only organizes your component better but also opens a world of reusability and flexibility.

Figure 2.9 is your visual guide to the way the Summary pattern transforms the traditional component structure into something more refined and efficient. The pattern is like before-and-after photos for your React components. So let's get on with it and see how this seemingly simple pattern can have a big effect on your React development.

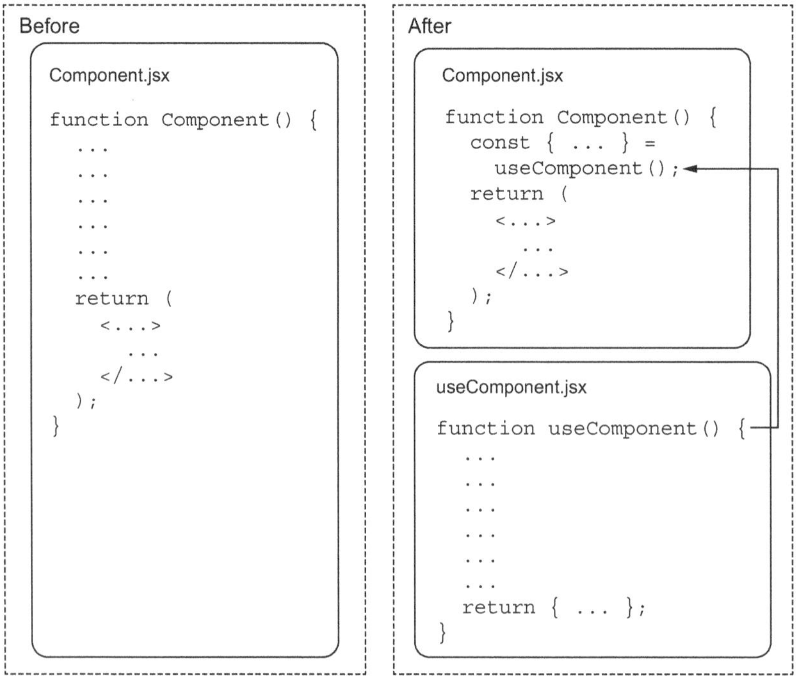

```
Before

Component.jsx

function Component() {
  ...
  ...
  ...
  ...
  ...
  ...
  return (
    <...>
      ...
    </...>
  );
}
```

```
After

Component.jsx

function Component() {
  const { ... } =
    useComponent();
  return (
    <...>
      ...
    </...>
  );
}
```

```
useComponent.jsx

function useComponent() {
  ...
  ...
  ...
  ...
  ...
  ...
  return { ... };
}
```

Figure 2.9   The essence of the Summary pattern captured in a simple diagram. Before, the component consisted of a bunch of code before the JSX and then a bunch of JSX. After, the component is a few lines before the JSX, and all the remaining code has been put in a custom hook specific to that component.

2.3.1 *A single custom hook*

We will start with a component that should be familiar to you: the `RadioGroup` component from listing 2.13 a few pages back. First, let's zoom in on the part of the component that comes before the return statement:

```
const [selectedValue, setSelectedValue] = useState("");
const handleChange = (value) => {
  setSelectedValue(value);
  if (onChange) {
    onChange(value);
  }
};
const contextValue = {
  name,
  selectedValue,
  onChange: handleChange,
};
```

This snippet isn't a lot of code, but it could be even less. The only value we need for the JSX is the `contextValue` at the end, so if we were to create a custom hook, all we'd need from it would be that object. So we could rewrite the code as

```
const contextValue = useContextValue({ name, onChange });
```

Note that we need to pass in both the `name` and `onChange` properties, as they're used by the context. And yes, we can easily create such a custom hook like so:

```
import { useState } from "react";
export function useContextValue({ name, onChange }) {
  const [selectedValue, setSelectedValue] = useState("");
  const handleChange = (value) => {
    setSelectedValue(value);
    if (onChange) {
      onChange(value);
    }
  };
  return {
    name,
    selectedValue,
    onChange: handleChange,
  };
});
```

We've essentially moved these lines to a new function. That's it. But the result is a much cleaner `RadioGroup` component, as you can see in the following listing.

Listing 2.14   The `RadioGroup` component summarized

```
import { RadioGroupContext } from "./contexts";
import { Option } from "./Option";
import { Details } from "./Details";
import { useContextValue } from "./useContextValue";
```

```
export function RadioGroup({ children, name, onChange }) {
  const contextValue =
    useContextValue({ name, onChange });         ┐  Prepares for the JSX return
  return (                                       │  in a single line invoking the
    <div                                         ┘  new custom hook
      style={{
        display: "flex",
        flexDirection: "column",
        alignItems: "flex-start",
      }}
    >
      <RadioGroupContext.Provider value={contextValue}>
        {children}
      </RadioGroupContext.Provider>
    </div>
  );
}
RadioGroup.Option = Option;
RadioGroup.Details = Details;
```

Example: radio-summary

This example is in the `ch02/radio-summary` folder. You can use that example by running this command in the source folder:

```
$ npm run dev -w ch02/radio-summary
```

Alternatively, you can go to this website to browse the code, see the example in action in your browser, or download the source code as a zip file: https://reactlikea.pro/ch02-radio-summary.

That's it. This example seems deceptively simple, and it is. But your code will look so much more impressive with this one small change. Trust me!

Note that we removed more lines than just the few inside the component. We also got rid of an import because we no longer need `useState` in this file. Yes, we did add a new import for the custom hook, but often, we can remove more than one import.

2.3.2 *Better results with more complexity*

Let's look at a more complex component with many more dependencies and more regular hooks. This time, we're building a user profile component; the user can see and edit their user data as well as update their preferences (such as theme and notifications). The result looks like figure 2.10. (Please imagine that it looks pretty, with some professional styles.)

To implement this page, we have a hook to access our API functionality from a shared place, called `useAPI`. We also have components to render the user data, user data edit form, and user preferences (equally obviously named). So let's see what this

Figure 2.10 The user profile page in view mode and edit mode, respectively

component looks like in a common setup. We put all the basic and custom hooks used directly in the component itself.

Listing 2.15 User profile before summarizing

```
import { useState, useEffect } from "react";
import { UserDataForm } from "./UserDataForm";
import { UserDetails } from "./UserDetails";
import { UserPreferences } from "./UserPreferences";
import { useAPI } from "./useAPI";
export function LongUserProfile({ userId }) {
  const [userData, setUserData] = useState(null);
  const [editMode, setEditMode] = useState(false);
  const [userPreferences, setUserPreferences] =
    useState({
      theme: "light",
      notifications: true,
    });
  // Fetching user data
  const api = useAPI();
  useEffect(() => {
    api
      .fetchUser(userId)
      .then((response) => response.json())
      .then((data) => setUserData(data));
  }, [api, userId]);
  // Initializing user preferences
  useEffect(() => {
    const storedPreferences = localStorage.getItem("userPreferences");
    if (storedPreferences) {
```

Creates three stateful values using useState

Accesses the API using a custom hook

Registers three effects using useEffect

```
      setUserPreferences(JSON.parse(storedPreferences));
    }
  }, []);
  // Updating user preferences
  useEffect(() => {                      ◁──┐  Registers three effects
    localStorage.setItem(                    │  using useEffect
      "userPreferences",
      JSON.stringify(userPreferences)
    );
  }, [userPreferences]);
  // Toggle edit mode
  const toggleEditMode =
    () => setEditMode(!editMode);
  // Update preferences                       Creates callbacks to
  const updatePreferences =                   be used in the JSX
    (newPreferences) =>
      setUserPreferences(newPreferences);
  if (!userData) return <div>Loading...</div>;
  return (
    <div>
      <h1>User Profile</h1>
      {editMode ? (
        <UserDataForm
          userData={userData}
          onChange={setUserData}                    ◁──┐
        />                                              │
      ) : (                                             │
        <UserDetails userData={userData} />             │
      )}                                                │  Uses callbacks created above
      <button onClick={toggleEditMode}>        ◁──     the JSX to add interactivity
        {editMode ? "Save Changes" : "Edit Profile"}    where required
      </button>                                         │
      <UserPreferences                                  │
        preferences={userPreferences}                   │
        onPreferencesChange={updatePreferences}  ◁──┘
      />
    </div>
  );
}
```

Now let's move all the logic before the (first) return to a custom hook.

Listing 2.16 User profile custom hook

```
import { useEffect, useState } from "react";
import { useAPI } from "./useAPI";
function useFetchUserData(userId) {          ◁──┐  Creates a small custom
  const [userData, setUserData] = useState(null); │  hook for part of the logic
  const api = useAPI();
  useEffect(() => {
    // API call to fetch user data
    api
      .fetchUser(userId)
```

```
      .then((response) => response.json())
      .then((data) => setUserData(data));
  }, [api, userId]);
  return userData;
}
export function useUserProfile(userId) {
  const [editMode, setEditMode] = useState(false);
  const [userPreferences, setUserPreferences] = useState({
    theme: "light",
    notifications: true,
  });
  const userData = useFetchUserData(userId);
  useEffect(() => {
    const storedPreferences = localStorage.getItem("userPreferences");
    if (storedPreferences) {
      setUserPreferences(JSON.parse(storedPreferences));
    }
  }, []);
  useEffect(() => {
    localStorage.setItem(
      "userPreferences",
      JSON.stringify(userPreferences)
    );
  }, [userPreferences]);
  const toggleEditMode = () => setEditMode(!editMode);
  const updatePreferences = (newPreferences) =>
    setUserPreferences(newPreferences);
  return {
    userData,
    editMode,
    userPreferences,
    toggleEditMode,
    updatePreferences,
  };
}
```

Creates the main custom hook that captures all the logic required

Returns all the values needed by the component for display

With that task done, our base component looks like the following listing.

Listing 2.17 User profile after summarization

```
import { useUserProfile } from "./useUserProfile";
import { UserDataForm } from "./UserDataForm";
import { UserDetails } from "./UserDetails";
import { UserPreferences } from "./UserPreferences";
export function CompactUserProfile({ userId }) {
  const {
    userData,
    editMode,
    userPreferences,
    toggleEditMode,
    updatePreferences,
  } = useUserProfile(userId);
  if (!userData) return <div>Loading...</div>;
```

Destructs all the values from the custom hook. Even though this destructuring takes up many lines, we still save a ton overall.

```
    return (
      <div>
        <h1>User Profile</h1>
        {editMode ? (
          <UserDataForm
            userData={userData}
            onSave={toggleEditMode}
          />
        ) : (
          <UserDetails userData={userData} />
        )}
        <button onClick={toggleEditMode}>
          {editMode ? "Save Changes" : "Edit Profile"}
        </button>
        <UserPreferences
          preferences={userPreferences}
          onPreferencesChange={updatePreferences}
        />
      </div>
    );
}
```

Example: user-summary

This example is in the `ch02/user-summary` folder. You can use that example by running this command in the source folder:

```
$ npm run dev -w ch02/user-summary
```

Alternatively, you can go to this website to browse the code, see the example in action in your browser, or download the source code as a zip file: https://reactlikea .pro/ch02-user-summary.

That's a much shorter component! We went from 58 to 34 lines (ignoring empty lines) in the component file. We did add a second file, so the total line count has increased, but each file is short and condensed and has a simple, single purpose—a huge improvement and a much cleaner component. The best part is that if you're an experienced developer, you might not even have to look inside the `useUserProfile` hook because what it does is obvious based on the return values and how they're used—an instant LGTM (Looks Good To Me) in the pull-request code review!

NOTE   The example in listings 2.16 and 2.17 would be even cleaner if we also adopted the Provider pattern and wrapped all the child components in a provider. But I'll leave that task as an exercise for you.

2.3.3   *Multiple hooks required*

Let's create a simple task manager this time around. You can see it at different stages in figure 2.11. Let's implement it in a single big component, as shown in listing 2.18.

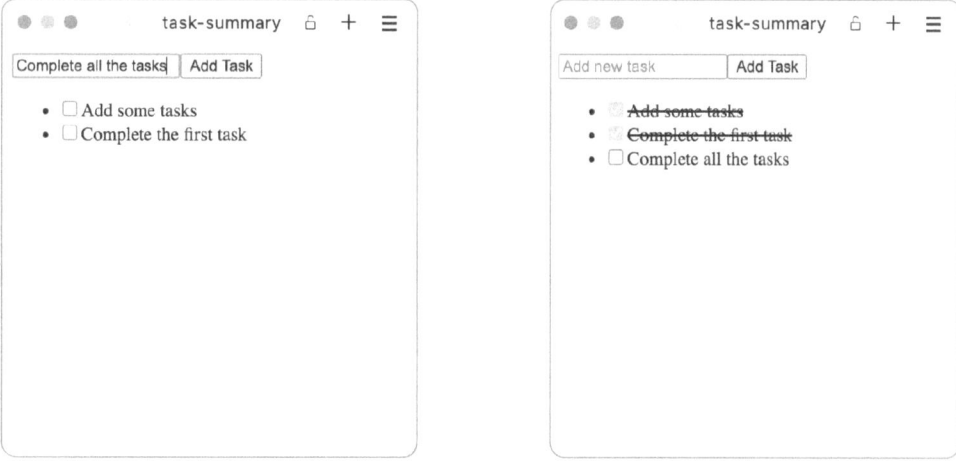

Figure 2.11   The task manager in action. We can add, see, and complete tasks. What else would we ever want to do?

Listing 2.18   Task manager before summarization (excerpt)

```
import { useState, useCallback } from "react";
export function LongTaskManager() {
  const [newTask, setNewTask] = useState("");
  const [tasks, setTasks] = useState([]);
  const handleNewTaskChange = (e) => {
    setNewTask(e.target.value);
  };
  const addTask = (task) => {
    if (task.trim() !== "") {
      setTasks((prevTasks) => [
        ...prevTasks,
        { task, completed: false },
      ]);
    }
  };
  const toggleTaskCompletion = useCallback(
    (index) => {
      setTasks((prevTasks) =>
        prevTasks.map((task, i) =>
          i === index ? { ...task, completed: !task.completed } : task
        )
      );
    },
    [],
  );
  const handleSubmit = (e) => {
    e.preventDefault();
    addTask(newTask);
```

Wraps a callback in a memoization hook. This code doesn't do anything in this instance, as we'll discuss in chapter 3, but it's included for the example.

```
    setNewTask("");
  };
  return (
    ...         ◁────┐  The returned JSX is quite straightforward but
  );                 │  skipped here for brevity. You can see it in the
}                    │  attached task-summary example or in listing 2.21.
```

Nothing here is surprising. You should be able to write this component, and most developers would do it something like listing 2.18. But we can do better: we have 20-plus lines of logic before the return that can be reduced significantly for improved overview!

Although we could extract the entire logic into a single hook, and nothing is stopping us, the logic kind of splits into two groups of code. One group deals with the task list and with adding and toggling tasks inside it; the other deals with the add-new-task form and its internal logic required to update the form's state and handle the submit. These two nonoverlapping responsibilities make it a prime candidate for two separate hooks, though they won't be completely separate because the form-handling hook needs to know about the `addTask` function from the task-list hook. The following listing shows how we could move the task-list logic to a separate hook.

Listing 2.19 Task-list custom hook

```
import { useCallback, useState } from "react";
export function useTaskList() {
  const [tasks, setTasks] = useState([]);
  const addTask = (task) => {
    if (task.trim() !== "") {
      setTasks((prevTasks) => [
        ...prevTasks,
        { task, completed: false },
      ]);
    }
  };
  const toggleTaskCompletion = useCallback((index) => {
    setTasks((prevTasks) =>
      prevTasks.map((task, i) =>
        i === index ? { ...task, completed: !task.completed } : task
      )
    );
  }, []);
  return { tasks, addTask, toggleTaskCompletion };  ◁──┘ Returns the three
}                                                        properties we need
```

Next is the `useNewTask` hook, which takes the `addTask` function from the `useTaskList` hook as an argument.

Listing 2.20 New-task custom hook

```
import { useState } from "react";              ┐  Accepts the addTask function to be
export function useNewTaskInput(addTask) {  ◁──┘  passed in by the main component
  const [newTask, setNewTask] = useState("");
```

```
  const handleNewTaskChange = (e) => {
    setNewTask(e.target.value);
  };
  const handleSubmit = (e) => {
    e.preventDefault();
    addTask(newTask);
    setNewTask(""); // Reset input after adding task
  };
  return {
    newTask,                      Returns the three
    handleNewTaskChange,          properties we need to
    handleSubmit                  handle adding tasks
  };
}
```

The following listing shows the new compact task manager with the logic summarized into two hooks.

Listing 2.21   The optimized task-list manager

```
import { useNewTaskInput } from "./useNewTask";
import { useTaskList } from "./useTaskList";
export function CompactTaskManager() {
  const { tasks, addTask, toggleTaskCompletion } =    Invokes the task-list
    useTaskList();                                      custom hook first
  const {
    newTask,                      Invokes the add-task custom
    handleNewTaskChange,          hook second, as it needs a
    handleSubmit                  value from the first hook
  } = useNewTaskInput(addTask);
  return (
    <div>
      <form onSubmit={handleSubmit}>
        <input
          type="text"
          value={newTask}
          onChange={handleNewTaskChange}
          placeholder="Add new task"
        />
        <button type="submit">Add Task</button>
      </form>
      <ul>
        {tasks.map((task, index) => (
          <li
            key={index}
            style={{
              textDecoration: task.completed ? "line-through" : "none",
            }}
          >
            <input
              type="checkbox"
              checked={task.completed}
              onChange={() => toggleTaskCompletion(index)}
              disabled={task.completed}
```

```
        />
        {task.task}
      </li>
    ))}
  </ul>
 </div>
 );
}
```

> **Example: task-summary**
>
> This example is in the `ch02/task-summary` folder. You can use that example by run-ning this command in the source folder:
>
> `$ npm run dev -w ch02/task-summary`
>
> Alternatively, you can go to this website to browse the code, see the example in action in your browser, or download the source code as a zip file: https://reactlikea .pro/ch02-task-summary.

The choice between using a single hook or multiple hooks is completely arbitrary, of course, and up to the developer in charge. In this instance, a single hook might have been okay, but I prefer a two-hook version for this example.

2.3.4   *How useful is the Summary pattern?*

In conclusion, the Summary pattern stands out for its ability to streamline and orga-nize React components. After exploring its application through single or multiple cus-tom hooks, we see that this pattern is a key player in enhancing code clarity and maintainability.

The strength of the Summary pattern lies in its versatility and scalability. Whether we're simplifying a component with a single hook or orchestrating several hooks for more complex scenarios, it offers a tailored approach to managing component logic. This pattern not only cleans up code but also fosters a mindset of reusability, making it invaluable for larger projects in which consistency is crucial.

In essence, the Summary pattern may be understated, but its contribution to creat-ing efficient, manageable React applications is undeniable. It exemplifies the princi-ple that effective solutions often lie in simplicity and thoughtful organization.

Summary

- Effective software development mirrors core principles of architecture, empha-sizing stability, structure, and use of appropriate patterns.
- The Provider pattern in React centralizes and simplifies data management, making it indispensable for global state control in complex applications.
- By using the Provider pattern, React developers can pass data and functions efficiently through component hierarchies, enhancing organization and functionality.

- The Composite pattern in React offers a strategic approach to managing complex UI structures, enabling modular and flexible component architecture.
- Embracing the Composite pattern allows for dynamic and complex UI designs, fostering component reusability and structural integrity in React projects.
- The Summary pattern in React focuses on reducing code clutter by abstracting logic into custom hooks, leading to cleaner, more maintainable components.
- Implementing the Summary pattern enhances the readability and scalability of React components, contributing to efficient and collaborative coding practices.
- In React development, adhering to foundational design patterns such as Provider, Composite, and Summary ensures the creation of robust and innovative applications.
- Mastering these React design patterns gives developers the tools to build diverse and stable digital structures, much like in physical construction.

Optimizing React performance

Navigating the complex world of React development requires more than just coding skills; it also demands an in-depth understanding of how React components behave and render. Have you ever pondered why a component re-renders or perhaps why it refuses to do so? The answers are often hidden in the subtle interplay of component relationships, state changes, and React's internal rendering logic.

Dispelling common myths about React rendering is essential. The idea that component re-renders are triggered only by property changes, for example, is a misconception that could lead developers astray. Understanding these nuances is key to writing efficient and effective React code.

Two of the central topics when it comes to (mis)understanding how React renders are memoization and dependency arrays. *Memoization*—a cornerstone in React optimization—is a technique centered on rendering efficiently and avoiding unnecessary recalculations. Using React's `memo()`, `useMemo`, and `useCallback` hooks effectively can significantly enhance your application's performance.

At the core of React's reactive nature are *dependency arrays*, which are used in hooks like `useEffect` and `useMemo`. These arrays are crucial in determining how and when your components update, making them fundamental to your React toolkit. It's important to balance optimization with practicality, however. Overoptimizing sometimes introduces complexity without tangible benefits, making it crucial to optimize judiciously.

This chapter delves into the intricacies of React's rendering process, offering insights into optimization strategies, the role of memoization, and the effective use of dependency arrays. Embark on this journey to deepen your understanding and mastery of React, ensuring that your applications are not just functional but also optimally efficient.

> **NOTE**   The source code for the examples in this chapter is available at https:// reactlikea.pro/ch03.

3.1   *Understanding React rendering*

To optimize React rendering, we need to understand it first. A functional component will render for one of three reasons:

- The component has just been *mounted*. (It was not in the component tree before and is now.)
- The parent component just re-rendered.
- The component uses a hook that has flagged this component for re-render.

That's it. If none of these things happens, your component will not re-render, and that's a guarantee. If any one of the three happens, your component will re-render for sure. But React might batch rendering after several of these things happen. If a state value changes *and* the parent component re-renders, for example, the component might re-render once, or it might re-render twice. That process is controlled by React and depends on subtle timing details.

You should have a fairly good understanding of all these things by now with your basic knowledge of React, so I won't go into detail. But I will discuss some misconceptions about this list. In particular, I'll go over these two myths:

- *React re-renders a component if the properties change.* Technically, that statement is not true, and that technicality matters.
- *In React 18 using Strict Mode, React mounts every component twice.* The reality is slightly different.

Let's discuss these two myths because they are important.

3.1.1 Changing properties is irrelevant

There's a common belief in React circles that components re-render because their properties change, but that's not the case, as we can prove in two ways:

- We can create a component that has properties that change but doesn't re-render.
- We can create a component that is rendered many times with the same properties and that re-renders every time.

Both of these situations are easy to imagine. First, we need a component that clearly shows whether it re-renders. Let's create that component as shown in the following listing.

Listing 3.1 A component that highlights re-renders

```
import { useEffect } from "react";
import { useRef } from "react";
export function Rerenderable() {
  const isFirst = useRef(true);            Sets the isFirst ref to false in an
  useEffect(() => {                        effect that, as always, runs
    isFirst.current = false;       <───┘   after the current render
  }, []);
  const style =
    { color: isFirst.current ? "red" : "blue" };   Results in a different render
  const text = isFirst.current                     on first render versus
    ? "First render" : "Not first render";         subsequent renders
  return <p style={style}>{text}</p>;
}
```

Next, let's create two components that use this component to highlight the two points.

Listing 3.2 Triggering re-renders against the myth

```
import { useRef, useState } from "react";
import { Rerenderable } from "./Rerenderable";
function RerenderWithoutPropsChange() {
  const [, setCount] = useState(0);      <───   Initializes state, but we need
  return (                                       to update it, not read it
    <div>
      <button
        onClick={() => setCount((c) => c + 1)}>   <───  Updates state to
        Click to re-render                              force a re-render
      </button>
      <Rerenderable />   <───   Embeds the re-renderable
    </div>                      component without any props
  );
}
function NoRerenderWithPropsChange() {      Defines a ref, which we can update
  const count = useRef(0);        <───┘     without triggering a re-render
  return (
    <div>                                        Updates the value
      <button onClick={() => count.current++}>   <───┘  inside the ref
```

```
        Click to re-render
      </button>
      <Rerenderable count={count.current} />          ◁──┐ Includes the re-renderable
    </div>                                                 component with a property
  );                                                       extracted from inside the ref
}
export default function App() {
  return (
    <main>
      <h4>Re-renders without changing properties</h4>
      <RerenderWithoutPropsChange />
      <h4>No re-render with changing properties</h4>
      <NoRerenderWithPropsChange />
    </main>
  );
}
```

> **Example: rerender**
>
> This example is in the `ch03/rerender` folder. You can use that example by running this command in the source folder:
>
> ```
> $ npm run dev -w ch03/rerender
> ```
>
> Alternatively, you can go to this website to browse the code, see the example in action in your browser, or download the source code as a zip file: https://reactlikea .pro/ch03-rerender.

The point of the application in listing 3.2 is that if the myth were true, the `Rerenderable` inside `RerenderWithoutPropsChange` would never re-render because the properties never change. Likewise, the `Rerenderable` component inside `NoRerenderWith-PropsChange` should re-render even though the parent doesn't because the property passed to it updates. Neither of those things happens, as you can see in figure 3.1.

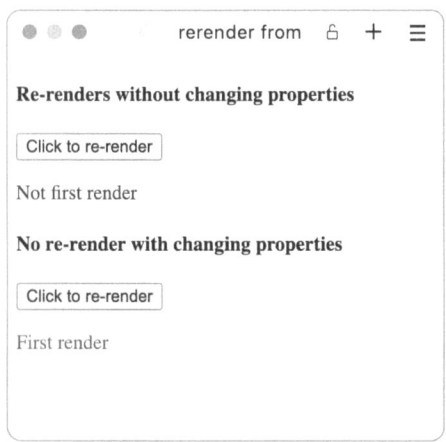

Figure 3.1 The result of clicking both buttons. If the myth were true, the top component would not re-render, whereas it clearly does, and the bottom component would re-render, whereas it clearly doesn't.

What does this mean? React components re-render when their parents do regardless of which properties they take, where those properties come from, or how those properties potentially update.

3.1.2   *Repeated function calls in Strict Mode while in development*

In Strict Mode during development using React 18 or later, React does several tricks to see whether your components are well designed, including running a bunch of functions multiple times. The reality can be tricky. It seems that components mount twice, but they don't; they render twice. Also, effects, initializers, and updaters are run twice (not every time, but sometimes). You don't gain anything directly from this feature, but it's a quirk of React that you need to be aware of. Let's create a sample component that uses a bunch of these features to see how it runs in a normal run versus a Strict Mode development run.

Listing 3.3   A sample application with various effects

```
import { useEffect, useRef, useState } from "react";
let outsideCount = 0;
export default function App() {
  const ref = useRef(true);
  const [count, setCount] = useState(() => {
    console.log(
      "initializing count to", outsideCount
    );
    return outsideCount++;
  });
  console.log("rendering with ", count);
  useEffect(() => {
    console.log(
      "effect first time?", ref.current
    );
    ref.current = false;
    setCount((c) => {
      console.log(
        "setting count from ", c, " to ", c + 1
      );
      return c + 1;
    });
    return () => console.log("cleaning up");
  }, []);
  useEffect(() => {
    console.log("effect every time?", count);
    return () => console.log("cleaning up every time");
  }, [count]);
  return <h1>What is the count? {count}</h1>;
}
```

Logs out what happens in various stages of the component life cycle

First, let's examine the output when we run this component under normal circumstances. For this purpose, we can run the component with React 17, run it without Strict Mode, or run it in a production environment. The easiest solution is to remove Strict Mode, so we will modify `main.jsx` as shown in the following listing.

Listing 3.4 Running without Strict Mode

```
import ReactDOM from "react-dom/client";
import App from "./App.jsx";
ReactDOM.createRoot(document.getElementById("root")).render(
  /*<React.StrictMode>*/                    Removes Strict Mode by hiding these
  <App />                                   JSX nodes inside comment blocks
  /*</React.StrictMode>*/
);
```

> ### Example: strict-mode
> This example is in the `ch03/strict-mode` folder. You can use that example by running this command in the source folder:
>
> ```
> $ npm run dev -w ch03/strict-mode
> ```
>
> Alternatively, you can go to this website to browse the code, see the example in action in your browser, or download the source code as a zip file: https://reactlikea.pro/ch03-strict-mode.

So what's the output? It's kind of what we would expect:

```
initializing count to 0
rendering with  0
effect first time? true
setting count from  0  to  1
effect every time? 0
rendering with  1
cleaning up every time
effect every time? 1
```

Let's draw what happened in a (surprisingly complex) diagram (figure 3.2).

Now let's see how the output changes when we re-enable Strict Mode (by reverting `main.jsx` to the original):

```
initializing count to 0
rendering with  0
initializing count to 1
rendering with  1
effect first time? true
setting count from  1  to  2
effect every time? 1
cleaning up
cleaning up every time
effect first time? false
effect every time? 1
setting count from  2  to  3
rendering with  3
setting count from  2  to  3
rendering with  3
cleaning up every time
effect every time? 3
```

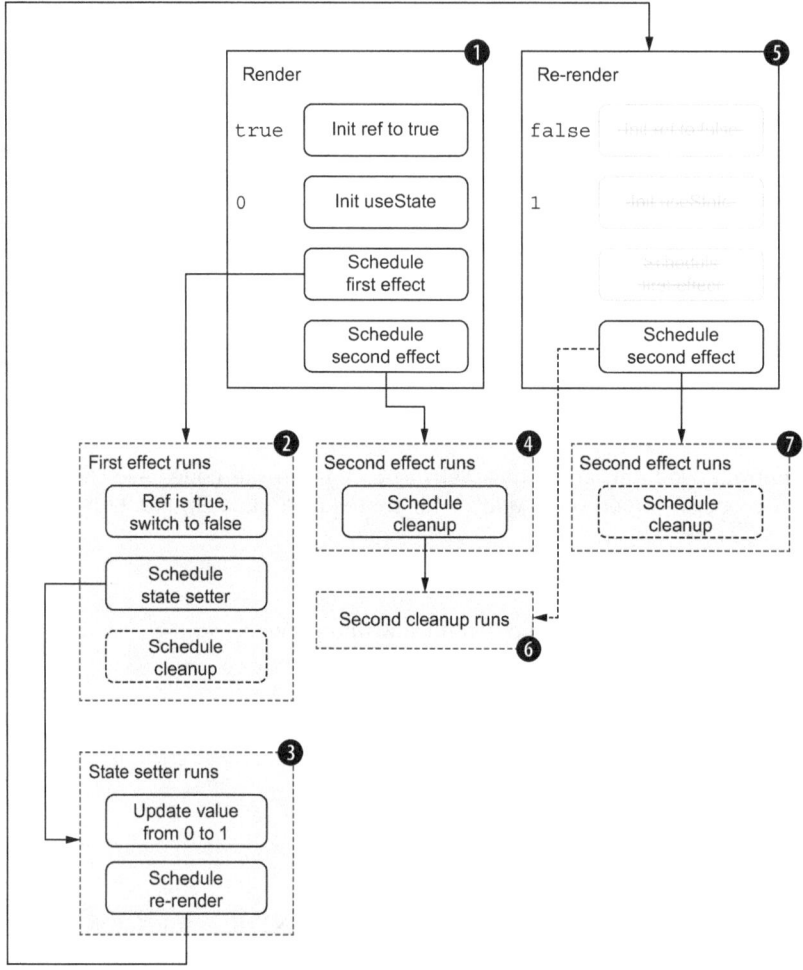

Figure 3.2   The flow of the component under normal circumstances. The large numbers are the order in which the various parts run. On the initial render (1), state is initialized and both effects are scheduled (steps 2 and 4), and when the first effect runs (2), it schedules a setter (3), which, in turn, schedules a re-render. On the re-render (5), the state is not reinitialized and the first effect doesn't run, but the second effect does run (7), making sure to clean up first (6). Note that two of the scheduled cleanups never run (the ones with a dashed border) because those effects are never rescheduled in this application's life cycle.

That code has a lot more lines of output! We see multiple initializers, and we see the first effect running multiple times but with different output. Strict Mode even cleans up the first effect, though we normally wouldn't expect that to happen before the component unmounts because it's scheduled with an empty dependency array. Let's try to diagram what happens during Strict Mode in figure 3.3, but beware—it's getting complicated!

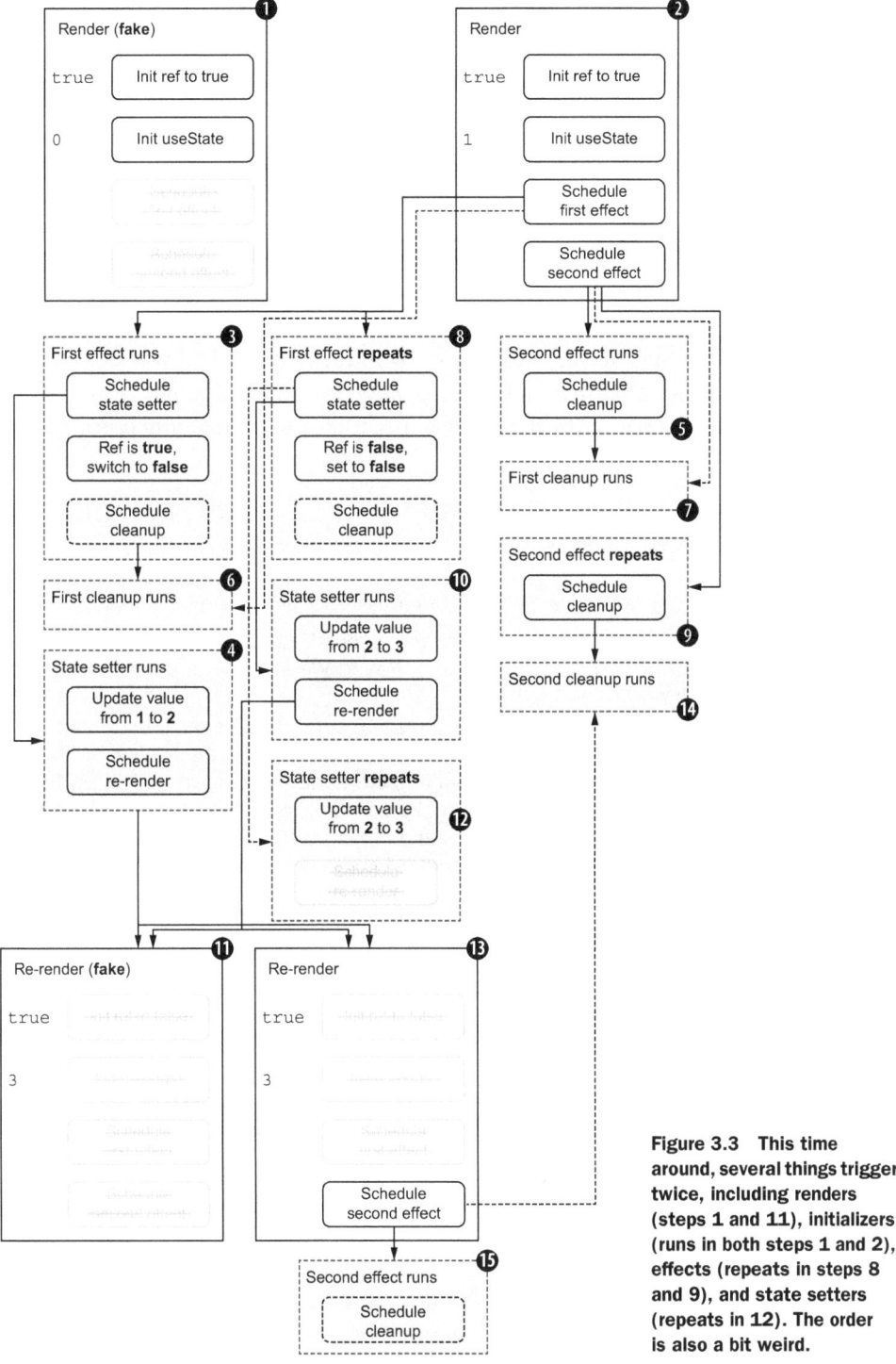

Figure 3.3   This time around, several things trigger twice, including renders (steps 1 and 11), initializers (runs in both steps 1 and 2), effects (repeats in steps 8 and 9), and state setters (repeats in 12). The order is also a bit weird.

Figure 3.3 is the most complex diagram I have ever made. Getting it right took me a long time, and I already knew most of this stuff, so don't worry too much if you don't understand it completely.

React executes all those different types of functions in seemingly arbitrary order and with seemingly arbitrary repeats to allow you to catch potential bugs before they become production problems. React reserves the right to create smarter components in the future, when offstage components might suspend while they're not displayed (such as when they're outside the viewport or in an inactive browser window). Only when those components are redisplayed will they reanimate. You must allow all these functions to rerun so your components will reinitialize correctly.

Though that example seems to involve new worries, they're mostly edge-case situations anyway. Stick to the main takeaway in this section, and you should be safe from most problems. That main takeaway is *make sure that renders, initializers, effects, and state setters are pure functions.* By that, I mean it's crucial that these functions have no outside inputs or outside effects.

Where did we go wrong?

In our example in listing 3.3, the count ends up at 3 with Strict Mode even though it goes only to 1 in production. Why? Well, we're doing two things wrong:

- *The initializer has outside inputs and outside effects.* It reads from and updates a variable outside the scope of React. We should not do that. Truth be told, I did it only to break things.
- *The effect is not pure.* Sure, the state setter is pure, as it updates from the old value to that value + 1, but the effect is not pure, as it changes the state. To do things correctly, we should decrement the state in a cleanup function. To be fair, however, it doesn't make sense to increment a state value in an effect, so this example is made up. In reality, you'd increment based on a user action such as a pointer click, keyboard press, or form submission, and the events would trigger only once.

TIP   Some known problems can arise from effects running twice. The React documentation has a great list of suggestions on how to circumvent these problems at https://mng.bz/oeoZ.

3.2 *Optimizing performance by minimizing re-rendering*

Several times, I have mentioned the importance of minimizing unnecessary renders. But how important is it to minimize re-rendering, and what tools can we use?

JavaScript tries to run at about 60 frames per second in most browsers, which is only 16 milliseconds (ms) per frame. Each time React renders one or more components, that counts as one frame. So if your entire React render takes more than 16 ms, your browser will start to treat your script as slow and start dropping frames. For some applications, this situation won't matter, but if you have a lot of animations and other moving elements, it will matter, and users will notice.

Secondarily, response time matters. Research shows that a user interface should update within 0.1 second for reaction to seem instantaneous to the user. If your UI is slower, your users will notice, which might result in their double-clicking buttons because the first click doesn't work, or they may simply leave in annoyance because the app feels slow.

There are many ways to optimize JavaScript applications in general and React applications in particular, and I'm not going to cover all of them—only the ones that are particularly relevant to React. One method that I've already discussed is minimizing state updates. We want to make sure that we update the component state only when the resulting component output must change.

Another common tool in the React toolbox is memoization, which I've already mentioned a few times. In this section, you're going to see a lot more examples.

NOTE With the introduction of React 19, an experimental feature known as the React Compiler aims to automatically handle memoization, potentially making manual techniques like `memo()`, `useMemo()`, and `useCallback()` obsolete. While this feature promises to simplify performance optimizations by automating them, it remains experimental and is not yet widely adopted, so understanding and applying traditional memoization methods is still relevant for current development practices.

What is memoization?

Memoization involves remembering the last input and output of a *pure* function and, if the function is invoked with those same inputs the next time around, returning the already calculated output rather than calling the function again. Note that it makes sense only for a pure function whose return value depends solely on its inputs—never any outside information or randomness.

This process can sometimes be considered to be caching. But whereas caching often remembers many different values for many different inputs, memoization normally remembers only the latest call to a given function, checks whether the next call is equivalent, and then reuses the previous answer.

React has a `memo()` function that can memoize a component, but it doesn't work for noncomponent functions. If you want to memoize regular functions and not just React components, you should install a package such as `memoizee` (note the two es):

```
import memoize from 'memoizee';
const rawAddition = (a, b) => a + b;
const addition = memoize(rawAddition);
```

In this example, if we invoked the unmemoized function, `rawAddition()`, with the same values again and again, the calculation would be performed over and over. But if we invoked the memoized variant, `addition()`, with the same values again and again, the calculation would be performed only the first time, and the response would be cached. The cached response would be returned for the subsequent invocations as long as the inputs remained the same.

We can memoize bits of React applications in three ways:

- We can memoize an entire component.
- We can memoize a bit of JSX.
- We can memoize a property to be passed to a component.

I will discuss all these approaches with examples in the following subsections. After going through examples that require memoization, I'll discuss the hooks that we use to achieve this purpose in more technical detail.

3.2.1 *Memoize a component*

I've already mentioned something that you might find a bit weird: when a component renders, all child components also render, whether they have changed or not. This forced rendering of all children includes child components that are completely self-contained and don't take properties, they only render a static bit of JSX. Also, component-accepting properties will render even if they're given the same properties again.

We can use the `memo()` function from the React module to memoize an entire component. Then, if the component is invoked again with the same properties (or lack thereof), it will not render again but use the same response that was already calculated once.

In such a case, React optimizes the reconciliation of your component into the browser's document object model (DOM) and realizes that no new information has been created, so the DOM does not even need to be compared to the JSX. React knows that, because the JSX is not just similar but exactly the same, the DOM will already be correct. Such optimizations can save a lot of time!

Let's create a to-do list application that allows users to add to-dos. While the user is typing in the input field, we will update the internal state of the title of the to-do to be added. This approach is common for a controlled input field, but it causes a lot of renders. For our first attempt, we will implement the to-do application without memoization.

Listing 3.5 A to-do list without memoization

```
import { useState } from "react";
function Items({ items }) {          ◁─┐  Our Items component renders
  return (                              │  the items it receives; it does
    <>                                  │  not have any state itself.
      <h2>Todo items</h2>
      <ul>
        {items.map((todo) => (
          <li key={todo}>{todo}</li>
        ))}
      </ul>
    </>
  );
}
function Todo() {
  const [items, setItems] = useState(["Clean gutter", "Do dishes"]);
```

```
  const [newItem, setNewItem] = useState("");
  const onSubmit = (evt) => {
    setItems((items) => items.concat([newItem]));
    setNewItem("");
    evt.preventDefault();
  };
  const onChange =
    (evt) => setNewItem(evt.target.value);
  return (
    <main>
      <Items items={items} />
      <form onSubmit={onSubmit}>
        <input value={newItem} onChange={onChange} />
        <button>Add</button>
      </form>
    </main>
  );
}
function App() {
  return <Todo />;
}
export default App;
```

> **The Todo component does have state, and is updated every time the user types in the input field.**

> **Because the state updates on every key entered, the JSX returned in the to-do list is also regenerated every time, causing the Items component to render every time.**

Example: todo-simple

This example is in the `ch03/todo-simple` folder. You can use that example by running this command in the source folder:

```
$ npm run dev -w ch03/todo-simple
```

Alternatively, you can go to this website to browse the code, see the example in action in your browser, or download the source code as a zip file: https://react-likea.pro/ch03-todo-simple.

If we spin this code up in the browser, we see that it works and is a decent attempt at a simple to-do application. But if we open the performance tools in our browser of choice to see what happens every time a user types in the input field, we see that the browser can spend up to 5 ms handling the keypress event. Now, 5 ms may not sound like a lot of time, but remember that we have only 16 ms per frame, and we're already spending about a third of that time handling a single input field. If other things are happening in the application, we'll quickly run behind. Let's try to memoize the Items component by using the `memo()` function imported from the React module.

Listing 3.6 A to-do list with memoization

```
import { memo, useState } from "react";
const Items = memo(
  function Items({ items }) {
  return (
    <>
      <h2>Todo items</h2>
```

> **Remember to import memo().**

> **Apply it to the whole component.**

```
      <ul>
        {items.map((todo) => (
          <li key={todo}>{todo}</li>
        ))}
      </ul>
    </>
  );
});
function Todo() {
  const [items, setItems] = useState(["Clean gutter", "Do dishes"]);
  const [newItem, setNewItem] = useState("");
  const onSubmit = (evt) => {
    setItems((list) => list.concat([newItem]));
    setNewItem("");
    evt.preventDefault();
  };
  const onChange = (evt) => setNewItem(evt.target.value);
  return (
    <main>
      <Items items={items} />
      <form onSubmit={onSubmit}>
        <input value={newItem} onChange={onChange} />
        <button>Add</button>
      </form>
    </main>
  );
}
function App() {
  return <Todo />;
}
export default App;
```

Example: todo-memo

This example is in the `ch03/todo-memo` folder. You can use that example by running this command in the source folder:

```
$ npm run dev -w ch03/todo-memo
```

Alternatively, you can go to this website to browse the code, see the example in action in your browser, or download the source code as a zip file: https://reactlikea .pro/ch03-todo-memo.

With this minor optimization, our render for every keypress drops to about 2 ms simply because we don't need to render the whole list every time, looping over every entry and creating a new JSX element for every to-do item that's already in the list. That change saves us a significant amount of time with a minimal amount of work. Extra good job, us!

NOTE In React 19, we have an improved way to handle forms: using actions, which is a new kind of combined effect and callback. Using an action for this form would have simplified the code quite a bit, but because we're using React 18, we'll stick with this slightly more verbose code.

3.2.2 Memoize part of a component

In the preceding section, the items were rendered in a different component, so we had the luxury option of memoizing the entire component. But we won't always have that option. Sometimes, the relevant part of the JSX covers multiple components. Suppose that we did not have an `Items` component but instead rendered the list items directly in the `Todo` component. What can we do?

We can do two things:

- Move the section of the component that is often unchanged to a new, separate component and memoize that component, which would take us directly back to listing 3.6.
- Use the `useMemo` hook to memoize the JSX directly in the parent component, as shown in the following listing.

Listing 3.7 A to-do list with memo hook

```
import { useMemo, useState } from "react";    ◁── Imports useMemo() rather than memo()
function Todo() {
  const [items, setItems] = useState(["Clean gutter", "Do dishes"]);
  const [newItem, setNewItem] = useState("");
  const onSubmit = (evt) => {
    setItems((items) => items.concat([newItem]));
    setNewItem("");
    evt.preventDefault();
  };
  const itemsRendered = useMemo(          ◁──┐ Renders the item's JSX
    () => (                                   │ inside the useMemo hook
      <>
        <h2>Todo items</h2>
        <ul>
          {items.map((todo) => (
            <li key={todo}>{todo}</li>
          ))}
        </ul>
      </>
    ),                   ┌── Adds items as a dependency of
                         │   the hook. If not, the list never
    [items]      ◁──┘   updates even as you add items.
  );
  const onChange = (evt) => setNewItem(evt.target.value);
  return (
    <main>
      {itemsRendered}
      <form onSubmit={onSubmit}>
        <input value={newItem} onChange={onChange} />
        <button>Add</button>
      </form>
    </main>
  );
```

```
}
function App() {
  return <Todo />;
}
export default App;
```

> **Example: todo-usememo**
>
> This example is in the `ch03/todo-usememo` folder. You can use that example by running this command in the source folder:
>
> ```
> $ npm run dev -w ch03/todo-usememo
> ```
>
> Alternatively, you can go to this website to browse the code, see the example in action in your browser, or download the source code as a zip file: https://reactlikea .pro/ch03-todo-usememo.

Once again, typing in the input field results in a render time of only 2 ms. If you remove the `useMemo` hook and render the items directly inline in the component, runtime jumps back up to 3-4 ms per event—less than before because we use fewer components but still more than 2 ms.

We could argue about which version of the to-do application has the cleanest code. I probably prefer the version that uses a memoized component (listing 3.6), but others might prefer the one in listing 3.7. The two different approaches allow us to choose either option as we see fit.

3.2.3   *Memoize properties to memoized components*

Let's go back to our to-do application in listing 3.6 but add a new requirement. We always want to display the to-do item `Complete todo list` at the top of the list, regardless of what is in the list of items.

> **Listing 3.8   A to-do list with a fixed item (excerpt)**

```
...
function Todo() {
  ...
  return (
    <main>
      <Items
        items={["Complete todo list", ...items]} />        ◁──────┐
      ...                                                          │
    </main>                          The only change from listing 3.6 is this line.
  );                                  Instead of passing items as the property, we
}                                        create a new array with a fixed item at the
...                                    start and then the rest of the items as before.
```

If you spin this code up in a browser and check the run time per keypress event, you see that it jumps back up to around 5 ms again. What happened?

The problem is that even if the state value is identical (even referentially identical) on every render while we're typing, we create a new array inline on every render, which has the extra item in the front. Then we pass that new array to the memoized component, but because the passed value isn't referentially identical every time, the component has to do a full render.

The good news is that we already know how to fix this problem! We need to create a value in the component that changes only when the state value changes. We have the useMemo hook for that purpose. Let's apply it as shown in the following listing.

Listing 3.9   A to-do list with a memoized fixed item (excerpt)

```
...
function Todo() {
  ...

  const allItems = useMemo(() =>
    ["Complete todo list", ...items],
    [items]);
  return (
    <main>
      <Items items={allItems} />
      ...
    </main>
  );
}
...
```

> We memoize the inline-created array and save it in a variable, allItems. This hook depends on the items array, so only when that array changes do we need to update the allItems value.

> We pass the memoized property to the items component, which memoizes correctly and renders only when the list is updated with new content.

Example: todo-fixed

This example is in the ch03/todo-fixed folder. You can use that example by running this command in the source folder:

```
$ npm run dev -w ch03/todo-fixed
```

Alternatively, you can go to this website to browse the code, see the example in action in your browser, or download the source code as a zip file: https://react-likea.pro/ch03-todo-fixed.

We did it! We fixed the render, and the performance is back down to about 2 ms per render while typing.

To make this application better, we should be able to delete items from the list when it's complete. Let's add a callback to our items component that will be invoked on click with the relevant item to remove. We go back to a previous iteration of the to-do list to make things simpler. If we do this the naive way, we will have the same problem as before:

```
<Items
  items={items}
```

```
    onDelete={(item) => setItems(ls => ls.filter(i => i === item))}
/>
```

Because this function is defined inline in JavaScript, we essentially create a new function every time. You might think that it's the same function on each render because each function has an identical definition, but that's not how JavaScript works. Passing new properties on every render is a no-go when we're using memoization. We need our values to be referentially identical if memoization is supposed to kick in. We need to memoize this callback. What better way is there than the `useCallback` hook made for this purpose? See the following listing.

Listing 3.10   A to-do list with deletable items

```
import { memo, useCallback, useState } from "react";
const Items = memo(function Items({ items, onDelete }) {
  return (
    <>
      <h2>Todo items</h2>
      <ul>
        {items.map((todo) => (
          <li key={todo}>
            {todo}
            <button onClick={() => onDelete(todo)}>X</button>
          </li>
        ))}
      </ul>
    </>
  );
});
function Todo() {
  const [items, setItems] = useState(["Clean gutter", "Do dishes"]);
  const [newItem, setNewItem] = useState("");
  const onSubmit = (evt) => {
    setItems((items) => items.concat([newItem]));
    setNewItem("");
    evt.preventDefault();
  };
  const onChange = (evt) => setNewItem(evt.target.value);
  const onDelete = useCallback(
    (item) => setItems((list) => list.filter((i) => i !== item)),
    []
  );
  return (
    <main>
      <Items items={items} onDelete={onDelete} />
      <form onSubmit={onSubmit}>
        <input value={newItem} onChange={onChange} />
        <button>Add</button>
      </form>
    </main>
  );
}
```

> We memoize the callback in a hook. We could also use the useMemo hook, but this approach is simpler.

> We pass an empty dependency array because our only dependency is a state setter, which is a value known to be stable.

```
function App() {
  return <Todo />;
}
export default App;
```

Example: todo-delete

This example is in the `ch03/todo-delete` folder. You can use that example by running this command in the source folder:

```
$ npm run dev -w ch03/todo-delete
```

Alternatively, you can go to this website to browse the code, see the example in action in your browser, or download the source code as a zip file: https://react-likea.pro/ch03-todo-delete.

We're back where we wanted to be. Our component renders swiftly even while typing, because the "expensive" part of the component, which doesn't change during typing, is memoized properly.

Often, you will see that it is necessary to memoize properties when you start memoizing components. Property memoization is relevant for objects and arrays created inline, and even more so for functions, which is the primary reason for the existence of the `useCallback` hook and why it is used so often in React.

Memoization is not a job to leave to the end of a project when you notice that your application is a bit sluggish. Memoization is something you do while developing to ensure a smooth, optimal user experience. With the tools presented in this section, you should be able to apply this example to your own projects.

At the same time, premature optimization is also a problem. If you optimize things that are running well, you might end up with the opposite situation. You incur slight run-time penalties just by invoking optimization functions, and if they don't make the application faster, they make it slower.

If you're a new developer, don't optimize prematurely. But if you know what you're doing, feel free to memoize when you predict that it's going to matter.

3.2.4 *Memoization hooks in detail*

In this section, I'll describe uses and best practices for two memoization hooks in detail. In short, you can memoize any value with `useMemo` and functions in particular with `useCallback`. But when should you do so, and how do you make sure that the value updates correctly if necessary?

MEMOIZE ANY VALUE WITH USEMEMO

This hook memoizes values between renders and can be used for two different purposes (or both at the same time):

- To prevent expensive recalculations
- To maintain referential equality

Although the first concept is fairly easy to grasp, the second is a lot more complex. I discuss why referential equality matters in section 3.3, where I talk more about dependency arrays; I've also already touched on the topic a few times in this chapter. In this section, I introduce the hook and show how to memoize values to prevent expensive calculations.

useMemo takes a function and a dependency array. If any value in the dependency array has changed since the component was last rendered, the function will be executed, and the return value of said function will be the return value of the call to use-Memo. If no value in the dependency array has changed since the last render, the value returned in the last render will be returned again (figure 3.4).

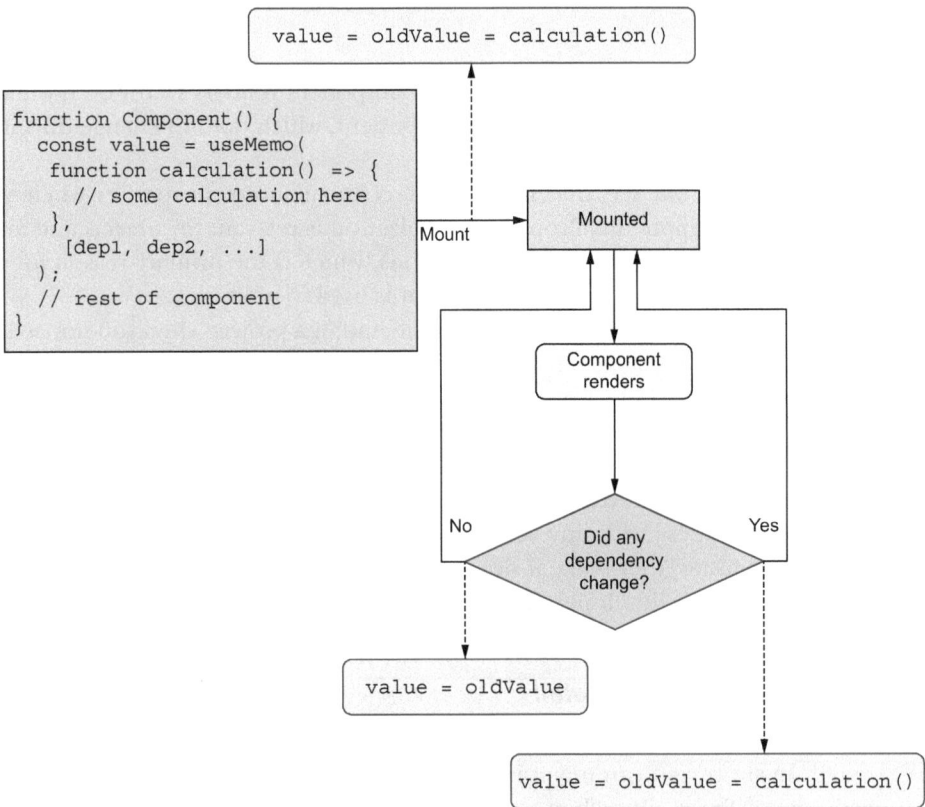

Figure 3.4   The useMemo flow. Note that oldValue doesn't exist in the component; it is an internal value accessible only to the React API and is not directly visible in the component.

Using this hook to avoid expensive recalculations is relatively simple to grasp. Suppose that we have a list of employees with some filters above the list. For this example, let's allow the user to see either all employees or only temporary workers.

We could perform this filtering of the employee list every time the component renders, but that process could be expensive, especially if the list contains 1,000 or more records. Instead, we'll use the useMemo hook to do the filtering only when either the source array or the filter changes value.

Listing 3.11 Memoized filtering

```
import { useMemo, useState } from "react";          ◁┐ We import the useMemo
function Employees({ employeeList }) {                 │ hook (along with useState)
  const [showTempOnly, setShowTempOnly] = useState(false); │ from the React package.
  const filteredList = useMemo(
    () =>
      employeeList.filter(({ isTemporary }) =>    The first argument is a function that
        showTempOnly ? isTemporary : true          performs filtering on the current array.
      ),
    [employeeList, showTempOnly]    ◁┐ The second argument is the dependencies of
  );                                  │ our calculation; it should be performed again
  return (                           │ only if either the list or the Boolean changes.
    <section>
      <h1>Employees</h1>
      <label>
        <input
          type="checkbox"
          onChange={() => setShowTempOnly((f) => !f)}
        />
        Show temp only?
      </label>
      <ul>
        {filteredList.map(({ id, name, salary, isTemporary }) => (
          <li key={id}>
            {name}: {salary} {isTemporary && "(temp)"}
          </li>
        ))}
      </ul>
    </section>
  );
}
function App() {
  const employeeList = [
    { name: "Bugs Bunny", salary: "$20,000", isTemporary: false },
    { name: "Daffy Duck", salary: "$15,000", isTemporary: false },
    { name: "Porky Pig", salary: "$17,000", isTemporary: true },
    ...
  ];
  return <Employees employeeList={employeeList} />;
}
export default App;
```

We invoke useMemo with the two arguments it takes.

Example: employees

This example is in the ch03/employees folder. You can use that example by running this command in the source folder:

(continued)
$ npm run dev -w ch03/employees

Alternatively, you can go to this website to browse the code, see the example in action in your browser, or download the source code as a zip file: https://reactlikea .pro/ch03-employees.

You can see this application in action in figure 3.5 with the Boolean flag turned on and off.

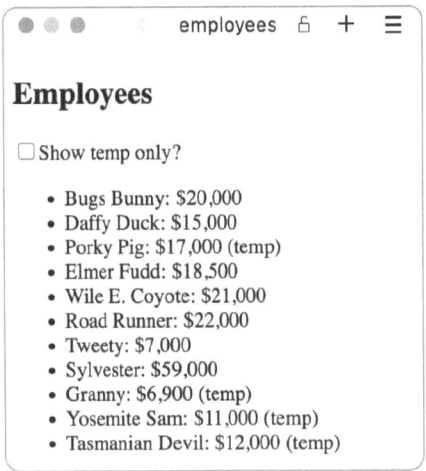
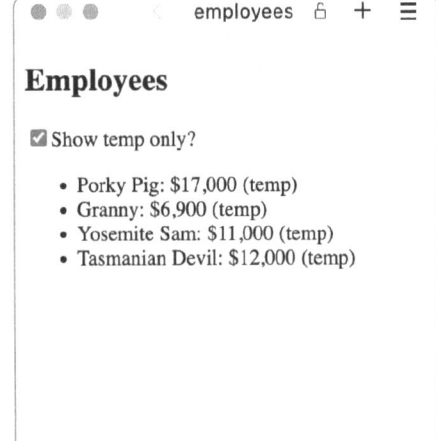

Figure 3.5 **The list of employees with and without the temporary employee filter enabled**

This example isn't a good one, however. Why? The only things that can change in this component are the list and the Boolean, so every time the component renders, one of those two (probably) changed. As a result, we need to do the calculation on every render because the dependencies always change. If we need to do the calculation on every render, using memoization is more expensive because of the overhead of calling extra functions. If our component had a bunch of other properties and state values, however, it could change independently of the state and property values, and our optimization would start to help a lot.

Suppose that the component had some other state that did not refer to the filtering of the list but to the sorting of the list. In that case, our filtering calculation would not be performed simply because we sorted the list differently. The filtering would be (re)applied only when we updated the Boolean filter flag or when the source array changed, which is what we want in this case.

The second use case, and probably the more common use case for `useMemo`, involves referential equality. I'll discuss this topic in section 3.3.

MEMOIZE FUNCTIONS WITH USECALLBACK

`useCallback` is one of the least necessary hooks built into React, as it's a simple extension of `useMemo`. It does the same thing as `useMemo` if `useMemo` is used to memoize a function. `useCallback` could be defined in terms of `useMemo` simply like this:

```
function useCallback(fn, deps) {
  return useMemo(() => fn, deps);
}
```

This definition is even stated directly in the React documentation. So why do both hooks exist? `useCallback` makes memoized callbacks where referential equality is desired, and is never used to prevent expensive calculations. Callbacks are most often defined inline in the component body like so:

```
const handleClick = useCallback(
  (evt) => {
    // handle evt and do stuff
  },
  [],
);
```

If we want to define this same memoized function using `useMemo`, we would do it this way:

```
const handleClick = useMemo(
  () => (evt) => {        ⟵┐  This notation looks
    // handle evt and do stuff  │  a little weird.
  },
  [],
);
```

That double-arrow notation in the second line is easy to forget—and forgetting it changes the meaning of the code. Rather than assign a function to `handleClick` as desired, if we forget the double arrow, we assign the result of invoking said callback, which is most likely `undefined`, as we rarely return anything from event handlers. Even though this hook can do only a subset of what `useMemo` can do, we will be using `useCallback` more than `useMemo` in the remainder of this book because we memoize functions more often than other types of values.

3.3   *Understanding dependency arrays*

We have used dependency arrays a few times already to restrict when various hooks are triggered. We use dependency arrays for effect hooks. An empty array in an effect hook indicates that it runs only on mount, whereas a nonempty array indicates that the hook runs on mount and every time the mentioned dependencies update. We also use dependency arrays for memoization hooks; we can create stable values by using empty dependency arrays, for example.

But how do dependency arrays work in practice? How do you specify the right elements in a dependency array, and how do you make sure that the dependencies don't update too often?

First, let's reiterate which hooks use these dependency arrays to define when the hooks should take effect: `useEffect`, `useCallback`, `useMemo`, and `useLayoutEffect`. These four hooks, and only these four, use dependency arrays to conditionally trigger their effect and/or execution.

There are three general classes of dependency arrays. You don't specify an array at all, you specify an empty array, or you specify a nonempty array. These classes are exemplified as follows:

```
useEffect(() => { ... });          ⟵──┤ No array
useEffect(() => { ... }, []);            ⟵──┤ Empty array
useEffect(() => { ... }, [id]);    ⟵──┤ Nonempty array
```

If you don't specify a dependency array, the hook should be triggered on every render regardless of which values update in the hook (if any). If you have an empty array, your hook triggers only on mount and never again (except for cleanup functions, which trigger on unmount, but that's not your hook; that's a side effect of running your hook).

If you specify a nonempty array, your hook triggers when any of the values in the array change on a render. Any single change triggers the hook. React uses referential equality to determine whether a value has changed.

Referential equality

In JavaScript (and many other languages), values come in two types: primitives and complex objects. JavaScript has seven primitive types (number, bigint, Boolean, string, symbol, `null`, and `undefined`) and one complex type (object). You may wonder, what about classes, regular expressions, arrays, and functions? They are also considered to be objects (though classes and functions in some sense are considered to be functions, which are a subtype of objects).

You can compare values to see whether they're strictly equal by using the triple-equals operator: `===`. The regular double-equals operator will do type conversion, so `"1" == 1`, but strict equality requires that the types be identical.

When you're comparing two primitive values, they are considered to be strictly equal if their values represent the same data, even if they are two different variables. You could compare `2 === 1+1`, for example, which would be true.

For complex types, however, strict equality means referential equality. Objects are considered to be identical only if they literally are the same object and updating one would also update the other. So `{} !== {}` and `[] !== []`, even though we're comparing two empty objects and arrays, respectively. They are not considered to be strictly equal, because they're not the same object (or array)—just similar data structures.

When we refer to React's using referential equality, we mean that React will use the strict equality operator to compare values and thus will consider objects or arrays to be identical only if they're references to the same object, and not merely two different values containing similar data.

3.3.1 What are dependencies?

Dependencies of a hook are a subset of all the variables and references that you use in the hook. A *dependency* is any local variable that exists locally in the component scope but not any variable that also exists outside the component scope. Figure 3.6 shows a few examples.

```
const one = 1;
function Component({ two }) {
  const three = 3;
  useEffect(
    () => {
      const four = three + 1;
      const sum = one + two + three + four;
    },
    [two, three],
  );
  // Rest of component
}
```

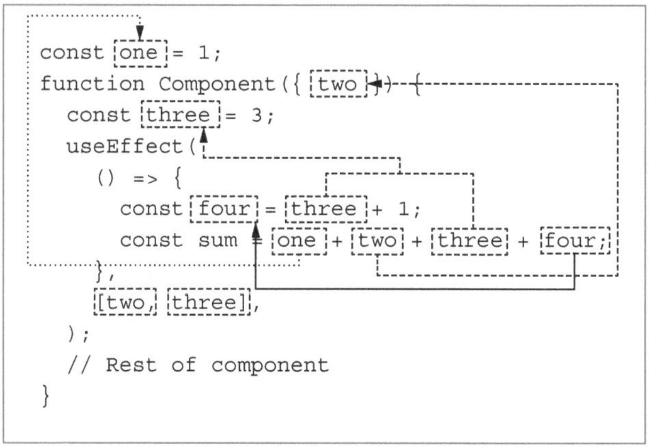

Figure 3.6 **This hook uses four variables inside named** one, two, three, **and** four. **Variable** one **comes from outside the component, as noted by the dotted arrow. Variables** two **and** three **come from inside the component but outside the effect, as noted by the dashed arrows. Variable** four **comes from inside the effect itself. Only variables** two **and** three **are relevant to add as dependencies, as you see in the dashed boxes at the bottom.**

Dependencies include any variable defined as a `const`, `let`, or `var` in the component, any functions defined inside the component, and any argument passed to the component (mostly properties, but potentially also forwarded references). Any function or variable defined outside the component or imported from other files is not relevant as a dependency for a hook. Finally, any variable defined inside the hook is not a dependency, as it does not exist in the outside component.

3.3.2   *Run on every render by skipping the dependency array*

Suppose that you want your effect to run on every render regardless of why a component re-renders. Maybe you want to track all the renders for tracking or statistical purposes. You could add a dependency array listing every single property and state value that exists, which would work if any of those values changed.

But remember that your component also re-renders because its parent component re-renders, and that parent-triggered render might not come with any change of a property or state value. So regardless of how many values you put in your dependency array, your effect will never run on every single possible render.

You have a simple solution: skip the dependency array. Don't supply any dependency array at all, and your effect will run on every render regardless of why the render happens:

```
function Component({ ... }) {
  useEffect(() => track('Component rendered'));
  ...
}
```

Note that we supply only a single argument to the `useEffect` function. We simply ignore passing a second argument.

You might ask, why run the effect in a hook at all? Why not just run the code inline, like so?

```
function Component({ ... }) {
  track('Component rendered');
  ...
}
```

Executing the tracking function inside an effect hook is recommended for optimization. The preceding `track` function might be a bit slow, and the responsiveness of this function call should not block your component from rendering. So by running the function in an effect, you decouple the execution of the effect from the rendering of the component.

MEMOIZATION WITHOUT DEPENDENCIES IS MEANINGLESS

Would you ever skip the dependency array for a memoization hook? If the memoization hook body runs for every render, the overhead of memoizing the value doesn't do anything. So you would never do that, as the code would be useless. If you use

```
const value = useMemo(() => someCalculation());
```

you might as well use this code, which is much more efficient and does the same thing:

```
const value = someCalculation();
```

NO DEPENDENCY ARRAY IS DIFFERENT FROM AN EMPTY ARRAY

Be aware that a missing dependency array is very different from an empty dependency array. The two values are polar opposites in the context of dependency arrays. A hook with an empty dependency array runs only once—on the initial mounting render of the component—and never again, whereas a hook without a dependency array runs on every single render of the component regardless of why it renders.

3.3.3   *Skip stable variables from dependencies*

If you have been extra attentive, you may realize that we sometimes cheat. We did not follow the best practice of always specifying all the variables used in a hook in the dependency array. We skipped that practice in listing 3.10. You get an extra gold star for noticing! I did point it out at the time, however, so maybe you get only a silver star. Here's the relevant section of the component in listing 3.10:

```
const [items, setItems] = useState(["Clean gutter", "Do dishes"]);
...
const onDelete = useCallback(
  (item) => setItems(                             ◁─── Here, we use the variable setItems,
    (list) => list.filter((i) => i !== item),          which is clearly defined outside the
  ),                                                    effect yet inside the component.
  []    ◁──── But we still specify an empty dependency
);              array. That's not allowed, is it?
```

What's going on here? Are we allowed to skip listing variables as dependencies? Yes, if the variable is a stable variable. The concept of a stable variable is quite an oxymoron because it's a variable that doesn't vary. If the variable always has the same value for every render of your component, it's irrelevant to put it in the dependency array because we know that it never changes. That's partially the reason why values from outside our component don't go in the dependency array. If we define a constant outside our component or import a constant from another file, we know that it's always the same constant for every render of our component, so even if we depend on it, we don't need to consider it to be a value that can change.

In the same way, we can have variables inside our component that we know are stable—variables that never change. When it comes to functions and objects, stable values are extra important because even if a function has the same body every time, that fact does not mean that it *is* the same value.

When it comes to hooks, React defines and specifically lists some return values as stable. If you compare the returned values from certain hooks, you see that not just similar functions or objects but the same function or object is returned. We can ignore adding these values as dependencies to make our components and hooks easier to read and understand.

This is the case for the setter function returned by `useState`. The value returned can change for every render, but the setter function is always the same function reference, which is why we don't need to include it in dependency arrays.

This is also the case for the object returned by `useRef`. The object is always the same, but the value of the `current` property changes and is dynamic.

If you use a `useRef` reference or a `useState` setter inside an effect hook (or a memoized hook), you can specify it in the dependency array, but you don't have to. Both you and React know that both the reference and the setter are stable, so they never change and thus will never cause the execution of the hook to change. Specifying them as dependencies is optional. For consistency, I recommend that you either always or never include values known to be stable. (I never do.) Development teams often specify their choice in this matter in their coding standards.

You can make your own stable variables as well to make your components easier to read and understand, both for yourself as a developer and for the rest of the team. If you memoize a value in your component by using a hook, and you include an empty dependency array, the returned value is stable. A memoizing hook with an empty dependency array always returns the same value; thus, it can be considered to be stable.

Image this code for an incomplete component, in which we specify all dependencies even if they're known to be stable. The code becomes more verbose, sacrificing simplicity and understanding:

```
function Panel() {
  const [isOpen, setOpen] = useState(false);
  const toggleOpen = useCallback(        We use a component-scoped
    () => setOpen(open => !open),         variable . . .
    [setOpen],        . . . so we specify it
  );                   as a dependency.
  useEffect(
    () => {
      // Some effect here    We use another component-
      toggleOpen();          scoped variable . . .
    },
    [toggleOpen],      . . . so we specify it,
  );                    too, as a dependency.
  ...
}
```

Here, we specify `setOpen` as a dependency, even though (as just discussed) we can skip it because it is known to be stable; it never changes. If you are examining the code in the preceding component, however, it is not obvious that the effect runs only on mount because there is a dependency array. You have to track that dependency to check its origin, which might force you to track another list of dependencies.

If we skip the `setOpen` dependency from the `useCallback` hook, we will see that `toggleOpen` is now a stable value because it is defined in a memoizing hook with an empty dependency array. This value also will never change over the lifetime of the component, so we can skip the `toggleOpen` value from the dependency array of the effect hook. We can greatly simplify this component as follows:

```
function Panel() {
  const [isOpen, setOpen] = useState(false);
  const toggleOpen = useCallback(
```

```
    () => setOpen(open => !open),
    [],
  );
  useEffect(() => toggleOpen(), []);
  ...
}
```

We can supply an empty dependency array
for both hooks because we know that both
use only values known to be stable.

This version is much easier to read and understand because you instantly know that both hooks run only a single time due to their empty lists of dependencies.

3.3.4 Get help maintaining dependency arrays

Maintaining dependency arrays can be quite troublesome. Say you're editing some effect and adding a reference to a property the component receives, but you forget to update the dependency array—the whole component starts acting weird.

In chapter 4, we discuss developer tooling. One of those tools, ESLint, has a great rule that will help you keep those dependency arrays updated. ESLint gives you an error directly in your editor if you forget to add something to the dependencies that should be there. This feature is enabled by default, so installing the package should get you going.

Summary

- React components re-render when their parent components re-render regardless of the properties they receive.
- Misconceptions in React include beliefs about property changes and double rendering in Strict Mode, which often don't reflect actual behavior.
- Memoization in React optimizes performance by caching the results of function calls and rendering, reducing unnecessary recalculations.
- React's memo() function can be used to prevent unnecessary re-renders of components by comparing properties.
- The useMemo and useCallback hooks in React help optimize performance by memoizing complex calculations and functions.
- Dependencies in React hooks dictate when effects are rerun, which is crucial for optimizing performance and avoiding unnecessary updates.
- Strict equality, or referential equality, is key in React for determining whether hook dependencies have changed and re-calculation is necessary.
- React hooks such as useEffect, useCallback, useMemo, and useLayoutEffect use dependency arrays to manage hook updates.
- Omitting the dependency array in React hooks results in the hooks' running after every render, which can be useful for tracking renders or performance analysis.
- In React, stable variables such as useState setters and useRef objects don't need to be included in dependency arrays, as they don't change between renders.

- Premature optimization in React, such as unnecessary memoization, can lead to decreased performance due to the overhead of the optimization code.
- ESLint and other development tools are useful for maintaining accurate dependency arrays in React, ensuring that components behave as expected.

Better code maintenance
with developer tooling

This chapter covers

- Writing error-free code with linting
- Increasing productivity with formatting
- Making components more robust with property constraints
- Debugging React applications using developer tools

Code quality degrades over time—unfortunately, a hard fact of our chosen profession. As our web applications grow more complicated, maintaining code quality becomes harder and harder. This is especially the case for multideveloper projects, in which different people invariably do things in different ways, but it is also a problem for single-person projects. If you are working on the same codebase over time, you will pick up new ways of doing things, and these ways will most likely differ from the ones you followed earlier. You might open a file you haven't touched in months and suddenly wonder, "What's going on here?"

Although good comments, documentation, and code structure are all relevant solutions to the above problems, several external tools at your disposal will improve your code quality immensely without requiring you to change your ways or even do more work.

This chapter is a bit special, in that it does not cover anything that's directly related to React or required when writing React. If you're playing with React on your own in smaller projects, you probably don't need much of the contents of this chapter; you can safely skip it until you feel more confident in your coding. If you're joining a small development team, you will need most of this material, so you might as well get ahead of the curve by learning it now. If you're looking to become a professional React developer, this content is practically mandatory.

We will use some of the tools presented here in future chapters, but I'll make sure to refer to the relevant material and give a brief recap where applicable in case you decide to skip this chapter for now. Here in chapter 4, I will introduce four concepts for better code maintenance and the tools that can help you obtain these new improvements:

- *Linting*—Linting is the process of automatically checking your source code for minor programmatic and stylistic errors. We will carry out this task with the `eslint` tool.
- *Formatting*—Formatting is the process of automatically adhering to predefined stylistic coding standards. We will carry out this task with the `prettier` tool.
- *Property constraints*—Property constraints are ways of making components more robust and easier to use by specifying types and ranges for valid properties. We will perform this task by using the built-in feature `.propTypes` combined with the external package `prop-types`.
- *Debugging*—Debugging with React Developer Tools (an external browser plugin) allows you to inspect and debug your React components more effectively, helping you identify and fix problems in your application's UI and state. We will explore the powerful features of React Developer Tools to streamline your debugging process.

NOTE   There's a slight overlap in the responsibility and performance of each of these guiding concerns; I will get more into that topic later.

The Venn diagram in figure 4.1 shows the reach and responsibilities of the four key concerns, which we can think of as guideposts to keep us in line as we write our code.

With these four guideposts configured in your project, you will find errors and problems long before committing your code to your teammates. Did you misspell a variable? Your linter can point that problem out to you. Are you unsure of the best practice for adding newlines inside a long and convoluted piece of code? Your formatter will solve that problem for you automatically. Are you passing the wrong type of property to a component? Property types will highlight this situation. Are you unable to figure out why your component renders all the time? Developer tools will tell you.

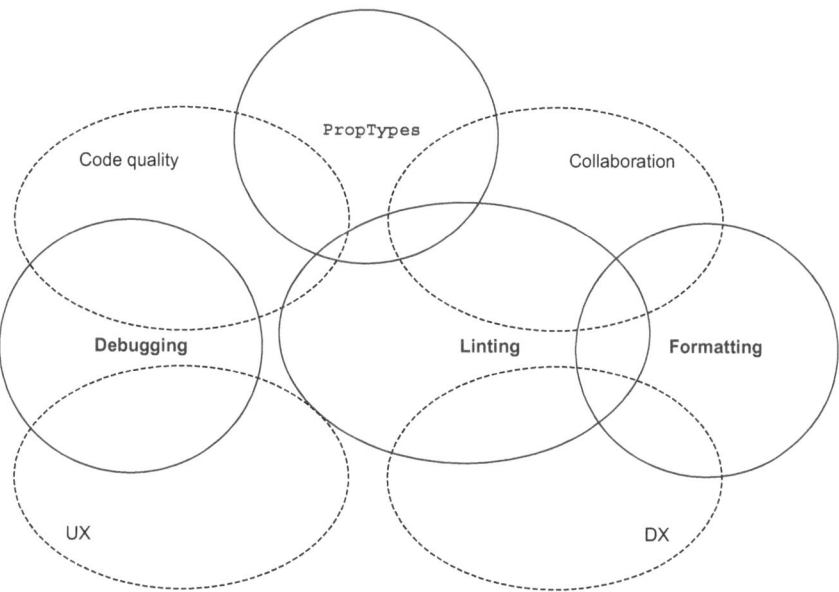

Figure 4.1   Effective software development requires paying attention to code quality, collaboration, user experience (UX), and developer experience (DX), represented here as ovals with dotted lines. The overlapping ovals with solid lines show how our four guideposts affect the outcome of each of these four areas. Notice how the responsibilities overlap.

A lot of teams are using at least one of these tools, if not all four, and these tools are often configured by default in many setups in common web development frameworks. In fact, some of these tools are so standard that most editors have built-in support for them and almost expect them to be used because their use has become so omnipresent in modern web development.

In this chapter, we will go through each of the four concepts, discussing the reason for using each tool and what problem it solves, as well as some more technical details about how to set it up, with links to packages and modules that are relevant to your editor.

One thing I can promise you: After you've been using any (or all) of these tools in a React project, you may not want to go back. Things tend to get a whole lot easier with tooling!

> **NOTE**   The source code for the examples in this chapter is available at https://reactlikea.pro/ch04.

4.1   *Reducing errors with linting*

If you have some lint on your clothes, you can use a lint roller to get rid of them. That tool allows you clean your clothes effectively with minimal effort. In the same way, if you have some minor stylistic or bad-practice problems in your source code, you use a linter tool to get rid of them effectively with minimal effort. Figure 4.2 highlights the responsibilities of linting, with only the relevant parts in focus.

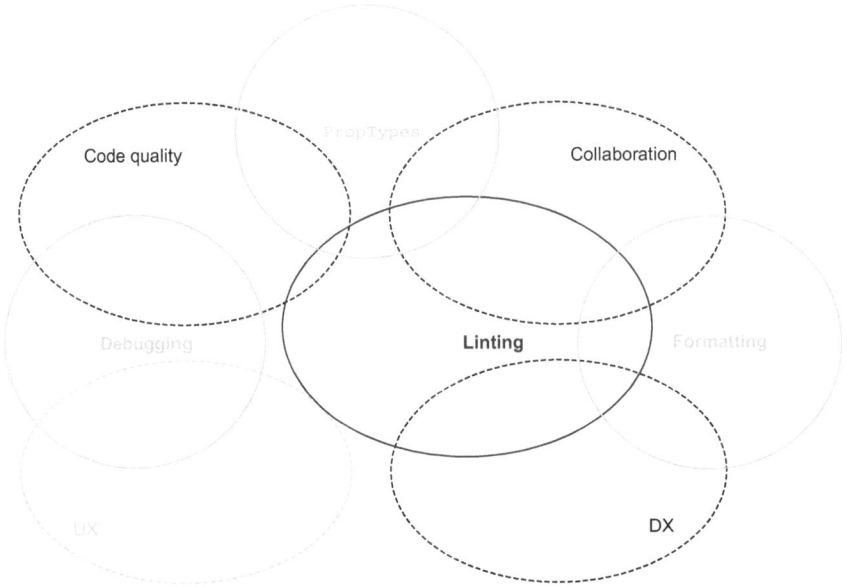

Figure 4.2   Linting affects several aspects of software development, including code quality, collaboration, and DX.

Here's an inexhaustive list of the types of problems that linting can help you solve automatically:

- Potential coding errors due to disambiguation (language weirdness), such as disallowing duplicate keys in an object literal (which doesn't work as expected anyway)
- Best practices such as requiring multiple returns in the same function to return the same type of variable (which makes the result consistent)
- Stylistic rules, such as requiring newlines at the end of a file

Code linting is becoming more and more popular, to the point where it's almost standard in most projects these days. The primary linter tool used today is ESLint, so that's the one I'll cover in this section.

4.1.1   *Problems solved by ESLint*

Suppose that you work on a large team, and to make things smoother, you create a coding style guideline that you want all your developers to follow. ESLint is one of the first tools for JavaScript that allows you to codify such a style in enforceable rules, which will be applied automatically to all the code for every developer, regardless of their setup.

You can not only set these rules to inform developers when (and how) they're breaking the style guide but also have ESLint fix a huge percentage of these violations automatically. You can set your system up so that it tries to fix the code as you commit it to the central repository.

4.1.2   ESLint configurations

ESLint consists of more than 300 rules, and you can specify how you want each rule to be enforced in your project. You can also specify the severity of violating a rule. Sometimes, not doing something according to your ruleset is a straight-up error. At other times, you may find that a warning is sufficient, but you might allow the violation if the developer in question finds it to be proper in the given situation.

Suppose that you want your code to be formatted with semicolons at the end of every statement line or that you want your code to never have semicolons. Those rules are two sides of the same coin. You specify a configuration for the rule named `semi`. If you want to enforce semicolons where applicable and enforce them as an error otherwise, you'd configure the rule as

```
semi: ["error", "always"]
```

Conversely, if you want to enforce the rule that nobody can put semicolons anywhere, you'd configure the rule as

```
semi: ["error", "never"]
```

Then you can go over every rule in the ESLint ruleset and specify your preference as you've agreed on with the team. That approach does sound like a lot of work, though, so you could opt for an existing group of configurations that someone else made and recommends.

ESLint itself has a recommended ruleset that includes configurations for most of the rules. You can extend this ruleset and vary it as your organization sees fit. You can find other predefined rulesets; the best known is probably the great set from Airbnb derived from its extensive style guide, which the company gladly posts online for anyone to copy or be inspired by:

- *ESLint rules* (https://eslint.org/docs/latest/rules)—Includes a list of configurations included in the ESLint recommended ruleset
- *Airbnb style guide* (https://github.com/airbnb/javascript)—Contains information about how to use it in ESLint as well

4.1.3   How to get started using ESLint

To get started using ESLint, follow these three steps:

1. Initialize ESLint in your project.
2. Modify the default configuration file, potentially extending a predefined ruleset and/or custom rule configurations.
3. Enforce the rules in your editor and your build.

STEP 1: INITIALIZE ESLINT CONFIGURATION

To carry out this step, you use `npm`:

```
npm init @eslint/config
```

When it's installed and configured, you're ready to start using the tool.

STEP 2: MODIFY THE CONFIGURATION FILE

As you run the initializer in step 1, a configuration file is added to the root of your project in your desired format. This file is named `<root>/.eslintrc.{js,yml,json}` (with the extension following your choice of format). Note the initial dot in the filename. In this file, you can extend an existing ruleset by adding an `extends` property (shown here in JSON):

```
{
  "extends": "eslint:recommended",
}
```

Also, you can include rules by listing them in a `rules` block:

```
{
  "rules": {
    "semi": ["error", "always"],
    "quotes": ["error", "double"]
  }
}
```

The configuration doesn't take any more work, and you don't even need to do the second part if you're happy with a predefined ruleset.

STEP 3: ENFORCE RULES IN YOUR EDITOR AND BUILD

All the popular editors have a package for ESLint to enforce automatically as you write your code. If your code editor has some form of package manager for extensions, it most likely has an ESLint package. Editors with ESLint support include the classic editors (such as VIM and Emacs) as well as modern ones (such as Visual Studio Code and Brackets).

ESLint is also easy to include in your existing build setup regardless of which setup you use. ESLint works with esbuild (the default build tool used in Vite), webpack, rollup, grunt, gulp, and many other tools. You can see all the integrations for both your editor and your build setup at https://mng.bz/ng65.

4.2   *Increasing productivity with formatters*

Tabs or spaces? Come on—I know you have an opinion, so out with it! But do you wanna know a secret? I don't—not anymore. Since the introduction of Prettier, a commonly used code autoformatter, I don't care one bit. Figure 4.3 highlights the responsibilities of formatting, with only the relevant parts in focus.

Although tabs versus spaces is probably the most hotly contested problem, it is not alone. Other purely formatting-related choices that you can make in your code include

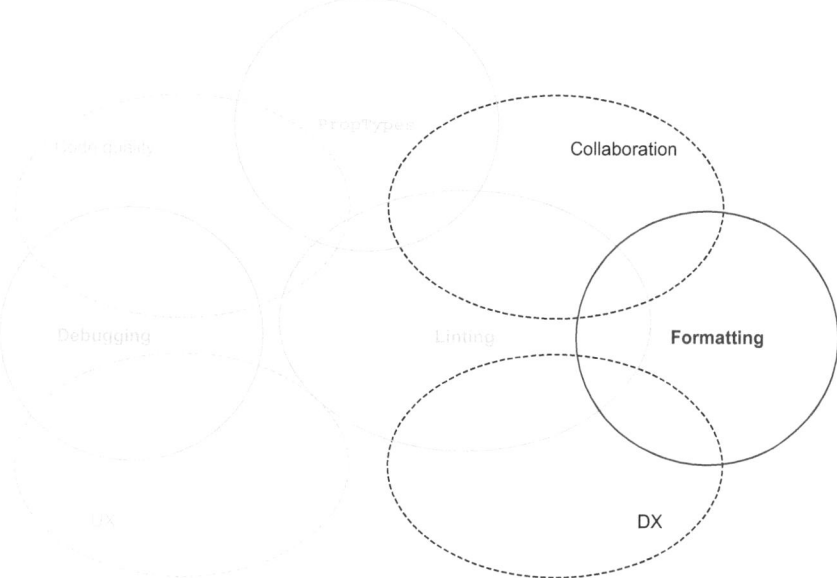

Figure 4.3 Formatting affects two aspects of software development: collaboration and DX.

- *Single or double quotes*
  - Either `var welcome = "Hello";`
  - Or `var welcome = 'Hello';`
- *Newline or space after function definition*
  - Either `function Component() {`
  - Or `function Component()`
    `{`
- *Space inside brackets in object literals*
  - Either `{property: 1}`
  - Or `{ property: 1 }`
- *Space inside parentheses around function arguments*
  - Either `useState(0)`
  - Or `useState( 0 )`

Sure, none of these matters are relevant to the performance of the code—only to DX. As I've stated again and again, however, DX matters—a lot. It is the difference between joining a project and being productive on day one versus spending days or even weeks getting up to speed and learning the customs of a new project (not that formatting alone takes weeks to master, of course).

Figure 4.4 shows how Prettier can format a messy piece of code into something much more consistent. More important, formatting choices need to be uniform within a project. Everything else leads to pure anarchy. If one file uses tabs and another uses spaces, you're in for a long day at work!

Figure 4.4   A snippet of code before and after Prettier takes a crack at it. This example uses the default settings in Prettier. The "after" code still is not elegant code, as it could be structured better, but at least the formatting is consistent.

4.2.1   *Problems solved by Prettier*

First, know that Prettier is an *opinionated* ruleset. The makers of Prettier have an opinion about how code should be formatted, and they aren't shy about it. How code should be formatted is constantly up for discussion, of course, but at its base, Prettier is an opinion, so your team doesn't need to have one.

I've worked on development teams that discussed coding standards and style guidelines *ad nauseam*. With Prettier, you eliminate this discussion by referring to the result of *someone else's* discussion. Prettier is that result. A lot (and I mean *a lot*) of developers all over the world, working on all sorts of projects and teams, have weighed in. Prettier is the result and the consensus choice.

The number of problems that Prettier solves is impossible to list, but one of its best features is that you never have to worry about formatting your files again. Often, you have stylistic design choices to make as a developer. Take this code snippet, for example:

```
const someCars = cars.filter((car) => car.make === "Fiat");
```

This snippet could have been formatted in many ways. All of the following variants do the same thing:

You could add newlines before method invocations.

You could add or remove parentheses around single-argument arrow functions.

```
const someCars = cars
  .filter((car) => car.make === "Fiat");
const someCars = cars.filter(car => car.make === "Fiat");
const someCars = cars.filter((car) => car.make === 'Fiat');
const someCars = cars.filter(
  (car) => car.make === "Fiat"
);
const someCars = cars.filter( ( car ) => car.make === "Fiat" );
```

You could use single quotes rather than double quotes.

You could add some line breaks around function arguments

You could add extra spaces around function arguments and parameters.

All these choices are purely stylistic. Some people prefer one style; others prefer another. Style makes no difference after the code is compiled. With Prettier, however, you don't have to make a single one of those choices. You invoke the formatter in your editor, and *voilà*—the correct style is applied automatically. With the default settings in Prettier, you'd get the following result (identical to the original statement):

```
const someCars = cars.filter((car) => car.make === "Fiat");
```

If you try to format this snippet in any other way and run Prettier, your code immediately reverts to this example.

You may be thinking, "But what if the line is longer? I don't want all my code to run on in long lines!" Well, you're in luck. Prettier is smart. It analyzes the code and figures out the best way to format any piece of code so that it looks great (under the given ruleset) and doesn't simply follow specific rules as a dumb machine. So although Prettier would format the preceding code as stated, suppose that the code was a little bit more complex, like this:

```
const someCars = originalListOfCars.filter((car) => car.make === "Fiat"
  && !car.isPickup);
```

If you apply Prettier with the default rules, that code would suddenly become

```
const someCars = originalListOfCars.filter(
  (car) => car.make === "Fiat" && !car.isPickup
);
```

Prettier decided that this line is too long and that breaking it up with the method argument on a newline is the best formatting for the code in question. What if we make this example a bit more complex?

```
const someCars = originalListOfCars.filter(
  (car) => car.make === "Fiat" && !car.isPickup
  ➥&& !car.isHatchback && car.cylinders >= 6
);
```

Prettier once again decides that this line is too long and breaks up the code like this:

```
const someCars = originalListOfCars.filter(
  (car) =>
    car.make === "Fiat" &&
    !car.isPickup &&
    !car.isHatchback &&
    car.cylinders >= 6
);
```

Prettier does not have simple rules like those in ESLint, which say that any array with more than *X* elements has to be in multiple lines and so on. Instead, Prettier adapts dynamically to the code in question and uses whatever formatting looks best (with *best* being an opinion, of course).

4.2.2 *Nonstandard rules with Prettier configuration*

Although uniformity is good, there are a lot of different people on this planet. Getting the whole world to agree on tabs versus spaces or single versus double quotes is an uphill battle. The good folks behind Prettier initially had the best intentions of unifying the world behind a single standard, but they've since relented; now they allow an ever-growing number of rules to be customized in each setup. So now it is possible to specify whether your particular project wants to use tabs or spaces, single or double quotes, and so on. Not all the internal rules are customizable, but the most hot-button ones are.

You can apply the configuration options when invoking Prettier on the command line or—better yet—by writing them in a configuration object. Prettier loads in the configuration options by using the `cosmiconfig` library, so you can load it in several ways. One of the most common ways is to format the object as JSON and store it in a file named `.prettierrc` or `.prettierrc.json` located at the root of your project. (Note the leading `"."` in the filename, which is common for configuration files like this one.)

> **TIP** See more about how to store the configuration object at https://prettier
> .io/docs/en/configuration.html.

Suppose that you want to format your files with Prettier, but you want your project to use tabs rather than the default spaces, and you want to exclude semicolons at the end of statements. (Yes, some people want that format. Go figure!) You can set those options on the command line like so:

```
$ prettier --use-tabs --no-semi src/
```

Alternatively, you can create a file located at `<root>/.prettierrc.json` with the following contents:

```
{
  useTabs: true,
  semicolon: false
}
```

Prettier will format your code according to your custom rules but keep everything else in the Prettier ruleset. You've now opined on top of the already opinionated library.

> **TIP** To customize your setup, you have to know what the options are, of course, and you can see the full list on the Prettier documentation website right here: https://prettier.io/docs/en/options.html.

Prettier allows a single case of rule customization, which you can do without configuring it specifically or even globally for your project. This rule is about whether the keys of an object go on separate lines or the entire object is defined on a single line (if it fits). Take this piece of code:

```
const car = { make: "Fiat", model: "500", isPickup: false };
```

Prettier will format the code this way if that's how you typed it. But if you added optional newlines before each property, Prettier would allow that option:

```
const car = {
  make: "Fiat",
  model: "500",
  isPickup: false,
};
```

Prettier is even clever enough to know when you want to change from one style to the other. Let's say you have the entire object defined in a single line. If you add a newline before the first property and invoke Prettier, the tool will guess that you want each property to be on a separate line:

```
const car = {
  make: "Fiat", model: "500", isPickup: false };   ⟵—  The newline at the start of the second
                                                        line instructs Prettier that you want the
                                                        properties to be on separate lines.
```

Conversely, if you have the object on multiple lines and want it to be more compact, you can remove the newline before the first property, and Prettier will inline the whole thing:

```
const car = {make: "Fiat",        ⟵—  The lack of a newline before the first
  model: "500",                         property instructs Prettier that you
  isPickup: false,                      want the object to be on a single line.
};
```

Note that this option works only if the object fits on a single line. If it doesn't, Prettier will always format it on multiple lines.

This feature is readily available to ensure consistency between objects. If you have an array with multiple objects, some of which are formatted on multiple lines because the contents are longer than others, you can ensure that all objects are formatted on multiple lines to make the code look more consistent. Compare the code snippet

```
const cars = [
  { make: "Fiat", model: "500" },
```

```
  {
    make: "BMW",
    model: "Individual M760i xDrive Model V12 Excellence THE NEXT 100 YEARS",
  },
];
```

with this code snippet, which forces the first object to be formatted on multiple lines as well:

```
const cars = [
  {
    make: "Fiat",
    model: "500",
  },
  {
    make: "BMW",
    model: "Individual M760i xDrive Model V12 Excellence THE NEXT 100 YEARS",
  },
];
```

This latter version does take up more space but looks better with both objects being styled identically. You can play with the examples in this section in the `prettier` example.

Example: prettier

This example is in the `prettier` folder. You can use that example by running this command in the source folder:

```
$ npm run dev -w ch04/prettier
```

Alternatively, you can go to this website to browse the code, see the example in action in your browser, or download the source code as a zip file: https://react-likea.pro/ch04-prettier.

4.2.3   How to start using Prettier

Getting started with Prettier normally requires up to four steps, the second and fourth of which are optional but often used:

1 Add Prettier to your project as a package.
2 Add a configuration file if you want to deviate from the standard configuration.
3 Enforce formatting in your editor.
4 Enforce formatting on code commits.

STEP 1: ADD PRETTIER AS A PACKAGE

You use npm for this step:

```
npm install --save-dev prettier
```

After it's installed, you're ready to start using the tool.

STEP 2: OPTIONALLY ADD A CONFIGURATION FILE

If you want to deviate from the standard ruleset, feel free to add a configuration file. By convention, this file is saved to `<root>/.prettierrc` in the root of your project. Refer to section 4.2.2 for the available configuration options.

STEP 3: ENFORCE FORMATTING IN YOUR EDITOR

Prettier works in most text editors that allow you to install custom packages. So whether you use Visual Studio Code, Atom, Sublime Text 3, or some other editor, search your package manager for Prettier to find the proper package. You can also check out this page, which has direct links to the relevant packages: https://prettier.io/docs/en/editors.html.

STEP 4: OPTIONALLY ENFORCE FORMATTING ON CODE COMMITS

Sometimes, files are changed outside your editor, or a code merge results in files being combined in a way that violates your formatting ruleset. To make sure that you *never, ever* commit any code that violates your formatting ruleset, a common approach is to make sure to run your formatter on any changed files before a commit is approved. To do this, you use what is known as a *precommit hook* (which is a version control hook and not at all related to React hooks), which runs a bit of code before any commit is affected.

Note that this step is optional; not every project needs it. You have many ways to achieve this task, depending on your setup and which other tools you have in your stack, but one of the easiest ways is to use a tool named `lint-staged`.

If you have already run the command for installing `lint-staged` in your project, it automatically picks up the fact that you also have Prettier set up, and it will start validating your changed files against your Prettier ruleset. If you haven't installed it, the command to install `lint-staged` is as follows:

```
npm install --save-dev lint-staged
```

> **TIP**   To see a list of other options for using Prettier in a precommit hook, see this page: https://prettier.io/docs/en/precommit.html.

4.2.4   *Alternative formatters*

Prettier has become the industry standard, and although it was a bit controversial at first, it is mostly a nonissue now. Some alternatives do exist, though, and formatting guidelines can be solved by other tools:

- *ESLint*—ESLint has quite a few rules available related to formatting, and even common standard ESLint setups come with several of these rules enabled. If you use both ESLint and Prettier, make sure that they don't have competing rules!
  - *ESLint formatting rules*—https://eslint.org/docs/user-guide/formatters
- *StyleLint*—This tool also lints your project, but only for style-related problems, so it is basically a formatter. You can even run StyleLint with your Prettier ruleset, if that's what you like, using the aptly named package `stylelint-prettier`.
  - *StyleLint*—https://stylelint.io

  – *StyleLint using Prettier*—https://github.com/prettier/stylelint-prettier

• *EditorConfig*—EditorConfig is a basic tool for formatting rules that almost all editors support out of the box. It's not really a tool but a configuration file that you put in the root of your project; it dictates some simple rules for your files to obey, such as whether you're using tabs or spaces. The tool has limited language support, but you often see it used in projects anyway (in combination with other tools), as it gives you a good baseline set of formatting rules even without installing all the extra packages that other tools require.

  – *EditorConfig*—https://editorconfig.org

4.3   Making components more robust with property constraints

As your application grows more complex, you may not know exactly how a given component works when you need to use it. Suppose that you know you have an `Input` component in your codebase, but you didn't create it and haven't used it before. How would you go about figuring out which properties to pass and which values to assign to them?

Checking the entire code inside a given component can be time consuming, so you might read the component definition. Let's say the `Input` component is defined as follows:

```
function Input({ name, label, value, change }) { ... }
```

The first three properties—`name`, `label`, and `value`—seem to be straightforward. They're most likely strings that you need to pass in. But what about that last one, `change`? Is that a change callback function or maybe a Boolean that indicates whether the value can be changed? Although you could have hoped for better naming that would have made the answer more obvious (such as calling it either `onChange` or `readonly`), you could also guess or use your intuition.

Another example is a date-display component that takes a `date` property. Is this date supposed to be a `Date` object, a string with the date already formatted, or even a timestamp with milliseconds since a certain date as a number? It's hard to tell directly from the component definition unless we explicitly name the property `dateString`, `dateObject`, or `timestampNumber`. But adding type information as part of the variable name is a terrible practice, mostly because it's not enforced anywhere, so it might not even be true.

Here's a related problem: what about required versus optional properties? When you read a component definition, you can't tell which properties are required to make the component work and which are optional to add functionality. Let's go back to our `Input` component, which might take properties for specifying whether the input is read-only or has a maximum or minimum value. These properties would most likely be optional, but can you be sure?

Finally, what happens when your components are passed the wrong properties, either in terms of wrong types or missing required properties? Most of the time, the components fail silently, but sometimes, you get JavaScript errors because the component tries to invoke a method on a property that isn't set. Wouldn't it be nice if you could be warned if any component anywhere in your application received a wrong property?

Those examples are a lot of different problems. Would you believe that all of them have a single solution? They do, and it's built into React, though you need an additional library to make it work. The answer is .propTypes, a configuration object appended to any component that tells React which property types it should expect your component to have. Figure 4.5 highlights the responsibilities of PropTypes, with only the relevant parts in focus. Let's dive in!

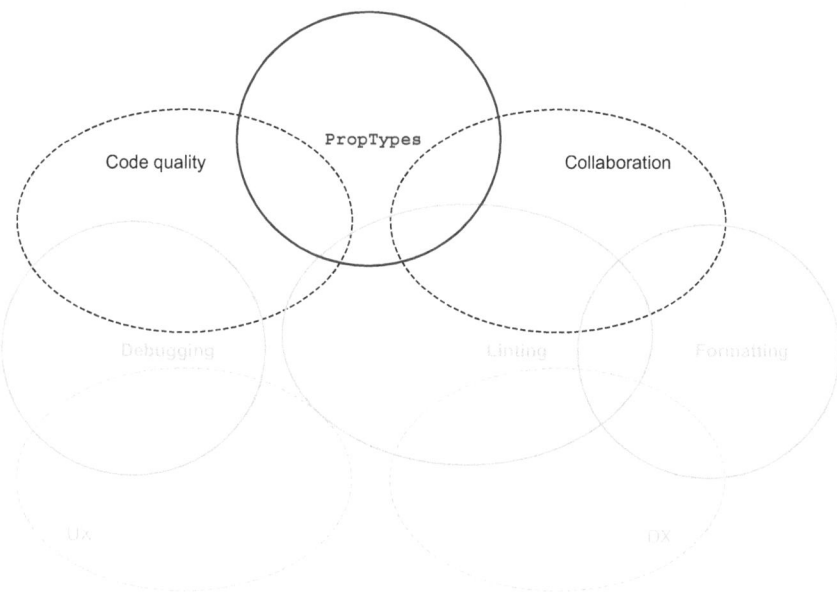

Figure 4.5 PropTypes **affects two aspects of software development: collaboration and code quality.**

> **NOTE** .propTypes is no longer supported as of React 19 and will be ignored. If you do not need to use property types, feel free to skip this section and go straight to section 4.4. If you are working on a codebase that uses React 19 or want to make sure you're prepared for anything, however, reading this section might be helpful.

4.3.1 How to apply property types

Going back to our fictional Input component from earlier in this chapter, let's see how we can apply property types to it correctly. The component takes four properties; the first three are strings, and the last one is a function. Following is the full component, including the property types:

```
import PropTypes from 'prop-types';
function Input({ name, label, value, onChange }) {
  return (
    <label>
      {label}
      <input name={name} value={value} onChange={onChange} />
    </label>
  );
}
Input.propTypes = {
  name: PropTypes.string,
  label: PropTypes.string,
  value: PropTypes.string,
  onChange: PropTypes.func,
};
export default Input;
```

First, we import the PropTypes library.

The component takes four properties and is otherwise defined as usual.

After the component definition, we add a property to the component function: propTypes, which is an object with a key named the same as each property that the component takes.

Three of the keys in the propTypes object are set to the value PropTypes.string, indicating that the relevant property should be a string.

The last key in the propTypes object is set to the value PropTypes.func, which indicates that the onChange property is expected to be a function. Note the abbreviated spelling of function.

As you can see, we add a property to the component after the definition. This value is set directly on the component definition function. Defining values on a function this way may look a bit weird, but it works well for this purpose.

The keys of the property-types object are the names of all the properties that the component takes, and the values are variables taken from the PropTypes library. This library includes a ton of values that you can use to define all sorts of properties with everything from simple types (such as strings and numbers) to complex and nested structures (such as lists of a certain type or objects with specific attributes).

GENERAL TYPES

The *PropTypes* library, of course, has support for all the simple types that we know and use every day: Booleans as PropTypes.bool, strings as PropTypes.string, and numbers as PropTypes.number. PropTypes also have support for symbols using PropTypes.symbol. These symbols are a special type of JavaScript variable that we don't use much in React. Then, of course, you can use functions (as PropTypes.func), arrays (as PropTypes.array), and objects (as PropTypes.object).

Note the special spelling of a few of these functions. They're called PropTypes.bool and PropTypes.func, not .boolean and .function.

SPECIFIC TYPES

But what if you have a component that takes an object of a specific type? Suppose that you have a component that displays a user with their name and age. The component expects a user object with a name property (which should be a string) and an age property (which should be a number). That object is called a *shape* in PropTypes lingo, and you define it like this:

```
function UserDisplay({ user }) {
  ...
}
```

This component takes a single property, but we need it to be structured in a specific way.

```
UserDisplay.propTypes = {
  user: PropTypes.shape({
    name: PropTypes.string,
    age: PropTypes.number,
  }),
};
```

The shape consists of two properties, a string and a number, respectively.

We define the property as a shape, which is further defined by another property-types object.

This example can be nested, so you could have a shape with a property that was another shape. You can also specify that an array has to be of a certain type. So if you have a component that takes an array of numbers, you would use the value `Prop-Types.arrayOf(PropTypes.number)`. You could combine this array notation with the previous shape to create a component that shows a list of users with full property validation performed by React:

```
function Users({ userList }) {
...
}
Users.propTypes = {
  userList: PropTypes.arrayOf(
    PropTypes.shape({
      name: PropTypes.string,
      age: PropTypes.age,
    }),
  ),
};
```

As you can see, that code quickly becomes quite complex to maintain. (What if users are changed so they have both a first name and a last name?) You can store your types in a shared file somewhere, so your components could look like this:

```
// types.js
export const UserType = PropTypes.shape({
  name: PropTypes.string,
  age: PropTypes.age,
});
// UserDisplay.js
import { UserType } from './types';
function UserDisplay({ user }) {
...
}
UscrDisplay.propTypes = {
  user: UserType,
};
// Users.js
import { UserType } from './types';
function Users({ userList }) {
...
}
Users.propTypes = {
  userList: PropTypes.arrayOf(UserType),
};
```

We can define the type as a regular variable in a central file.

Then we import the type as any other variable . . .

. . . and use the type where appropriate.

This example only scratches the surface of what the `PropTypes` library can do. You can even create custom validators if you have some special components. Check the documentation for the `PropTypes` library at https://mng.bz/v8Mp.

REQUIRED PROPERTIES

One final aspect of the `PropTypes` library that I want to introduce here is the notion of required versus optional properties, which often go hand in hand with default property values. Suppose that we have a component that can display data for a car. Some cars have sunroofs, but most cars do not, so we can set the default value for a sunroof to `false`; then we need to set the property only for cars that have a sunroof. All cars have a make and model, however, so those properties do not have default values and are required for all instances of the car component.

We can specify this relationship by appending the suffix `.isRequired` to the required property types in the `propTypes` object and leave it out for the optional ones. We can do that like so:

```
function Car({ make, model, hasSunroof = false }) {          The car component takes
...                                                          three properties; the last
}                                                            one has a default value.
Car.propTypes = {
  make: PropTypes.string.isRequired,         The two required property types
  model: PropTypes.string.isRequired,        have the suffix .isRequired.
  hasSunroof: PropTypes.bool,          The last optional property
};                                     type does not have this suffix.
```

Any type of property can be made required, even nested or complex property types. Note that there's no requirement that optional properties have defaults and required properties don't. Those details are up to you to track.

4.3.2 Drawbacks of using property types

You may have a few problems with using property types; the main one is the fact that validation happens only at run time. You have no error messages as you type the code—only when you run the code. This situation delays valuable feedback, which, in turn, slows your development efficiency.

Another problem with property types is that you have type safety only for components, not all the other things in your codebase. Those other things can be hooks, functions, external libraries, and much more. Therefore, the solution is only partial.

Compare both of these drawbacks with TypeScript, which we get to in chapter 5. TypeScript offers in-editor type safety for your entire application, which is why it is a more widely adopted solution today than merely using property types.

Finally, and most important, property types are not supported in React 19. Using property types does not cause any errors, but the `.propTypes` property will be ignored, and no validation will happen at run time. If you are using property types today and considering upgrading to React 19, you might as well switch to TypeScript, if you haven't already, to get at least the same level of type safety.

4.3.3 Default property values

A concept related to .propTypes was once fairly common, and you may still see it in live codebases today. This concept concerns default values for properties. This specific method is mostly irrelevant today, but it may be good to know about it in case you come across it in your work or are working on a codebase with class-based components. If neither situation applies to you, feel free to skip this section and go straight to section 4.4.

You may be thinking, "We already use default values for properties; we can specify them directly in the component definition. So what the heck are you going on about?" First, you don't need to get so aggressive! Second, yes, that is true today, but it wasn't back in the days of class-based components.

For a class-based component, there was (and still is) no elegant way to set a default value for a property, so the React team created one for you: the .defaultProps object, which you can apply to a component the same way that you assign .propTypes to a component. Look at this component, which has a link with a default target:

```
function MenuItem({ label, href, target="_self" }) {        ◁──┐  The property target
  return (                                                       has a default value:
    <li>                                                         the string "_self".
      <a href={href} title={label} target={target}>
        {label}
      </a>
    </li>
  );
}                                   Note how we
MenuItem.propTypes = {        ◁──┘ added propTypes.
  label: PropTypes.string.isRequired,        We don't specify the target property as
  href: PropTypes.string.isRequired,         a required value because we have a
  target: PropTypes.string,        ◁──────── default value in case it is not specified.
};
```

But if we were to create this same component as a class-based component, we'd have a different way to add this default property value:

```
class MenuItem extends React.Component {
  render() {
    return (
      <li>
        <a
          href={this.props.href}
          title={this.props.label}
          target={this.props.target}        ◁──┐  Remember that properties in class-based
        >                                        components are never defined anywhere, such
          {this.props.label}                     as when we destructure them in the functional
        </a>                                     component definition. We use them when
      </li>                                      necessary directly from the this.props object.
    );
  }
}
```

```
MenuItem.propTypes = {
  label: PropTypes.string.isRequired,
  href: PropTypes.string.isRequired,
  target: PropTypes.string,
};
MenuItem.defaultProps = {
  target: "_self",
};
```

We still specify the target property as not required because we want a default value for it.

The new thing here is adding an object named defaultProps to the component variable. That object contains default values for properties where relevant. Note that we specify only the properties that have default values; required properties never do.

Now these two variants of the `MenuItem` component are identical. You can specify the `target` property or leave it out and have the component use a default value.

You probably already know how you can add default property values to a functional component by using the destructuring syntax, and you've seen how you can add default property values to any component by using the `.defaultProps` object. You may wonder what would happen if you did both things. This question is why we can't have nice things; you want to burn the whole thing down!

Well, don't worry; nothing bad happens. There's no need to do both things, which would only make your component difficult to use. If you did, the component would still work. But the defaults specified in the functional component definition will be ignored if the same property names are specified in the `.defaultProps` object.

Consider a concrete example. We want to create a greeting component that says "hi" to the user by name. If the user hasn't provided a name, we want to display a default name, `"Stranger"`. Due to a slight mixup with multiple developers working on this component over time, a default property value was specified in two ways, both as a destructuring default and as part of a `.defaultProps` object:

```
function Greeting({ name="Stranger" }) {
  return <h1>Hello {name}</h1>;
}
Greeting.propTypes = {
  name: PropTypes.string,
};
Greeting.defaultProps = {
  name: "Anonymous",
};
```

We set a default value for the name property to "Stranger" in the component definition.

We also set the default value for the name property to "Anonymous" by using defaultProps.

What happens then? As I just mentioned, the value listed in `.defaultProps` takes precedence. In this instance, if you use this component and don't specify a value for the name property, the greeting would become `<h1>Hello Anonymous</h1>`.

But don't do this. Using `.defaultProps` is technically possible for functional components but not recommended. It might even become a warning in future versions of React. For now, this practice is valid but not recommended. If you have a codebase with only functional components, there's no need to use `.defaultProps`, so stick with destructured default values.

As of React 19, in fact, `.defaultProps` is no longer supported for functional components and will be ignored. You can still use the `.defaultProps` object for class components, as no reasonable alternative is available.

4.3.4   *How to get started using property types*

To begin using property types, you need to do only a limited amount of setup: install the `prop-types` packages. Use `npm` with the following command:

```
npm install --save prop-types
```

Using default property values with the `.defaultProps` object requires no setup. This functionality is entirely built into React. If you want to make sure that you remember to use property types throughout your project, you can apply two useful ESLint rules:

- `react/prop-types` throws an error by default if a component uses properties that are not defined in the `.propTypes` object or if the `.propTypes` object is missing.
- `react/no-unused-prop-types` throws an error by default if you have a `.prop-Types` object that defines properties, which aren't used in your component.

4.4   *Debugging applications with React Developer Tools*

Despite your using all of the preceding tools, and maybe even more, bugs will creep into your code—a sad fact of software development. Over time, bugs happen. They're unavoidable and not a direct reflection of your skills as a developer, only an unwanted consequence of lines of code plus time.

Your ability to find the source of a bug and fix it efficiently, however, *is* a reflection of your experience and ability as a developer. Luckily, React has some good tools that allow you to quickly identify root causes of common (and uncommon) bugs. Figure 4.6 highlights the responsibilities of debugging, with only the relevant parts in focus.

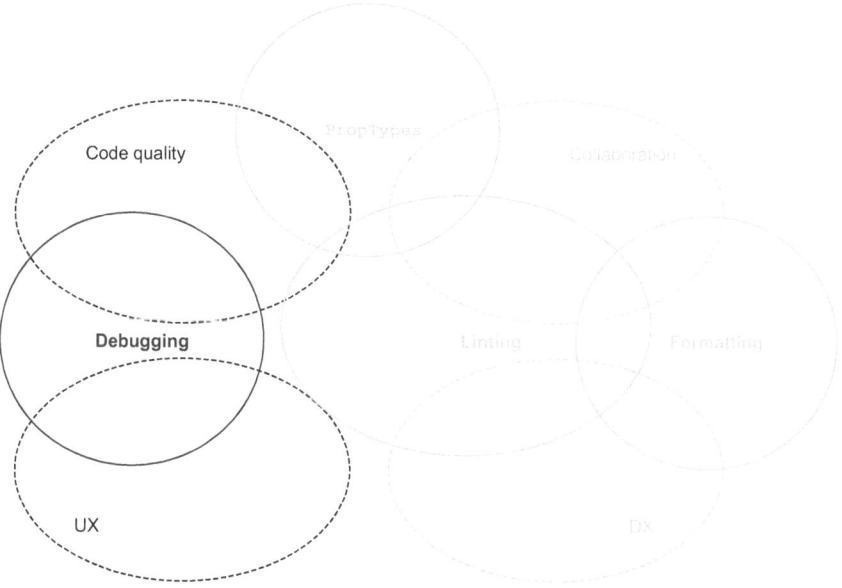

Figure 4.6   Debugging affects two aspects of software development: code quality and UX.

Our two main weapons in React are the developer tools built into our browser and the React Developer Tools. Although I won't cover your browser's developer tools (please check your browser documentation for information), I will go over React Developer Tools, a browser extension available directly for the Google Chrome, Mozilla Firefox, and Microsoft Edge browsers and indirectly for all other browsers.

4.4.1   Problems solved by debugging

Most of the problems we've dealt with so far in this chapter are related to static code analysis. Linters and formatters operate on source code only and have no idea about what happens when the code is running.

Debugging is the opposite situation. You operate a debugger in the live browser environment where your application code is running. A debugger can inspect the values of variables as they change over time, pause script execution, monitor when certain functions are running or lines of code are executed, and even hotswap new code into the running application.

The React Developer Tools plugin consists of two separate tools: the components inspector and the profiler. These tools work differently and are used for different purposes, but combined, they give you all the insights you require. I'll focus more on the components inspector because it's more useful and you'll reach for it more often. The profiler is a more specialized tool for a smaller range of problems. Using these tools, you can do the following:

- See why certain application states are reached by tracking down the exact values of variables over time.
- Identify the properties with which a certain component is instantiated by using the components inspector.
- Use the profiler to find which components are rendering too frequently or too slowly.
- Visualize which components are rendering and track down why by using the rendering highlighter in the components inspector.
- Inspect the full component tree by using the components inspector.

These tools will equip you to solve a lot of problems in your React application. To unsuspecting team members, you might even seem like a debugging wizard wielding these tools, which are immensely powerful when you fully understand them.

4.4.2   How to get started using React Developer Tools

React Developer Tools is a browser plugin for the most common browsers. But the tool also works as an application running separately from your browser as long as you make sure to connect your React application to an extra web server. You don't want to take this approach if you can avoid it, though, so go for the plugin if it exists for your browser.

INSTALLATION IN CHROME, FIREFOX, AND EDGE

For Chrome, Firefox, and Edge, React Developer Tools can be installed as a plugin directly from the browser's plugin store:

- *Chrome*—https://mng.bz/4J7R
- *Firefox*—https://mng.bz/QZ56
- *Edge*—https://mng.bz/X1X9

After you installed the plugin, you're basically done. Open any local React application running in development mode (the default when you're running it locally), and you can start using the plugin.

INSTALLATION IN OTHER BROWSERS

For other browsers, including Apple's Safari, you have to do three things to get the plugin running:

1. Install React Developer Tools via npm as a global package.
2. Launch React Developer Tools as a separate application via a command in your terminal.
3. Manually connect your web page with your development version of a React application to the React Developer Tools application.

First, you need to install the application:

```
$ npm install -g react-devtools
```

Notice the -g flag, which installs the package as global rather than local for a single specific application. Next, you need to launch the tool with this simple command:

```
$ react-devtools
```

This command launches an application that looks like an instance of developer tools inside a browser but is an independent application. This application won't be connected to anything until you complete step 3 (connect your HTML page with a local React application to this tool).

The standalone tool will run a web server on port 8097, and we simply need to load a script from there; that script takes care of everything else. So add the following HTML snippet to the <head> section of your application (which for most applications in this book requires updating the file in <root>/index.html):

```
<script src="http://localhost:8097"></script>
```

Include this snippet as the first thing inside <head>, and you should be good to go. When you reload your React application in your browser, you should see the React Developer Tools application connect to your React application and allow you to debug it.

Note that this approach has some drawbacks, including the fact that you need to have an extra application running. Also, and slightly more troublesome, you can have only one instance of React Developer Tools running, so you can debug only one React application at a time.

4.4.3   *Using the components inspector in React Developer Tools*

The first tool in the React Developer Tools plugin is the easiest to understand, use, and benefit from: the components inspector. This tool is incredibly powerful, and I won't cover everything it does, but I'll go over the most important bits. It allows you to

- Inspect the entire component tree (with or without HTML nodes)
- Easily and quickly see which nodes are memoized
- Inspect and manipulate component props
- Inspect and manipulate some stateful hooks and their values

INSPECTING THE COMPONENT TREE

Let's see how we can use the components inspector tool to inspect the component tree in various ways. For this example, let's reuse a simple application from chapter 2 with a React context, memoization, and some hooks so we can see how they show up in the inspector. In particular, let's look at listing 4.1. This code is the first iteration of the dark mode application (using native React context only), with a slight change to introduce an extra-simple component, `Title`. Figure 4.7 shows the slightly modified application running.

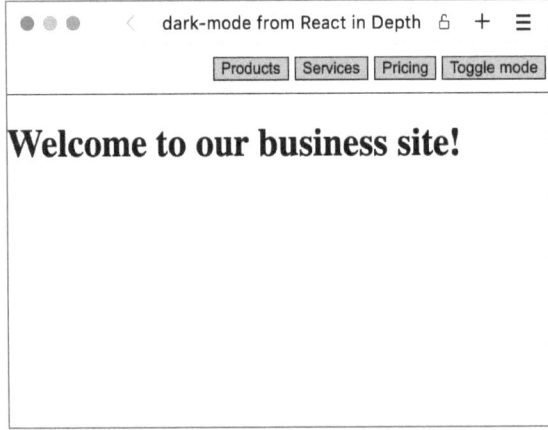

Figure 4.7   The application looks the way it did before, with a large "Welcome" headline and a dark mode toggle button in the top-right corner (which also still works as expected).

Listing 4.1   Dark mode application with React context

```
import { useContext, useState, createContext, memo } from "react";
const DarkModeContext = createContext({});
function Button({ children, ...rest }) {
  const { isDarkMode } = useContext(DarkModeContext);
  const style = {
    backgroundColor: isDarkMode ? "#333" : "#CCC",
    border: "1px solid",
    color: "inherit",
  };
  return (
```

```
      <button style={style} {...rest}>
        {children}
      </button>
    );
}
function ToggleButton() {
  const { toggleDarkMode } = useContext(DarkModeContext);
  return <Button onClick={toggleDarkMode}>Toggle mode</Button>;
}
const Header = memo(function Header() {
  const style = {
    padding: "10px 5px",
    borderBottom: "1px solid",
    marginBottom: "10px",
    display: "flex",
    gap: "5px",
    justifyContent: "flex-end",
  };
  return (
    <header style={style}>
      <Button>Products</Button>
      <Button>Services</Button>
      <Button>Pricing</Button>
      <ToggleButton />
    </header>
  );
});
const Title = memo(function Title({ isPrimary = false, children }) {
  const Heading = isPrimary ? "h1" : "h2";
  return <Heading>{children}</Heading>;
});
const Main = memo(function Main() {
  const { isDarkMode } = useContext(DarkModeContext);
  const style = {
    color: isDarkMode ? "white" : "black",
    backgroundColor: isDarkMode ? "black" : "white",
    margin: "-8px",
    minHeight: "100vh",
    boxSizing: "border-box",
  };
  return (
    <main style={style}>
      <Header />
      <Title isPrimary>Welcome to our business site!</Title>
    </main>
  );
});
function App() {
  const [isDarkMode, setDarkMode] = useState(false);
  const toggleDarkMode = () => setDarkMode((v) => !v);
  const contextValue = { isDarkMode, toggleDarkMode };
  return (
    <DarkModeContext.Provider value={contextValue}>
      <Main />
    </DarkModeContext.Provider>
  );
```

The new thing in this application compared with the same example in chapter 2 is this simple component. It's used only once but takes a Boolean property for the purpose of the example.

Uses the Title component and sets the Boolean flag to true to render it as a primary headline

```
}
export default App;
```

> **Example: dark-mode**
>
> This example is in the `dark-mode` folder. You can use that example by running this command in the source folder:
>
> ```
> $ npm run dev -w ch04/dark-mode
> ```
>
> Alternatively, you can go to this website to browse the code, see the example in action in your browser, or download the source code as a zip file: https://reactlikea .pro/ch04-dark-mode.

Next, take a look at figure 4.8 to see React Developer Tools open in the components inspector.

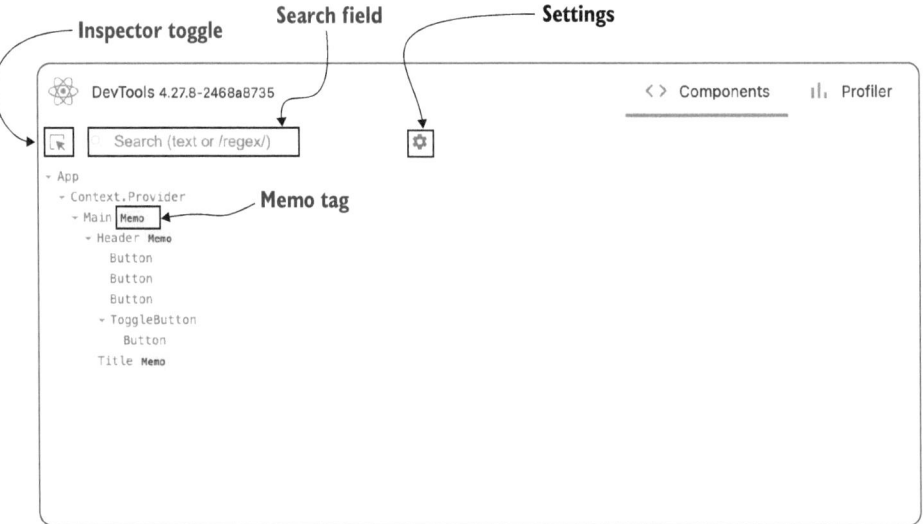

Figure 4.8   The initial view in the components inspector as you connect to the dark mode application. You can see the entire component tree on the left and an empty inspector on the right. Notice that several extra tools are included: the inspector toggle, a search field, a settings gear, and a small tag highlighting memoized components.

The components inspector includes a few extra tools (annotated in figure 4.8) that you will find useful, including the inspector toggle, which allows you to select a component in your application visually like inspecting HTML nodes in the regular document object model (DOM) tree browser, and the search field at the top, which allows you to filter the tree to view the matching subset (including searching by regular expressions). These tools are straightforward to use, so I recommend that you play around with them to see how they aid you.

The settings gear, annotated in figure 4.7, allows you to toggle additional modes and options in the components inspector. You can show all regular HTML nodes in the components tree, which are hidden by default. Figure 4.9 shows how to toggle that option; figure 4.10 shows the resulting component tree.

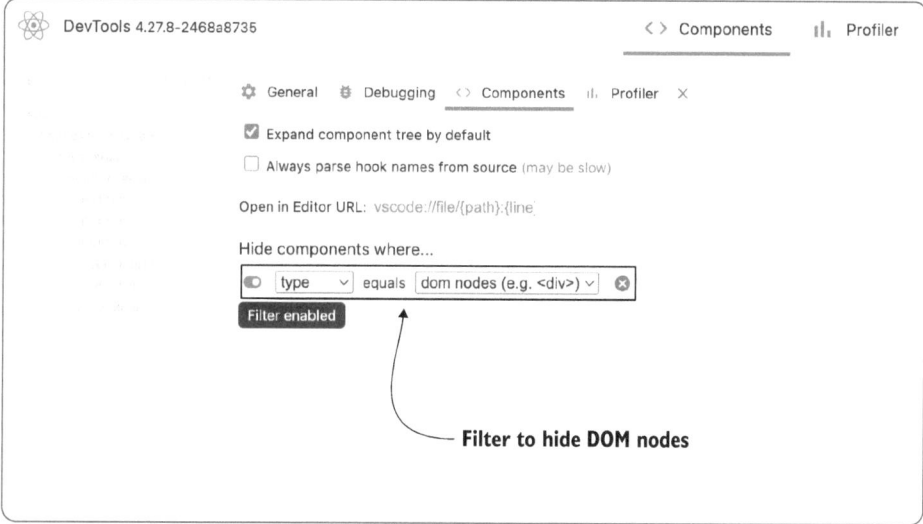

Figure 4.9   On the components tab of the components inspector's settings dialog box, you can disable the filter that hides all HTML nodes by default. You can use this same dialog box to add filters that hide other types of components, such as all memoized components, all class components, all contexts, and other types of components.

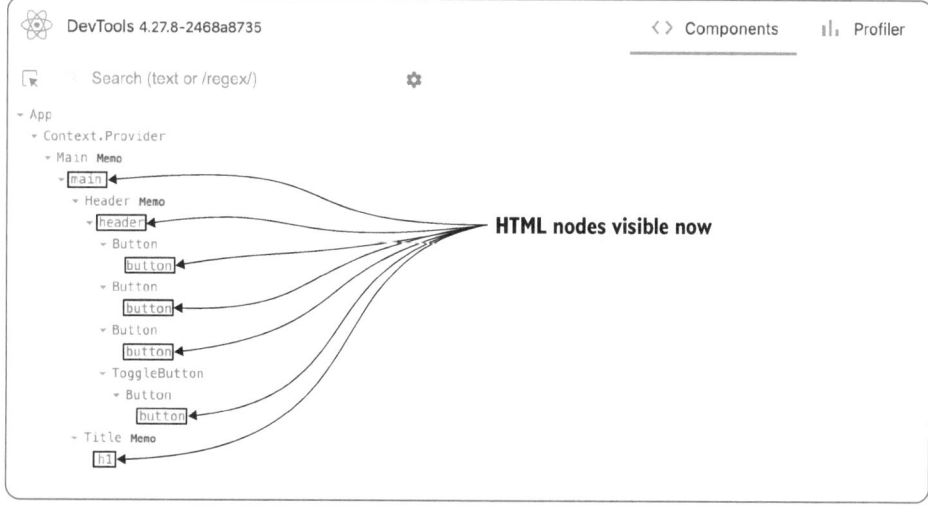

Figure 4.10   With the default HTML node filter disabled, the component tree is expanded to include all the HTML nodes.

INSPECTING COMPONENTS

When you click a component in the component tree on the left side of the inspector, you see all the properties of said component, as well as information about the hooks used in it. Figure 4.11 shows a simple component without hooks: the `Title` component.

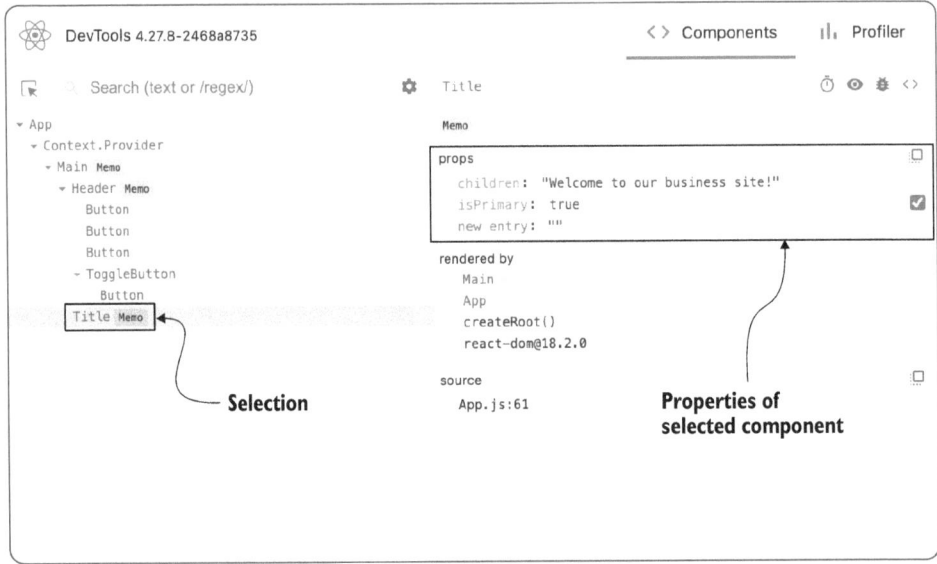

Figure 4.11   **The `Title` component is selected in the component tree, and all the properties are displayed on the right side.**

Besides viewing the properties, we can edit them directly and inline right in the components inspector. We can input strings and numbers directly in the input field when it's focused, and we can use the check box to toggle Booleans. Objects are a bit more tricky to manipulate directly but can be manipulated to some extent. We can't use this method to edit functions, however, because of scope and other concerns. Let's update the `Title` text and disable the primary headline Boolean flag, as shown in figure 4.12.

Manipulating components this way causes the relevant components to re-render instantly and update the view. If the parent component ever re-renders, of course, our changes would be overridden. We could trigger that activity in this case by toggling dark mode. Changing the values directly in the inspector is a temporary local change, not a change of the application. The resulting application looks like figure 4.13 until the parent component re-renders and resets the properties to their "real" values.

INSPECTING STATEFUL COMPONENTS

The root `App` component in the dark mode application is stateful, using the `useState` hook. Let's see how we can interact directly with that state without going through the

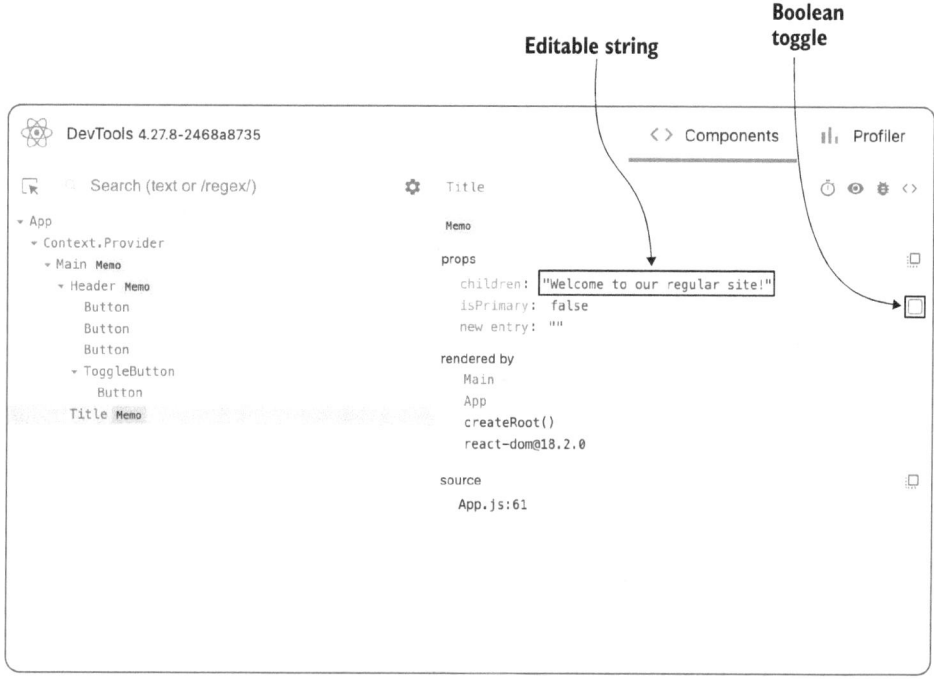

Figure 4.12 **We can update strings directly and toggle Booleans.**

Figure 4.13 **Manipulating component properties in the components inspector causes the specific components to re-render immediately.**

regular setter function. Using the components inspector, we can inspect a stateful component and see the state directly, as well as manipulate it. If we manipulate the state, the component will re-render with the new state as though it were updated correctly (figure 4.14).

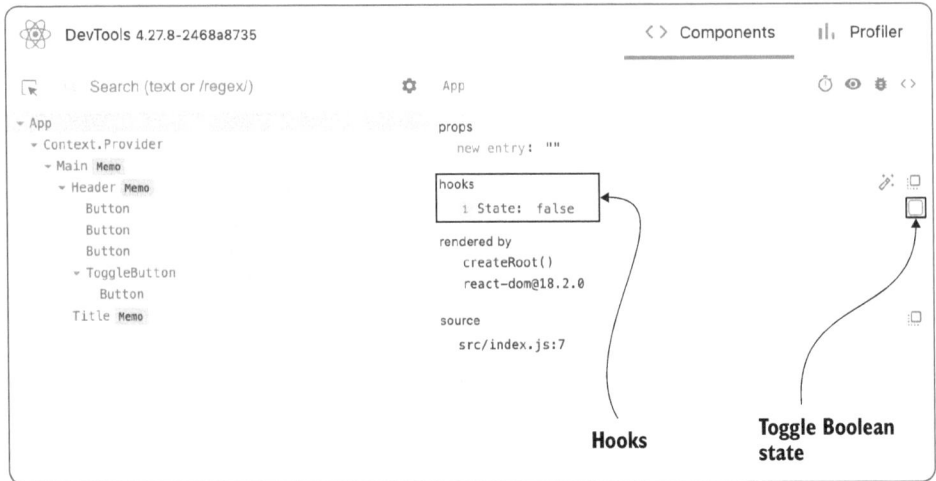

Figure 4.14   **When you're inspecting a stateful component with a** useState **or** useReducer **hook, you can interact with the state directly through the components inspector. You can manipulate the value, just as you can manipulate properties, as shown in figure 4.12.**

If you consume a context, your component also becomes stateful, and you can use the components inspector to inspect the context state. But you cannot update the context state directly by using the inspector from a context consumer; you have to go through the context provider and manipulate the value property from there instead (figure 4.15).

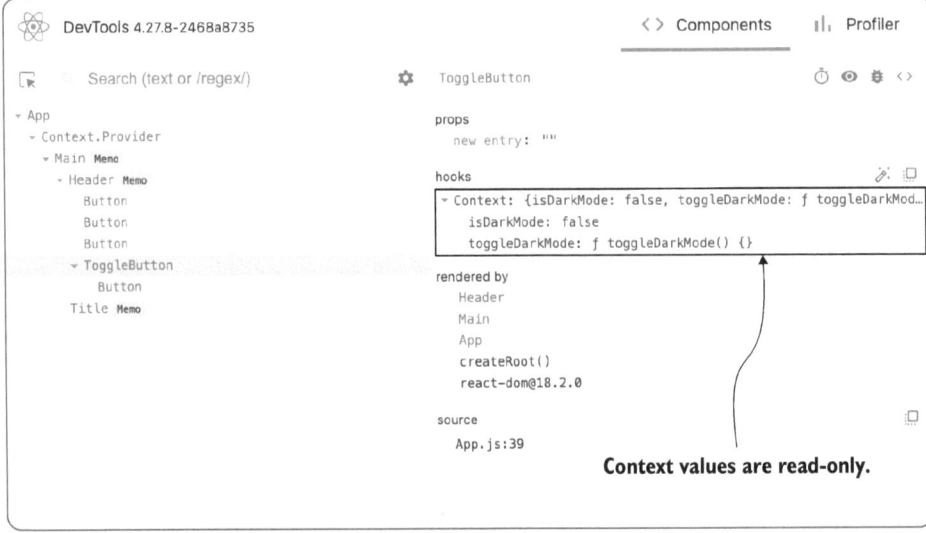

Figure 4.15   **You can see but not modify the value of a context when you're inspecting a context consumer.**

If instead you highlight the nearest context provider inside the components inspector's tree view, you can manipulate the value property as shown in figures 4.11 and 4.12.

4.4.4   *Using the profiler in React Developer Tools*

The profiler tool is the lesser-used tool in the React Developer Tools utility belt. This tool is a lot more complex and is used for specific purposes. It's comparable to the built-in performance as provided by your browser's regular developer tools.

Suppose that you have an application that is acting slow. When you click a specific button, the application freezes for about half a second before the click is registered and the resulting update happens. Why? That situation is where the profiler comes in.

In the profiler tool, you can start a recording before you click the button, keep the recording going while the button action takes place, and stop the recording afterward. Then you can look through the recording to see what happens: which functions are invoked, which components re-render and why, if tracking re-rendering is enabled, which effects run when, which events are invoked on what components, and many other details. The interface is complex, with a lot of information that can be hard to understand; the only good way to learn it is through experience.

Try to debug the dark mode application from listing 4.1. Start a recording in the profiler, toggle the dark mode button, and then stop the recording. The result should look something like figure 4.16.

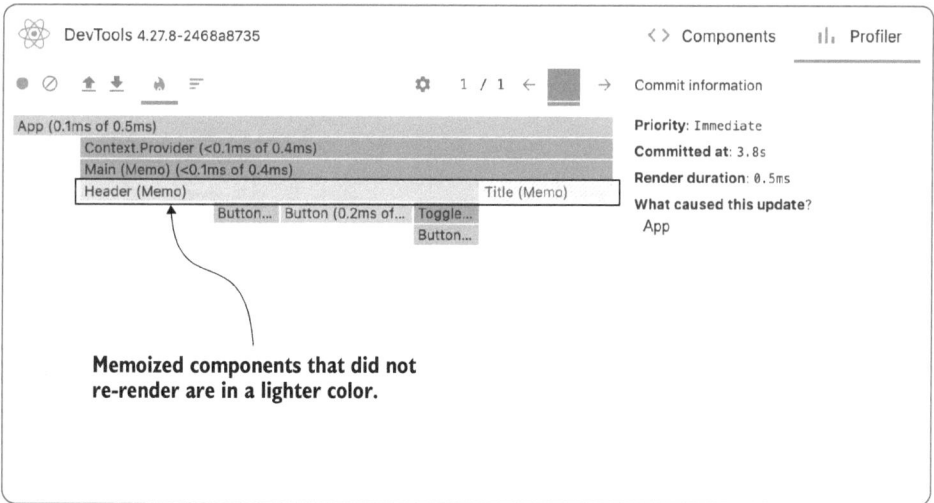

Figure 4.16   The result of a React profiler recording session, displaying which components re-render, when, and for how long, as well as how the renders cascade through the component tree. The lightly shaded components (`Header` and `Title`) are so colored because they didn't render. (They're memoized and had no changes.) All the other components displayed in the view did re-render for some reason.

If you enable the setting to track why components re-rendered in the profiler settings menu (shown in figure 4.17), inspecting the button inside the toggle button allows you to see stats for that component (figure 4.18).

The profiler recording session, shown in figure 4.18, displays a particular component (in this case, Button).

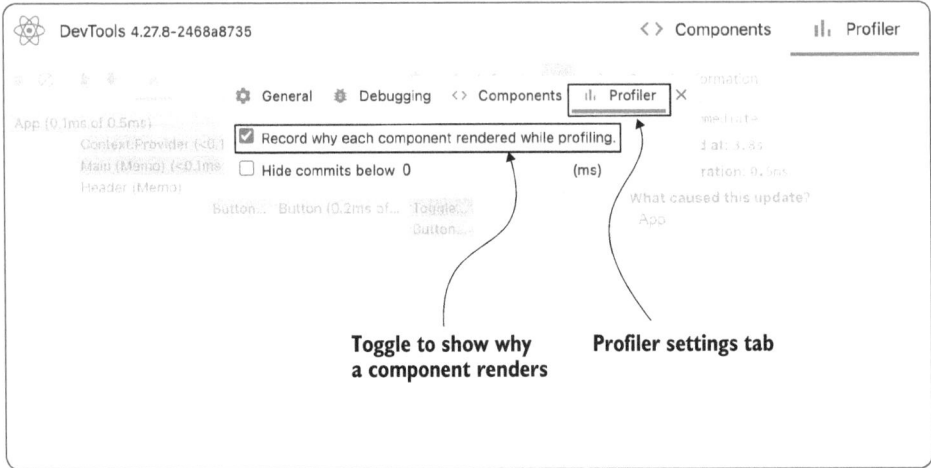

Figure 4.17   You can enable the setting to track why components re-render in the settings for the profiler tool.

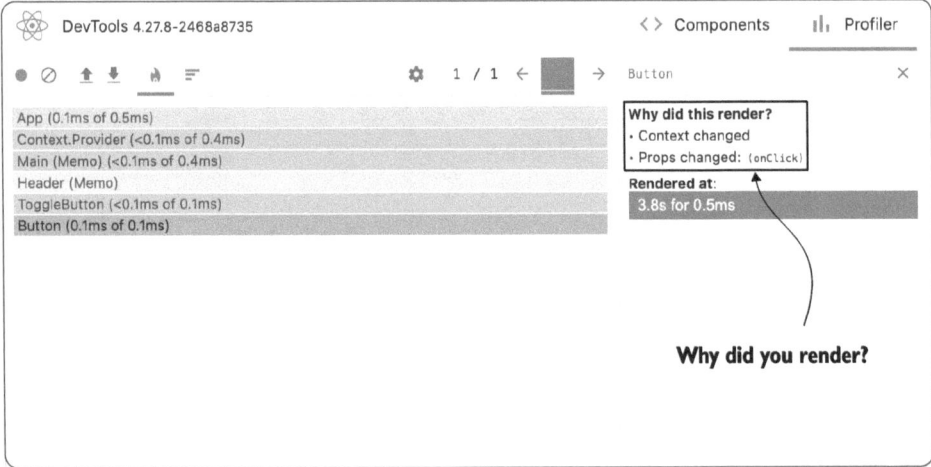

Figure 4.18   When we inspect this component, we see that it is rendered for two reasons: it consumes a context that has updated, and its properties have been updated. Either event would be sufficient to cause a re-render, but in this case, both happened. We can also see that the component re-rendered for a whopping 0.5 milliseconds, which seems to be the smallest unit of time that's trackable in the profiler.

As mentioned, the profiler is a complicated debugging tool that requires a bit of experience to fully understand, so play around with it if you want to master it. Using this tool in small applications that you understand can be a good way to go about learning.

4.4.5 *Alternatives and other tools*

Depending on your stack and the other technologies in use, a few other libraries may be relevant for you. Here's a brief list of libraries and tools that might apply to your application:

- If you're using Redux or any of the derived libraries (such as Redux Toolkit or RTK-Query), Redux DevTools is a must-have for debugging. You can find it at https://github.com/reduxjs/redux-devtools.
- If you're using React Native, the React Native Debugger is a great bridge application that allows you to use tools such as React Debugging Tools even while running React Native applications. You can get it at https://github.com/jhen0409/react-native-debugger.
- If you're using Electron to build React apps as desktop applications, Reactotron is the library for you. It works as a bridge between your Electron-wrapped application and the regular developer tools, like the React Native Debugger. Get it at https://github.com/infinitered/reactotron.
- If you need to re-create and debug errors experienced by other people, consider using Replay.io. This tool is a freemium service, but at the free level, you're able to debug only locally. If you subscribe at higher pricing tiers, you can re-create and debug error sessions experienced by other users. Even at the free tier, it's an awesome debugging tool inspired by Redux DevTools, but it works regardless of your state management library. Read more at https://www.replay.io.

If you're using other complex technologies in your stack, they may also have some dedicated debugging tools, so remember to search for them. Good luck debugging!

Summary

- Although React and JavaScript, in general, are great on their own, both can become significantly more pleasant to work with if you introduce some developer tooling to assist with managing complexity.
- Linting is great for enforcing style guides and reducing errors. ESLint is among the most popular linters available.
- Formatters reduce discussion and time spent on stylistic debates and fully automate the process of formatting the code as agreed on. Prettier is the tool most commonly used for formatting.
- React has a built-in system for validating property types passed to all the components in the codebase, but it is an older system that has significant drawbacks compared with TypeScript.

- The React Developer Tools plugin includes a powerful components inspector tool that allows users to inspect and manipulate component props, memoized nodes, and stateful hooks. The inspector provides features such as searching and filtering components, toggling modes and options, and highlighting memoized components.
- The profiler tool, although more complex, helps with understanding application performance by recording and analyzing function invocations, component re-renders, effects, events, and more. You need experience to use it and fully understand its capabilities.
- These four utilities have overlapping responsibilities, but you might see several or all of them applied to projects in the wild. You'll even see quite a few later in this book.

TypeScript: Next-level JavaScript

This chapter covers

- Using best practices with React and TypeScript
- Introducing static typing with TypeScript
- Reducing errors and increasing documentation with types

As we venture further into the realm of professional React development, we come across a pivotal tool in our arsenal: TypeScript. This chapter marks a significant step in enhancing your skills and understanding as a developer. TypeScript, often referred to as "JavaScript with superpowers," opens the door to a new world of possibilities in terms of robust, statically typed code and cleaner, more maintainable applications.

Over the past few years, TypeScript has gained widespread adoption in the JavaScript community. Its ability to catch bugs at compile time, provide improved code navigation and autocompletion, and enhance collaboration between developers has made it a go-to choice for building modern web applications. In this chapter, we will embark on a journey to understand TypeScript's fundamentals, its advanced features, and its application within the React ecosystem.

119

NOTE   The source code for the examples in this chapter is available at https://reactlikea.pro/ch05.

5.1   The importance of TypeScript

Trying to introduce TypeScript in a few chapters is like trying to explain all of calculus in a single math class. TypeScript is a huge topic, well deserving of complete books, and a lot of great literature about it is already available.

TypeScript is the bigger sibling of JavaScript. TypeScript can do everything Java-Script does, but it also does much more—namely, static typing and type safety checks. See figure 5.1 for an overview. TypeScript can be transpiled to JavaScript, losing all its additional functionality in the conversion, but as static typing and type safety checks can be validated before the code runs, you still get all the value that you can from it, while producing JavaScript in the end.

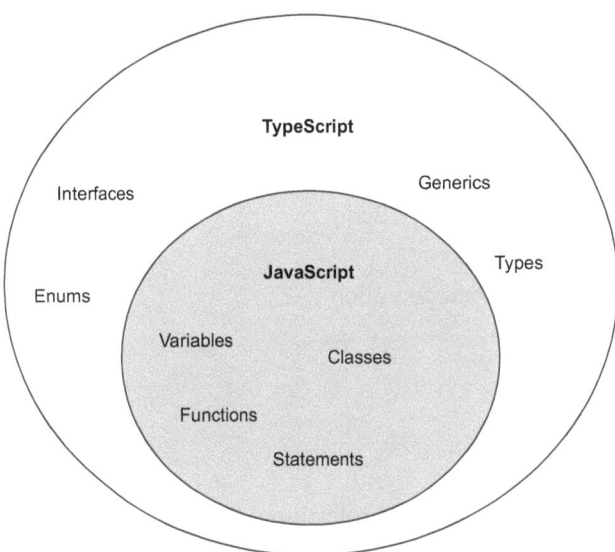

Figure 5.1   TypeScript contains all the features that JavaScript does, including variables, functions, classes, and statements. It also contains new features, including types, enums, interfaces, and generics.

Many React-based development teams have moved to exclusive use of TypeScript, which is the future of JavaScript in general and React in particular. That said, a ton of teams still aren't using it, and you can get by fine without knowing it, but your options will expand greatly if you add TypeScript to your skill set.

Before I proceed, it's important to note that our exploration of TypeScript and its integration with React is extensive, spanning two chapters. In this chapter, we'll delve into TypeScript's fundamental and advanced features in the context of React applications, setting the stage for our discussion of integrating TypeScript with React in chapter 6. So get ready to bolster your skills as we embark on this journey across TypeScript's terrain. While we're focusing on React, it's important to note that all these principles apply outside the world of React, making this knowledge universally valuable.

Whether you're a seasoned React developer or just getting started, the knowledge you gain in this chapter and the next one will be invaluable. TypeScript empowers developers to write more reliable, scalable, and maintainable code. It reduces the likelihood of runtime errors and simplifies collaboration on larger codebases. I'll take you through TypeScript's core concepts, its integration with React, advanced techniques that use generics, and the practical application of TypeScript in real-world scenarios.

By the end of this chapter, you'll not only have the knowledge to work effectively with TypeScript but also understand its potential pitfalls and how to navigate them. So let's dive into the world of TypeScript, where the JavaScript of tomorrow meets the challenges of today's professional web development.

5.2 Introduction to TypeScript

TypeScript is your bridge to a world where code becomes more predictable and maintainable and less error prone. We'll dive deep into understanding the basics, starting with TypeScript files and their seamless integration with React, giving you the essential knowledge to bring static typing to your applications.

Next, we'll explore TypeScript's type system, an indispensable aspect of the language. I'll demystify static types and show you how to apply them effectively to your code. By the end of this section, you'll have a firm grasp of TypeScript's core concepts, enabling you to use its robust features to enhance the reliability and maintainability of your React applications. Let's begin your TypeScript journey and unlock the full potential of JavaScript in the professional development landscape.

5.2.1 TypeScript files and React

Before we get started with the details, let's briefly discuss file extensions. Although it's not a hard requirement, it's a common practice to save TypeScript in `*.ts` files rather than `*.js` files to signify that they contain source code in a (slightly) different language. Furthermore (and I haven't discussed this fact previously), some developers put React components (or files using JSX) in `*.jsx` files rather than plain `*.js` files, and those same people would put React TypeScript components in `*.tsx` files rather than `*.ts` files. Many TypeScript + React setups require you to do so and will fail if you put JSX in `*.ts` files. We will be using `*.ts` files for TypeScript without JSX and `*.tsx` files for TypeScript with JSX in this section for those very reasons.

5.2.2 Static types

The most basic feature of TypeScript is static typing. Let's start with an example, creating a single function intended to calculate the next number in the Fibonacci sequence by passing the two previous numbers to it:

```
function fibonacci(a, b) {
  return a + b;
}
```

If we implement this function in TypeScript, the type checker doesn't know the type of the two arguments, so it is unable to infer the return value of the response. Thus, we can call this function with whatever we want, and TypeScript won't help us:

```
const result = fibonacci(true, "Hi there");
```

But TypeScript will alert us that type information is missing, saying `Parameter 'a' implicitly has 'any' type`). For TypeScript to function, it needs a bit of information to get started. In particular, we need to specify the types of arguments passed to functions. We do that using a colon (`:`) followed by the type name. Primitive types' names can be lowercase (`number`) or capitalized (`Number`), but the names of complex types are generally capitalized. In this example, we need to specify that a and b are numbers:

```
function fibonacci(a:number, b:number) {
  return a + b;
}
```

Now, if we try to use the function as we did before, TypeScript will come to our assistance:

```
const result = fibonacci(true, "Hi there");
```

TypeScript reports that an `Argument of type 'boolean' is not assignable to parameter of type 'number'`. If we change the first argument to a number, TypeScript will report an error for the second parameter. If we use the function correctly, however, TypeScript will correctly infer the types of all variables:

```
const f0 = 0;
const f1 = 1;
const f2 = fibonacci(f0, f1);
const f3 = fibonacci(f1, f2);
```

Note that we don't have to add type information for any of these variables directly. We could have written const `f0: number = 0`, but we didn't have to. TypeScript knows that 0 has the type `number`. Also, we don't have to write that f2 has a type `number`, as TypeScript will correctly infer that the type returned from the Fibonacci function has the type `number`. TypeScript knows what all the built-in functions do, so it knows that the result of adding two numbers is itself a number. Similarly, it knows that the length of a string is a number and that the `number.toString()` method returns a string. For more complex functions, we can add type hints about what a function is supposed to return; TypeScript will validate that it does in fact return only that type.

If a variable can hold multiple types of values, you can specify that fact too. You can create your own type, which indicates exactly which values are allowed. If you have a first-name variable that starts as null but can take a specific value later, you can specify that situation like so:

```
type Name = null | string;
let firstName: Name = null;
```

You can even specify that a value can be any type, but that approach is almost always a bad choice. Instead, use the literal type `any`. If you want to indicate that you don't know the type of a given value (maybe it's returned by a third-party API), you can use the type `unknown`. Also, you can specify specific values allowed for a type, such as a status variable that can be only `LOADING`, `SUCCESS`, or `ERROR`:

```
type Status = "LOADING" | "SUCCESS" | "ERROR";
let status: Status = "LOADING";
```

If we later try to assign the value `status = "COMPLETE"`, TypeScript will report this assignment as an error because that value is not valid:

```
Type '"COMPLETE"' is not assignable to type 'Status'.
```

When we're adding type information to a functional React component, we create a custom complex type, specifying the name and types of the properties passed to that function this way:

```
type PersonProps = {
  name: string;
  age: number;
};
function Person({ name, age }: PersonProps) {
  ...
}
```

We can also use an interface rather than a type, which is common practice for props definitions. A slight technical difference between interfaces and types exists, but we won't cover that difference here. Just know that you'll often see the previous example written this way instead:

```
interface PersonProps {
  name: string;
  age: number;
}
function Person({ name, age }: PersonProps) {
  ...
}
```

Note the slightly different notation for an interface in that it doesn't use an assignment (no equals sign). If you have optional properties, you indicate that fact by adding a question mark in the type or interface for the properties object. In the following example, both `name` and `age` are optional, and we assign a default value to the `name` when destructuring the properties but not to the `age`:

```
interface PersonProps {
  name?: string;
  age?: number;
}
function Person({ name = "Anonymous", age }: PersonProps) {
  ...
}
```

5.2.3 Employee display

Let's create an about page listing the employees of a fictional company. For that task, we need a simple component to display a single employee using TypeScript. We want to display this component in a card-like style, as a rounded rectangle with a bit of drop shadow. All these things come together in the file `EmployeeCard.tsx`, where we define the main employee-card component. You can see this file in the following listing.

Listing 5.1 An employee card using TypeScript

```
import "./employee.css";                          We import some styles to
type Employee = {    ←  First, we define a type for an employee.    make the card look good.
  name: string;          (You might have that type somewhere
  title: string;         central in your application.)
};
interface EmployeeCardProps {    ←  Then we define the interface for this specific
  item: Employee;              component, which takes an item of the employee type.
}
function EmployeeCard({ item }: CardProps) {    ←  We apply this interface to
  return (                                          the object of properties
    <section className="employee">                 received in the component.
      <h2 className="employee__name">
        {item.name}    ←
      </h2                  We can use values on the item object
      <h3 className="employee__title">    validated by TypeScript because of the type
        {item.title}       information we've added to the application.
      </h3>    ←
    </section>
  );
}
export default EmployeeCard;
```

Note that this property is required, as we don't include a question mark in the definition.

We also have some supporting files to make this application work with `App.tsx`, `app.css`, and `employee.css`, as you can see in the next three listings.

Listing 5.2 The main application displaying a single employee card

```
import EmployeeCard from "./EmployeeCard";
import "./app.css";
function App() {
  return (
    <main>
      <EmployeeCard item={{     Here, we use our employee-card component. Note that we
        name: "Willy Wonka",    don't need to specify that this item object is of the correct type.
        title: "Candy King"     TypeScript checks the object and validates that it has the
      }} />                      required values and types—and only those values and types.
    </main>
  );
}
export default App;
```

Listing 5.3   Base styles for our employee page

```
@import url("https://fonts.googleapis.com/css2?family=Open+Sans:wght@300 ");
* {
  box-sizing: border-box;
}
body {
  background-color: #eee;
  font-family: "Open Sans", sans-serif;
}
main {
  display: flex;
  align-items: center;
  justify-content: center;
  margin: 2em;
}
```

Listing 5.4   Styles specific to the employee card

```
.employee {
  background: white;
  flex: 0 0 300px;
  border-radius: 1em;
  padding: 1em 1.5em;
  box-shadow: 4px 4px 2px rgba(0 0 0 / 0.2);
}
.employee__name {
  margin: 0 0 0.5em;
  font-size: 24px;
}
.employee__title {
  margin: 0;
  text-transform: uppercase;
  font-size: 16px;
  color: #222;
}
```

What does this code look like in a browser? Well, as expected, it looks like a nicely styled employee card (figure 5.2).

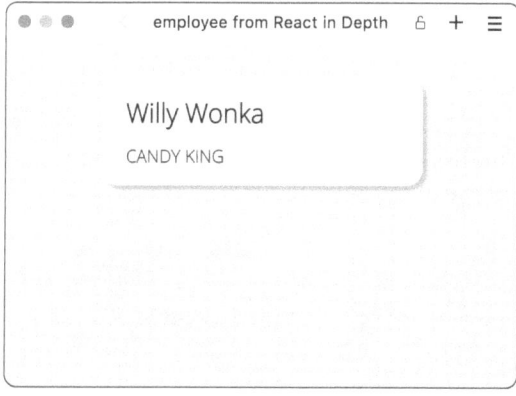

Figure 5.2   Our employee card in action. Nobody can tell from the screenshot that we used TypeScript behind the scenes, and they're not supposed to, but *we* know, so we appreciate the result a bit more. Also, Willy Wonka is king here.

> **Example: employee**
>
> This example is in the `employee` folder. You can use that example by running this command in the source folder:
>
> $ npm run dev -w ch05/employee
>
> Alternatively, you can go to this website to browse the code, see the example in action in your browser, or download the source code as a zip file: https://reactlikea .pro/ch05-employee.

5.2.4   Optional properties

Let's extend the example a bit by adding an optional website property to the employee type and then display it in the component if present. We could add that property as shown in the following listing.

Listing 5.5   An employee card with an optional website link

```
import "./employee.css";
export type Employee = {
  name: string;
  title: string;
  website?: string;     ⟵──  Adds the optional property
};                             with a question mark
interface EmployeeCardProps {
  item: Employee;
}
function EmployeeCard({ item }: CardProps) {
  return (
    <section className="employee">
      <h2 className="employee__name">{item.name}</h2>
      <h3 className="employee__title">{item.title}</h3>
      {item.website && (
        <h4 className="employee__link">             Renders the optional
          Web: <a href={item.website}>{item.website}</a>    property using a
        </h4>                                               logical AND expression
      )}
    </section>
  );
}
export default EmployeeCard;
```

We can use this new component to display two different employees—one with a website and one without a website—on the about page.

Listing 5.6   A new main application displaying two employees

```
import EmployeeCard, { type Employee } from "./EmployeeCard";
import "./app.css";
```

```
function App() {
  const employees: Employee[] = [
    {
      name: "Wayne Campbell",
      title: "Host Extraordinaire",
      website: "https://extremepartytime.com",
    },
    {
      name: "Garth Algar",
      title: "Tech Wizard",
    },
  ];
  return (
    <main>
      {employees.map((employee) => (
        <EmployeeCard
          key={employee.name}
          item={employee}
        />
      ))}
    </main>
  );
}
export default App;
```

Defines Wayne with his cool website. (Note: this site isn't Wayne's, but check it out anyway!)

Defines Garth without a website

Renders a list of employees using the map function

Rendering these two cool characters should look like figure 5.3.

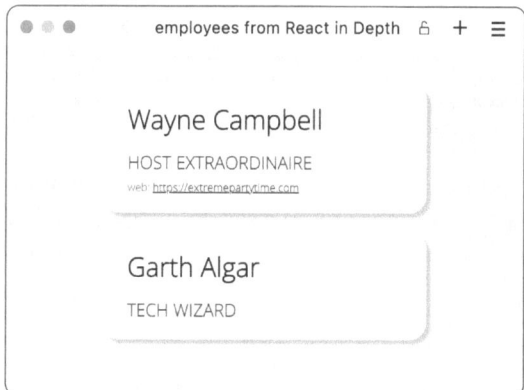

Figure 5.3 Rendering two infamous employees as card components. Only the first shows the optional website link. Go ahead and click it! I dare you!

Example: employees

This example is in the `employees` folder. You can use that example by running this command in the source folder:

```
$ npm run dev -w ch05/employees
```

(continued)

Alternatively, you can go to this website to browse the code, see the example in action in your browser, or download the source code as a zip file: https://reactlikea .pro/ch05-employees.

5.3   *Advanced TypeScript with generics*

Generics is a well-known concept in the world of static typing, known from other, more complex, strongly typed languages such as Java and C#. A *generic type* takes another type as an argument. An array can be a generic type, for example; it's a list of something, but what it contains is unspecified until we *do* specify it. A number array is an instantiation of this generic type, with the array specifically said to contain numbers and only numbers.

   Generics are used for all sorts of tricks in TypeScript and are especially important in React as well. In this section, we'll go over a bunch of important generic types that are built into TypeScript and React and that you'll often use in applications. Also, I'll go over some best practices that many React TypeScript teams use every day while creating large React applications:

- Typing `children`
- Extending interfaces
- Spreading props
- Optional and required properties
- Either/or properties
- Forwarding refs and memoizing components
- Typing hooks (covered in chapter 6)

Finally, we can make our own generics—not just for functions, but for complete React components. We can make a React component to take several properties that have to be in sync but aren't specified from the start. This process is fairly complex, so we'll save that task for section 5.4.

5.3.1   *Understanding generic types*

Let's create a function that returns the middle element of an array and should work with any array. As we saw in section 5.2.2, we can make it untyped, which is the same as typing it as `any`:

```
function getMiddle(list) {
  const mid = Math.floor(list.length / 2);
  return list[mid];
}
```

We can invoke this function on a list of numbers and store the result in a string, and it would compile:

```
const one: string = getMiddle([0, 1, 2]);
```

But we can see that this example is wrong; it's a list of numbers, so of course the middle item will also be a number, not a string. We can signify this fact by making the `get-Middle` function *generic*—that is, we can say that the function works with some type (which we may or may not put restrictions on), and then we can use this generic type to say that the function accepts an array of that type and returns a value of that type. The type can change with each invocation. To accomplish this task, we use angle-bracket notation (`<Type>`):

```
function getMiddle<Type>(list: Type[]): Type {
  const mid = Math.floor(list.length / 2);
  return list[mid];
}
```

Now, if we try the same thing as before, we get an error:

```
const one: string = getMiddle([0, 1, 2]);
```

TypeScript reports an error with the `one` variable:

```
Type 'number' is not assignable to type 'string'.
```

If we assign the type to a properly typed variable, it will work. Then we can invoke the function with different types of arrays and get different types out:

```
const one: number = getMiddle([0, 1, 2]);
const apple: string = getMiddle(['pear', 'apple', 'banana']);
```

This code works as expected and is powerful, also in React. Note that in the invocations of `getMiddle`, the generic type argument is *inferred* by the value arguments to the function. We can also specify that argument explicitly, but we rarely have to. This code works as it did before:

```
const one: number = getMiddle<number>([0, 1, 2]);
```

If we specify a more specific set of types as the type argument, TypeScript loosens the definition of the return type. If we specify manually that we're invoking the function with an array of numbers or strings, we need to type the return value specifically as `number | string` to make the type system happy:

```
const one: number | string = getMiddle<number | string>([0, 1, 2]);
```

Note that we introduced this complexity ourselves. I use this example only to explain what would happen. We'll specify type arguments manually in later examples because the inferred type is not specific enough or because that approach makes typing easier.

5.3.2 *Typing children*

Let's create a heading component. We will use this component on a fictional website to display identical headings on all the pages, and we can easily update the headline styling in a single central place. Let's create the component without TypeScript first, using plain JavaScript:

```
function Heading({ children }) {
  return <h1 style={{ backgroundColor: "hotpink" }}>{children}</h1>;
}
```

That component is neat and simple; we know how to create it. We use the special property `children` to allow the component to be used as `<Heading>Title here</Heading>`. But how do we type this property? In this case, the heading of a page is probably a string, so let's type it as a string:

```
interface HeadingProps {
  children: string;
}
function Heading({ children }: HeadingProps) {
  return <h1 style={{ backgroundColor: "hotpink" }}>{children}</h1>;
}
```

That code seems fine, right? Well, yes. If we use this component like `<Heading>Hello</Heading>`, it works well. But what if we want to include dynamic values like `<Heading>Hello {name}</Heading>`? Now we get an error from TypeScript:

```
Type 'string[]' is not assignable to type 'string'.
```

That error does kind of make sense. Now we pass two string children to the component; the first is the string `"Hello "`, and the second is the value of the variable `name`. So we can modify the type to accept either a string or an array of strings like so:

```
interface HeadingProps {
  children: string | string[];
}
```

On one page, however, we need to use the heading to display a dynamic number, and at a different place. we might pass in a Boolean by using a logical AND expression, as in these two examples:

```
<Heading>You have {messages.length} new messages</Heading>
<Heading>There are {isValid && 'no'} errors</Heading>
```

Both examples are classic React patterns, showing how we pass things as child nodes to other components. But both examples fail with new errors:

```
Type 'number' is not assignable to type 'string'.
Type 'boolean' is not assignable to type 'string'.
```

Again, those errors make a lot of sense. Let's amend the type to accept strings, numbers, Booleans, and even arrays of those types:

```
interface HeadingProps {
  children:
    | string
    | number
    | boolean
    | (string | number | boolean)[];
}
```

We have everything covered now, right? Let's say that we want to include some special formatting, such as a bold word, as in `<Heading>Hello <strong>World</strong></Heading>`. Then we get a new error:

```
Type 'Element' is not assignable to type 'string | number | boolean'.
```

We need to add one more thing: `JSX.Element`. What if we don't pass in anything, as in `<Heading />`? We also need to allow the property to be missing by making it optional. Combining all those changes, we arrive at this code:

```
interface HeadingProps {
  children?:
    | string
    | number
    | boolean
    | JSX.Element
    | (string | number | boolean | JSX.Element)[];
}
```

This example is getting out of hand, and we haven't considered a few more edge cases yet. Luckily, React has an exported type that includes all these cases *and* the extra ones we haven't discussed. That type, called `ReactNode`, can be imported from the React package as follows:

```
import { type ReactNode } from 'react';
interface HeadingProps {
  children?: ReactNode;
}
function Heading({ children }: HeadingProps) {
  ...
}
```

That code is a lot cleaner. We still have to make the property optional, but we don't have to enumerate all the different possibilities.

An easier approach is to use the built-in interface `PropsWithChildren` in React, which defines an interface that takes the `children` property as defined in the preceding example and nothing else. Using this interface, we can define the same component this way:

```
import { type PropsWithChildren } from 'react';
function Heading({ children }: PropsWithChildren) {
  ...
}
```

NOTE There's no real difference between typing the `children` property directly with `ReactNode` or having React type it automatically by using `Props-WithChildren`. I prefer the latter approach for brevity's sake, so I will use it throughout this book.

CHILDREN AND MORE

Now let's start using this heading component for both small and large headings. We'll add a new property, `isLarge`, that defaults to `false`, so we can specify when a particular heading has to be extra-prominent this way:

```
<Heading isLarge>This is important!</Heading>.
```

How do we add this new property to the props interface now that we've removed that interface and replaced it with a built-in one from React? Well, I didn't mention one thing about `PropsWithChildren`: it takes an *optional* generic type argument. Yes, even generic type arguments can be optional. In this case, the type argument is the interface for all the other, non-`children` props that the component accepts, and we can use it like so:

```
import { type PropsWithChildren } from 'react';    ⟵  Imports the
interface HeadingProps {                                PropsWithChildren type
  isLarge?: boolean;         Defines an interface defining    from the React package
}                            nonchildren props for the component
function Heading({
  isLarge = false, children                    Combines the two interfaces by passing
}: PropsWithChildren<HeadingProps>) {   ⟵     the props interface as a generic type
  return (                                      argument to PropsWithChildren
    <h1 style={{
      backgroundColor: "hotpink", fontSize: isLarge ? '48px' : '36px'
    }}>
      {children}
    </h1>
  );
}
```

The default value for the `PropsWithChildren` interface is an empty props interface, as though we invoked it with `PropsWithChildren<{}>`.

NOTE The default type argument is true only in React 18 and later. In React 17 and earlier, the interface does not have a default type argument, and if you want to use it for a component that accepts only the `children` property, you have to write it as `PropsWithChildren<{}>`. That code seems a bit clunky, but it works.

RESTRICTING CHILDREN TO CERTAIN TYPES IS NOT POSSIBLE

You may wonder whether we can use the type of the `children` property to restrict which types of elements are allowed. What if we want to create a `<TableRow>` component, and the only allowed child nodes are `<TableCell>` nodes? Unfortunately, React and TypeScript do not give you this opportunity. Typing `children` as `TableCell[]` may seem to be trivial, but it doesn't work for various reasons—first and foremost because JSX is syntactic sugar and doesn't exist in the eyes of the compiler.

Unfortunately, we cannot use TypeScript that way. There's no clever workaround for now, so make sure to design your components so that it's clear what kind of child nodes are valid.

5.3.3   *Extending interfaces*

Suppose that we have a generic button in our UI library that can render a string as the button label. We also have an icon variant of the button that allows the component to be rendered with both an icon and a label. Let's say that our button takes several properties, such as `color` and `size`:

```
interface ButtonProps {
  color: "primary" | "secondary";
  size: "large" | "medium" | "small";
  onClick?: () => void;
  disabled?: boolean;
  className?: string;
}
function Button({ ... }: PropsWithChildren<ButtonProps>) {
  return (...);
}
```

Note that this example is partial; we don't implement the button. Now let's look at how we would create the icon button. If we didn't use TypeScript, we would define it like this:

```
function IconButton({ icon, children, ...rest }) {
  return <Button {...rest}>{icon} {children}</Button>;
}
```

That is, we extract only the `icon` and `children` properties from the passed properties, using them combined as the children of the button component, and sending all other properties to the button as they are.

But if we want to type this feature, how do we specify that this icon button can take these six properties: the five properties that the button takes plus an icon, which is a React node? The naive way would be to specify all six properties again, but that approach seems like a bad idea from the start. It would work, of course, but the two definitions would be unsynchronized. If we update the button properties later, the icon button properties won't update automatically.

Instead, we can extend one interface when defining another one. To do so, we need a reference to the interface for the props of the original component. Let's assume that we exported it so we can import it:

Imports the component and the type for its properties from a different file

```
import { Button, type ButtonProps } from './Button';
interface IconButtonProps extends ButtonProps {
  icon: ReactNode,
}
function IconButton(
```

Defines the properties for the icon button by extending the button props interface and adding only the new property, icon

```
  { icon, children, ...rest }: PropsWithChildren<IconButtonProps>
) {
  return <Button {...rest}>{icon} {children}</Button>;
}
```

After using this icon button for a while, we find out that it works only with the large button style, so we don't want developers to try to specify a different button style—only the large one. Now we want the icon button properties to extend every property of the button except one. How do we do it? We omit the extraneous property, using the `Omit` interface from TypeScript itself:

```
import { Button, type ButtonProps } from './Button';
interface IconButtonProps
  extends Omit<ButtonProps, "size"> {          ◁─┐  Extends the button properties
  icon: ReactNode,                                 except the size property
}
function IconButton({ icon, children, ...rest }: IconButtonProps) {
  return <Button size="large" {...rest}>   ◁─┐  Hardcodes the size property to large while
    {icon} {children}                          making sure that the rest object will never
  </Button>;                                    contain a different definition of size
}
```

We can even omit multiple properties by passing in a union of multiple strings:

```
Omit<ButtonProps, "size" | "color">
```

We can also do the opposite: pick just a few properties, which might be easier than omitting several. Suppose that we want to extend only the `color` property from the button component. We could do that by omitting the `size`, `onClick`, `disabled`, and `className` properties. But it's easier to say that we pick only the `color` property like this:

```
Pick<ButtonProps, "color">
```

`Pick` is also a built-in interface provided by TypeScript. In all these examples, we extend the properties of another component by using a direct reference to an interface describing these properties. But what do we do if we don't have a reference to the interface for the properties—only the component? Cue next section (via a small detour).

5.3.4   Spreading props in general

In the preceding example, we made a component that extended another of our own components. But often, we make components that extend built-in components or even third-party components. Let's start with a component that has an HTML element inside it. We want to pass properties from outside the component to the HTML element.

We're going to create a `UserImage` component. This component takes some properties that are specific to this type of image, such as the `name` and `title` of the user, but it also takes properties that a regular image tag takes, such as `src`, `alt`, `width`, and `height`. We want to do something like this:

```
interface UserImageProps
  extends RegularImageProps {        ◁──  Tries to extend a regular
  name: string;                            image component, but
  title: string;                           RegularImageProps doesn't exist
}
function UserImage({ name, title, ...rest }: UserImageProps {
  return (
    ...
      <img {...rest} />     ◁──┐  The goal is to use the rest value this
    ...                        │  way and have TypeScript validate
  );                           │  that only valid props are passed.
}
```

In this example, we use a regular `<img />` tag, and we want TypeScript to validate that we can pass, say, `src` to our `UserImage` component but not a property such as `source` that doesn't exist for an image. We could type all the possible properties, but that list would be huge. In React, more than 200 possible properties are allowed for most HTML elements (mostly because of event handlers such as `onClick`, `onFocus`, and dozens more). As in section 5.3.3, we know that there must be a smarter way. But this time, we don't have a convenient interface directly describing the allowed properties. The `RegularImageProps` interface doesn't exist.

There is a better way: `ComponentProps`, and it's built into React. `ComponentProps` is a generic interface for which we must provide a type argument. This type argument is the type of component for which we want to know the properties' interface. In our example, that component is `img`, so we pass it in as a string:

```
import { type ComponentProps } from 'react';
interface UserImageProps extends ComponentProps<"img"> { ... }
```

We have a slight problem, however: this interface also allows the property `ref` for all components, but references aren't received as regular props inside the component (at least not before React 19). As a result, it doesn't make sense to type the props received by a component to include this property. We'll get back to typing references in section 5.3.8. A slightly longer interface, `ComponentPropsWithoutRef`, does exactly what it says:

```
import { type ComponentPropsWithoutRef } from 'react';
interface UserImageProps extends ComponentPropsWithoutRef<"img"> { ... }
```

Now we have our component fully functional, accepting the right props. Remember that we can also `Pick<>` or `Omit<>` from this interface to allow or disallow specific properties. Maybe we don't want the developer to pass in the `alt` property because we're going to set it ourselves:

```
import { type ComponentPropsWithoutRef } from 'react';
interface UserImageProps extends
  Omit<ComponentPropsWithoutRef<"img">, "alt"> {    ◁──┐  Extends all the properties
  name: string;                                         │  of an image element
  title: string;                                        │  except the alt property
}
```

```
function UserImage({ name, title, ...rest }: UserImageProps) {
  return (
    ...
      <img
        alt={`Profile image for ${name}`}
        {...rest}          <---  By not allowing the alt property, we
      />                         can be sure that our custom alt
    ...                          property will not be overridden.
  );
}
```

But what if we're extending a custom component? Can we still use the `Component-PropsWithoutRef`? Suppose that we have a `<Rating />` component from a third-party library that takes properties like those in this example (and might take even more properties):

```
<Rating icon="♥" max={6} value={4.3} label="4.3 hearts" />
```

We want to create a new `BookReview` component. We want to be able to pass in some specific things about the book, as well as some of the same properties that the `Rating` component takes, such as `value`, `label`, and `icon`. We would like to do this:

```
import { Rating, type RatingProps }    Imports a component and its
  from 'cool-rating-library';          type from a third-party library
interface BookReviewProps extends
  Pick<RatingProps, "value" | "label" | "icon"> {    <---  Creates a new type
  title: string;                                            from the type of the
  reviewer: string;                                         external component
  body: string;
}
function BookReview({ ... }: BookReviewProps) {
  ...
```

In this example, we depend on the external library to provide a type of the props of the component. What if we don't have it? Can we use `ComponentPropsWithoutRef`? We can't use it directly, as `ComponentPropsWithoutRef<Rating>` doesn't make sense. Here, `Rating` is a real JavaScript variable, not a TypeScript type. But we can do the naive thing and use `typeof`:

```
import { type ComponentPropsWithoutRef } from 'react';
import { Rating } from 'cool-rating-library';
type RatingProps =                                    typeof does exactly what it says:
  ComponentPropsWithoutRef<typeof Rating>;            returns the type of a given variable.
interface BookReviewProps extends
  Pick<RatingProps, "value" | "label" | "icon"> {  <---  Now we can use the type
  ...                                                     extracted from the component.
```

Let's turn this code into a full-blown example so we can play around with it. We'll create both components ourselves, but we won't expose the props type from the `Rating` component. We'll also get to play with CSS to make a fancy rating display. First, we have the `Rating` component.

Listing 5.7   Rating component

```
import { type PropsWithChildren } from "react";
import "./Rating.css";
interface StarsProps {
  count: number;
  faded?: boolean;
}
function Stars({
  count,
  faded = false,
  children,
}: PropsWithChildren<StarsProps>) {
  return (
    <span className={`rating__stars ${faded && "rating__stars--faded"}`}>
      {Array.from(Array(count).keys()).map((_, i) => (
        <span key={i} className="rating__star">
          {children}
        </span>
      ))}
    </span>
  );
}
interface RatingProps {
  icon?: string;
  value: number;
  max?: number;
  label?: string;
}
export function Rating({
  icon = "☆",
  value,
  max = 5,
  label = "",
}: RatingProps) {
  const percentage = Math.round((value / max) * 100);
  return (
    <div className="rating" title={label}>
      <Stars faded count={max}>
        {icon}
      </Stars>
      <div className="rating__overlay" style={{ width: `${percentage}%` }}>
        <Stars count={max}>{icon}</Stars>
      </div>
    </div>
  );
}
```

Defines the interface for the allowed props of the Rating component. Note that this interface is not exported, so it's not directly accessible from outside this file.

Then we have the `BookReview` component, which contains the `Rating` component.

Listing 5.8   `BookReview` component using the `Rating` component

```
import { ComponentPropsWithoutRef } from "react";
import { Rating } from "./Rating";
import "./BookReview.css";
type RatingProps =
  ComponentPropsWithoutRef<typeof Rating>;
type PickedRatingProps = Pick<
  RatingProps, "value" | "max" | "icon"
>;
interface BookReviewProps
  extends PickedRatingProps {
  title: string;
  reviewer: string;
  body: string;
}
export function BookReview({
  title,
  reviewer,
  body,
  ...rest
}: BookReviewProps) {
  return (
    <section className="review">
      <Rating max={5} {...rest} />
      <h3 className="review__title">{title}</h3>
      <h4 className="review__byline">By {reviewer}</h4>
      <p className="review__body">{body}</p>
    </section>
  );
}
```

- Creates a type RatingProps by extracting props of the Rating component
- Creates a type PickedRatingProps by picking specific props from RatingProps
- Creates the BookReviewProps interface by extending PickedRatingProps
- Adds props specific to the BookReview component

Finally, let's include some instances of the book review in our main application.

Listing 5.9   The main app with a few reviews

```
import { BookReview } from "./BookReview";
function App() {
  return (
    <div className="reviews">
      <BookReview
        title="Great book"
        reviewer="Anonymous"
        body="I loved the book"
        value={4.8}
      />
      <BookReview
        title="Mediocre Sci-fi"
        reviewer="Sci-fi Lover"
        body="The aliens are boring."
        value={3.3}
        icon="👽"
      />
```

- Creates the first review using only the required properties
- Creates a review with a custom icon

```
      <BookReview
        title="It's a classic!"
        reviewer="Hiro Protagonist"
        body="The perfect romance novel."
        value={9.2}
        max={10}
        icon="🖤"
      />
    </div>
  );
}
export default App;
```

Creates a review with both a custom icon, using 10 icons instead of the default 5

The result should look like figure 5.4.

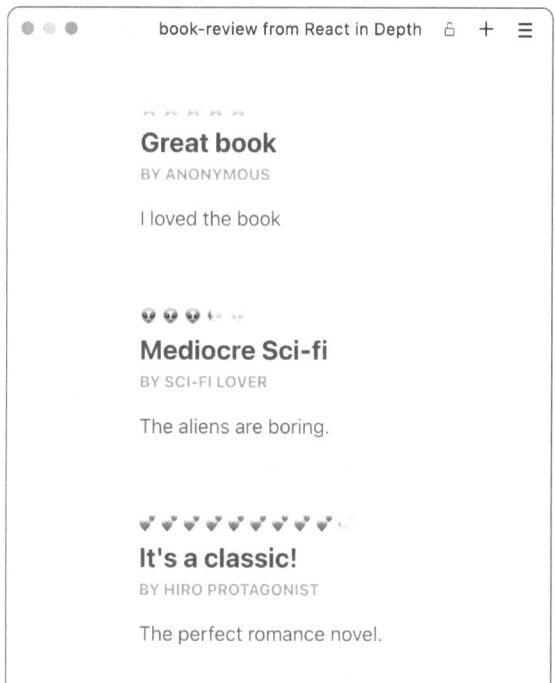

Figure 5.4   Three book reviews with slightly different rating displays. Varying the review icon with the genre looks cool, no? We can provide that function in a typesafe way even when the `BookReview` component exposes some properties of a third-party component.

Example: book-review

This example is in the `book-review` folder. You can use that example by running this command in the source folder:

```
$ npm run dev -w ch05/book-review
```

Alternatively, you can go to this website to browse the code, see the example in action in your browser, or download the source code as a zip file: https://reactlikea .pro/ch05-book-review.

5.3.5   *Restricting and loosening types*

When we extend an interface, we can restrict the interface, but we cannot loosen it. If we have the interface

```
interface Style {
  width: number | string;
}
```

we can extend it while restricting it, perhaps for a `number`-only type:

```
interface NumberStyle extends Style {
  width: number;
}
```

But we cannot go the other way and loosen it for a broader definition:

```
interface AnyStyle extends Style {
  width: number | string | null;
}
```

The preceding code would result in the following TypeScript error message:

```
Interface 'AnyStyle' incorrectly extends interface 'Style'.
  Types of property 'width' are incompatible.
    Type 'string | number | null' is not assignable to type
    'string | number'.
      Type 'null' is not assignable to type 'string | number'.
```

So what do we do? In this case, we could not extend the interface because it has only one property. But suppose that the interface has more than one property. If so, we can omit the original and add it as a new one:

```
interface AnyStyle extends Omit<Style, "width"> {
  width: number | string | null;
}
```

This code works! We can use it in our components in the same way when we want to extend the properties of another component but restrict or loosen a type. The `value` property of an input, for example, is an optional property that can be a string, a `number`, or `undefined`. We can define our own `StringInput` component that allows the `value` to be a string only (no numbers are allowed):

```
interface StringInputProps extends ComponentPropsWithoutRef<"input"> {
  value?: string;
}
export function StringInput(props: StringInputProps) {
  return <input type="text" {...props} />;
}
```

If we want to do the opposite by creating an input in which the `value` could also be a Boolean, we'd have to omit the `value` before redefining it to be a looser type:

```
interface AnyInputProps
  extends Omit<ComponentPropsWithoutRef<"input">, "value"> {
  value?: string | boolean;
}
export function AnyInput({ value, ...rest }: AnyInputProps) {
  return <input type="text" value={String(value)} {...rest} />;
}
```

5.3.6 *Using optional and required properties*

In the preceding example, I talked about restricting or loosening a type and mentioned adding more or fewer alternatives to a union type. But we can toggle another aspect of a property, whether or not it's required. We could have created the string input in such a way that the `value` was not optional but required, by omitting the question mark:

```
interface StringInputProps extends ComponentPropsWithoutRef<"input"> {
  value: string;
}
```

But we can't go the other way. Suppose that we wanted to extend our previous `Rating` component but make the `value` of the `BookReview` component optional:

```
interface BookReviewProps extends PickedRatingProps {
  value?: number;
}
```

This code would result in a TypeScript error message similar to the one in section 5.3.5 because we're effectively expanding the type to be `number` or `undefined`, and that kind of loosening is not allowed, so we'd have to omit it before redefining it.

Sometimes, all we want to do is make a specific property required instead of optional, but we don't want to change anything else about the type. Suppose that we want to add a button and must define `onClick`. The built-in optional type for the `onClick` property of a button is fairly long:

```
// Built-in type for button onClick property
onClick?: React.MouseEventHandler<HTMLButtonElement>;
```

We don't want to repeat the entire definition—only remove the question mark. So we can refer directly to the old definition that we can get via `ComponentPropsWithoutRef`:

```
type ButtonProps = ComponentPropsWithoutRef<"button">;
interface ButtonWithClickProps extends ButtonProps {
  onClick: ButtonProps["onClick"];
}
```

This code, however, would mean doing a lot of typing if we want to do the same thing for multiple properties:

```
type ButtonProps = ComponentPropsWithoutRef<"button">;
interface HoverButtonProps extends ButtonProps {
```

```
  onMouseOver: ButtonProps["onMouseOver"];
  onMouseMove: ButtonProps["onMouseMove"];
  onMouseOut: ButtonProps["onMouseOut"];
}
```

There's a smarter way. TypeScript has a built-in interface, `Required<>`, that makes all properties of another type required. That behavior is not what we want here, but we can use it to create our own utility interface that makes some properties required:

```
type RequireSome<T, K extends keyof T> = T & Required<Pick<T, K>>
```

Then we can create our `HoverButtonProps` much more elegantly:

```
type ButtonProps = ComponentPropsWithoutRef<"button">;
type RequireSome<T, K extends keyof T> = T & Required<Pick<T, K>>
type HoverButtonProps = RequireSome<
  ButtonProps,
  "onMouseOver" | "onMouseMove" | "onMouseOut"
>;
```

You're probably beginning to see the power of TypeScript. You can do programming by using types alone!

5.3.7 Using either/or properties

Let's create a product-card component that can be used on an e-commerce website, but we want to use the same component to display prices for both regular items and on-sale items. We want the result to look like figure 5.5.

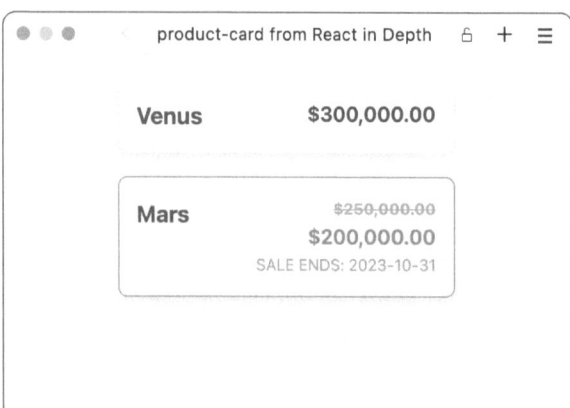

Figure 5.5 A product-card component that can be used for both regular items and on-sale items. Notice that the on-sale item has additional info, including the sale price and an expiry date.

We want to define a component that always requires some properties. Additionally, it will require some extra properties if another property has a certain value. We want the interface to match one interface or the other but not be some mix (figure 5.6).

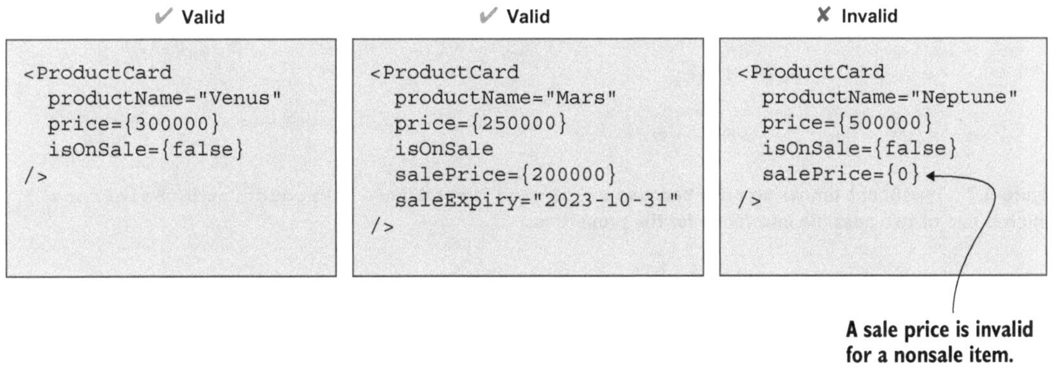

Figure 5.6 Valid and invalid property combinations for our product card

We know how to define these two interfaces separately:

```
interface ProductCardSaleProps {
  productName: string;
  price: number;
  isOnSale: true;
  salePrice: number;
  saleExpiry: string;
}
interface ProductCardNoSaleProps {
  productName: string;
  price: number;
  isOnSale: false;
}
```

To create the final props type for our component, we simply do the naive thing by making a union type of those two interfaces:

```
type ProductCardProps = ProductCardSaleProps | ProductCardNoSaleProps;
```

TypeScript is super clever. It knows that if the props received in the component has isOnSale set to true, the properties object must conform to the ProductCardSale-Props type, so it must have both salePrice and saleExpiry properties. Conversely, if isOnSale is false, it cannot have these properties. We can use an expression like this one:

```
{isOnSale && (
  <div className="sale-price">{props.salePrice}</div>
)}
```

Let's see how TypeScript knows about these types. Figure 5.7 shows a screenshot of a code snippet in Visual Studio Code with TypeScript support enabled; we're trying to access props.salePrice without checking props.isOnSale.

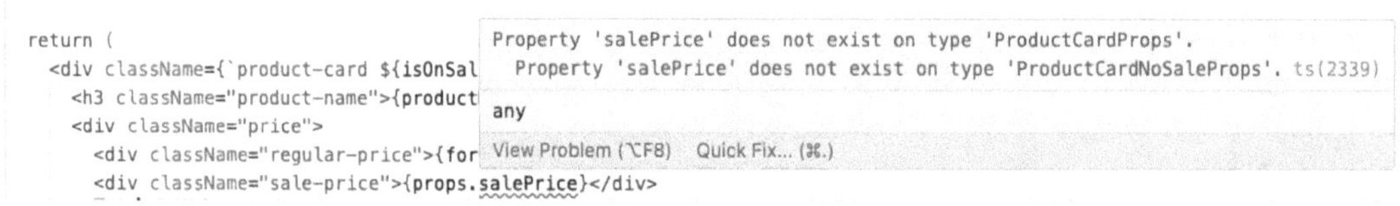

```
return (
  <div className={`product-card ${isOnSal     Property 'salePrice' does not exist on type 'ProductCardProps'.
    <h3 className="product-name">{producti        Property 'salePrice' does not exist on type 'ProductCardNoSaleProps'. ts(2339)
    <div className="price">                   any
      <div className="regular-price">{for   View Problem (⌥F8)   Quick Fix... (⌘.)
      <div className="sale-price">{props.salePrice}</div>
```

Figure 5.7   TypeScript throws an error because `salePrice` **is not defined in** `ProductCardNoSaleProps`, **which is one of two possible interfaces for the properties.**

Figure 5.8 shows how TypeScript knows that the props type must be the on-sale variant when we perform the check for `isOnSale` first.

```
return (
  <div className={`product-card ${isOnSale ? "on-sale" : ""}`}>
    <h3 className="product-name">{productName}</h3>
    <div className="price">
      <div className="regular-price">{formatPrice(price)}</div
      {isOnSale && (                        (parameter) props: ProductCardSaleProps
        <div className="sale-price">{props.salePrice}</div>
      )}
    </div>
  </div>
);
```

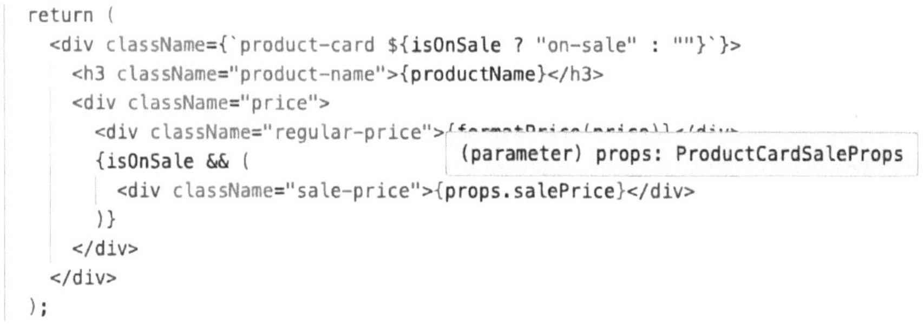

Figure 5.8   When we check for `isOnSale` **first, TypeScript is perfectly well aware that the original props object must be of type** `ProductCardSaleProps`, **so it must have the** `salePrice`, **and all is well here.**

The following listing shows the full component for a product card.

Listing 5.10   Product card with a discriminated union

```
import "./ProductCard.css";
interface ProductCardSaleProps {          ◁─┐  Creates the definition
  productName: string;                       │  for a sale item
  price: number;
  isOnSale: true;
  salePrice: number;
  saleExpiry: string;
}
interface ProductCardNoSaleProps {        ◁─┐  Creates the definition
  productName: string;                       │  for a nonsale item
  price: number;
  isOnSale: false;
}
type ProductCardProps =                        Combines the two definitions for
  | ProductCardSaleProps                       our final component props type
  | ProductCardNoSaleProps;
```

```
function formatPrice(price: number) {                Defines a small utility function
  return price.toLocaleString("en-US", {             to help format numbers nicely
    style: "currency",
    currency: "USD",
  });
}                                          Creates the component
export function ProductCard(                definition without destructuring
  props: ProductCardProps                   the props; we'll get to why that
) {                                         matters later in this section.      Destructs the props
  const { productName, price, isOnSale } = props;                                "manually" as a
                                                                                 separate statement
  return (
    <div className={`product-card ${isOnSale ? "on-sale" : ""}`}>
      <h3 className="product-name">{productName}</h3>
      <div className="price">
        <div className="regular-price">{formatPrice(price)}</div>
        {isOnSale && (                           Renders conditional JSX
          <>                                     depending on a property
            <div className="sale-price">
              {formatPrice(props.salePrice)}          Accesses optional properties
            </div>                                    in a typesafe way
            <div className="sale-expiry">
              Sale ends: {props.saleExpiry}
            </div>
          </>
        )}
      </div>
    </div>
  );
}
```

We can improve this code a bit. You may recognize the fact that we repeated a few
properties between the two interfaces. We defined `productName` and `price` in both
interfaces. Let's extract those properties to a base interface and update the resulting
type. The result would be the new types shown in the following listing.

Listing 5.11 Product-card types with base props (partial)

```
interface BaseProps {
  productName: string;         Creates an interface
  price: number;               with the shared props
}
interface ProductCardSaleProps {
  isOnSale: true;
  salePrice: number;           Creates the two variants by
  saleExpiry: string;          specifying only the props
}                              that vary between them
interface ProductCardNoSaleProps {
  isOnSale: false;
}
type ProductCardProps = BaseProps &
  (ProductCardSaleProps |      Creates the resulting component props type by merging
   ProductCardNoSaleProps);    the base props with the union of the two alternatives
```

Example: product-card

This example is in the `product-card` folder. You can use that example by running this command in the source folder:

```
$ npm run dev -w ch05/product-card
```

Alternatively, you can go to this website to browse the code, see the example in action in your browser, or download the source code as a zip file: https://reactlikea .pro/ch05-product-card.

A few minor things might have caught you off guard. We've strayed from some things that we normally do.

First, as you can see in the function declaration in listing 5.10, we don't spread the props as we normally do. We almost always spread the props in the definition, but we don't here. There are two reasons why we don't spread the props directly in the definition:

- We can't spread conditional props.
- TypeScript doesn't keep track of the relationship of props after spreading.

The first reason is easier to understand. We cannot spread the props object into the values `salePrice` and `saleExpiry` because the props object doesn't always contain these values. If we did spread them, what would their values be if the item is not on sale? What would happen if we used them anyway? TypeScript doesn't work this way. You cannot read something from an object that doesn't exist under every circumstance.

To explain the second reason, let's take a small detour. Why can't we spread the conditional props into a `. . .rest` object, as we sometimes do, and then, if the item is on sale, read the values from that object? Suppose that we took the following approach:

```
export function ProductCard({
  productName,
  price,
  isOnSale,
  ...rest
}: ProductCardProps) {
  ...
        {isOnSale && (
          ...
            {formatPrice(rest.salePrice)}
```

This code is essentially the same thing as listing 5.10, right? We try to read the sale price only from the `rest` object (which is the leftover properties after the product name, price and on-sale flag have been removed), if the item is on sale. So all should be well, shouldn't it?

Unfortunately, no. TypeScript is clever but not *that* clever. After we extract the leftover properties from the props object, TypeScript forgets where the value came from and assigns it a type that's not connected to the other extracted types for that object.

Even when we find out that `isOnSale` is `true`, TypeScript doesn't update its knowledge about the `rest` object; it still has the same union type and has not been narrowed. Compare the type of the props object in figure 5.8 with the `rest` object in figure 5.9.

```
expor (parameter) rest: {
  pro       salePrice: number;
  pri       saleExpiry: string;
  isO } | {}
  ...rest
}: ProductCardProps) {
  return (
    <div className={`product-card ${isOnSale ? "on-sale" : ""}`}>
      <h3 className="product-name">{productName}</h3>
      <div className="price">
        <div className="regular-price">{formatPrice(price)}</div>
        {isOnSale && (
          <>
            <div className="sale-price">
              {formatPrice(rest.salePrice)}
            </div>
            <div className="sale-expiry">
              Sale ends: {rest.saleExpiry}
            </div>
          </>
        )}
      </div>
    </div>
  );
}
```

```
export function ProductCard({
  productName,
  price,
  isOnSale,
  ...rest
}: ProductCardProps) {
  return (
    <div className={`product-card ${isOnSale ? "on-sale" : ""}`}>
      <h3 className="product-name">{productName}</h3>
      <div className="price"~
        <div className="reg (parameter) rest: {     orice)}</div>
        {isOnSale && (          salePrice: number;
          <>                     saleExpiry: string;
            <div className= } | {}
              {formatPrice(rest.salePrice)}
            </div>
            <div className="sale-expiry">
              Sale ends: {rest.saleExpiry}
            </div>
          </>
        )}
      </div>
    </div>
  );
}
```

Figure 5.9 When we extract the `rest` properties from the passed props, TypeScript disconnects the value of that object from the other properties extracted. So even when `isOnSale` is `true`, the type of the `rest` variable doesn't change.

Unfortunately, we have to do things a bit differently when we use discriminated unions, but taking that approach isn't the most common thing to do. Know that when you need discriminated unions, you have to change your habits a bit.

5.3.8 Forwarding refs

This section gets technical, and if you don't use reference forwarding much, you can skip it for now. When you need to, please come back to this section to get the inside scoop.

> **NOTE** In React 19, reference forwarding no longer matters. `forwardRef` is no more. In React 19, you can accept `ref` as a regular property in a functional component, and typing it is much easier because we no longer need to exclude the `ref` property from the properties object and type it separately.

Suppose that you want to create an input component, but to give an outside component access to the HTML element for the input field inside your component, you want to allow a reference to be forwarded to the input field.

In this example, we can say that the main component includes a login form and wants to place the user keyboard focus inside the username input field when the application component loads. The main component would look like this:

```
import { useEffect, useRef } from "react";
import "./App.css";
import { Input } from "./Input";
export default function App() {
  const username = useRef<HTMLInputElement>(null);
  useEffect(() => {
    username.current?.focus();
  }, []);
  return (
    <main>
      <h1>Login</h1>
      <form>
        <Input ref={username} label="Username" name="username" />
        <Input label="Password" name="password" type="password" />
      </form>
    </main>
  );
}
```

Our first attempt to create the input component looks like the following code snippet, which doesn't have the reference and is a basic input component:

```
import { ComponentPropsWithoutRef } from "react";
interface InputProps extends ComponentPropsWithoutRef<"input"> {
  label: string;
}
export function Input({ label, ...rest }: InputProps) {
  return (
    <label>
      <span>
        {label}
        <input {...rest} />
      </span>
    </label>
  );
}
```

To allow the main component to add a `ref` to the custom input component, two things have to happen:

- We need to accept such a reference inside our component.
- We need to pass that reference to the input element.

We achieve the first thing by using the React built-in function `forwardRef()`. The naive implementation is

```
export const Input = forwardRef(function Input(
  { label, ...rest }: InputProps,
  ref
) {
```

The second step is assigning this `ref` to the input element, which sounds easy enough:

```
<input ref={ref} {...rest} />
```

That code should be fine, right? But it doesn't work. TypeScript complains that

```
Type 'ForwardedRef<unknown>' is not assignable to type
'LegacyRef<HTMLInputElement> | undefined'.
  Type 'MutableRefObject<unknown>' is not assignable to type
  'LegacyRef<HTMLInputElement> | undefined'.
    Type 'MutableRefObject<unknown>' is not assignable to type
    'RefObject<HTMLInputElement>'.
      Types of property 'current' are incompatible.
        Type 'unknown' is not assignable to type 'HTMLInputElement | null'.
```

This error is a long way of saying that the `forwardRef` function told TypeScript that the `ref` belongs to an unknown element, and an input element is not unknown. To fix this problem, we need to tell TypeScript that the `ref` belongs to an input element and only to an input element. When we do, TypeScript allows us to assign that reference to the input element. We can take either of two approaches:

- Type the reference directly.
- Provide generic type arguments to the `forwardRef` function.

The simple solution is to type the `ref` argument inside the function. The type to use is `Ref<HTMLInputElement>`, where `Ref` is an interface from the React package:

```
import type { ComponentPropsWithoutRef, Ref } from "react";
import { forwardRef } from "react";
...
export const Input = forwardRef(function Input(
  { label, ...rest }: InputProps,
  ref: Ref<HTMLInputElement>
) {
```

That approach is simple, and it works. The other solution adds type arguments to `forwardRef` and takes two type arguments: the element type and the property type. We can provide those two arguments as type arguments and then remove them from the function definition:

```
export const Input = forwardRef<HTMLInputElement, InputProps>(
  function Input({ label, ...rest }, ref) {
```

The nice thing about this solution is that it doesn't require the extra `Ref` import. The not-so-nice thing is that the type arguments are in reverse order. First, we specify the element type, which is used in the type for the second argument of the component definition function. Second, we pass in the type for properties, which is the first argument. That process is a bit weird and hard to remember, so you might make mistakes (though TypeScript would scream at you if you reversed the order of the types by accident).

Pick whichever solution you prefer as long as you use it consistently. I prefer typing the arguments (the first solution), as I generally avoid providing type arguments whenever possible because it feels a bit forced. There's no substantial evidence to justify that choice—merely personal preference. In chapter 6, I'll address one extra caveat with regard to `forwardRef`.

Summary

- TypeScript offers a more predictable and maintainable approach to coding in React compared with coding in plain JavaScript.
- Different file extensions, such as `*.ts` and `*.tsx`, distinguish between regular TypeScript and React components with TypeScript.
- Static typing is a foundational feature of TypeScript, helping you catch type mismatches and enhancing code reliability.
- TypeScript allows you to create custom types, specify allowed values, and define optional properties.
- When designing React components with TypeScript, you can use both types and interfaces to define properties and their expected data types.
- Optional properties in TypeScript provide flexibility to data structures while ensuring consistent functionality.
- Generics in TypeScript allow for dynamic typing, making them crucial for advanced React applications.
- Using TypeScript with React, you can specify types for `children` properties by using the `ReactNode` type from React or the `PropsWithChildren` interface. This approach streamlines the process and covers all the valid child node types, including strings, numbers, Booleans, and JSX elements. `PropsWithChildren` not only types the `children` property but also wraps other potential props, making it a versatile choice.
- When extending interfaces in TypeScript, you can build on properties of an existing interface, ensuring that code isn't duplicated unnecessarily and remains easy to maintain.
- TypeScript enables you to gather props of built-in and custom components by using the `ComponentProps` and `ComponentPropsWithoutRef` utility types.
- Use TypeScript's discriminated unions for components with multiple configurations based on property values.
- TypeScript provides conditional type checking to ensure valid combinations of component properties.
- In TypeScript, using `forwardRef` in React requires correct typing of references, as the default type is considered to be unknown, necessitating explicit specification of the `ref` type for inner elements.

Mastering TypeScript with React

In this chapter, we delve deeper into the synergy between TypeScript, React components, and the broader application landscape. Imagine your React components as the tenants in a larger property; the application as a whole acts as the landlord. TypeScript takes center stage as the binding contract between these two entities, ensuring clarity, security, and smooth interactions. This chapter marks a crucial step in your journey to mastering the art of writing reliable, scalable, and maintainable React applications by enhancing the tenant–landlord relationship with TypeScript as the pivotal contract.

TypeScript brings clarity to the responsibilities and obligations of each party, making the entire development process more efficient and reliable. As you progress through this chapter, you'll discover how TypeScript reinforces this contract, making your React applications more robust and resilient. The chapter covers the following topics to round off your TypeScript edification (for now):

- Exploring the intricacies of typing React hooks to ensure that your components interact seamlessly with the world beyond
- Uncovering the power of well-typed React hooks as exceptional building blocks for shared functionality in your applications
- Discovering the practical application of generics in building a versatile and reusable component for data pagination
- Understanding the potential challenges and complexities of TypeScript integration and how to mitigate them

By the end of this chapter, you'll have not only a solid grasp of using TypeScript with React but also the knowledge to apply these concepts in various professional web development projects. Let's explore how TypeScript further elevates your React skills, making you a master of this powerful combination, including the exceptional potential of well-typed hooks as building blocks for shared functionality within your applications.

> **NOTE**   The source code for the examples in this chapter is available at https:// reactlikea.pro/ch06.

6.1   Using React hooks in TypeScript

Hooks play a central role in modern React development, which still holds true when TypeScript is introduced. Nevertheless, certain considerations apply to working with hooks in a typed environment; keeping type definitions clear is vital, and at times, some guidance is needed for the TypeScript interpreter.

Of the various hooks, two of the most fundamental—`useState` and `useRef`—can be surprisingly complex to type correctly. This conundrum is an interesting one because these hooks are among the most commonly used.

This section begins by addressing these two hooks, providing insights into typing them effectively. Then we'll explore React context, which is not overly complex but require some attention. Finally, we'll discuss effects, reducers, and memoization hooks. This list skips a few of the React hooks, but they aren't relevant to this discussion because they're extremely simple typewise or too advanced functionally to cover in this book.

6.1.1   Typing useState

The `useState` hook needs one piece of information for typing: the type of the state stored by using the hook. Sometimes, this information is trivial; at other times, the type of the data stored varies over time, and we need to inform the hook about all the potential types on initialization so we can use it in a typesafe manner.

INFERRING TYPE FROM INITIALIZER

Suppose that you're building an appointment-booking website. When an appointment arrives, the recipient can reject or accept the appointment and provide a message.

This task calls for a small component with two states. One state, `isAccepted`, is a Boolean that holds whether the appointment was accepted. Let's set it to `true` by default, as we assume that most recipients will accept appointments as booked. The second state, `message`, is a string with an optional reason or additional details. Let's set it to an empty string by default, indicating that no additional details are present. In pure JavaScript, here's how we would create these two state values in React:

```
const [isAccepted, setIsAccepted] = useState(true);
const [message, setMessage] = useState("");
```

In TypeScript, we'll do the same thing. This code works as well and as desired in TypeScript—nothing of note to discuss.

Imagine a slightly different scenario, however. This time, we won't assume anything about the response of the recipient, so we'll default the `isAccepted` value to `null`, indicating that no selection has been made yet. In plain JavaScript, we'd initialize the value this way:

```
const [isAccepted, setIsAccepted] = useState(null);
```

But if we do the same in TypeScript, we'll run into problems later. If we update the value by calling `setIsAccepted(true)`, we get this TypeScript error:

```
Argument of type 'true' is not assignable to parameter of type
'SetStateAction<null>'.
```

The error message says that we invoked the setter function (which is typed internally in React with the interface `SetStateAction`) with a value that did not match the expected one. `null` was expected, and we passed in a Boolean. We created a stateful variable that can hold only the value `null`.

TypeScript infers the value of the state contents from the initial value, and when we provided `boolean` as the initial value, the type was inferred as Boolean. But now that we're providing `null`, the type is inferred to be `null`, and only a single value has that type: `null` itself.

That result is no good, of course. We intended the type of the state contents to be `null` or `boolean`. We inform TypeScript of that by providing a type argument to `useState`:

```
const [isAccepted, setIsAccepted] = useState<null | boolean>(null);
```

Now our booking component works. The radio buttons for selecting whether the appointment is accepted or rejected are initially unselected but can update as the user interacts with the component. You can see the full code for this component in the following listing and the output in figure 6.1.

```
import { useState } from "react";
interface AppointmentResponseProps {
  onSubmit:
    (data: { isAccepted: boolean; message: string }) => void;
}
export function AppointmentResponse({
  onSubmit,
}: AppointmentResponseProps) {
  const [isAccepted, setIsAccepted] =
    useState<null | boolean>(null);
  const [message, setMessage] = useState("");
  const canSubmit = typeof isAccepted === "boolean";
  return (
    <div>
      <fieldset
        style={{
          display: "flex",
          flexDirection: "column",
          gap: "1em",
          width: "300px",
        }}
      >
        <legend>Appointment Response</legend>
        <div>
          <label>
            <input
              type="radio"
              name="is_accepted"
              checked={isAccepted === true}
              onChange={
                () => setIsAccepted(true)
              }
            />{" "}
            Accept
          </label>
          <label>
            <input
              type="radio"
              name="is_accepted"
              checked={isAccepted === false}
              onChange={
                () => setIsAccepted(false)
              }
            />{" "}
            Decline
          </label>
        </div>
        <label>
          Optional message:
          <input
            type="text"
            value={message}
            onChange={
              ({ target: { value } }) =>
                setMessage(value)
```

Creates the isAccepting state value using a type argument to allow both null and booleans to be passed in

Creates the message state value without a type argument because we'll pass in only strings anyway

Updates the state values as normal

```
          }
        />
      </label>
      <button
        disabled={!canSubmit}
        onClick={() => canSubmit && onSubmit({ isAccepted, message })}
      >
        Submit
      </button>
    </fieldset>
  </div>
  );
}
```

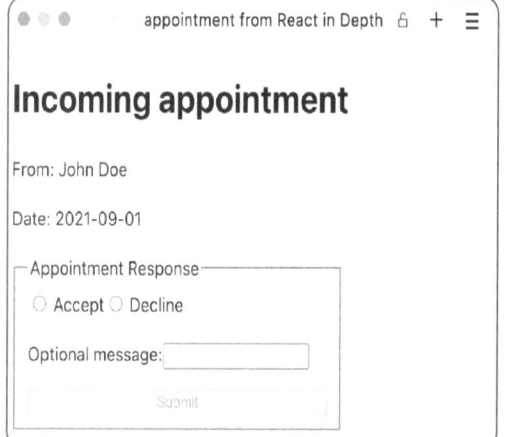 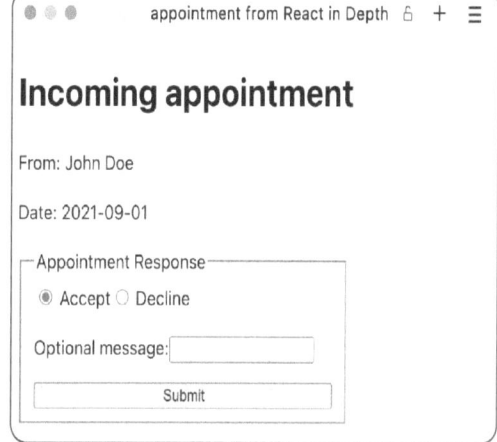

Figure 6.1 This appointment-response component is initially undecided (left) but can be updated as accepted or rejected (right). This component is powered by the state value, for which `null`, `true`, and `false` are the allowed values.

Example: appointment

This example is in the `appointment` folder. You can use that example by running this command in the source folder:

```
$ npm run dev -w ch06/appointment
```

Alternatively, you can go to this website to browse the code, see the example in action in your browser, or download the source code as a zip file: https://reactlikea .pro/ch06-appointment.

Note that instead of using a type argument, we could have cast the initializer to the desired type, in this instance to `null | boolean`:

```
const [isAccepted, setIsAccepted] = useState(null as null | boolean);
```

That code looks weird and feels wrong, so you probably won't see a lot of people using it, but it would work.

TYPING ARRAYS IN USESTATE

A related problem happens when you have arrays or objects in your state. Suppose that we're creating a small component, `TagForm`, to add tags to some object. This component might be used in a blog system to allow users to add tags to blog posts.

This component allows the user to type a tag and press Enter; then the tag is added to an internal list of tags and the input is cleared. All the current tags are displayed below the input.

For this task, we need two state values. One value is the value of the input, `newTag`, which is a string we'll initialize to the empty string. The other value is the list of tags, `tags`, an array of strings that we'll initialize to an empty array:

```
const [newTag, setNewTag] = useState("");
const [tags, setTags] = useState([]);
```

Again, we'll run into problems when we try to update this list of tags. The obvious update is

```
setTags((oldTags) => [...oldTags, newTag]);
```

but it results in this TypeScript error:

```
Argument of type '(oldTags: never[]) => string[]' is not assignable to
parameter of type 'SetStateAction<never[]>'.
  Type '(oldTags: never[]) => string[]' is not assignable to type
  '(prevState: never[]) => never[]'.
    Type 'string[]' is not assignable to type 'never[]'.
      Type 'string' is not assignable to type 'never'
```

As when we're creating a regular variable initialized to an empty array, we need to specify what the array can contain. Otherwise, TypeScript assumes that the array can contain nothing (which is an inane default, but it makes as much sense as any other assumption). The obvious solution is a type argument to `useState`:

```
const [tags, setTags] = useState<string[]>([]);
```

You can see the full source code for this application with a tag form in the `tag-form` example.

> ### Example: tag-form
> This example is in the `tag-form` folder. You can use that example by running this command in the source folder:
>
> ```
> $ npm run dev -w ch06/tag-form
> ```
>
> Alternatively, you can go to this website to browse the code, see the example in action in your browser, or download the source code as a zip file: https://reactlikea .pro/ch06-tag-form.

TYPING OBJECTS IN USESTATE

For objects, we do the same thing. Suppose that we want to create a map of which users are hidden from a given view. For this task, we have a state variable with a map from user id (which is a string) to a Boolean indicating whether the user is hidden.

Again, we cannot initialize the state to an empty object and assume that TypeScript can guess what we want to put there. We need to enter a type argument, such as one using the `Record` interface:

```
const [userVisibility, setUserVisibility] =
  useState<Record<string, boolean>>({});
```

This example is a common way of typing object maps, so you'll see it often.

6.1.2 *Typing useRef*

When using references in your components, you often run into the same problems as for states. TypeScript automatically infers the contents of the reference from the initializer, but if the initializer does not reflect the full picture of what you want to put there, you run into problems. In common cases, you deal with the problem by providing a type argument with the full picture:

```
const stringOrNullRef = useRef<string | null>(null);
const userArrayRef = useRef<User[]>([]);
```

This code works pretty much as expected if you do what you did for `useState` in section 6.1.1. But `useRef` has some surprises. We can type the first example slightly more simply:

```
const stringOrNullRef = useRef<string>(null);
```

`useRef` has a type overload for the specific case in which the type argument doesn't include `null` but the initializer is `null`. If that's the case, `useRef` expands the type argument to allow `null` implicitly.

But the catch is that the latter definition is a nonmutable reference. Nonmutable references can be passed on to elements, so something like the following would work:

```
const inputRef = useRef<HTMLInputElement>(null);
...
return <input ref={inputRef} />;
```

This example is a common use case of a special overload of `useRef`. We can leave | `null` out of the type argument and initialize the `ref` with `null`, and everything works as expected. But if we're creating references for mutable state and want to update that state directly, perhaps in an effect or a callback, this approach doesn't work.

Suppose that we want to create a component that remembers the position of the cursor while it's inside the component in a reference and clears that reference when the mouse leaves. We could implement that component as follows:

```
function MouseTracker() {
  const position = useRef<{ x: number; y: number } | null>(null);
  const onMouseLeave = () => {
```

```
    position.current = null;
  };
  const onMouseMove = (evt: MouseEvent) => {
    position.current = { x: evt.clientX, y: evt.clientY };
  };
  return (
    <div onMouseLeave={onMouseLeave} onMouseMove={onMouseMove}>
      ...
```

Notice that we initialize the reference with an explicit | `null` in the type argument. If we left that bit out, the example would not work—not because `null` wasn't allowed but because the reference would be immutable. No direct updates would be allowed, and we'd get this error:

```
Cannot assign to 'current' because it is a read-only property.
```

It's best to be explicit about the possible values of a mutable reference in the type argument to prevent this weird behavior.

> **NOTE**   In React 19, all references are mutable, so this error will no longer happen. You could safely skip | `null` in the preceding snippet, and the code would run without errors or warnings.

6.1.3   *Typing contexts and useContext*

Simple contexts are simple to type. Complex contexts are complex to type. If you use the basic context from React itself (not a selector-based one, as in chapter 2), you'll probably use the context only for fairly simple values.

   If we have a context that stores whether we're in dark mode on the website, the context value is a Boolean. For such a simple example, there's no difference between using TypeScript and plain JavaScript, as the types are easily inferred:

```
import { createContext, useContext } from 'react';
const DarkModeContext = createContext(false);    ⟵──┐  Dark mode is disabled
...                                                  │  by default.
function App() {
  const [isDarkMode, setDarkMode] = useState(false);
  ...
  return (
    <DarkModeContext.Provider value={isDarkMode}>
      ...
}
...
function SomeComponent() {
  const isDarkMode = useContext(DarkModeContext);
  ...
}
```

Nothing here should be too surprising. This example is how contexts work in JavaScript, and it works exactly the same way in a typesafe world. If we hover over the `DarkModeContext` variable in a TypeScript-capable editor, we can inspect the value and see that it is typed as `React.Context<boolean>`. The type of the context is inferred by the default value. TypeScript helps us provide the proper value. If we try to pass something non-Boolean to the provider, we'll get the usual TypeScript error about a type mismatch.

If we have a more complex context, such as an object with multiple values that we initialize to `null` but set it to a different value in the provider, we can provide a type argument to `createContext` about the expected type:

```
import { createContext, useContext } from 'react';
interface DarkMode {                    ◁──┐  Defines the interface for
  mode: 'light' | 'dark';                   │  the context contents
  toggle: () => void;
}
const DarkModeContext =                          Specifies the context type
  createContext<DarkMode | null>(null);  ◁──┘   using a type argument
function useDarkMode() {                 ◁────────────────────────────────┐
  const context = useContext(DarkModeContext);                            │
  if (!context) {                                                         │
    throw new Error(                                                      │
      "useDarkMode must be wrapped in DarkModeContext.Provider"           │
    );                                                                    │
  }                                  Defines a custom hook that returns the correctly typed
  return context;                    context. If the context value is null, the hook will throw;
}                                    thus, it will never return null. The context value would only
...                                  be null if we tried to access it outside the provider.
function App() {
  const [mode, setMode] = useState<"light" | "dark">("light");
  const toggle = () =>
    setMode((v) => (v === "light" ? "dark" : "light"));
  const contextValue = { mode, toggle };
  return (
    <DarkModeContext.Provider value={value}>  ◁──┐  Provides a value for the
      ...                                          │  context that matches
}                                                  │  the interface for it
...
function Button() {
  const { mode } = useDarkMode();  ◁──┐  Uses the context through
  ...                                  │  the custom hook
}
```

Here, we're provide a type argument to `createContext` to specify the range of possible values we can pass in, making TypeScript aware that the value provided in the main app file has the expected format. You can see this typesafe variant of the dark mode application in the `dark-mode` example.

Example: dark-mode

This example is in the `dark-mode` folder. You can use that example by running this command in the source folder:

```
$ npm run dev -w ch06/dark-mode
```

> **(continued)**
>
> Alternatively, you can go to this website to browse the code, see the example in action in your browser, or download the source code as a zip file: https://reactlikea .pro/ch06-dark-mode.

In both examples, we never add type hints to `useContext`. This hook simply returns a value of the same type, as is contained in the context. So this hook is super simple to use in TypeScript land.

6.1.4   *Typing effects*

Effects are trivial to type, as an effect is a function that takes no arguments and returns a function or nothing. None of the effect hooks takes any type arguments because none is ever needed:

```
useEffect(() => {
  // Effect goes here - no types needed anywhere!
}, []);
```

You can use `useEffect` and `useLayoutEffect` the same way in TypeScript and Java-Script. The only type-related thing to be mindful of is the fact that the effect function is allowed to return only `undefined` or a function (the cleanup function). If you return any other value, TypeScript will tell you that you made an error.

Suppose that we have a timer component with an effect that runs an interval if the timer is running. You might write this code in regular JavaScript:

```
useEffect(() => {
  if (!isRunning) {
    return false;
  }
  const interval = setInterval(
    () => { /* do something */ },
    1000,
  );
  return () => clearInterval(interval);
}, []);
```

Using `return false;` this way out of habit, not because it does anything, is not unheard of, and it's fine in JavaScript. But in TypeScript, you'll receive this slightly cryptic error message:

```
Argument of type '() => false | (() => void)' is not assignable to
parameter of type 'EffectCallback'.
  Type 'false | (() => void)' is not assignable to type 'void |
  Destructor'.
    Type 'boolean' is not assignable to type 'void | Destructor'.
```

TypeScript complains that your function returns something other than `void` or a `Destructor`, which is an effect cleanup function. To fix the problem, simply change the returns to `return;` like so:

```
useEffect(() => {
  if (!isRunning) {
    return;
  }
  const interval = setInterval(
    () => { /* do something */ },
    1000,
  );
  return () => clearInterval(interval);
}, []);
```

This mistake isn't a common one, but you might come across the preceding weird error message. If so, the fix is to make sure to return only valid values (nothing or a cleanup function) from your effect.

6.1.5   *Typing reducers*

A well-behaved reducer is easy to type, as it's a clean construction. The `useReducer` hook type follows the reducer in a straightforward manner. A small trick is required for generic reducers, however, because `useReducer` somehow forgets the generic argument.

> **NOTE**   In React 19, this situation has been fixed! No tricks are required, and you don't need type hints for `useReducer` even when generics are involved.

Suppose that we're setting out to build a revolutionary music-streaming application, bringing millions of songs to users worldwide. As part of our app's features, we want to empower users to create their own music playlists, curating their favorite tracks into personalized lists. Crafting a seamless experience is paramount. Users should be able to rearrange the order of songs in their playlists easily, placing their most-loved tracks at the top or moving others to the bottom as they see fit.

To accomplish this task, we need a way to manage the state of these playlists in our application's frontend. Instead of reinventing the wheel with every component or scenario, creating a custom hook dedicated to managing reorderable lists would be incredibly beneficial. This hook would encapsulate the logic needed to move songs up, down, or to specific positions within the playlist, ensuring a consistent and efficient user experience across the app. By building such a hook, which we'll call `useReorderable`, we can take our application one step closer to delivering an unmatched music-curation experience to our users.

We could create this hook specifically to reorder song items in a playlist array, but why not make it generic so that it can reorder any type of element in a list of such elements? Let's do just that. First, we define the state of the reducer, which is the list of elements:

```
type State<T> = T[];
```

Next, we need to define the actions as a discriminated union:

```
type Action =
  | { type: "moveUp"; index: number }
  | { type: "moveDown"; index: number }
  | { type: "moveToTop"; index: number }
  | { type: "moveToBottom"; index: number }
```

As you can see, the actions don't take a generic argument because the actions don't directly include the elements of the array—only manipulations done on those elements. Then, we need the main reducer function, which generally takes this form:

```
                    The reorder function is a reducer
                     with a generic type argument,
                       which can be any type.
                                                    A reducer function always takes two
                                                    arguments. The first argument is the current
function reorder<T>(                    ◁──┘        state of the data we're working on . . .
  state: State<T>,                         ◁──┘
  action: Action                       ◁──┐       . . . and the second argument is an
): State<T> {                         ◁──┘        action to apply to the current state.
  switch (action.type) {
    case "moveUp":                    The reducer function returns the new state of the data,
      ...                             which may or may not be the same state as before.
      // Return new array with the same elements in correct order
    ...
  }
}
```

At the end, we put the whole thing together in a custom hook, accepting the initial array and passing that and the reducer function into a `useReducer` call:

```
export function useReorderable<T>(initial: State<T>) {
  const [state, dispatch] = useReducer(reorder, initial);
  ...
}
```

Note that we don't add type hints to the `useReducer` function itself. We made the types perfectly clear when we created the reducer function, and as long as the type of the initial state matches the type of state the reducer works on, `useReducer` should be happy. Well, it is, but it isn't. If we hover over the state value in our editor, TypeScript reports the type as

```
const state: State<unknown>;
```

But that's wrong! The type is supposed to be `State<T>`, not `State<unknown>`. This result is where the trick comes in. We need to add a type hint to `useReducer` to inform it that the function is a reducer with a generic type argument.

> **NOTE** In React 19, this situation has been improved. The state is correctly inferred as `State<T>` when you call `useReducer` without type arguments, so these shenanigans aren't required anymore.

React has a built-in interface, `Reducer`, that takes two type arguments: the state and the action interface, both of which are readily available. So instead of making the previous simple attempt to create our custom hook, we have to make this slightly more complicated version:

```
import { type Reducer, useReducer} from 'react';
...
export function useReorderable<T>(initial: State<T>) {
  const [state, dispatch] = useReducer<
    Reducer<State<T>, Action>
  >(reorder, initial);
```

When we put everything together, our custom hook, `useReorderable`, looks like the following listing.

Listing 6.2 The `useReorderable` hook

```
import { useReducer } from "react";
type State<T> = T[];
type Action =
  | { type: "moveUp"; index: number }
  | { type: "moveDown"; index: number }
  | { type: "moveToTop"; index: number }
  | { type: "moveToBottom"; index: number }
  | { type: "moveToPosition"; index: number; targetIndex: number };
function reorder<T>(state: State<T>, action: Action): State<T> {
  const newState: T[] = [...state];
  switch (action.type) {
    case "moveUp": {
      if (action.index <= 0 || action.index >= newState.length) {
        return state;
      }
      // Swap previous element with index
      [newState[action.index - 1], newState[action.index]] = [
        newState[action.index],
        newState[action.index - 1],
      ];
      return newState;
    }
    case "moveDown": {
      if (action.index < 0 || action.index >= newState.length - 1) {
        return state;
      }
      // Swap next element with index
      [newState[action.index], newState[action.index + 1]] = [
        newState[action.index + 1],
        newState[action.index],
      ];
      return newState;
    }
    case "moveToTop": {
      if (action.index <= 0 || action.index >= newState.length) {
```

```
        return state;
      }
      // Move index to top
      const itemToTop = newState.splice(action.index, 1)[0];
      newState.unshift(itemToTop);
      return newState;
    }
    case "moveToBottom": {
      if (action.index < 0 || action.index >= newState.length) {
        return state;
      }
      // Move index to bottom
      const itemToBottom = newState.splice(action.index, 1)[0];
      newState.push(itemToBottom);
      return newState;
    }
    default:
      return state;
  }
}
export function useReorderable<T>(initial: State<T>) {
  const [state, dispatch] = useReducer<
    Reducer<State<T>, Action>
  >(reorder, initial);
  return {
    list: state,
    moveUp: (index: number) =>
      dispatch({ type: "moveUp", index }),
    moveDown: (index: number) =>
      dispatch({ type: "moveDown", index }),
    moveToTop: (index: number) =>
      dispatch({ type: "moveToTop", index }),
    moveToBottom: (index: number) =>
      dispatch({ type: "moveToBottom", index }),
  };
}
```

> **We return a cleaner API than the raw dispatch function to make the hook easier to use.**

Now let's get back to our revolutionary music-streaming application. We need to put this new hook to use. In the following listing, we have a playlist component that allows a user to reorder the songs in a playlist. We've added some nice icons and a CSS file for styling but didn't include the latter here.

Listing 6.3   A playlist component with items to reorder

```
import {
  BiSolidUpArrowAlt as Up,
  BiSolidDownArrowAlt as Down,
  BiSolidArrowToTop as Top,
  BiSolidArrowToBottom as Bottom,
} from "react-icons/bi";
import { useReorderable } from "./useReorderable";
```

```tsx
import "./playlist.css";
interface Song {
  id: number;
  title: string;
  artist: string;
}
interface PlaylistProps {
  songs: Song[];
}
export function Playlist({ songs }: PlaylistProps) {
  const {
    list,
    moveUp,                          Uses the custom
    moveDown,                        useReorderable hook
    moveToBottom,                    exactly as defined
    moveToTop,
  } = useReorderable(songs);

  return (
    <ol>
      {list.map((song, index) => (
        <li key={song.id}>
          <span>{index + 1}</span>
          <p>
            <strong>{song.title}</strong> by <em>{song.artist}</em>
          </p>
          <button onClick={() => moveUp(index)}>
            <Up />
          </button>
          <button
            onClick={() => moveDown(index)}
          >
            <Down />
          </button>                      Defines reorder buttons
          <button                        for each song. The CSS file
            onClick={() => moveToTop(index)}    will make them look nice.
          >
            <Top />
          </button>
          <button
            onClick={() => moveToBottom(index)}
          >
            <Bottom />
          </button>
        </li>
      ))}
    </ol>
  );
}
```

In the main application, we pass in an array of actual songs. The result looks like figure 6.2.

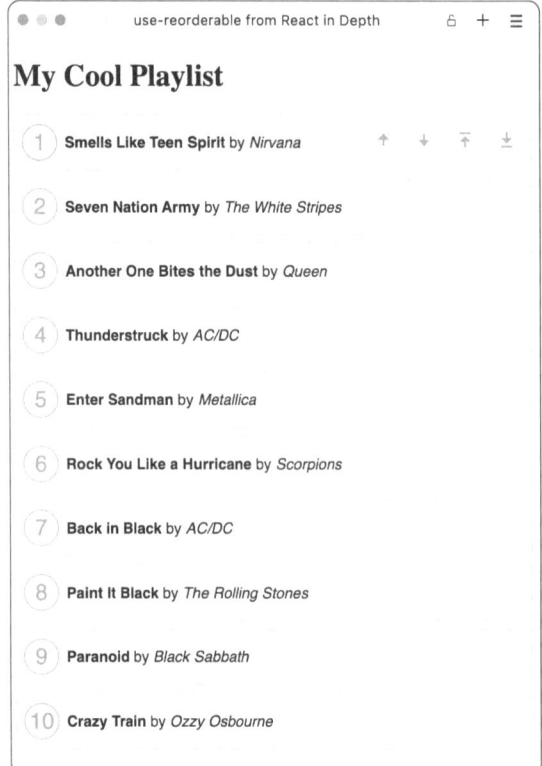

Figure 6.2   My playlist after I prioritized songs a bit. All this fairly complex functionality is covered by a simple custom hook using a generic reducer and the properly typed `useReducer` **hook. TypeScript is awesome.**

Example: use-reorderable

This example is in the `use-reorderable` folder. You can use that example by running this command in the source folder:

```
$ npm run dev -w ch06/use-reorderable
```

Alternatively, you can go to this website to browse the code, see the example in action in your browser, or download the source code as a zip file: https://reactlikea .pro/ch06-use-reorderable.

Now we can use this generic hook for reordering list items in other places. Do you want to have a list of your favorite album covers? Do you want to reorder the tracks currently queued up to play next? This example shows the power of custom hooks and TypeScript in action!

6.1.6   *Typing memoization hooks*

React has three memoization hooks, but only one of them—`useCallback`—is interesting from a TypeScript perspective. `useMemo` and `useDeferredValue` are identical in TypeScript compared with plain JavaScript.

TYPING USECALLBACK

Let's go back to the playlist, which is suboptimal from a performance perspective. Suppose that a user has 1,000 songs in a playlist and then swaps the positions of two of them. Because the rendering of every item happens directly in the playlist component, every item has to re-render. But for 998 of the songs, nothing changes, so we could have memoized them, with a great performance boost. To do this, we have to restructure things a bit by following these steps:

1 Create a new `PlaylistItem` component to handle a single song in a list.
2 Pass a single callback to the playlist item that takes both the index and the type of action to perform.
3 Rework the `useReorderable` hook so that it exports the dispatch function, as we're going to use it directly in the single callback.

Step 3 is the easiest one. We'll return the `useReducer` output directly (but still need the type hint from section 6.1.5):

```
export function useReorderable<T>(initial: State<T>) {
  return useReducer<Reducer<State<T>, Action>>(reorder, initial);
}
```

The following listing shows how we can implement the `PlaylistItem` component.

Listing 6.4 A single playlist-entry item

```
import {
  BiSolidUpArrowAlt as Up,
  BiSolidDownArrowAlt as Down,
  BiSolidArrowToTop as First,
  BiSolidArrowToBottom as Last,
} from "react-icons/bi";                          Notice that we've moved some
import { Song } from "./types";          ◁────── commonly used types to a shared file.
import { MouseEvent, memo } from "react";
interface PlaylistItemProps {                     The single callback function has
  song: Song;                                     a slightly complicated
  index: number;                                  signature, but it should make
  move: (index: number) =>                        sense to you at this point.
    (evt: MouseEvent<HTMLButtonElement>) => void;
}
export const PlaylistItem =
memo(function PlaylistItem({          ◁──── Defines the playlist item as
  song,                                     a memoized component
  index,
  move,
}: PlaylistItemProps) {
  const onClick = move(index);
  return (
    <li>
      <span>{index + 1}</span>
      <p>
        <strong>{song.title}</strong> by <em>{song.artist}</em>
      </p>
```

```
      <button name="up" onClick={onClick}>
        <Up />
      </button>
      <button name="down" onClick={onClick}>
        <Down />
      </button>
      <button name="first" onClick={onClick}>
        <First />
      </button>
      <button name="last" onClick={onClick}>
        <Last />
      </button>
    </li>
  );
});
```

> Uses the callback on each button identically. The action to perform will be deduced from the button name.

The only thing left to do is rewrite the main playlist component so that it uses the new `useReorderable` hook and then renders the list of items, passing in a callback for each item. First, let's do this without memoization.

Listing 6.5   A simplified playlist component

```
import { useReorderable } from "./useReorderable";
import "./playlist.css";
import { ActionType, Song } from "./types";
import { PlaylistItem } from "./PlaylistItem";
interface PlaylistProps {
  songs: Song[];
}
export function Playlist({ songs }: PlaylistProps) {
  const [list, dispatch] = useReorderable(songs);
  return (
    <ol>
      {list.map((song, index) => (
        <PlaylistItem
          key={song.id}
          song={song}
          index={index}
          move={(index) => (evt) => {
            const type =
              evt.currentTarget.name as ActionType;
            dispatch({ type, index });
          }}
        />
      ))}
    </ol>
  );
}
```

> Defines the move callback inline as it is passed to each playlist-entry item

When we define the callback inline, we don't need to add types to the arguments used in the functions because they can be inferred by the context in which the callback is used. TypeScript can infer the types from the type of the `move` property in the playlist item props interface.

But now we want to add memoization to the callback. Note that the callback is currently defined inside a loop, which we can't do with a hook, so we can't use `move={use Callback(...)}`. That attempt would violate the rules of hooks. So we have to define the function above the return statement, which also means that we have to add type information to the function arguments, as TypeScript no longer has the context of the `move` property near the definition. The following listing shows one solution.

Listing 6.6 The playlist with a memoized callback

```
import { useReorderable } from "./useReorderable";
import "./playlist.css";
import { ActionType, Song } from "./types";
import { PlaylistItem } from "./PlaylistItem";
import { MouseEvent, useCallback } from "react";
interface PlaylistProps {
  songs: Song[];
}
export function Playlist({ songs }: PlaylistProps) {
  const [list, dispatch] = useReorderable(songs);
  const handleMove = useCallback(
    (index: number) =>
      (evt: MouseEvent<HTMLButtonElement>) => {        Adds type information to
        const type = evt.currentTarget.name as ActionType;   the function arguments
        dispatch({ type, index });                       inline inside the
      },                                                 useCallback hook
    [dispatch]
  );
  return (
    <ol>
      {list.map((song, index) => (
        <PlaylistItem
          key={song.id}
          song={song}
          index={index}
          move={handleMove}
        />
      ))}
    </ol>
  );
}
```

Example: playlist

This example is in the `playlist` folder. You can use that example by running this command in the source folder:

```
$ npm run dev -w ch06/playlist
```

Alternatively, you can go to this website to browse the code, see the example in action]in your browser, or download the source code as a zip file: https://reactlikea .pro/ch06-playlist.

The result is a fully optimized playlist-reordering application. If you try to check re-rendering by using React Developer Tools for the latest version (linked in the "Example: playlist" sidebar), you'll see that if you swap two playlist entries, only those entries will re-render; the rest will be unchanged.

As always, there's more than one way to skin a cat. All of the following statements are functionally identical ways to add type information to the callback:

```
// Define the function arguments in the function definition
const handleMove = useCallback(
  (index: number) => (evt: MouseEvent<HTMLButtonElement>) => {
    const type = evt.currentTarget.name as ActionType;
    dispatch({ type, index });
  },
  [dispatch]
);
// Define the function type generally as a type argument to useCallback
const handleMove = useCallback<
  (index: number) => (evt: MouseEvent<HTMLButtonElement>) => void
>(
  (index) => (evt) => {
    const type = evt.currentTarget.name as ActionType;
    dispatch({ type, index });
  },
  [dispatch]
);
// Defines the function type on the target variable
const handleMove: (
  index: number
) => (evt: MouseEvent<HTMLButtonElement>) => void = useCallback(
  (index) => (evt) => {
    const type = evt.currentTarget.name as ActionType;
    dispatch({ type, index });
  },
  [dispatch]
);
```

More abstractly, you can do the same thing in these three ways:

```
// Define the function arguments in the function definition
const callback = useCallback((a: Type) => {}, []);
// Define the function type generally as a type argument to useCallback
const callback = useCallback<(a: Type) => void>((a) => {}, []);
// Define the function type on the target variable
const callback:(a: Type) => void = useCallback((a) => {}, []);
```

I prefer the first method, but you might come across the other variants in the wild.

TYPING USEMEMO AND USEDEFERREDVALUE

useMemo and useDeferredValue are even easier to work with, as the value returned from each hook simply has the same type as the value returned by the callback passed to the hook. These callbacks never take arguments, which makes things even simpler. In short, you use these hooks the same way in TypeScript and regular JavaScript.

NOTE As mentioned in chapter 3, with the introduction of the new React Compiler, memoization is no longer required once React Compiler becomes stable and standard in all projects. However that might take some time and many projects will not use React Compiler for quite some time so this information is still important to know.

6.1.7 Typing the remaining hooks

All the other hooks in React are seldom used and are extremely simple or quite complicated typewise, so we'll skip them for now. In the rare case in which you do need them in a TypeScript project, look them up in the React documentation, and you should be able to make sense of them.

6.2 Generic pagination: An example

So far, we've seen a ton of examples of using generics to make functions more versatile. Generics come up in hooks all the time. But components are functions, so can components be made generic too? Yes, they certainly can.

To create a useful React application by using generic components, we're going to create an application with a significant number of components, so it's not completely trivial. Grasping everything will require greater effort, but the result will be well worth the trouble.

We want to create a component that can display a list of items with pagination if there are many items. We want to display four items per page, and if there are more, we want little numbers below the component to allow the user to go to page 1 of the results, page 2 of the results, and so on (figure 6.3).

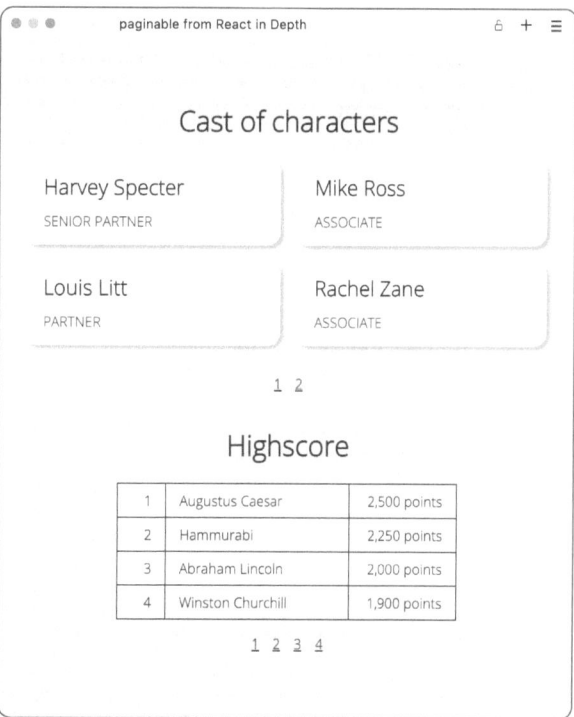

Figure 6.3 Pagination used for a list of employee cards and a high score. This application shows how to use generics to apply similar functionality to different types of objects, as long as they follow the proper interfaces.

We want to create this component so that it works with any type of content, however. We want to make it generic. We will pass the component a list of items of something, and we will also supply a renderer for each something that needs to be displayed. That something is what we want our generic type to be. We can use this pagination component to display a list of employees, using the `EmployeeCard` component that we created in chapter 5 (section 5.2.3). We can also use the same component to display a `paginable` high-score list, as shown in figure 6.3. The following listing shows how.

Listing 6.7   A generic pagination component

```tsx
import { FC, useState } from "react";
import "./paginable.css";
const PERPAGE = 4;
interface PaginableProps<Type> {
  items: Type[];
  Renderer: FC<PaginableItemProps<Type>>;
  className?: string;
}
interface PaginableItemProps<Type> {
  item: Type;
  index: number;
}
export function Paginable<Type>({
  items,
  Renderer,
  className,
}: PaginableProps<Type>) {
  const [currentPage, setCurrentPage] = useState(0);
  const startOffset = currentPage * PERPAGE;
  const endOffset = (currentPage + 1) * PERPAGE;
  const subset = items.slice(startOffset, endOffset);
  const numPages = Math.ceil(items.length / PERPAGE);
  const pages = Array.from(Array(numPages)).map((k, v) => v);
  return (
    <section className={className}>
      {subset.map((item, index) => (
        <Renderer
          key={index}
          item={item}
          index={index + startOffset}
        />
      ))}
      {numPages > 1 && (
        <ol className="pagination">
          {pages.map((page) => (
            <li className="pagination__item" key={page}>
              {page === currentPage ? (
                page + 1
              ) : (
                <button
                  className="pagination__link"
                  onClick={() => setCurrentPage(page)}
```

Now things really start to get complicated. First, the type of the Paginable component will be generic, as it will vary with the type of props received.

The first property of the paginable is a list of items of a given type.

The second property is a functional renderer component, which takes props that match the type of elements in the array in the first property.

These other props that the renderer component takes are themselves generic.

First, the renderer gets an item of the given type.

Second, the renderer receives an index, which is the position of the rendered item in the array.

We put this type magic together when we require the received props of the component to conform to the specified interface.

Finally, we can use the renderer component directly by invoking it with an item and an index because we specified that it has to accept those properties.

```
                >
                  {page + 1}
                </button>
              )}
            </li>
          ))}
        </ol>
      )}
    </section>
  );
}
```

We can use this pagination component for an employee list in an application like this:

```
import { EmployeeCard } from "./EmployeeCard";
import { Paginable } from "./Paginable";
import { Employee } from "./types";
const EMPLOYEES: Employee = [
  { name: "Harvey Specter", title: "Senior Partner" },
  ...,
];
function App() {
  return (
    <main>
      <h1>Cast of characters</h1>
      <Paginable
        className="employee-list"
        items={EMPLOYEES}
        Renderer={EmployeeCard}
      />
    </main>
  );
}
export default App;
```

Before we go see this application in action, let's create something else to paginate so we can see generics at play. Let's create a high-score list with entries, each with a position, name, and score. We create the entry as shown in the following listing.

Listing 6.8   A high-score entry list

```
import "./highscore.css";
import { Entry } from "./types";
interface EntryProps {
  item: Entry;
  index: number;
}
export function HighscoreEntry({ item, index }: EntryProps) {
  return (
    <div className="highscore-entry">
      <p className="highscore-entry__pos">
        {index + 1}
      </p>
```

A high-score entry consists of a name and some point value, which is a type we import from a central file.

For this component, we also need the index of the entry in the overall list, as that will be the position in the high-score list.

The index is incremented by 1, as the top spot in a high-score list is generally called #1, not #0.

```
      <p className="highscore-entry__name">
        {item.name}
      </p>
      <p className="highscore-entry__points">
        {item.points.toLocaleString("en-US")}
        points
      </p>
    </div>
  );
}
```

> The name is printed as is.

> The points are formatted with a bit of built-in JavaScript functionality to add thousands separators to the list.

The following listing shows two different paginable components.

Listing 6.9   The main application

```
import "./app.css";
import { EmployeeCard } from "./EmployeeCard";
import { HighscoreEntry } from "./HighscoreEntry";
import { Paginable } from "./Paginable";
import { Employee, Entry } from "./types";
const EMPLOYEES: Employee[] = [
  { name: "Harvey Specter", title: "Senior Partner" },
  { name: "Mike Ross", title: "Associate" },
  { name: "Louis Litt", title: "Partner" },
  { name: "Rachel Zane", title: "Associate" },
  { name: "Donna Paulsen", title: "Legal Secretary" },
  { name: "Jessica Pearson", title: "Managing Partner" },
  { name: "Katrina Bennett", title: "Associate" },
];
const ENTRIES: Entry[] = [
  { name: "Augustus Caesar", points: 2500 },
  { name: "Hammurabi", points: 2250 },
  { name: "Abraham Lincoln", points: 2000 },
  { name: "Winston Churchill", points: 1900 },
  { name: "Nelson Mandela", points: 1800 },
  { name: "Catherine the Great", points: 1700 },
  { name: "Ashoka", points: 1600 },
  { name: "Marcus Aurelius", points: 1500 },
  { name: "Lech Wał?sa", points: 1400 },
  { name: "Hatsheput", points: 1300 },
  { name: "Charles de Gaulle", points: 1200 },
  { name: "Eleanor of Aquitane", points: 1100 },
  { name: "Ivan the Terrible", points: 1000 },
];
function App() {
  return (
    <main>
      <h1>Cast of characters</h1>
      <Paginable
        className="employee-list"
        items={EMPLOYEES}
        Renderer={EmployeeCard}
      />
```

> We instantiate the Paginable component for the employee list first with all the correct props.

```
      <h1>Highscore</h1>
      <Paginable
        className="highscores"
        items={ENTRIES}
        Renderer={HighscoreEntry}
      />
    </main>
  );
}
export default App;
```

We do the same thing for the high score. Note that TypeScript would warn us directly inline if any entry in the high-score list was wrong or if the HighscoreEntry component did not accept the correct properties.

Putting everything together in the browser, we get what we set out to get in figure 6.4. We can even navigate the two lists separately, such as with the cast list on page 2 and the high score on page 3 (figure 6.4).

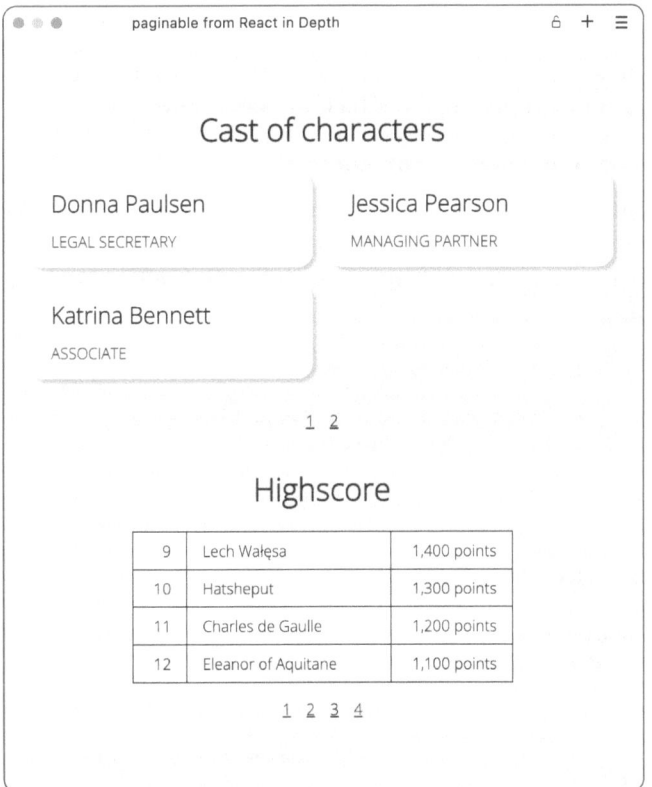

Figure 6.4 Here, we see pagination in action as we did in figure 6.3. This time, we've progressed the page differently in the two lists, demonstrating that pagination happens independently in each component.

I strongly urge you to check out this example on your own, as you'll fully appreciate how TypeScript makes it possible only when you start to play around with it. The errors you get when typing something wrong are mind-blowing, and the code-completion hints you get when you might not expect them are helpful.

Note that this code is complicated. It's okay if you don't fully understand it; a lot is going on here. This example is meant only to inspire you to seek more information. As I mentioned, I could have dedicated this whole book to TypeScript, and it would have been just as long and comprehensive.

Also, the rabbit hole goes a lot deeper. TypeScript has some crazy options that enable you to program your types with a programming syntax inside the type system to make dynamic, extensible types. Remember, TypeScript never runs in the browser in the final application; it runs only in your editor and in your compiler to make sure that it will run correctly. What you can do with TypeScript, and what TypeScript can do for you, is quite amazing.

Generic components, such as `Paginable`, have one small gotcha. Two built-in functions in the React core API don't play well with generic components, and you need to work a bit around the problem (or hope that it will be fixed in a future release, which is likely).

If you memoize or forward a reference to a generic component, your type argument for the component will be "forgotten." Unfortunately, we have to fix that ourselves to get back the generic functionality, which we want to do.

6.2.1 *Forwarding a reference to a generic component*

Suppose that we want to allow the main application to add a reference to the `paginable` list in the `Paginable` example. We want to allow the parent component to pass in a reference to a section element and then assign that reference to `<section>` inside the component:

```
import { forwardRef, Ref, FC, useState } from "react";
...
export const Paginable = forwardRef(function Paginable<Type>(
  { items, Renderer, className }: PaginableProps<Type>,
  ref: Ref<HTMLElement>,
) {
  ...
  return (
    <section ref={ref} className={className}>
```

This example should work for this component, right? No. Whether or not we pass in a reference, we get a TypeScript error in our main application when we pass a `Renderer` property to `Paginable`:

```
Type '({ item }: CardProps) => Element' is not assignable to type
'FC<PagenableItemProps<unknown>>'.
  Types of parameters '__0' and 'props' are incompatible.
    Type 'PagenableItemProps<unknown>' is not assignable to type
    'CardProps'.
      Types of property 'item' are incompatible.
        Type 'unknown' is not assignable to type 'Employee'.
```

Suddenly, the type argument is `unknown` when we expected it to be the type of item that we're rendering: `Employee`. But when we apply `forwardRef` to the component, the type argument is somehow "forgotten" and replaced by `unknown`. Now we can no longer achieve our goal of matching the items with the renderer.

The problem is that `forwardRef` does not return a component with the same type that you pass into it. We do not expect exactly the same type, but just because we want to pass references to the component doesn't mean that we want to change anything else.

Two solutions are available. The first is good for one-off (or maybe two-off) occasions, but if you have many generic components, the latter might be your go-to:

- Cast the component to the correct type after applying `forwardRef`.
- Augment the type of `forwardRef` in the schema for React globally in your application.

To cast the type, we need to think about how a component without `forwardRef` is different from one with `forwardRef`. The only difference is that the component with a reference takes all the same properties and returns the same value, but it also takes a `ref` property typed to the specific type of element. To type such a function, still with a generic type, we need the following complex expression:

```
function PaginableWithoutRef<Type>(         ◁──────────
  { items, Renderer, className }: PaginableProps<Type>,
  ref: Ref<HTMLElement>
) {
...
}
const Paginable =
  forwardRef(PaginableWithoutRef) as <Type>(
    p: PaginableProps<Type>
      & RefAttributes<HTMLElement>
) => ReturnType<typeof PaginableWithoutRef>;
```

Defines the original component in a separate statement

Creates the exported component by wrapping the original in forwardRef and then casting it to a similar component that also allows ref attributes

This code looks clunky, mostly because it's overly complex and comes out of nowhere. But despite the way the code looks, it works. If you have to type the code several times, it becomes a bit annoying, and you might forget it. Also, the code can be confusing to new developers, so you should add a comment to explain what's going on.

An alternative to adding this type cast in every generic component with a forwarded `ref` is to augment the schema for the React namespace. Yes, we can do that. We can redefine the types for external libraries, including those of React, because we "know better" than React. The React team made an error in its types, and we are allowed to fix it and are capable of fixing it.

To augment the schema, we create a TypeScript definition file (`*.d.ts`) somewhere in the source tree, such as `<root>/react-augmented.d.ts`. Note that we have to do this only once globally; then it should work for all components. In that file, we include the following:

```
import React from "react"
declare module "react" {
  function forwardRef<T, P = {}>(
    render: (props: P, ref: ForwardedRef<T>) => ReactElement | null
  ): (props: P & RefAttributes<T>) => ReactElement | null;
}
```

This code does the same thing as for the single instance, but abstractly, so it works for all instances.

> **NOTE**   As I've mentioned a few times, `forwardRef` is no longer required in React 19. Not having to jump through these hoops to type a generic component is another great benefit of this improvement in React 19.

6.2.2   *Memoizing a generic component*

Memoizing a generic component has the same problems and the same fixes. If we tried to memoize the `Paginable` example this way,

```
import { memo, FC, useState } from "react";
...
const Paginable = memo(function Paginable<Type>(
  { items, Renderer, className }: PaginableProps<Type>
) {
```

we'd run into the same error as with the `forwardRef` example. The fixes are the same: cast to the proper return type or augment React globally.

   The first option is even easier for memoized components, as they don't change their signature. A memoized component is identical to the original typewise, so we can cast to the type of the original:

```
function PaginableWithoutMemo<Type>(
   ...
const Paginable = memo(PaginableWithoutMemo)
  as typeof PaginableWithoutMemo;
```

This example looks better than the reference example, but it would still be annoying to duplicate. The augmentation solution looks like this:

```
import React from "react"
declare module "react" {
  function memo<T, R>(Component: (props: T) => R): (props: T) => R;
}
```

> **NOTE**   This type fix isn't included in React 19. This is probably due to the work on the new experimental React Compiler, which when fully ready removes the need for memoization altogether. Read more about React Compiler here: https://react.dev/learn/react-compiler.

You can merge this example with the `forwardRef` augmentation in the same file, if you're using both in your codebase:

```
import React from "react"
declare module "react" {
  function forwardRef<T, P = {}>(
    render: (props: P, ref: ForwardedRef<T>) => ReactElement | null
  ): (props: P & RefAttributes<T>) => ReactElement | null;
  function memo<T, R>(Component: (props: T) => R): (props: T) => R;
}
```

6.3 Drawbacks of using TypeScript

Although TypeScript is great and beloved by many developers, starting to use it is not consequence free. The drawbacks of TypeScript are complexity and learning curve, which are two sides of the same coin:

- New developers, even strong React developers, without the required level of TypeScript experience will have a longer time getting familiar with the codebase and might even require dedicated training.
- The project inevitably ends up with more lines of code. Those extra lines are there to ensure that the lines you already had have less errors, so they shouldn't be a problem.
- Finally, it takes more time to write code in TypeScript than in JavaScript because you write more code and have to think a bit more about how you write that code. But with the result being a more bug-free application, you should make that time up easily in less maintenance.

Overall, the advantages win out over time, but if you cannot bear the investment (in terms of training and extra time spent) up front, you may want to delay introducing TypeScript to your codebase until you can make such a commitment.

Some people might argue that the extra value TypeScript provides is irrelevant if you're a great developer. Daniel Heinemeier Hansson of Ruby on Rails fame made that argument in a controversial post about dropping TypeScript at https://mng.bz/y8ep. But in that post, Hansson missed teamwork. On a team, nobody (not even the best 10× Distinguished Engineer) knows the entire codebase, and TypeScript is currently the most efficient way to get hints about the things you don't know, so you're able to work with it quickly and confidently. To me, and to most of the rest of the JavaScript community, TypeScript is a godsend.

6.4 TypeScript resources

The important aspects of using TypeScript are understanding it fully and using its strengths to make your applications more resilient. The following books are great ways to learn more about TypeScript in general:

- *TypeScript Quickly*, by Yakov Fain and Anton Moiseev (https://www.manning.com/books/typescript-quickly)
- *TypeScript in 50 Lessons*, by Stefan Baumgartner of *Smashing Magazine* (https://typescript-book.com).

If you want to learn more about React and TypeScript in combination, check out these resources:

- React and TypeScript, a five-hour online course by Steve Kinney at Frontend Masters (https://mng.bz/MZqQ)
- React & Redux in TypeScript Complete Guide, an online reference guide by various contributors hosted at GitHub (https://mng.bz/aEGj)

Summary

- React hooks, particularly `useState` and `useRef`, require nuanced typing in TypeScript for optimal utility.
- Typing the `useState` hook in TypeScript properly ensures correct state inference and prevents type errors during state updates.
- When typing `useRef` in TypeScript, being explicit with types prevents problems with type inference and mutability. Although shorthand methods are available, they might result in immutable references, which can't be updated directly.
- Contexts in TypeScript can be typed based on their expected values, ensuring type safety. Simple contexts have straightforward typing, and complex contexts may require interfaces and type arguments. `useContext` itself remains straightforward to use with inferred types from the provided context.
- Effects in TypeScript are easy to use, similar to JavaScript. The main typing consideration is ensuring that effects return only `undefined` or a cleanup function; any other return value will cause a TypeScript error.
- Using TypeScript with React's `useReducer` allows for the creation of typesafe, versatile hooks for managing complex state transitions in applications.
- Using generic reducers in React's `useReducer` with TypeScript can be challenging and requires extra type arguments, but it provides a robust solution for managing abstract state structures.
- In TypeScript, the `useCallback` hook can be typed in various ways: directly defining the function arguments, providing a type argument to `useCallback`, or setting the type on the target variable.
- Both `useMemo` and `useDeferredValue` in TypeScript function similarly to their JavaScript counterparts, with the return type being consistent with the callback's output.
- Just as TypeScript can be used to create generic functions, React components (which are essentially functions) can also be made generic. Generic components allow us to create versatile components that can adapt to different types of content as long as they adhere to the expected interfaces.
- Although TypeScript enhances the development experience, some challenges occur when combining TypeScript's generic components with certain React functionalities, such as `forwardRef` and `memo`. When you use these functions with generic components, TypeScript may "forget" the type, causing type mismatches. Solutions involve casting the component to the correct type post-function application or augmenting React's type definitions to handle generics correctly.
- TypeScript can pose a learning curve for new developers, demanding an initial time investment and potentially specialized training, but TypeScript's hints and guidance enhance code collaboration, outweighing its complexity with valuable advantages.

CSS in JavaScript 7

This chapter covers

- Making your applications look great
- Evaluating the many ways to add styling
- Exploring three ways to style a component

Creating functional apps is a good start, but ensuring that they look gorgeous as well is going to make users love using your apps. Making HTML websites look good is the job of CSS, which is notoriously different from HTML and JavaScript, which we are using in the world of React.

We will be examining three different ways of styling React applications and evaluating their strengths and weaknesses:

- CSS files and class names
- CSS Modules
- Styled-components

I will cover them in this order, which is their order of complexity and learning curve. The first option requires almost no new knowledge, so you can start right away even if you know only React and CSS. I've excluded the most complex options because you would have to read a lot of documentation to start; they use methods and concepts far from regular CSS to achieve a similar result.

But why are there so many ways of styling React and web applications in general? Why don't all of us developers agree on the best way and stick with that? Well, the "best way" to style a React application is an unsolved problem. A styling solution has many requirements, depending on what you're building, who's building it, who your target audience is, and (of course) personal preference and professional sentiments.

In this chapter, I aim to demonstrate, compare, and evaluate three approaches so you will be equipped to select the best one for your project. After some preliminary discussion of CSS in general, I'll show you how to implement a simple React application with each of the three methods so you can learn not just how to implement each method but also when and why to use one over another.

NOTE   The source code for the examples in this chapter is available at https://reactlikea.pro/ch07.

7.1   *Styling with concerns*

CSS has existed in its current form since the mid-1990s, so its use and incorporation in web development are well established at this point. In older web development, HTML, CSS, and JavaScript were often implemented independently, and JavaScript was more an add-on than a key component.

Modern web development, however, relies heavily on JavaScript, and with React and many other frameworks, the output HTML is defined directly inside the JavaScript application. In React, we write HTML inside JavaScript via JSX. Moving HTML into the JavaScript application allows us to closely link the script and the underlying document that it works on, making it much easier to keep them in sync and update one when the other is rewritten.

But CSS and HTML have the same problem of interconnectedness. If you update your HTML without the new structure's being reflected in CSS, your application might at best look wrong or at worst be unusable. So when we can move our HTML into our JavaScript components, why not also move the CSS in there? Compare the three scenarios in figure 7.1. The goal of CSS-in-JS technologies is to allow your web developers to define all, or almost all, of the parts of a component in a single place.

CSS-in-JS is a controversial topic. Many developers have a strong opinion about it, and some developers swear by certain paradigms and hate others. I will try my best to give you an unbiased overview of the various concepts and technologies, though of course I have my own preferences as well. (See whether you can guess which way I lean.)

If you and your team love using CSS, you're good to go. Keep using it by all means. But if you experience friction, bugs, and/or headaches, which cause velocity to go down or deadlines to slip, you may want to look for an alternative, depending on your goals and preferences.

People have many concerns about their styling solutions—and by *many*, I mean *many*! Not all the concerns apply to all projects, all teams, or all developers, and different people may have different desired outcomes for the same concern.

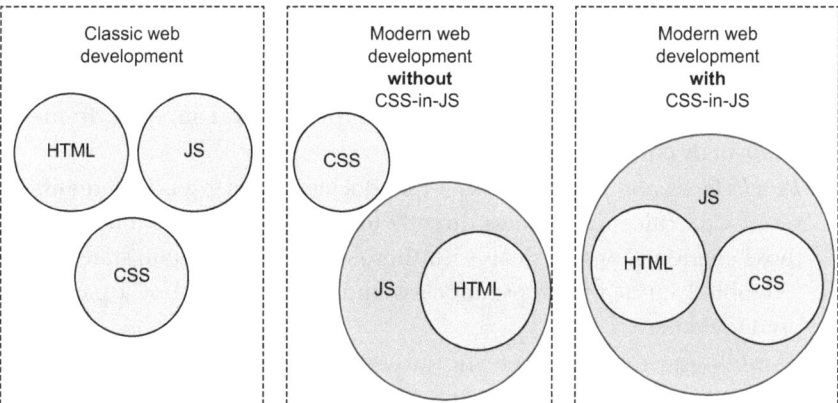

Figure 7.1 In classic web development, the three technologies are developed more or less independently. But in modern web development, either HTML alone or HTML and CSS gets bundled with the JavaScript, as the JavaScript is the main protagonist of our web application narratives.

In this chapter, I've grouped the different concerns into three main categories: CSS language features, developer experience, and web application development. First, I'll talk a bit about each category.

7.1.1 CSS language features

This category includes CSS language features that affect how easy it is to implement a given design. All these concerns are also valid in regular CSS as written in CSS files, but often with complications:

- *Specificity*—Specificity means making sure that the right rules apply to the right elements with the correct priority. The specificity of a rule is its priority. If two rules apply to an element, the least specific rule applies first and the more specific rule applies second. If you have a button that is normally green, but you want it to be purple in a single place, you must make sure that the rule for the button's being purple in that single place is more specific that the regular green rule; otherwise, the button will still be green. The green color would override the purple one, as the more specific rule applies last.
- *Collision*—Collisions happen when applications grow large and developers accidentally give things the same names. Because CSS is not hierarchical, all the rules live in the same global namespace. If you try to create two different rules for a `.wrapper` class, both rules will apply to both elements even though you wanted one rule to apply to one element and the other rule to apply to another element. You can prevent collisions through sensible naming, but if you have hundreds of components, checking whether you've already used a `.group` class on some other component can be a daunting task.

- *Composition/nesting*—This principle specifies the rules for only one element as it relates to another element. The styling of the body of an element in an accordion, for example, depends on whether that entire accordion element is expanded. Specifying nested rules is super elegant in some frameworks and annoyingly complex in others.

- *Pseudoclasses and psuedoelements*—Pseudoclasses and pseudoelements are a subset of CSS rules that relates directly to specific elements, but only to parts of those elements, or that deals with those elements in certain states. You can style a disabled input with a pseudoclass and the first word of a paragraph with a pseudoelement.

- *At-rules*—At-rules are a specific subset of CSS rules that start with the @ sign (hence, the name). The reason why they're special in this context is that they cannot be applied inline and have to live in a CSS block somewhere in the document. In more practical terms, these rules often aren't specific to one or two elements; they work on groups of (possibly unrelated) elements, such as media queries, or describe features related to individual properties of other rules, such as keyframe rules for animations.

- *Conditional rules*—These rules apply to an element under some circumstances. You might have a push button that has one styling when it's not activated and another styling when it's activated.

- *Dynamic rules*—These rules are declarations applied to an element with a value derived from JavaScript. You might have a range slider in your application that controls the opacity of an element, so you need to be able to apply any dynamic opacity to an element from JavaScript.

- *Vendor prefixes*—These experimental features have to be enabled with a prefix to work in various browsers. They used to be common in web development, but browsers rarely use them anymore. But some new CSS features still must be used through vendor prefixes, so it's nice to use a styling solution that knows exactly when and where to apply the prefixes automatically. Don't rely on that approach too heavily, though. Many of the specialized features that require vendor prefixes are pseudoelements (such as scrollbars), and as far as I'm aware, they're rarely automatically vendor prefixed by any existing solution.

7.1.2   *Developer experience*

The concerns that are related to developer experience (DX) are about making sure that development is smooth and efficient for all team members, both new and experienced, especially when teams grow large, with many people working on the same codebase. All of the following concerns are important for efficient collaboration:

- *Colocation*—This principle involves moving related bits of code close together. For React, specifically, it makes sure that everything related to a component is located as close to that component as possible. Optimally, styles and JSX are located in the same file close to each other or at least in files in the same folder.

At the extreme other end of the spectrum are styles located in some central CSS file far from the components that use the rules. Colocation is important for DX, as it makes it much easier for a developer to understand and maintain components that they haven't worked on before.

- *Familiarity*—Familiarity is about the learning curve. Imagine a new hire on your team who knows web development, CSS, HTML, and React. How quickly will they be able to contribute to your project, including maintaining and expanding the styling of your components?

- *Complexity*—Complexity is bad. Unnecessary complexity is extra bad. Web applications are complex, so CSS probably has to be complex too. But if your styling solution has too many moving parts, it might easily break down, be misconfigured, lead to bad behaviors, or be circumvented for convenience. Your solution should make your team members want to use it, not try to get around it.

- *Scaling*—Scaling involves team and project size. Having all your styles in a single CSS file might be great when you're building your own small website, but if 50 developers all need to update lines in the same file, which has more than 10,000 lines, your pull requests will get complex quickly!

- *Readability*—Readability is important to being able to scan a component quickly and understand what's going on. Can you determine which styles apply to a given element after you've found the rules? This concern may seem trivial, but some popular libraries out there, such as Tailwind, challenge readability.

- *Debugging*—Debugging concerns being able to work your way back from what you see in the browser. If you notice that a specific element has the wrong color, are you able to (quickly) find the specific line of source code that made it that color?

- *Encapsulation*—This concern is important for code reuse. If you use the same UI library in multiple projects, it's helpful if your styles are encapsulated inside the UI library and don't leak out to the surrounding project, requiring duplication of setup.

- *Theming*—Theming involves creating reusable UI libraries and distributing and customizing them for each project in an organization or even as a public library. How difficult is it to make the primary accent color of all the components in the library green rather than the default blue? Can you change all the bits and pieces of the library without too much hassle as a library consumer without knowing anything about the library internals?

7.1.3   Web application development

Web applications are supposed to be fast and efficient to use. Modern web applications use a bunch of tricks to make them even faster and serve them to the target audience as fast as possible by bundling and reusing bits and pieces. This topic is a huge one (and a moving target as browsers get smarter), but your styling approach matters for several reasons:

- *Bundle size*—This concern is trivially important. If your styles are 30 KB instead of 10 KB, your page loads slower. Some approaches are a lot more expensive in terms of bundle size than others.
- *Performance*—Performance concerns both how fast your project compiles and how fast your styles are applied to your components. Some approaches have no compilation overhead, whereas others do. Similarly, some approaches have some runtime overhead when you view the page as a visitor, whereas others do not. You must weigh these choices as the project developer.
- *Cacheability*—This concern is important for speeding up revisits to your applications. If your styles can be cached, returning users will have a much smoother experience than they would otherwise.
- *Code splitting*—Code splitting is important for minimizing the number of bytes sent to a user when they visit each part of the website. If your stylesheet for the entire website is 100 KB, but you use only about 2 KB of that on a specific page, you're sending 98 KB of wasted content to a user who sees only that page. It would be a lot better to split your styles so that only the specific styles used on a specific page are sent to the user.
- *Maintenance*—Maintenance is about (among other things) dead-code elimination. You want to make sure you're shipping only styles that are used in your application, not styles left in there from a feature you deleted a long time ago. Some approaches make style use hard to determine, whereas others have it built in.

7.1.4   *Why not inline styles?*

Many examples in this book so far have used inline styles. By *using inline styles*, I mean using the React feature of assigning styles to HTML elements by setting the `style` property of an element to some object, like this:

```
return <h1 style={{ color: 'hotpink' }}>Welcome!</h1>;
```

Why are we not even considering that option, then? Well, as you look through the lists of concerns in the preceding sections, you may start to see the problems.

Almost none of the CSS language feature concerns are options with inline styles, which have no pseudoclasses or pseudoelements, no at-rules, no nested rules, and so on. What's more, these features aren't merely nice to have but essential for any useful web application that you or anyone else would want to build.

For these reasons, inline CSS is all but useless except for tiny examples and early prototypes. Tiny prototypes happen to be exactly what we're building in this book, but if we ever wanted to expand any of those examples or deploy them to a real website, we'd find a better method. If you take only one thing away from this chapter, let it be this: you should always use a better approach to CSS than inline styles.

We implemented the example application by using inline styles, and you can check it out in the `ch07/inline` folder. When you do, you'll see that it falls short on many features. It has no animations (which require at-rules), no hover states (which require pseudoclasses), and a much larger file size than all the other examples (because the CSS is duplicated in full for every single button instance). Even in this tiny example application, the problems start piling up fast.

Example: inline

This example is in the `inline` folder. You can use that example by running this command in the source folder:

```
$ npm run dev -w ch07/inline
```

Alternatively, you can go to this website to browse the code, see the example in action in your browser, or download the source code as a zip file: https://reactlikea .pro/ch07-inline.

7.1.5   *What about existing UI libraries?*

You may be considering another option: rather than build all your styles yourself, you can use an existing UI library. You could consider using three types of UI libraries for a React application:

- Full React component libraries ready to import and use. Material UI is an example (https://mui.com).
- Opinionated stylesheets, in which several component designs have already been implemented in CSS, waiting for us to apply the proper class names to our application. Bootstrap is an example (https://getbootstrap.com).
- Unopinionated (utilitarian) stylesheets, which allow you to create almost anything from base class names. Tailwind CSS is an example (https://tailwindcss .com).

Although all these options are great for various React applications, I'm not going to cover them in this chapter, as I don't feel that they're good solutions for this particular application. Feel more than free to investigate them yourself to see whether they might match your requirements.

The first two types of UI libraries are opinionated and already have designs for a button. These two libraries work best if you want your buttons to look they way they prescribe. You do have some wiggle room, but if you want a unique design, you'll rarely go for one of these types, which is why I feel that they come up short in this instance.

The last type—the utilitarian approach—is getting a lot of traction lately. Tailwind CSS is popular because you can get started fast and don't have to write any CSS, though you still have almost the full capabilities of CSS at your disposal.

The type of application we're building here, however, does not lend itself well to the Tailwind approach. Because we have a single component with a lot of variability and styles to apply, using Tailwind would get messy. I implemented the target application in Tailwind for reference, however, and you can see the result in the repository.

> **Example: tailwind**
>
> This example is in the `tailwind` folder. You can use that example by running this command in the source folder:
>
> ```
> $ npm run dev -w ch07/tailwind
> ```
>
> Alternatively, you can go to this website to browse the code, see the example in action in your browser, or download the source code as a zip file: https://reactlikea.pro/ch07-tailwind.

7.2   *The example button application*

We need a good example project to test the solutions. Because we want to demo a wide variety of the concerns mentioned in the preceding sections, we cannot create a simple application that contains all of them. If we wanted to go that way, we'd have to create an application with at least 15 to 20 components, to illustrate all the aspects that we want to highlight. Although React can handle that task, book pages are less flexible, so we'd need a lot of pages for the source code for each example application.

So rather than go for a single application, we're going to create a minimal UI library and some example uses of said library with a single UI component: a button. In essence, we're going to create five variants of our button, allowing the application to style the button slightly differently in different use cases (figure 7.2).

Figure 7.2   **The target application that we are going to implement in three ways. The application is only five versions of a button, but it will give us a ton of information about and insight into the technology in question.**

Imagine that we know about a target application in which our button will be used. The button must serve several purposes throughout the application, and we have been given some design specifications that our UI library and button must support.

I'll go over the variants in this section and explain which problems they deal with. Note that we're going to challenge mostly the CSS language feature problems, as those are the ones we can see directly. As we go about implementing those variants, we'll discuss which other problems the various solutions make easy or hard to solve. The five variants of a button that our UI library has to support are as follows:

- *The normal button*—This button has a pink background with white text and a forward-pointing chevron. When you hover over the button, the chevron bounces forward in a looping animation. The chevron also needs some styling to be sized and positioned correctly.
- *The outline button*—This button is used as an alternative, less important button. it might be used for a confirm box, in which the confirm button is the primary one and the cancel button is this outline button. This outline button has a pink outline, pink text, and a transparent background.
- *The disabled button*—We need the button to work as a submit button for forms as well, so we need the button to be shown in a disabled state. When it's disabled, the button does not receive any pointer events (including hover), and it's faded to 50% opacity.
- *The wide button*—In a few places, we're going to need a button that has a custom width rather than the fixed width of the normal button. We can use this button in a shopping cart sidebar, where we want the checkout button to be as wide as the sidebar. We'll implement this button by passing in a `width` property to the button and use that value as a pixel value for the button width.
- *The custom button*—On a few occasions, we need to be able to customize the button and break all the regular rules if we so desire. We may want the button to be taller, a different color from normal, to have rounded corners, or a box shadow. We want to be able to pass custom styles to the button and have them applied.

Note that all these variants can be applied together. Thus, we could use the UI library to create a disabled outline button with a custom width or an outline button with a border radius applied via the custom styling option.

We're going to create a simple application for all the examples, using the button from our simple UI library (refer to figure 7.2). We'll create the applications identically, following this general recipe:

```
import Button from "./Button";
function App() {
  return (
    <>
      <fieldset>
        <legend>Normal button</legend>
```

```
        <Button>Send</Button>
    </fieldset>
    <fieldset>
      <legend>Outline button</legend>
      <Button outline>Send</Button>
    </fieldset>
    <fieldset>
      <legend>Disabled button</legend>
      <Button disabled>Send</Button>
    </fieldset>
    <fieldset>
      <legend>Wide button</legend>
      <Button width={400}>Send</Button>
    </fieldset>
    <fieldset>
      <legend>Custom button</legend>
      <Button hasCustomStyle>Send</Button>
    </fieldset>
  </>
  );
}
export default App;
```

The normal button instance is passed zero properties.

The outline button instance is passed only a Boolean outline property.

The disabled button instance is passed only a Boolean disabled property.

The wide button is passed a width property with the value 400.

The custom button is going to be passed custom styles in some way or another. This implementation will vary with the choice of styling methodology. The hasCustomStyle property is only an example, of course; we would need to pass those custom styles to the component in some fashion for it to make sense.

7.3   *Method 1: CSS files and class names*

Using CSS files and class names is the old method of styling any web application, and it's the well-established norm that all the other CSS-in-JS technologies are rebelling against. This method can be considered the *nonmethod*. It is how "classic" web applications are built, so we can build our React-based web applications that way too.

I include this method so you can better understand what the other approaches are rebelling against, when it still makes sense to use this classic approach, what it does well, and, in particular, what it doesn't do well.

7.3.1   *How class names work*

I don't need to explain this part, which is how CSS has been done for 25 years, so I trust you know how it works. Figure 7.3 illustrates the relationship between JSX and the applied style.

Do note one thing, however: you have no guarantee that `card.css` contains the class names used in `Card.js`. It could be referring to any class names defined in any CSS files imported anywhere in the project. Often, it makes sense to group JavaScript and CSS files as shown in figure 7.3, but grouping isn't a requirement and isn't enforced by React or the bundler. I'll get back to that topic in section 7.3.5.

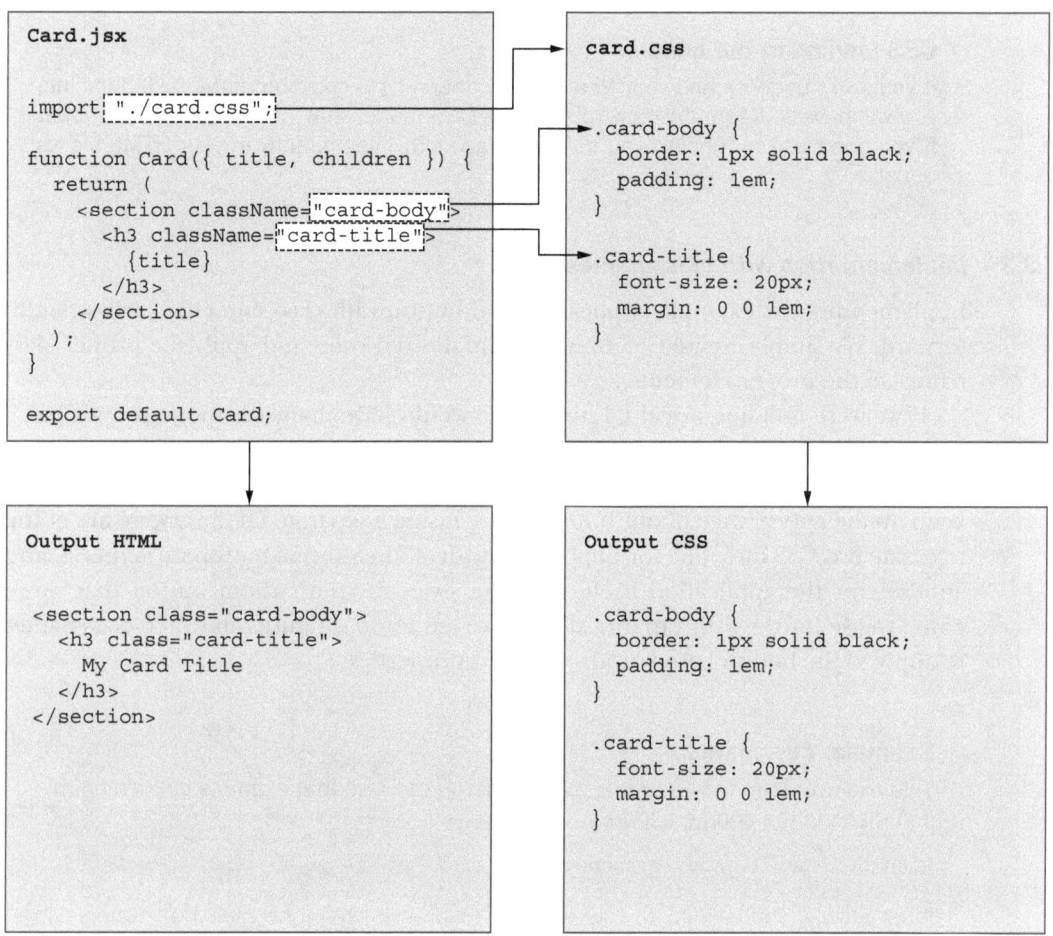

Figure 7.3 How JSX elements are styled when you use CSS files and class names. You can import a CSS file directly from a JavaScript file and then use CSS class names directly in your JSX. The resulting HTML and CSS looks exactly like what you type.

7.3.2 Setup for class name project

If you use Vite to initialize your project, you can use CSS files and class names right out of the box. The only slightly tricky thing about using CSS files in React development is that you can import the CSS files directly in the JavaScript files. Normally, you would have an HTML file with references to both CSS files and JavaScript files, but because we use a bundler (esbuild, built into the Vite setup), we can "import" the CSS files in the JavaScript files, and the bundler will turn the combined code into separate CSS and JavaScript files, correctly inserted into the document. Note that this process involves some technical details that your setup docs in the background, so you don't have to worry about it.

> **CSS loading in the bundler**
>
> If you don't use Vite and your React setup doesn't support automatic CSS bundling, you will have to figure out how to set up a CSS loader that works with your bundler. If you don't use a bundler, you can reference CSS files directly in your HTML file as usual.

7.3.3 *Implementation with class names*

Implementing the example application and button with class names is fairly straightforward. We simply create CSS files with the desired rules and apply the proper class names to the proper elements.

If we were building a real UI library, we would have many components, not just a button, and we'd have very clear separation of the library and the application. In this example, we have only two files, and we pretend that one of them is the UI library. To keep up the appearance of our button being inside a separate UI library, we are going to create two CSS files: one for the button, with all the normal button variant CSS, and another for the application itself, with the styles for the custom button that we're going to use for the fifth variant. All we have left to do is figure out which class names to apply to the button based on the relevant properties.

> **Example: classnames**
>
> This example is in the `classnames` folder. You can use that example by running this command in the source folder:
>
> ```
> $ npm run dev -w ch07/classnames
> ```
>
> Alternatively, you can go to this website to browse the code, see the example in action in your browser, or download the source code as a zip file: https://reactlikea .pro/ch07-classnames.

APP.JSX

In the main application, we load the styles for our custom button and apply the class name to that custom button. Otherwise, we use the predetermined button variants. The source for `App.jsx` is in the following listing.

Listing 7.1 `src/App.jsx` with class names

```
import Button from "./Button";
import "./app.css";          ◁─┐  First, we load the application
function App() {               │  stylesheet by importing the file.
  return (
    <>
      <fieldset>
```

```
      <legend>Normal button</legend>
      <Button>Send</Button>
    </fieldset>
    <fieldset>
      <legend>Outline button</legend>
      <Button outline>Send</Button>
    </fieldset>
    <fieldset>
      <legend>Disabled button</legend>
      <Button disabled>Send</Button>
    </fieldset>
    <fieldset>
      <legend>Wide button</legend>
      <Button width={400}>Send</Button>
    </fieldset>
    <fieldset>
      <legend>Custom button</legend>
      <Button className="custom-button">        ◁──┐  Then we add a custom class
        Send                                         │  name to the custom button.
      </Button>
    </fieldset>
  </>
 );
}
export default App;
```

APP.CSS

The application stylesheet could contain other rules, but for this simple application, it contains only the rule for the custom button. Note that there's no direct synchronization between the rules defined in this CSS file and the rules used in the main application; we have to maintain that synchronization manually. If we misspell the class name in either file, no error will appear at either compile time or run time. The only indication of an error would be the fact that the button isn't styled. The source for app.css is in the following listing.

Listing 7.2 `src/app.css` **with class names**

```
.custom-button {            ◁──┐  The rule for a custom
  background-color: purple;      │  purple button
  border-color: purple;
}
```

BUTTON.JSX

This section shows how to choose the styles to apply to the button element based on the properties of the component. We solve the normal button and the outline button by applying class names. We solve the disabled button in CSS only through pseudo-classes. Finally, we solve the wide button with inline styles. We could have used a CSS variable, but the result would have been comparable in terms of complexity. The source for Button.jsx is in the following listing.

Listing 7.3   `src/Button.jsx` with class names

```
import "./button.css";                 ◁──    We need to import the style sheet,
function Button({                              and we check manually which class
  children,                                    names are used in the stylesheet.
  outline = false,
  disabled = false,
  className = "",
  width = null,
}) {
  const classNames = [          ◁──
    "button",
    outline ? "button--outline" : "",         ◁──
    className,                    ◁──
  ].filter(Boolean);
  const style = width
    ? { width: `${width}px` }
    : null;
  return (
    <button
      className={classNames.join(" ")}
      style={style}
      disabled={disabled}
    >
      {children}
      <svg
        className="button__icon"              ◁──
        version="1.1"
        xmlns="http://www.w3.org/2000/svg"
        xmlnsXlink="http://www.w3.org/1999/xlink"
        viewBox="0 0 490 490"
      >
        <polygon
          points="240.112,0 481.861,245.004 240.112,490
                  8.139,490 250.29,245.004 8.139,0"
          fill="currentColor"
        />
      </svg>
    </button>
  );
}
export default Button;
```

We generate a final class name for the button element by creating an array of class names and merging them.

First, we always apply the button class name.

Then we apply the button--outline only if the outline property is true.

Finally, we append any custom class name to the component as well.

We also have to create a style object if there is a custom width property.

We apply the class name and style object to the button element, and we're all set.

The inline Scalable Vector Graphics (SVG) element also needs some styles, which we apply with a simple class name.

BUTTON.CSS

This file is plain CSS, using all the rules and declarations we need to style the button. The source for `button.css` is in the following listing.

Listing 7.4   `src/button.css` with class names

```
.button {
  display: flex;
  background: hotpink;
  color: white;
  border: 2px solid hotpink;
```

```
      margin: 1em 2em;
      padding: 1em 2em;
      font-size: 120%;
      width: 250px;
      cursor: pointer;
      gap: 10px;
      justify-content: center;
      align-items: center;
    }
    .button__icon {
      width: 16px;
      height: 16px;
      position: relative;
    }
    .button:hover .button__icon {
      animation: bounce .2s ease-in-out alternate infinite;
    }
    @keyframes bounce {
      from {
        left: 0;
      }
      to {
        left: 10px;
      }
    }
    .button--outline {
      border-color: hotpink;
      background-color: transparent;
      color: hotpink;
    }
    .button:disabled {
      opacity: 0.5;
      pointer-events: none;
    }
```

We can use pseudoclasses and composition.

We can use at-rules.

We can use pseudoclasses.

7.3.4   *Strengths of the class names approach*

The strengths of this approach are relatively obvious, but a few of them may come as a surprise due to the way the application is bundled:

- We can use all features of CSS because that's what we're writing—plain old CSS.
- This approach is familiar and understandable to all team members who have ever tried to use CSS. You don't have to do any onboarding; the team is up and running in seconds.
- Debugging is easy because you can see which classes apply to which elements in the browser and (ideally) find the same classes in your CSS files somewhere. Which CSS file includes a specific class may not be obvious, but a search will probably reveal it. If your bundler is set up correctly, source maps in your browser developer tools may tell you which file and line contained the original style (even though your bundler will have merged the files into a different CSS file).
- Because you can import stylesheets into the individual components that use them, you get some level of maintenance and code splitting for free. If you do

not include a specific component in your application, the stylesheets included in that component will not be bundled with your application, so you won't be loading any unused styles. Also, if you lazy load (delay load) some components to optimize browser rendering, the styles for those components will also be lazy loaded.

- This approach is fast, with almost no overhead in compile time mostly because your CSS files aren't analyzed; they're included in the bundle as is. Also, this approach has zero runtime overhead because it is regular CSS files and class names. Nothing has to be calculated on the fly.

7.3.5   *Weaknesses of the class names approach*

The topic of this section is the entire reason why CSS-in-JS exists. This regular approach, although it's easy to work with and well understood, has several weaknesses. For many developers, those weaknesses are significant enough that they've created hundreds of alternative methods for styling complex web applications. Let's deal with the most important weaknesses first:

- *There is no synchronization between CSS files and components.* Yes, you might include a `button.css` file in your `Button.js` component file, but you have no guarantee or validation that the styles included in the CSS file are the ones used in the component, and vice versa. If you misspell a class name, nothing helps you check it. If you have unused classes in your CSS file, no pruning occurs.

- *The split of the component between a CSS file and a JavaScript file requires a lot of context switching.* As you're developing the component, you have to switch back and forth between the two files and remember class names and HTML structure to make sure that you style your application as desired.

- *Collisions are likely.* As your application grows, many components might be named `Group` because the concept of a group can be used in many contexts. But you can have only one CSS class named `.group`. If you accidentally reuse that class name in a new component, errant styles will apply to your component (and you'll probably have broken the original). This problem can be tricky to track down. Even worse, if you embed your React application in a regular website (maybe you created a small calculator module that can be reused on many pages), the CSS classes used on the website might collide with the classes in the application, and vice versa. You have to apply some complex naming schemes to prevent collisions (one popular approach is BEM [http://getbem.com]), but even that precaution probably won't be enough.

- *If you need to use dynamic values, you need to use inline CSS.* This situation may occur if you have a `width` variable in JavaScript that you need to apply to an element.

- *Specificity can be a problem.* Rules defined in the same CSS file will be output in that order in the final document. But in what order will rules defined in different CSS files be output? A system exists, but it can be hard to understand. We happen to be lucky in this case because the rule for `.custom-button` apparently was defined after the rule for `.button`, but we can't depend on luck at scale.

Following are a few lesser but still important problems:

- *If you use basic CSS as I advocate in this section, you're not using a preprocessor.* That is, the CSS you write is the CSS that will be used in the browser. Preprocessors such as Less and Sass allow you to use fancy features that aren't supported in normal CSS. In this setup, none of those options is available, so you're limited to what CSS normally offers. To a CSS purist, that situation might be a plus, but to most other developers, it's a minus.
- *Theming is tricky.* You can use CSS variables, which all major browsers today support, but you have to manage your variables manually and remember the names of the variables that will be used throughout your application.
- *This approach scales acceptably, but only to a point.* Because of the single global namespace, collisions make collaboration difficult on a large scale.
- *Dead-code removal has to be done by hand.* It is impossible to tell automatically whether a given rule is used anywhere in your application.

7.3.6   When (not) to use CSS files and class names

This approach is good for small-to-medium-size projects that aren't too complex or dynamic. When your application, team, and ambitions grow, along with the need for more complex structures, you will probably have to look for a different solution. You will also find that most established teams use some other approach, for all the reasons stated in section 7.3.5.

7.4   Method 2: CSS Modules

This approach is a small extension of the regular CSS file and class name approach that addresses some of the problems I pointed out in section 7.3.5. This concept is called *CSS Modules*, and it primarily deals with the problems of colocation and collisions. CSS Modules still use CSS files, which you write as you normally would. But those files will be parsed, and the class names will be extracted and regenerated as new unique names. All other aspects stay the same.

7.4.1   How CSS Modules work

The syntax and setup for using CSS Modules is almost identical to using class names and CSS files. We are still using CSS files, but we're going to make sure that they use the `.module.css` extension rather than `.css`. The file extension `.module.css` instructs the bundler to handle them using the CSS Modules plugin instead of the regular CSS plugin. Figure 7.4 shows how we're going to be using this approach.

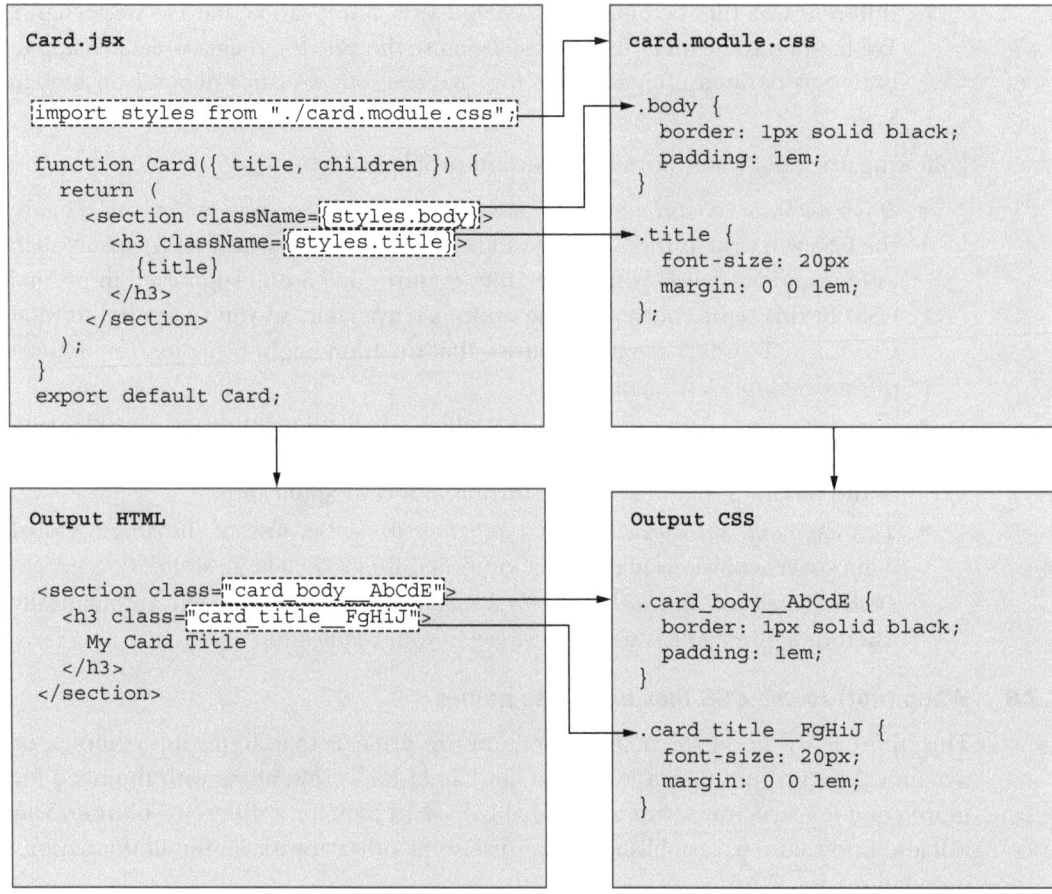

Figure 7.4   The relationship between the component and the CSS Module. We can use whatever class names we want in the module, and we refer to those class names in the component as direct variables. The resulting output will replace these class names in both the CSS file and the module with some autogenerated class names, partially based on the CSS Module filename, the class name, and some randomly generated padding to prevent collisions.

As you see in figure 7.4, CSS Modules is a clever library. When you import a CSS Module into a JavaScript file, the bundler converts the CSS files to an object with a key for each class defined in the module, and each key maps to a dynamic class name. This dynamic class name is generated based on the module filename, the class name in the module, and some random information.

7.4.2   *Setup for CSS Modules project*

Support for CSS Modules is built into any Vite setup by default. All you have to do is name your CSS files `*.module.css`, and you're good to go.

If you aren't using a Vite-based setup, you need to find a plugin for CSS Modules that works with your bundler. For webpack, you can use the `css-loader` plugin, and for everything else, you can use `postcss` and the `postcss-modules` plugin:

- `css-loader`—https://github.com/webpack-contrib/css-loader
- `postcss`—https://github.com/postcss/postcss
- `postcss-modules`—https://github.com/madyankin/postcss-modules

7.4.3 *Source code with CSS Modules*

Implementing the button application with CSS Modules is a straightforward evolution from the class name version. We simply rename the CSS files from `*.css` to `*.module.css`; we simplify the CSS class names because we no longer have to worry about collisions; and we replace the static filenames with the imported dynamic style names. In this section, I'll go over the files to show how we do all these things.

> **Example: cssmodules**
>
> This example is in the `cssmodules` folder. You can use that example by running this command in the source folder:
>
> `$ npm run dev -w ch07/cssmodules`
>
> Alternatively, you can go to this website to browse the code, see the example in action in your browser, or download the source code as a zip file: https://reactlikea .pro/ch07-cssmodules.

APP.JSX

We change the CSS import and the filename passed to the custom button. Otherwise, everything is standard. The source for `App.jsx` is in the following listing.

Listing 7.5 `src/App.jsx` with CSS Modules

```
import styles from "./app.module.css";          ◁────  We import the module to
import Button from "./Button";                          the named variable styles.
function App() {
  return (
    <>
      <fieldset>
        <legend>Normal button</legend>
        <Button>Send</Button>
      </fieldset>
      <fieldset>
        <legend>Outline button</legend>
        <Button outline>Send</Button>
      </fieldset>
      <fieldset>
        <legend>Disabled button</legend>
        <Button disabled>Send</Button>
      </fieldset>
      <fieldset>
        <legend>Wide button</legend>
        <Button width={400}>Send</Button>
      </fieldset>
```

```
      <fieldset>
        <legend>Custom button</legend>
        <Button className={styles.customButton}>    ◁──────  We use the styles variable
          Send                                               to apply the dynamic class
        </Button>                                            name to the custom button.
      </fieldset>
    </>
  );
}
export default App;
```

APP.MODULE.CSS

The only change we make in the main CSS file of the application (besides the file-name) is to use a class name that works better in JavaScript as an identifier. Before, the class name was `custom-button`, and although we can use it in JavaScript as `styles['custom-button']`, it is easier to type `styles.customButton` if we change the class name similarly.

We also need to change another thing. When we imported the CSS files in the previous application by using plain CSS files, we were lucky that the files were appended in the correct order, with the button CSS first and the app CSS second. That result meant that the app CSS applied last and thus had higher specificity. For this CSS Module application, the loader happens to load our rules in the opposite order, so the app CSS rules are loaded first, which means that they have lower specificity. To make sure that the custom button rule is applied to override the regular button styles, we need to increase the specificity of the selector or make the declarations important. We choose to do the former, using a tag name, so the final selector becomes `button.customButton`. The source for `app.module.css` is in the following listing.

Listing 7.6   `src/app.module.css` with CSS Modules

```
button.customButton {                ◁──────  Before, we had .custom-button. Now, we rename
    background-color: purple;                 it .customButton to make it work better as a
    border-color: purple;                     JavaScript identifier. Finally, we add the button
}                                             tag name to raise the specificity of this rule;
                                              otherwise, it would not work correctly. We could
                                              also have solved this problem with !important.
```

BUTTON.JSX

The implementation of the button using CSS Modules is almost identical to the implementation using class names, except that we get the class names from the import rather than the strings. Changing the import and the class name is generally all it takes to switch to using CSS Modules. The source for `Button.jsx` is in the following listing.

Listing 7.7   `src/Button.jsx` with CSS Modules

```
import styles from "./button.module.css";    ◁──────  We import the class names
function Button({                                     from the CSS Module.
  children,
```

```
  outline = false,
  disabled = false,
  className = "",
  width = null,
}) {                                          We change all the instances of
  const classNames = [                        string class names to the class
    styles.normal,                            names returned by the import.
    outline ? styles.outline : "",
    className,
  ].filter(Boolean);
  const style = width                  We still need inline styles for dynamic values.
    ? { width: `${width}px` }
    : null;
  return (
    <button
      className={classNames.join(" ")}
      disabled={disabled}
      style={style}
    >
      {children}
      <svg
        className={styles.icon}
        version="1.1"
        xmlns="http://www.w3.org/2000/svg"
        xmlnsXlink="http://www.w3.org/1999/xlink"
        viewBox="0 0 490 490"
      >
        <polygon
          points="240.112,0 481.861,245.004 240.112,490
                  8.139,490 250.29,245.004 8.139,0"
          fill="currentColor"
        />
      </svg>
    </button>
  );
}
export default Button;
```

BUTTON.MODULE.CSS

The button CSS is identical except that we can use less complex class names because
we don't have to worry about collisions. We can use .outline for the outline button
rather than .button--outline or .buttonOutline. The source for button.module
.css is in the following listing.

Listing 7.8   `src/button.module.css` with CSS Modules

```
.normal {
    display: flex;
    background: hotpink;
    color: white;
    border: 2px solid hotpink;
    margin: 1em 2em;
    padding: 1em 2em;
```

```
        font-size: 120%;
        width: 250px;
        cursor: pointer;
        gap: 10px;
        justify-content: center;
        align-items: center;
}
.icon {
        width: 16px;
        height: 16px;
        position: relative;
}
.normal:hover .icon {
        animation: bounce .2s ease-in-out alternate infinite;
}
@keyframes bounce {
        from { left: 0; }
        to { left: 10px; }
}
.outline {
        border-color: hotpink;
        background-color: transparent;
        color: hotpink;
}
.normal[disabled] {
        opacity: 0.5;
        pointer-events: none;
}
```

> Note that we can make selectors composed of multiple class names. CSS Modules will replace each class name with the correct output class name.

7.4.4   *Strengths of CSS Modules*

The strengths of using CSS Modules are the same as the strengths of using regular CSS and class names, but some of the weaknesses of the latter method have been fixed. In particular, compared with the first method we tested, CSS Modules gives us the following benefits:

- *Synchronization between CSS files and components*—Because we're not betting on strings happening to match up but using actual variables, we can be sure that we use the correct class names in our components.
- *Look, Mom, no collisions*—Because the final class names will be autogenerated, we don't have to worry about coming up with unique names for our classes. We can have a `.wrapper` class in every component, and the bundler will make sure that they all have unique names in the final product.
- *Easy dead-code elimination*—Dead-code elimination is often easier, as you can be fairly certain that a given rule is used only by components that import the CSS Module file in which it exists. If a CSS Module contains a rule that is no longer used in any component importing that module, it can be safely removed (most of the time, at least).

7.4.5 Weaknesses of CSS Modules

Some of the weaknesses of the classic, class names method persist in CSS Modules:

- We still have our component split into two files. Even for a tiny component, we need to switch back and forth between the JavaScript file and the CSS file to get the full picture.
- We still need to use inline CSS for dynamic values.
- Specificity and source order are still problems, as we aren't in control of the order of the CSS rules in the final output.

Additional weaknesses include the following:

- Debugging is harder. If you are testing the application in the browser and find a component that's wrongly styled, it's trickier to track down the offending CSS, as you can't search for the rule that you see in the output. The original rule in your source code will be different. Browser source maps will get you closer, but the process can still be tricky.
- CSS Modules are slightly more complex than plain CSS files, so new developers need an introduction to this system if they are unfamiliar with it.
- Composition of rules is harder. You cannot refer directly to class names from other modules, as those class names will not remain the same in the final output. So you have to isolate your styles inside each component and cannot apply styles inside a different component without using some weird tricks that are specific to CSS Modules.

7.4.6 When (not) to use CSS Modules

Despite the previously mentioned weaknesses, CSS Modules are a stable method for larger applications. When CSS Modules came out, they quickly gained traction as the best way to work with CSS in larger codebases, and you will still find it used in many codebases. That being said, it does have some weaknesses that other systems have solved better.

Suppose that you're on a project using CSS Modules, and the team is doing fine. In that case, you don't need to change things just for the sake of change. If you have the opportunity to define the styling method for a new project, however, CSS Modules may be what you want if you can live with or at least work around the weaknesses. If not, newer alternatives are available.

7.5 Method 3: Styled-components

Styled-components is the natural extension of CSS Modules, taking the concept to the next step. CSS Modules have CSS files and class names, but those class names are local variables, not class names in the final CSS. So why not skip having class names, create elements directly with a given set of styles already applied, and use those elements directly in your component?

What do I mean? Well, imagine that we could import the HTML-element-with-class directly from the CSS file as shown in figure 7.5.

CSS Modules	New fancy idea?

```
card.module.css

.body {
  border: 1px solid black;
  padding: 1em;
}

.title {
  font-size: 20px;
  margin: 0 0 1em;
}
```

```
card.fancy.css

section.body {
  border: 1px solid black;
  padding: 1em;
}

h3.title {
  font-size: 20px;
  margin: 0 0 1em;
}
```

```
Card.js

import styles from "./card.module.css";


function Card({ title, children }) {
  return (
    <section className={styles.body}>
      <h3 className={styles.title}>
        {title}
      </h3>
    </section>
  );
}
```

```
Card.js

import {
  Body, Title
} from "./card.fancy.css";

function Card({ title, children }) {
  return (
    <Body>
      <Title>
        {title}
      </Title>
    </Body>
  );
}
```

Figure 7.5   The structure on the left is what CSS Modules give us. But what if we could skip some of that extra work and go to the version on the right, where we don't have to type the class names and can import the CSS directly as components?

Figure 7.5 illustrates the general idea behind styled-components. Additionally, styled-components eliminates the need for CSS files and allows you to specify the components with CSS directly in the main JavaScript file.

7.5.1   How styled-components works

Styled-components allows you to define HTML JSX elements with styles applied directly in your component JavaScript files. See the example in figure 7.6.

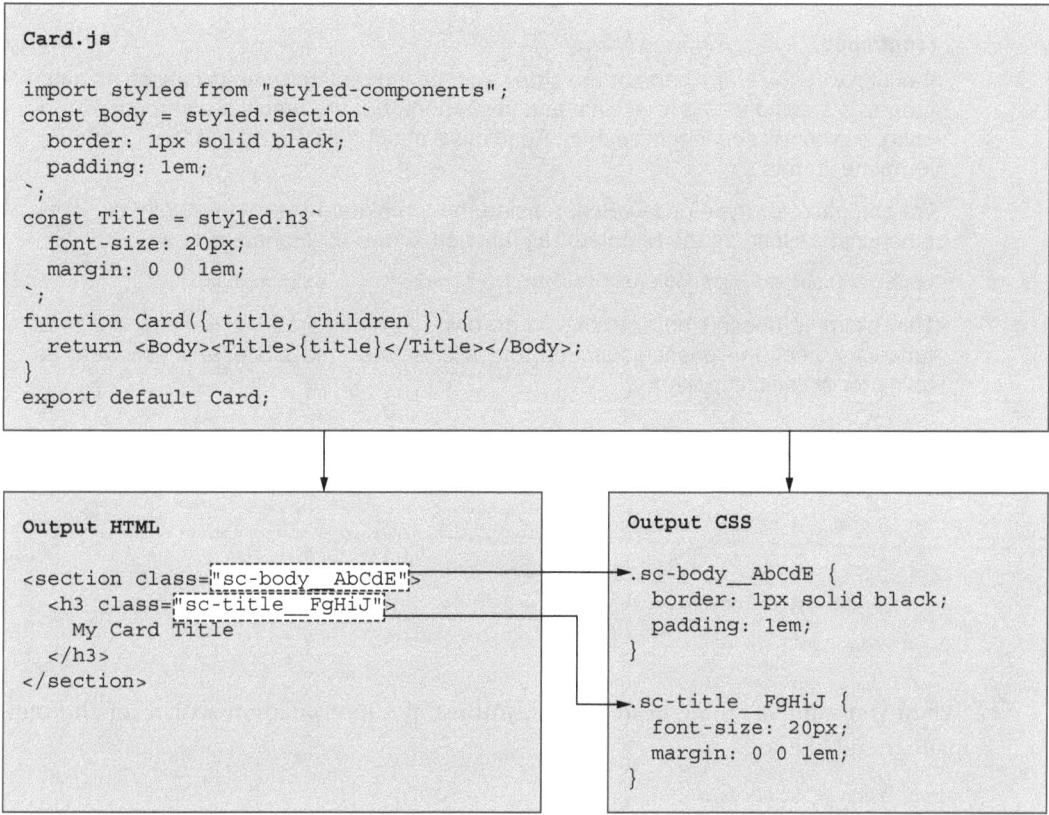

```
Card.js

import styled from "styled-components";
const Body = styled.section`
  border: 1px solid black;
  padding: 1em;
`;
const Title = styled.h3`
  font-size: 20px;
  margin: 0 0 1em;
`;
function Card({ title, children }) {
  return <Body><Title>{title}</Title></Body>;
}
export default Card;
```

```
Output HTML

<section class="sc-body__AbCdE">
  <h3 class="sc-title__FgHiJ">
   My Card Title
  </h3>
</section>
```

```
Output CSS

.sc-body__AbCdE {
  border: 1px solid black;
  padding: 1em;
}

.sc-title__FgHiJ {
  font-size: 20px;
  margin: 0 0 1em;
}
```

Figure 7.6 **We have a single source file and can define CSS directly applied to the relevant JSX elements. The file is a bit more complex overall, but the resulting JSX is clean.**

You might say, "Well, that's good for these examples, but what about pseudoclasses, composition, and so on?" Don't worry. Styled-components has got you covered with nested syntax from tools such as Less and Sass.

String template literals

How does this backtick syntax in `styled.section``` work?

Backticks are used in JavaScript to create *string template literals*, a great way to create complex multiline strings, especially with interpolation. You can interpolate regular JavaScript variables into a string template literal with the `${}` syntax like so:

```
const name = 'World';
const message = `Hello ${name}!`;
```

What's this extra notion of adding the backticks right after another variable, as in `styled.section`````? This syntax is a *tagged template literal*. It allows you to call a

> **(continued)**
>
> function with the literal parts of the string and the interpolated values passed as arguments. It's complicated to explain and implement, but the result is a smooth experience, as you will see in this section. Read more about the concept at https://mdn.io/template-literals.
>
> We can pass any type of JavaScript inside the template by using interpolation, even functions, as long as the template tag function knows how to interpret it:
>
> ```
> const message = messageBuilder`Hello ${person => person.name}!`;
> ```
>
> This example doesn't do anything on its own, as it requires the `messageBuilder` function to call the passed function, but it illustrates the process, which we'll be using for styled-components.

If you need to add a pseudoclass such as `:hover` or `:disabled`, you do it like so:

```
const Submit = styled.button`
  background-color: red:
  &:hover {
    background-color: blue;
  }
`;
```

When you want to create nested rules, you use the interpolation syntax for the template literal like so:

```
const Icon = styled.img`
  width: 32px;
`
const Submit = styled.button`
  background-color: red:
  & ${Icon} {
    width: 24px;
  }
`;
```

You can combine all these tricks to create all the rules you need. You can even create dynamic rules that use properties passed to the components to generate the CSS on the fly, using interpolation with a function receiving all components passed:

```
const Submit = styled.button`
  background-color: ${({ color }) => color};
`;
function MyForm() {
  return (
    <Submit color="red">Red submit!</Submit>
  );
}
```

You can also extend a definition by wrapping another component in the `styled` function:

```
const Submit = styled.button`
  background-color: green;
`;
const AngrySubmit = styled(Submit)`
  background-color: red;
`;
```

Here, we create a component with `styled``` and then wrap that component in `styled()`. Styled-components will automatically stack the two rules on top of each other with the proper specificity and source order. But if you wrap a custom component that you create yourself with `styled()`, the library will generate a class name for you and pass it into the component in question as a `className` property. We will use this trick in listing 7.9.

When it comes to at-rules, even more tricks are available. If you need to create keyframes for an animation, you can use a specific function (which we'll look at in listing 7.10). For media queries, you can create those inline as well like pseudoclasses. Finally, if you still need to create global rules (maybe you need to style the `html` or `body` element), another function for adding simple global CSS applies everywhere.

That's a lot of information in a short time. I'm only trying to give you a sense of what you can do and how you can do it, and I'm still covering only the bare minimum capabilities. There's a lot to learn about styled-components, and the best way is to read the documentation at https://styled-components.com.

7.5.2   *Setup for styled-components project*

Support for styled-components is not baked into Vite, but it is still easy to install. You simply install the module by using npm:

```
$ npm install --save styled-components
```

Then you can start importing from the package and using it as we saw in section 7.5.1.

7.5.3   *Source code with styled-components*

React components implemented with styled-components tend to be lengthy because the CSS is included in the same file as the React component code. This length is a feature of the library, however; related bits of code are placed as close together as possible to make updating the component easier. If you are restyling a component, you'll likely be changing both the CSS and the HTML (JSX) structure. With this library, both CSS and HTML are conveniently located next to each other.

Example: styled

This example is in the `styled` folder. You can use that example by running this command in the source folder:

```
$ npm run dev -w ch07/styled
```

> *(continued)*
>
> Alternatively, you can go to this website to browse the code, see the example in action in your browser, or download the source code as a zip file: https://reactlikea .pro/ch07-styled.

APP.JS

To apply a custom style to another component, we use the trick mentioned in section 7.5.1: wrapping a component in the `styled` function and applying the CSS by using the tagged template. Then our component will be invoked with a class name that we pass to the relevant JSX. The latter part goes inside the button. For now, we're worried only about how to style the button. The source for `App.js` is in the following listing.

Listing 7.9   `src/App.js` with styled-components

```
import styled from "styled-components";
import Button from "./Button";
const CustomButton = styled(Button)`
  background-color: purple;
  border-color: purple;
`;
function App() {
  return (
    <>
      <fieldset>
        <legend>Normal button</legend>
        <Button>Send</Button>
      </fieldset>
      <fieldset>
        <legend>Outline button</legend>
        <Button outline>Send</Button>
      </fieldset>
      <fieldset>
        <legend>Disabled button</legend>
        <Button disabled>Send</Button>
      </fieldset>
      <fieldset>
        <legend>Wide button</legend>
        <Button width={400}>Send</Button>
      </fieldset>
      <fieldset>
        <legend>Custom button</legend>
        <CustomButton>Send</CustomButton>
      </fieldset>
    </>
  );
}
export default App;
```

We add custom styles to an existing component by wrapping it in the styled function and get a new "enhanced" component back.

We can include the CSS directly inline.

Finally, we use this "enhanced" component like normal in JSX.

BUTTON.JSX

This part is where all the magic happens. There's no CSS file anymore; all the CSS exists inline in the button component JavaScript file.

Note that we add an animation to the CSS. We also specify that the component will still accept a class name because, under the hood, styled-components still generates CSS files with classes and applies those classes to the elements in question. The source for `Button.jsx` is in the following listing.

Listing 7.10 src/Button.jsx with styled-components

```
import styled, { keyframes } from "styled-components";
const Icon = styled.svg`
  width: 16px;
  height: 16px;
  position: relative;
`;
const bounce = keyframes`
  from { left: 0; }
  to { left: 10px; }
`;
const Normal = styled.button`
  display: flex;
  background: hotpink;
  color: white;
  border: 2px solid hotpink;
  margin: 1em 2em;
  padding: 1em 2em;
  font-size: 120%;
  width: 250px;
  cursor: pointer;
  gap: 10px;
  justify-content: center;
  align-items: center;
  ${(({ $width }) =>
    $width && `width: ${$width}px`
  };
  &:hover ${Icon} {
    animation: ${bounce} 0.2s ease-in-out
      alternate infinite;
  }
  &[disabled] {
    opacity: 0.5;
    pointer-events: none;
  }
`;
const Outline = styled(Normal)`
  border-color: hotpink;
  background-color: transparent;
  color: hotpink;
`;
function Button({
  children,
```

> To add an animation with custom keyframes, we use the util function keyframes from the styled-components library.

> We can include custom properties from the JSX in the generated CSS by using interpolated functions, which have access to all the properties.

> We can use composed rules, nested rules, pseudoclasses, and all sorts of selectors directly in the CSS declaration.

> Uses the bounce animation by interpolating the value returned from the keyframes function

> We can even extend one class with the rules of another (so this element will have both classes applied) to avoid duplicating rules.

```
      outline = false,
      disabled = false,
      className = null,
      width = null,
    }) {
      const Element = outline ? Outline : Normal;
      return (
        <Element
          disabled={disabled}
          $width={width}
          className={className}
        >
          {children}
          <Icon
            version="1.1"
            xmlns="http://www.w3.org/2000/svg"
            xmlnsXlink="http://www.w3.org/1999/xlink"
            viewBox="0 0 490 490"
          >
            <polygon
              points="240.112,0 481.861,245.004 240.112,490
                      8.139,490 250.29,245.004 8.139,0"
              fill="currentColor"
            />
          </Icon>
        </Element>
      );
    }
    export default Button;
```

> When we use an element styled with styled-components, we can pass in HTML properties (disabled and className) as well as properties used to generate the resulting CSS ($width). Prefixing properties with $ is a way to make sure that they don't go into the output HTML. $-prefixed properties are called transient properties.

7.5.4   *Strengths of styled-components*

Proponents of styled-components often promote several attributes as key benefits of this framework. Here are the highlights:

- Colocation is superb because you have the styles right next to the elements you're styling.
- Specificity is not a problem because the library takes care of it for you. If you extend one rule by another rule, the library makes sure to include them in the right order so that the rules apply correctly.
- You can use the full feature set of CSS seamlessly.
- No collisions occur, so you never have to worry about coming up with unique class names or meaningful selectors.
- Nesting is often eliminated or kept to two levels, making your selectors much shorter, which in turn means that the browser can apply the CSS much faster.
- Because you write the CSS inside JavaScript files, you can use JavaScript to do more complex calculations if you need to.

7.5.5   *Weaknesses of styled-components*

This library has a a couple of drawbacks, of course, and I want to highlight the following:

- Because the CSS is generated at compile time, extensive use of styled-components makes your application build slower. The overhead normally is not significant, but it is something to watch out for.
- There is an unclear separation of concerns, with CSS "logic" spread between both components and CSS rules. If you have conditional values, you can place the condition in either CSS or JavaScript; different developers on the same team might do things differently.
- Debugging is a bit harder because you just see a class name in the production HTML and can't immediately track it back to a CSS file, but you have to rely on source maps.
- Because you have CSS directly inside the component files, these files tend to get longer—sometimes a lot longer. Compare `Button.jsx` in the class names example (~40 lines) with the `styled` example (~70 lines). Generally, you can mitigate more lines of code by creating more, smaller components or even moving all the `styled` components to a separate file (such as `Component.styled.js`) and importing the elements from there.
- Because you are writing CSS-in-JS, it can be hard to revert to plain CSS files when you have a complex codebase, so evaluate your options carefully before committing to a library.
- It can be hard to see whether a JSX node is a component or a styled HTML element. You might see `<Heading>Expenses</Heading>` in a component and not know whether `Heading` is a styled HTML element or a different complex component. But maybe it's okay that you can't tell. Also, modern editors often give you inline hints about the element source.

7.5.6   *When (not) to use styled-components*

Styled-components is great for complex designs with many one-off components but is often considered less ideal for component libraries or web applications with unified and streamlined designs, such as dashboards and admin interfaces. The library is versatile and popular, so you can't go wrong with using it, but you may want to consider the alternatives before committing to it on a huge project.

7.6   *One problem, infinite solutions*

As I mentioned earlier, there is no one best way to style a React application because applications and developers are different. What works for one application and one team might be a terrible choice for another team.

In this section, I summarize five ways of styling an application:

- Inline CSS
- CSS files and class names

- CSS Modules
- Styled-components
- Tailwind CSS

I included the full source code for these methods in the online repository so you can check it out for yourself. I carefully dissected three of these approaches in this chapter; I implemented the other two (inline CSS and Tailwind CSS) but didn't describe them here to save space. Those implementations are linked in sections 7.1.4 and 7.1.5 if you want to check them out.

Table 7.1 is my admittedly subjective review of various attributes. I rate each attribute as being a feature of the approach ($\checkmark$), a problem (X), or something that the approach is neutral about or that has both ups and downs (!).

Table 7.1 Evaluating CSS methods on several attributes

Category and attribute	Inline CSS	CSS files	CSS Modules	Styled-components	Tailwind CSS
Folder	inline	classnames	cssmodules	styled	tailwind
CSS language features					
Specificity	!	X	!	$\checkmark$	X
Collisions	$\checkmark$	X	$\checkmark$	$\checkmark$	$\checkmark$
Composition	X	!	$\checkmark$	$\checkmark$	!
Pseudoclasses	X	$\checkmark$	$\checkmark$	$\checkmark$	!
Pseudoelements	X	$\checkmark$	$\checkmark$	$\checkmark$	!
At-rules	X	$\checkmark$	$\checkmark$	$\checkmark$	!
Conditional rules	X	X	X	$\checkmark$	$\checkmark$
Dynamic rules	$\checkmark$	X	X	$\checkmark$	$\checkmark$
Vendor prefixes	X	X	X	$\checkmark$	$\checkmark$
DX					
Colocation	$\checkmark$	!	!	$\checkmark$	$\checkmark$
Familiarity	$\checkmark$	$\checkmark$	$\checkmark$	!	X
Simplicity	!	$\checkmark$	!	!	X
Scaling	X	X	!	$\checkmark$	$\checkmark$
Readability	!	$\checkmark$	$\checkmark$	!	X
Debugging	$\checkmark$	$\checkmark$	!	$\checkmark$	!
Encapsulation	X	!	!	$\checkmark$	$\checkmark$
Theming	X	!	!	$\checkmark$	$\checkmark$

Table 7.1   Evaluating CSS methods on several attributes *(continued)*

Category and attribute	Inline CSS	CSS files	CSS Modules	Styled-components	Tailwind CSS
Web application development					
Bundle size	X	✓	✓	!	!
Performance	X	!	!	✓	✓
Cacheability	X	✓	✓	!	✓
Code-splitting	!	!	!	✓	✓
Maintenance	!	✓	✓	✓	X

You may notice that styled-components has the fewest drawbacks in table 7.1. I often use and strongly recommend this library for many projects, but I use different approaches in different projects, depending on other factors. Styled-components is like IBM: nobody gets fired for using it because it is safe. But check your alternatives.

One final note on this topic: these libraries are only a few of many. Dozens of other libraries are available, with all sorts of approaches developed by teams and developers who had all sorts of weird requirements or restrictions. New libraries pop up every month. By the time you read this book, a new approach might be the cool kid on the block. So although no one solution fits every project, at least some solution is likely to fit each individual project.

Summary

- You have many ways to style a web application in general and a React application in particular.
- CSS-in-JS refers to different ways of writing CSS inside your JavaScript files. It's a popular, easy way to write components and styles at the same time. But not all styling libraries use this approach.
- Using CSS files and class names is the old approach but still valid for smaller projects. Although it doesn't scale well, this tried-and-true approach doesn't require extra training for new team members.
- CSS Modules are a minor extension to regular CSS files. Rather than plain class names as written in the CSS file, the CSS declarations are preprocessed, and autogenerated unique class names are used instead with minimal effect on DX. It doesn't solve all the problems of regular class names, but it scales better.
- Styled-components is a modern CSS-in-JS approach to web application styling. With styled-components, you write your CSS directly inside your JavaScript files next to the components that need it. This approach leads to a much better overview of small components, as you can see JavaScript, HTML, and CSS at a glance. For larger components, however, the benefits diminish.

- Each individual library or approach has benefits and drawbacks. Although I can't recommend any single solution for every project, I recommend going with styled-components for medium-to-large-size projects because I feel that it has the most benefits and the fewest drawbacks. But remember that this recommendation is subjective and depends on a lot of things that I don't know about your project.

Data management
in React

This chapter covers

- Introducing the importance of data management
- Evaluating various data management libraries
- Building the data layer of an application in five ways

We've been using data in all the apps we've built, from the value of an input field to the list of items in a to-do application. I've introduced several ways to handle data as well. We've used `useState` for single data values and `useReducer` for more complex multivalue state. We've also discussed how React context can help you distribute and manipulate your data throughout your application in meaningful yet simple ways.

But there are many more ways to manage data in an application. Especially as applications grow large and complex, it can make sense to use a more structured approach to data management rather than sprinkle `useState` hooks all over the codebase with no clear structure behind them.

By *data management*, I mean the process of storing, reading, and modifying data locally in the application as the user goes about their business in the application. Data in this context can be different things, including UI state (whether the menu is open or closed), form state (what is currently entered in each input), and application state (the movie object that you can edit). Data can also include read-only data, such as all the articles in the blog section of the application.

Data management is one of those topics that cause developers to turn to third-party libraries and break from using pure React. They make this change partly for historical reasons: back in the days before hooks and context, using React alone for data management was too much of a pain. Developers also look for other libraries partly for convenience: the community has built a lot of elegant solutions to the data management problem. Different solutions are governed by different computer science principles, and if you or your team members subscribe to those same principles, those libraries will fit your project like a glove.

One data management library, Redux, is almost synonymous with React. This library was introduced in the earliest days of React and shaped the way data management worked in React for many years. It is still incredibly popular.

The downside of Redux is the amount of boilerplate code you have to write. Redux adheres to the functional coding principle of reducing state, and because it was initially strict in its application of this principle, it required a lot of moving parts to get going. If you needed Redux for a small list of items to read from, append to, and delete from, you had to create up to seven files with various configurations, action creators, stores, reducers, and more.

Redux has since become a lot more accessible in the form of Redux Toolkit (RTK), which is a much leaner library with a lower requirement for boilerplate, automating and serializing a lot of the complexity of classic Redux. Redux has also shaped how we handle data in pure React. The `useReducer` hook is inspired directly by Redux (and RTK in particular), and you'll see in this chapter that it works almost identically.

Alternatives to Redux have popped up over the years, and in this chapter, we're also going to look at one of the most bare-bones alternatives: zustand, which uses the same principles as Redux but takes the complexity all the way to zero (sacrificing scaling somewhat).

Finally, we're going to discuss a completely different approach to data management: using a state machine. A state machine is a flow management tool, but it comes with built-in data management, so it will work well for our application. The state-machine tool we'll be using is XState, and the library that connects XState to React is `@xstate/react`.

Wait—what application? Yes, we're going to build an application in this chapter so we can see how to build the data layer in five ways. But the twist this time is that we're not going to display all the code. We want to build a larger application with about 15 components, and the source code alone would take up too many pages, so I've provided the full source code only in the online repository.

In this chapter, I will discuss only how to modify the data layer of the application and leave the presentation layer intact. We'll have a clear boundary between presentation and data management so we can replace one part without touching the other.

> **NOTE**   The source code for the examples in this chapter is available at https:// reactlikea.pro/ch08.

8.1   Creating a goal-tracking application

All right, let's get to the application. This time, we're building a life-organizing tool—nothing less than that. A productivity and life-priority philosophy says that you should start doing something only if you can commit to doing it 100 times. If you want to start running, you should commit to running for at least 100 days. If you want to write a book, you should commit to at least 100 writing sessions. I'm not going to question or address this philosophy so much as adhere strictly to it. Thus, we'll create a tool for organizing doing something 100 times. You can do multiple things 100 times, of course.

Our inspiration comes from the aptly named website https://do100things.com, and in this project, we will create an application that looks somewhat like that website. I've already done that work and put it up at https://100.bingo for you. You can see the final product in figure 8.1.

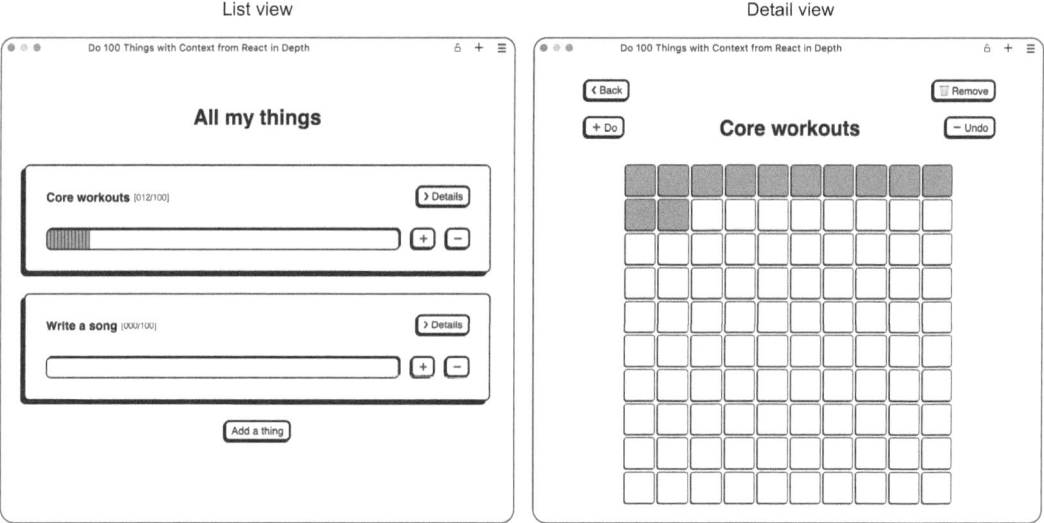

Figure 8.1   The final goal-tracking application. On the left, you see list view, where all the things are shown, and on the right, you see detail view for a single thing. We've been working on our six-packs and completed 12 sessions of core workouts. The songwriting career, however, isn't going too well.

As mentioned, I created the base application in an online repository, and we'll use all the components in this chapter. In the base repository, I created the application by using the basic `useState` hook. Using just this hook works, but it's not ideal.

In this chapter, I'll discuss how to manage this application's data by using the following methods:

- `useState` (+ context)
- `useReducer` (+ `useReduction`, `useContextSelector`, and Immer) and context
- RTK (+ Immer)
- zustand (+ Immer)
- XState (+ `xstate/react`) and context

8.2   *Building the application architecture*

We're building something rather simple, but because of styling (we're using styled-components), I've split it into tiny components to make getting an overview easier. From a top-down perspective, the application is structured with a presentation layer (called *things* because we're doing things in this application) and a data layer (called *data*). The application is bound together by the main `App` component, which includes the data provider on the outside and the presentation top-level component on the inside. You can see this overall structure in figure 8.2.

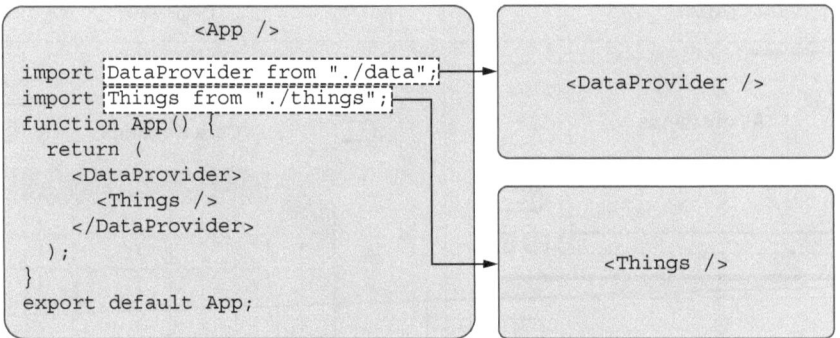

Figure 8.2   **The application architecture with the main application and the two parts. The top part on the right is the data layer, and the bottom part is the presentation layer. The app on the left is merely the glue that holds the whole thing together; it doesn't do anything.**

The structure of the data layer will vary with each implementation; it won't vary much, but we still have some wiggle room. The structure of the presentation layer, however, is fixed. We will use the same components with the same lines of codes in all the applications (with one notable exception in the XState variant in section 8.7.1.).

So let's see the structure of the presentation layer. First, we have two views to display: list view and single-item detail view. List view contains several things (literally) and a form for adding a new thing. Detail view has some buttons up top and a full grid of all the things you have done and must do. Figure 8.3 shows the conceptual structure.

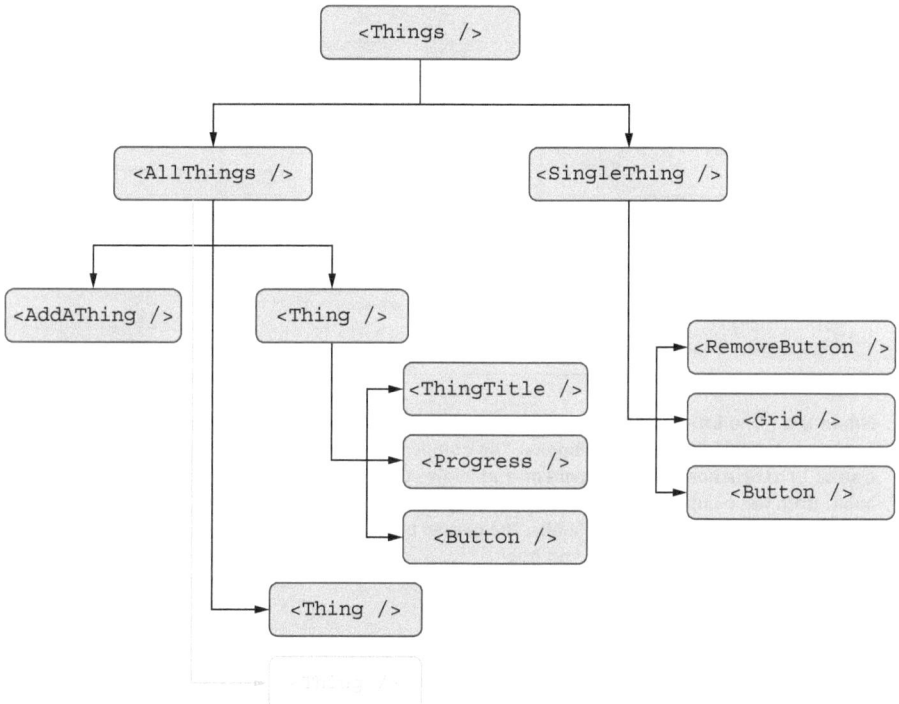

Figure 8.3   The conceptual structure of the presentation layer consists of a large number of components, with some being general purpose (such as Button, Grid, **and** Progress**) and others being application specific (such as** AllThings, ThingTitle, **and** RemoveButton**).**

The most interesting part is how these components interact with the data layer. There are four such interactions:

- The top-level Things component needs to know whether to display list view or detail view.
- The list view AllThings component needs to get an array of all the things.
- The AddAThing component needs to be able to add a thing to the data layer.
- The two components concerned with displaying a single thing—Thing and SingleThing—need to be able to get data for that thing and access some functions to interact with that thing.

We will create four custom hooks that expose a specific API to the presentation layer so that the relevant components can do their things. Figure 8.4 illustrates these interactions.

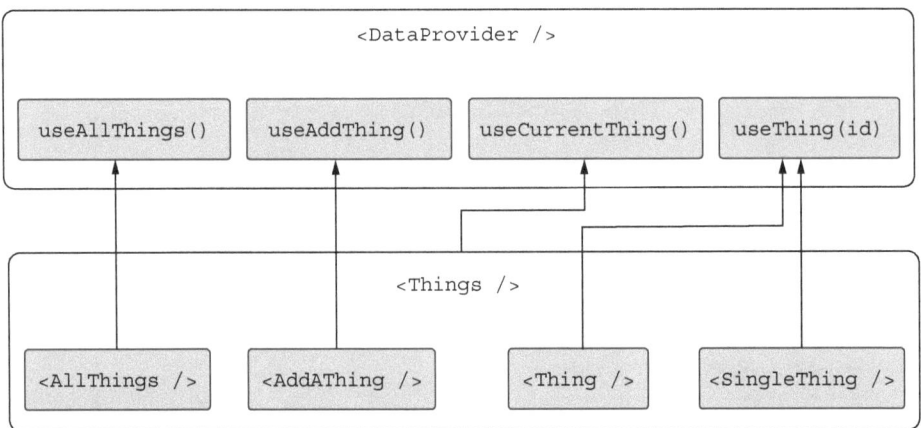

Figure 8.4 **The interactions between the presentation layer and the data layer happen in five components, using four custom hooks. The component that displays all things uses the useAllThings hook. The component that allows the user to add a thing uses the useAddThing hook. Both the component that displays a single thing and the component that displays a thing in a list use the useThing hook. Finally, the overall component that displays either a list or a single thing uses the useCurrentThing hook.**

We expect the following behavior from the four hooks:

- useCurrentThing must return either the id of the current single thing being displayed or null if the list is to be displayed.
- useAllThings must return an array of the ids of all the things in the order in which they were created.
- useAddThing must return a function that accepts a single parameter—the name of a thing to add—and should in turn add that thing to internal data storage.
- useThing is the most complex hook. It must return an object with the thing in question (the id of which is passed in as a parameter to the hook) and also functions for manipulating said thing: seeThing, seeAllThings, doThing, undoThing, undoLastThing, and removeThing.

The following list describes the latter functions in detail:

- seeThing()—Should store the id of the thing as the current thing (switching from list view to detail view for that thing)
- seeAllThings()—Should clear the id of the current thing (switching from detail view to list view).

- `doThing()`—Should append a new entry to the list of the number of times this particular thing has been done
- `undoThing(index)`—Should remove a specific entry (denoted by the index in the list) of the number of times this thing has been done
- `undoLastThing()`—Should remove the last entry in the list of the number of times this thing has been done
- `removeThing()`—Should remove the entire thing and switch to list view if this thing was the current thing

We've built the presentation layer around this simple API. Many of the components are dumb and present only what they've been told to present via props, but a few use this limited API to tap into the data layer to show or manipulate data. Our main obligation from here on out is to create the data layer and make sure that each implementation exports its data and functions according to this API.

One final requirement for the data layer is that we want data to be persisted locally on the computer displaying the application. So if you reload the page, all your data and state are kept intact, including remembering whether you're in list view or detail view. We're adding this requirement because

- It makes the application feel more real because you can reload and your data will still be there.
- It challenges the data layer to come with a built-in solution.

We'll see how the five methods stack up against one another regarding this requirement as well.

8.3   Managing data in pure React

We already know that we can manage data by using `useState` and distribute it throughout our application by using context. In this application, we need two different data items—a list of things and a current thing—so we're going to use the `useState` hook twice. We're also going to need some functions for manipulating the data, which will be wrappers for our state setters.

8.3.1   Context

We're going to shove all this code into a context by using the Provider pattern from chapter 2. Then we can retrieve the relevant data items and data manipulation functions as needed, using the `useContext` hook. Figure 8.5 is a rough outline of how this process is going to work.

What's left is creating all the actions, which are wrappers of `setThings` and `setCurrentThing` as appropriate according to the specifications. When it comes to persisting state to local storage, we have to do that work ourselves. Fortunately, writing data is fairly easy, and `useEffect` is the perfect tool. Whenever the state changes, we persist it to local storage. Reading data is even easier: we initialize the two `useStates` based on local storage data if they exist or reasonable defaults if they don't exist.

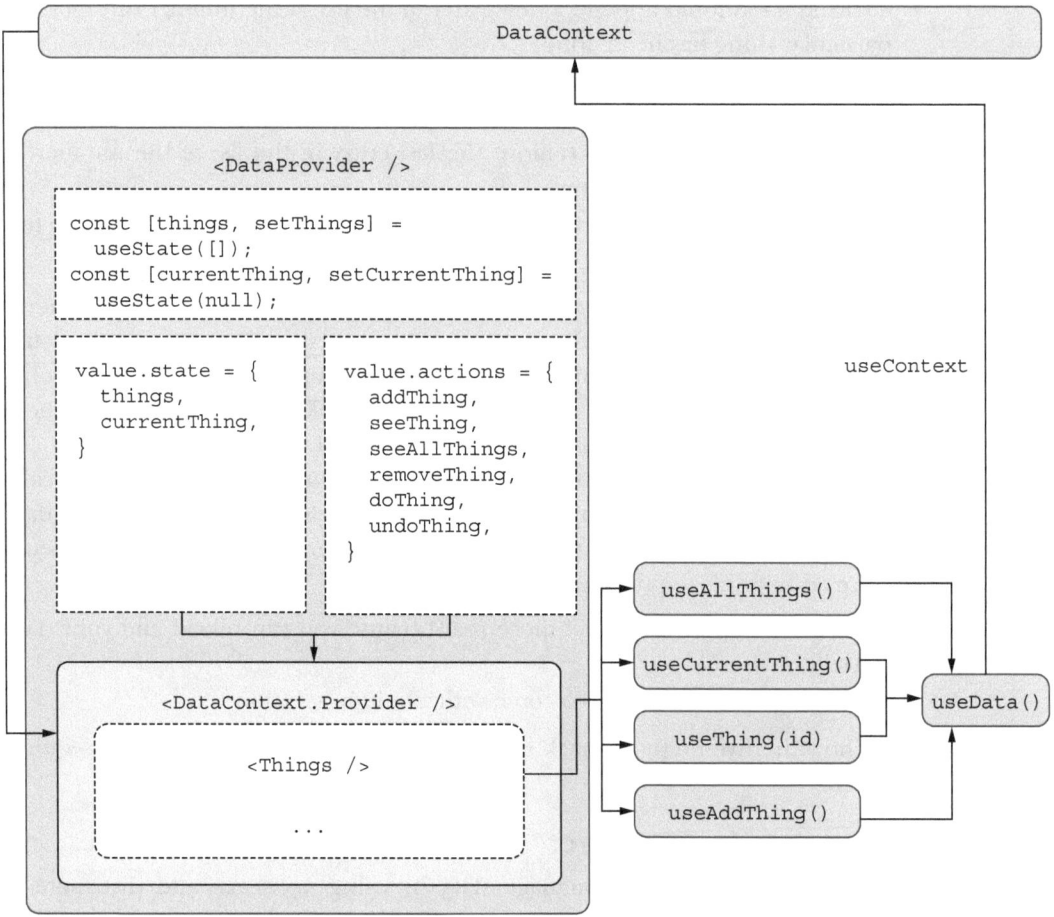

Figure 8.5 We wrap the entire application in a context with the relevant content, and we extract that content by using our custom hooks from said context. The dotted component represents the entire presentation layer, which uses the four hooks. The four hooks in turn use the `useData` hook, consuming the context via `useContext`.

8.3.2   Source code

We have eight files in the data structure, including the index file, but only two files contain anything of significance, and one of them is tiny. All the data storage and manipulation happens in `DataProvider.jsx`, and retrieving data or functions from the context happens in `useData.js`, which is a trivially simple file.

> **Example: context**
>
> This example is in the `context` folder. You can use that example by running this command in the source folder:
>
> ```
> $ npm run dev -w ch08/context
> ```

Alternatively, you can go to this website to browse the code, see the example in action in your browser, or download the source code as a zip file: https://reactlikea .pro/ch08-context.

DATAPROVIDER.JSX

The data provider is the heart of the application, as it both contains and distributes the state to whomever needs it, as well as defines functions that allow components to manipulate the state as needed. See figure 8.6 and listing 8.1.

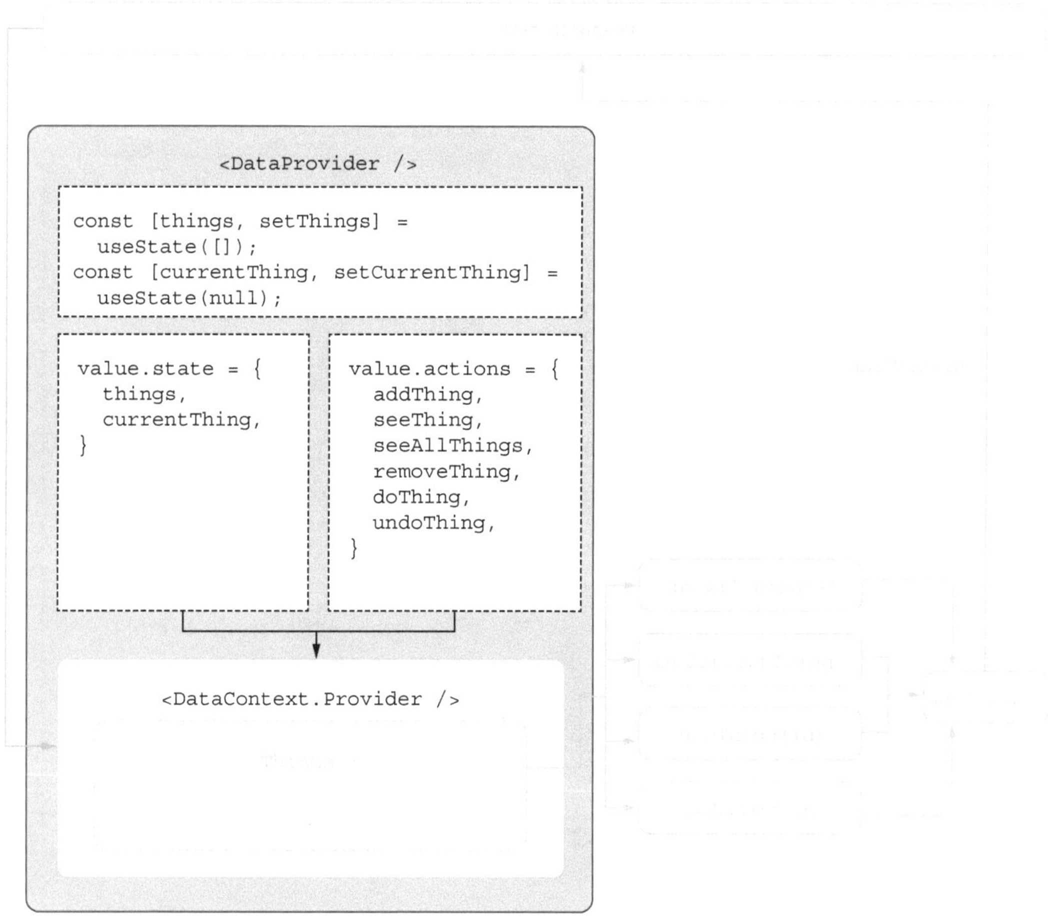

```
                        <DataProvider />
  ┌─────────────────────────────────────────────────┐
  │ const [things, setThings] =                      │
  │   useState([]);                                  │
  │ const [currentThing, setCurrentThing] =          │
  │   useState(null);                                │
  └─────────────────────────────────────────────────┘

  ┌──────────────────────┐ ┌──────────────────────────┐
  │ value.state = {      │ │ value.actions = {        │
  │   things,            │ │     addThing,            │
  │   currentThing,      │ │     seeThing,            │
  │ }                    │ │     seeAllThings,        │
  │                      │ │     removeThing,         │
  │                      │ │     doThing,             │
  │                      │ │     undoThing,           │
  │                      │ │ }                        │
  └──────────────────────┘ └──────────────────────────┘

              <DataContext.Provider />
```

Figure 8.6   The data provider highlighted

Listing 8.1   src/data/DataProvider.jsx

```
import { useState, useCallback, useEffect } from "react";
import { v4 as uuid } from "uuid";
```

```
import { DataContext } from "./DataContext";
const STORAGE_KEY = "100-things-context";
const INITIAL_STATE =
  JSON.parse(
    localStorage.getItem(STORAGE_KEY)
  ) ||
    { things: [], currentThing: null };
export function DataProvider({ children }) {
  const [things, setThings] =
    useState(INITIAL_STATE.things);
  const [currentThing, setCurrentThing] =
    useState(INITIAL_STATE.currentThing);
    useEffect(
      () =>
        localStorage.setItem(
          STORAGE_KEY,
          JSON.stringify({ things, currentThing })
        ),
      [things, currentThing]
  );
  const addThing = useCallback(
    (name) =>
      setThings((ts) => ts.concat([{ id: uuid(), name, done: [] }])),
    []
  );
  const seeThing = setCurrentThing;
  const seeAllThings = useCallback(
    () => setCurrentThing(null),
    []
  );
  const removeThing = useCallback((id) => {
    setThings((ts) => ts.filter((t) => t.id !== id));
    setCurrentThing((cur) => (cur === id ? null : cur));
  }, []);
  const editThing = useCallback(
    (id, cb) =>
      setThings((ts) =>
        ts.map((t) => (t.id === id ? { ...t, done: cb(t.done) } : t))
      ),
    []
  );
  const doThing = useCallback(
    (id) => editThing(id, (done) => done.concat(Date.now())),
    [editThing]
  );
  const undoThing = useCallback(
    (id, index) =>
      editThing(id, (done) =>
        done.slice(0, index).concat(done.slice(index + 1))
      ),
    [editThing]
  );
  const value = {
    state: {
      things,
```

First, we load the previous state of the system from local storage if it exists.

Then, we create the two data values, using useState with the defaults.

In an effect in useEffect, we persist any change to either state value to local storage.

The six data manipulation functions are carefully crafted wrappers of the two state setter functions, setThings and setCurrentThing.

Finally, we put all the state and functions inside the context, which we wrap around the rest of the application.

```
      currentThing,
    },
    actions: {
      addThing,
      seeThing,
      seeAllThings,
      doThing,
      undoThing,
      removeThing,
    },
  };
  return (
    <DataContext.Provider value={value}>
      {children}
    </DataContext.Provider>
  );
}
```

Finally, we put all the state and functions inside the context, which we wrap around the rest of the application.

USEDATA.JS

This hook feeds the other hooks that require values from the context (figure 8.7 and listing 8.2).

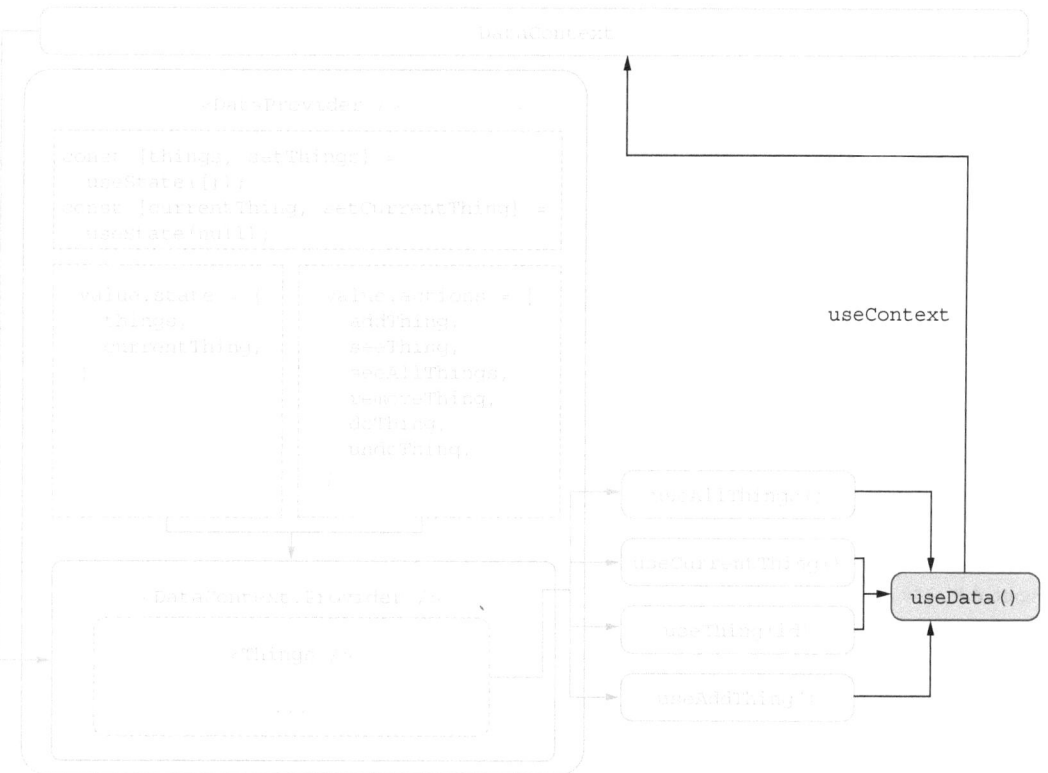

Figure 8.7 The useData hook highlighted

Listing 8.2 `src/data/useData.js`

```
import { useContext } from "react";
import { DataContext } from "./DataContext";
export function useData() {
  return useContext(DataContext);
}
```

> In this version, we retrieve the entire context, which also means that any component using this hook will re-render any time anything inside the state changes.

DATACONTEXT.JS

This file is the plain context, implemented with React's built-in method (figure 8.8 and listing 8.3).

Figure 8.8 The data context highlighted

Listing 8.3 `src/data/DataContext.js`

```
import { createContext } from "react";
export const DataContext =
  createContext({ state: {}, actions: {} });
```

> The default context contains no state values or functions.

USEALLTHINGS.JS

When we need to display all the things in our presentation component, we use this hook to extract them from the context (figure 8.9 and listing 8.4).

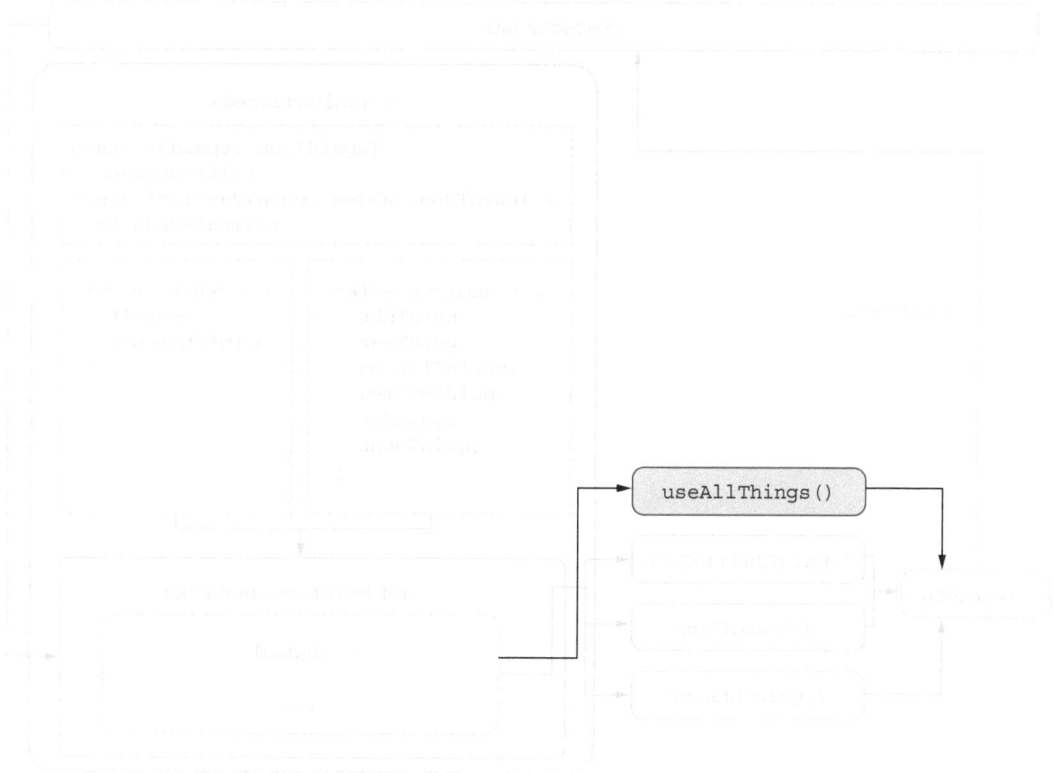

Figure 8.9 The `useAllThings` hook highlighted

Listing 8.4 `src/data/useAllThings.js`

```
import { useData } from "./useData";
export function useAllThings() {
  return useData().state.things
    .map(({ id }) => id);
}
```

| Per specification, useAllThings must return an array of ids only, so we map the existing things to get only that property.

USETHING.JS

When we want to interact with a single thing in the presentation layer, we go through the useThing hook, passing it the id of the thing in question (figure 8.10 and listing 8.5).

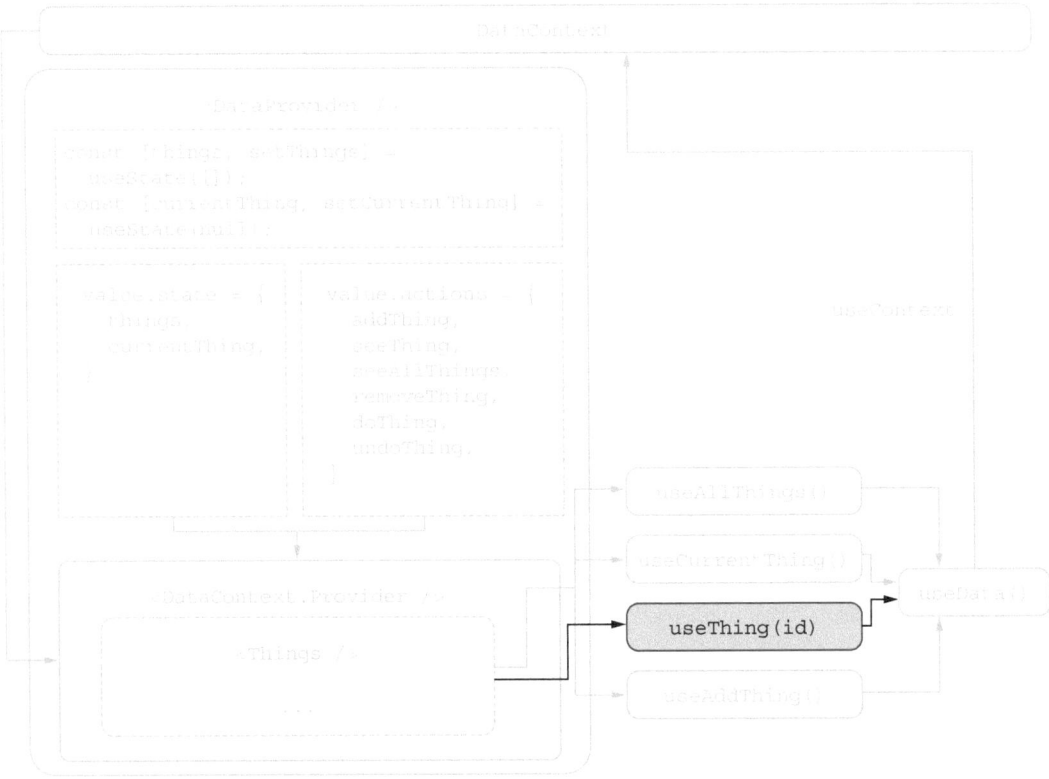

Figure 8.10   The `useThing` hook highlighted

Listing 8.5   `src/data/useThing.js`

```
import { useData } from "./useData";
export function useThing(id) {
  const {
    state: { things },
    actions: {
      seeThing,
      seeAllThings,
      doThing,
      undoThing,
      removeThing,
    },
  } = useData();
  const thing = things.find((t) => t.id === id);
  return {
    thing,
    seeAllThings,
    seeThing: () => seeThing(id),
    removeThing: () => removeThing(id),
    doThing: () => doThing(id),
```

`useThing` is the most complex hook, where we have to retrieve the list of things and almost all the functions from the context.

Returns the relevant thing from the entire array

We specialize these five functions with respect to the passed id and return them as specified.

```
    undoThing: (index) => undoThing(id, index),
    undoLastThing:
      () => undoThing(id, thing.done.length - 1),
  };
}
```

△ **We specialize these five functions with respect to the passed id and return them as specified.**

USEADDTHING.JS

Adding a new thing requires invoking the right callback from the context (figure 8.11 and listing 8.6).

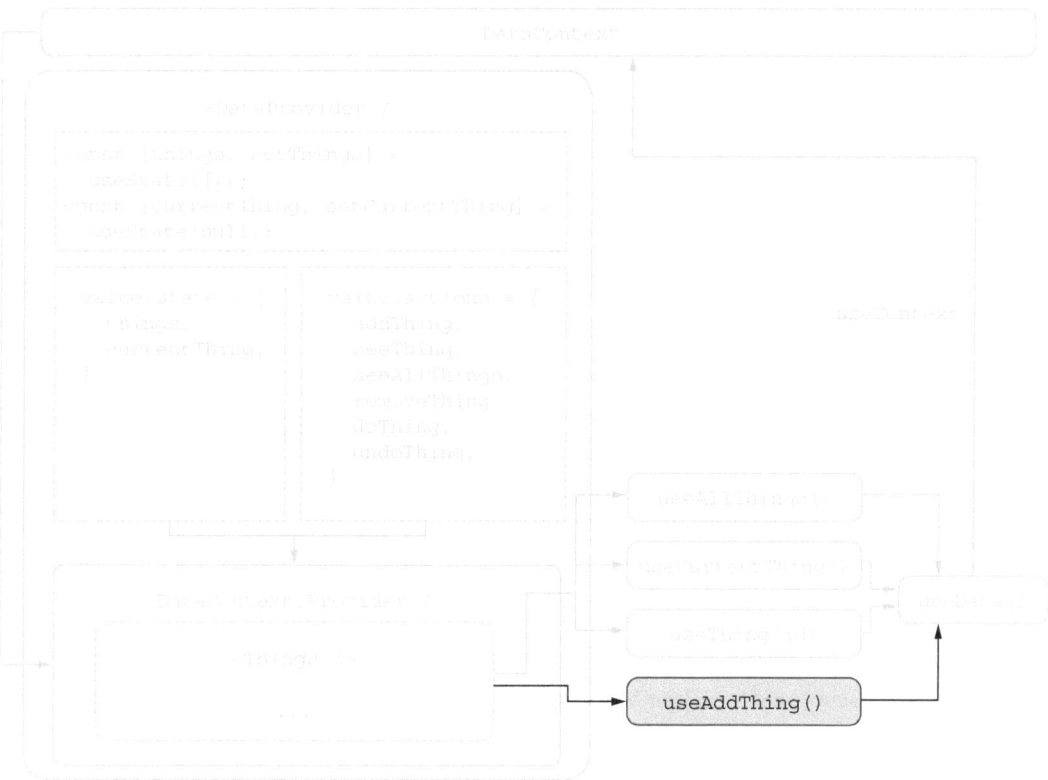

Figure 8.11 The `useAddThing` **hook highlighted**

Listing 8.6 `src/data/useAddThing.js`

```
import { useData } from "./useData";
export function useAddThing() {
  return useData().actions.addThing;
}
```

◁── **This hook returns a single function from the context.**

USECURRENTTHING.JS

To determine whether we're displaying list view or detail view, we have this hook to return the id of the current thing or `null` if nothing is currently selected (figure 8.12 and listing 8.7).

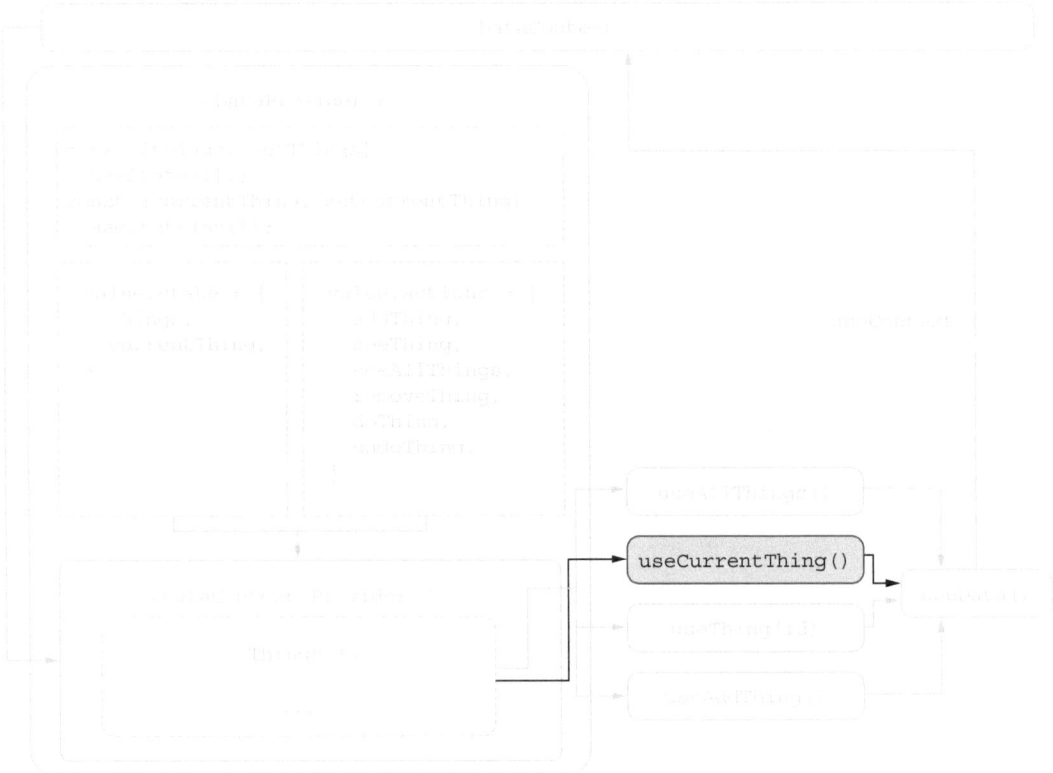

Figure 8.12   The `useCurrentThing` **hook highlighted**

Listing 8.7   `src/data/useCurrentThing.js`

```
import { useData } from "./useData";
export function useCurrentThing() {
  return useData().state.currentThing;
}
```

◁— **Likewise, this hook returns a single state value from the context.**

INDEX.JS

This file exports all the externally accessible parts of the data package, as shown in the following listing.

Listing 8.8   `src/data/index.js`

```
export { DataProvider } from "./DataProvider";
export { useAddThing } from "./useAddThing";
export { useAllThings } from "./useAllThings";
export { useThing } from "./useThing";
export { useCurrentThing } from "./useCurrentThing";
```

8.4   *Reducing data state*

The code in the `DataProvider` in listing 8.1 is a bit messy and spaghetti-like. It can be hard to follow the logic, and it tends to be hard to maintain code like that in the long run. But we've already seen a better way to maintain complex state in chapter 2: the Provider pattern. We're also going to use three external libraries, one of which was also introduced in chapter 2:

- `useReduction`—Allows us to write reducers in React with less boilerplate
- `useContextSelector`—Consumes partial contexts, minimizing re-renders
- *Immer*—Allows us to write immutable code without all the hassle

To get an idea of the overall structure compared with the implementation using `useState` (figure 8.5), see figure 8.13.

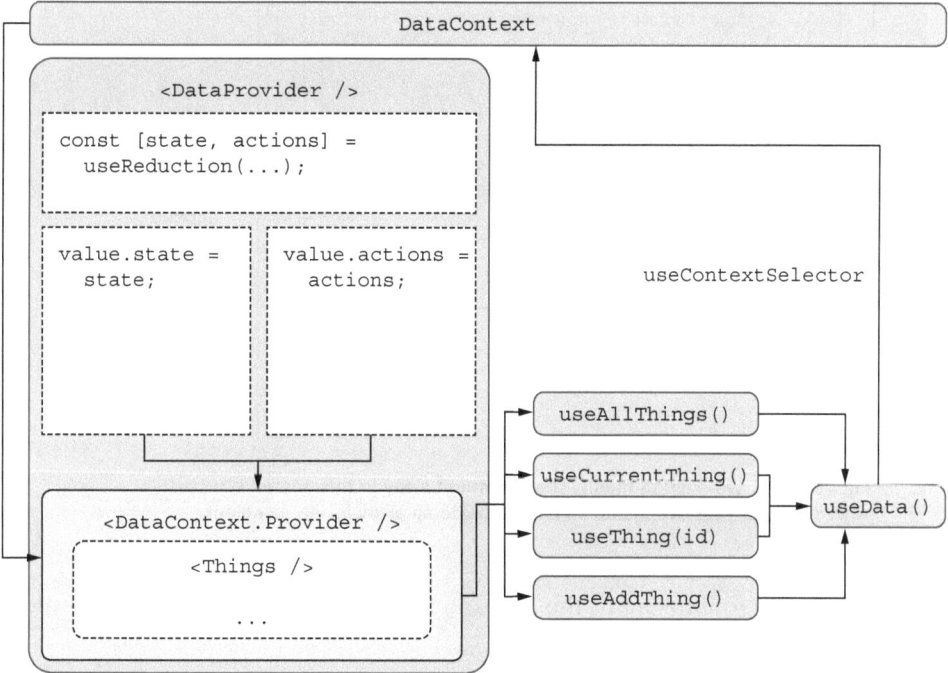

Figure 8.13   The provider and context are used in the same fashion now, but defining the state and the actions is a lot simpler with the `useReduction` package. We also get better performance when we use `useContextSelector` to write the hooks.

8.4.1   Immer: Writing immutable code mutably

In this application, we need to create a reducer that, among other things, handles the `doThing` action. This action takes an `id` of the thing to do and appends a new entry to that thing's list of the number of times this has been done. You can see the structure of the state and what we need to do in figure 8.14.

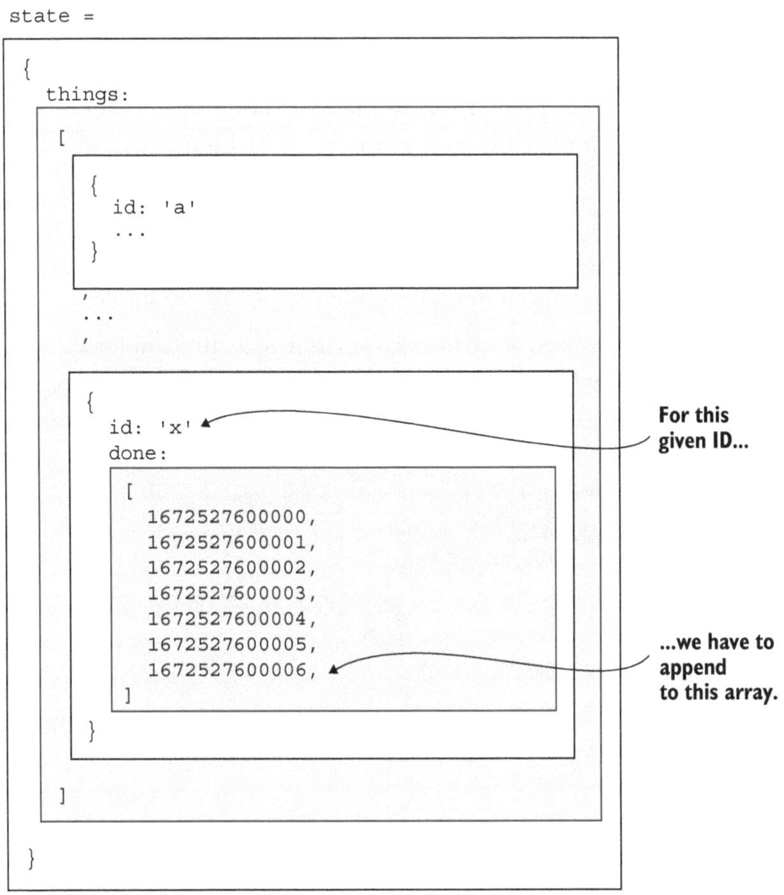

Figure 8.14   We need to modify the innermost array in this nested structure, where the array resides inside an object inside an array inside an object.

If we were to implement the `doThing` function as mutable code, we would do something like this:

```
doThing: (state, {payload: id}) => {
  const thing = state.things.find((thing) => thing.id === id);
  thing.done.push(Date.now());
}
```

Because we're writing an immutable reducer, however, we cannot mutate an array or an object directly, and in the preceding code, we're mutating a nested array directly. Instead, we have to create and use a new array. But because the array exists inside an object, we also have to create a new object, and because that object exists inside another array, we have to create yet another array, which again is inside another object. So this same code in immutable land looks like this:

```
doThing: (state, {payload: id}) => {
  const thingIndex = state.things.findIndex((thing) => thing.id === id);
  const thing = state.things[thingIndex];
  const newThing = {
    ...thing,
    done: thing.done.concat([Date.now()])
  };
  const newThings = [
    ...state.things.slice(0, thingIndex),
    newThing,
    ...state.things.slice(thingIndex + 1),
  ];
  return {...state, things: newThings};
}
```

> We create a copy of the object with a copy of the array with an extra item appended.

> We put the copy of the object inside a copy of the things array in place of the old one.

> Finally, we put the things array inside a copy of the state object.

That's a lot of code compared with the mutable alternative. What if we could get the best of both worlds—write code in the simplest way possible as mutable code but still get the benefits of immutability? That's exactly what Immer does. It allows you to mutate a proxy object directly, and it "plays back" your mutations as immutable alterations of the original object. The process sounds complex, and is (using some sheer JavaScript magic), but all we need to care about is the fact that it works. With the `produce()` function from Immer, we can write an immutable reducer like so:

> We wrap the function in produce() and accept a draft argument. We use the variable draft to denote that this object is not the actual state object, but a proxy for it that we are allowed to change directly.

```
import produce from 'immer';
...
doThing: produce(((draft, {payload: id}) => {
  const thing = draft.things.find((thing) => thing.id === id);
  thing.done.push(Date.now());
})
```

> We mutate the draft and any objects inside it directly.

I must admit that even I don't fully understand how Immer works on the inside. It uses some kind of proxy object combined with setters and getters to record all the changes being made to the draft object and repeats these changes to the actual state object immutably. To be honest, Immer is kind of like dark matter in the sense that it clearly exists, but we don't know how. Well, I don't, but I guess some very clever people do.

8.4.2   *Source code*

The structure is almost identical to the version from section 8.3.1, with the same eight files. A lot of those files are different, however, because now we can use the added capabilities we get from using external libraries, making both the application and the code leaner and more efficient. Once again, we need to persist the data manually. But this time, we already have a combined state object, so we serialize that object in and out of local storage without too much hassle.

> **Example: reducer**
>
> This example is in the `reducer` folder. You can use that example by running this command in the source folder:
>
> `$ npm run dev -w ch08/reducer`
>
> Alternatively, you can go to this website to browse the code, see the example in action in your browser, or download the source code as a zip file: https://reactlikea .pro/ch08-reducer.

DATAPROVIDER.JSX

The data provider has the same responsibility as before, but this time, we use a reducer rather than pure `useState` hooks. Otherwise, we expose the same data and callbacks.

Listing 8.9   `src/data/DataProvider.jsx`

```
import { useEffect } from "react";
import { v4 as uuid } from "uuid";
import { produce } from "immer";
import useReduction from "use-reduction";
import { DataContext } from "./DataContext";
const STORAGE_KEY = "100-things-reducer";
const INITIAL_STATE = JSON.parse(localStorage.getItem(STORAGE_KEY)) || {
  things: [],
  currentThing: null,
};
const reducers = {
  seeThing: produce(
    (draft, { payload: newThing }) => {
      draft.currentThing = newThing;
    }
  ),
  seeAllThings: produce((draft) => {
    draft.currentThing = null;
  }),
  addThing: produce(
    (draft, { payload: name }) => {
      draft.things.push({ id: uuid(), name, done: [] });
    }
  ),
  removeThing: produce(
    (draft, { payload: id }) => {
      const index = draft.things.findIndex((thing) => thing.id === id);
      if (index !== -1) {
        draft.things.splice(index, 1);
```

This time, we're creating all the data manipulation functions as reducers, using Immer's produce() function.

```
          if (id === draft.currentThing) {
            draft.currentThing = null;
          }
        }
      }
    ),
    doThing: produce(
      (draft, { payload: id }) => {
        const thing = draft.things.find((thing) => thing.id === id);
        thing.done.push(Date.now());
      }
    ),
    undoThing: produce(
      (draft, { payload: { id, index } }) => {
        const thing = draft.things.find((thing) => thing.id === id);
        thing.done.splice(index, 1);
      }
    ),
};
export function DataProvider({ children }) {
  const [state, actions] = useReduction(INITIAL_STATE, reducers);
  useEffect(
    () => localStorage.setItem(STORAGE_KEY, JSON.stringify(state)),
    [state]
  );
  const value = { state, actions };
  return (
    <DataContext.Provider value={value}>
      {children}
    </DataContext.Provider>
  );
}
```

This time, we're creating all the data manipulation functions as reducers, using Immer's produce() function.

USEDATA.JS

We still have this intermediate hook to access values in the context, but this time, we use the useContext hook from the useContextSelector library.

Listing 8.10 src/data/useData.js

```
import { useContextSelector } from "use-context-selector";
import { DataContext } from "./DataContext";
export function useData(selector) {
  return useContextSelector(
    DataContext,
    selector,
  );
}
```

Accessing the context via a selector for improved performance

DATACONTEXT.JS

Similarly, we have to define the context by using the useContextSelector library, as shown in the following listing.

Listing 8.11 `src/data/DataContext.js`

```
import {
  createContext,
} from "use-context-selector";
export const DataContext = createContext({});
```

> Here, we remember to create the context by using the createContext function from the third-party library, not the default one in React itself.

USEALLTHINGS.JS

Accessing values from the context is much cleaner when we use a selector.

Listing 8.12 `src/data/useAllThings.js`

```
import { useData } from "./useData";
export function useAllThings() {
  return useData( ({ state }) => state.things)
    .map(({ id }) => id);
}
```

> We select the array as is inside the selector and manipulate it outside for optimization reasons. If the array doesn't change, doing it this way doesn't cause a re-render. If we did the mapping inside the selector, we would always generate a new array, so we would always re-render.

USETHING.JS

When we need to access multiple values from the context, we can do so in separate calls to the `useData` hook.

Listing 8.13 `src/data/useThing.js`

```
import { useData } from "./useData";
export function useThing(id) {
  const thing = useData(({ state }) =>
    state.things.find((t) => t.id === id)
  );
  const {
    seeThing,
    seeAllThings,
    doThing,
    undoThing,
    removeThing,
  } = useData(({ actions }) => actions);
  return {
    thing,
    seeAllThings,
    seeThing: () => seeThing(id),
    removeThing: () => removeThing(id),
    doThing: () => doThing(id),
    undoThing: (index) => undoThing({ id, index }),
    undoLastThing: () =>
```

> Because we can select only one thing at a time by using the default selector function, we split the selector into two parts. Remember that the whole actions object can be considered stable, as it is returned in full by the reducer hook.

```
        undoThing({ id, index: thing.done.length - 1 }),
    };
}
```

USEADDTHING.JS

This file is another simple value retrieval from the context.

Listing 8.14   `src/data/useAddThing.js`

```
import { useData } from "./useData";
export function useAddThing() {
  return useData(({ actions }) => actions.addThing);
}
```

USECURRENTTHING.JS

This file is yet another simple value retrieval from the context.

Listing 8.15   `src/data/useCurrentThing.js`

```
import { useData } from "./useData";
export function useCurrentThing() {
  return useData(({ state }) => state.currentThing);
}
```

INDEX.JS

This file is identical to the first iteration.

Listing 8.16   `src/data/index.js`

```
export { DataProvider } from "./DataProvider";
export { useAddThing } from "./useAddThing";
export { useAllThings } from "./useAllThings";
export { useThing } from "./useThing";
export { useCurrentThing } from "./useCurrentThing";
```

8.5   *Scaling data management with Redux Toolkit*

Because we know how the React hook `useReducer` works, we already know how Redux works. Redux is the source of the `useReducer` functionality and came long before hooks were ever conceived of. Originally, Redux was rather boilerplate heavy, and creating a simple application with a Redux store often required creating a ton of configuration and functions that were almost trivial. For all the trivial cases, Redux comes in a much more compact edition known as RTK, which works almost exactly like `useReduction`, which we've just seen in section 8.4. `useReduction` is also based on how RTK works. So although we haven't used Redux in this book, we've used tools based on it, so we can get started easily.

8.5.1   How does Redux work?

To understand Redux, it's important to understand the Redux cycle. Redux has a store with reducers that are invoked from action creators dispatching actions. You can see the cycle depicted in figure 8.15.

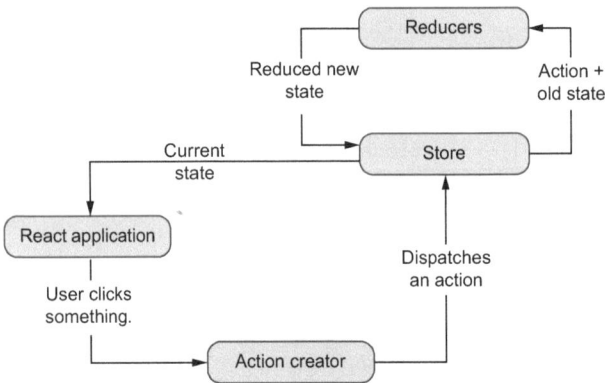

Figure 8.15   The simplified Redux cycle. State is kept in the store. The state defines how the application is rendered. When the user interacts with the application, actions are dispatched, and the store sends them to the relevant reducer along with the old state. The newly reduced state is updated in the store and sent back to the application, and the cycle repeats.

In classic Redux, you define action creators, actions, and reducers separately; in RTK, you define them all at the same time. So if you define a reducer named `increment`, you automatically get an action creator named `increment()`, which dispatches an action that invokes that reducer.

The Redux store is split into slices. Each slice consists of its own reducers, actions, and action creators. What makes up a slice is a decision made by the developer. Normally, we put related items in the same slice. If we added a menu that could be opened and a dark mode toggle, we could put those values in a `ui` slice. If we added authentication, we could put user data and login status in an `auth` slice. For this application, we have only a single slice of data, so we will call that slice `data`.

When we apply the Redux methodology to our data layer, we get what you see in figure 8.16. Redux comes with its own provider (which internally uses a React context), so we do not need to create our own context. Redux also comes with its own selector hook, `useSelector`, so we don't need to use the `useContextSelector` module.

NOTE   To be honest, Redux is basically the same as context + `useReduction` + `useContextSelector`.

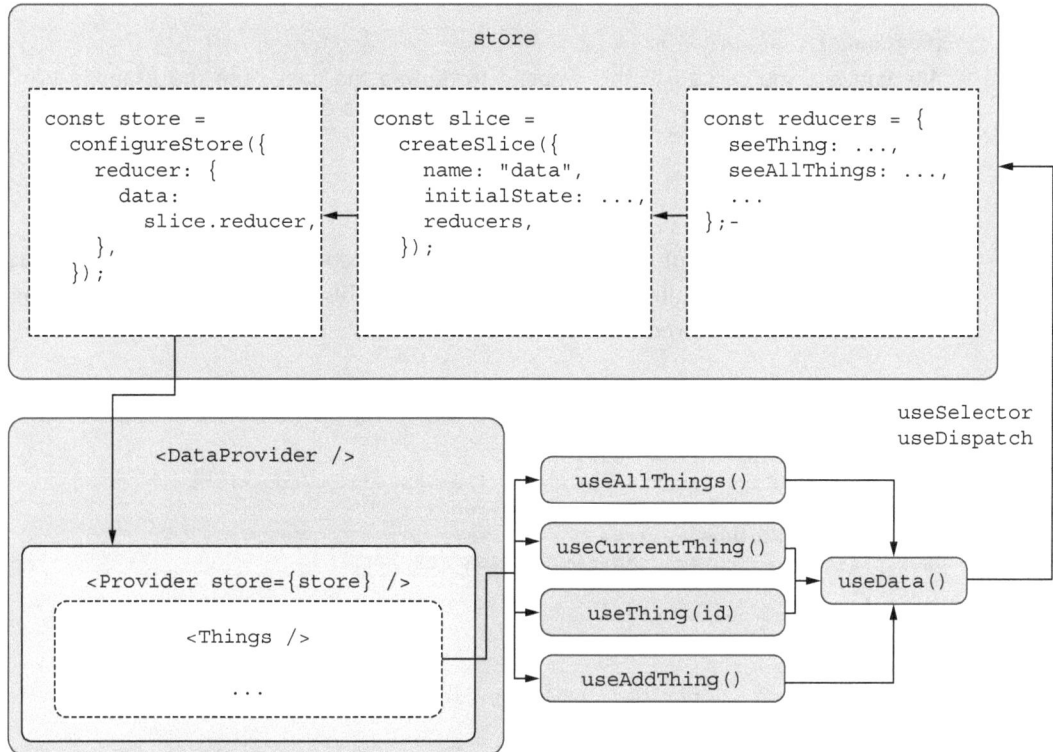

Figure 8.16   The data layer looks like this when we use Redux. Redux comes with a built-in provider, and `useSelector` and `useDispatch` hooks, which we'll use in our four main hooks to read and update state, respectively.

8.5.2   Source code

RTK has Immer built into its reducers, so we can more or less copy and paste the reducers from the previous implementation, as they are essentially identical and work the same way. To read the persisted state, we need to read the state from local storage manually as we define the slice of data. To write state, we need to listen for updates to the store, using the aptly named method `store.subscribe`, which takes a callback that triggers every time anything inside the store updates. Listing 8.18 shows how we can use this function to store the state.

> **Example: redux**
>
> This example is in the `redux` folder. You can use that example by running this command in the source folder:
>
> ```
> $ npm run dev -w ch08/redux
> ```

(continued)

Alternatively, you can go to this website to browse the code, see the example in action in your browser, or download the source code as a zip file: https://reactlikea .pro/ch08-redux.

STORE.JS

The store is the central hub for this application—where we define the main reducer, which manipulates the state as required. Note that this process is similar to using `useReduction` to create a reducer.

Listing 8.17 `src/data/store.js`

```javascript
import { v4 as uuid } from "uuid";
import { createSlice, configureStore } from "@reduxjs/toolkit";
export const STORAGE_KEY = "100-things-redux";
const getInitialThings = () =>
  JSON.parse(localStorage.getItem(STORAGE_KEY)) || {
    things: [],
    currentThing: null,
  };
const reducers = {
  seeThing: (draft, { payload: newThing }) => {
    draft.currentThing = newThing;
  },
  seeAllThings: (draft) => {
    draft.currentThing = null;
  },
  addThing: (draft, { payload: name }) => {
    draft.things.push({ id: uuid(), name, done: [] });
  },
  removeThing: (draft, { payload: id }) => {
    const index = draft.things.findIndex((thing) => thing.id === id);
    if (index !== -1) {
      draft.things.splice(index, 1);
      if (id === draft.currentThing) {
        draft.currentThing = null;
      }
    }
  },
  doThing: (draft, { payload: id }) => {
    const thing = draft.things.find((thing) => thing.id === id);
    thing.done.push(Date.now());
  },
  undoThing:
    (draft, { payload: { id, index } }) => {
      const thing = draft.things.find((thing) => thing.id === id);
      thing.done.splice(index, 1);
    },
};
const dataSlice = createSlice({
```

> We create the reducers' mutating state without a worry because we know that they will be wrapped with Immer.

> The reducers are passed into our main slice, which also has a name and an initial value loaded from local storage.

```
  name: "data",
  initialState: getInitialThings(),
  reducers,
});
```

> That slice is passed to our store, which is exported for the data provider.

```
export const store = configureStore({
  reducer: {
    data: dataSlice.reducer,
  },
});
export const actions = dataSlice.actions;
```

> Finally, we also export the actions as defined in our slice.

DATAPROVIDER.JSX

The data provider doesn't have to do anything in this iteration except provide the store from Redux. Because we also need to persist the state to local storage, however, we do that here.

Listing 8.18   `src/data/DataProvider.jsx`

```
import { useEffect } from "react";
import { store, STORAGE_KEY } from "./store";
import { Provider } from "react-redux";
export function DataProvider({ children }) {
  useEffect(
    () =>
      store.subscribe(() =>
        localStorage.setItem(
          STORAGE_KEY,
          JSON.stringify(store.getState().data)
        )
      ),
    []
  );
  return (
    <Provider store={store}>
      {children}
    </Provider>
  );
}
```

> We use the provider given to us by the react-redux package, which is a wrapper for a regular React context provider.

> To persist data on change to local storage, we subscribe to the store. Note that this subscribe method returns an unsubscribe function, which the effect also returns, so it will clean up after itself.

> We put the store and the provider together surrounding the entire application.

USEDATA.JS

To read data from the store, we use the Redux selector hook.

Listing 8.19   `src/data/useData.js`

```
import { useSelector } from "react-redux";
export function useData(selector) {
  return useSelector(selector);
}
```

> Redux comes with its own selector function, so we use that function.

USEALLTHINGS.JS

This file retrieves a single value from the store.

Listing 8.20   `src/data/useAllThings.js`

```
import { useData } from "./useData";
export function useAllThings() {
  return useData((store) => store.data.things)      ◁─┐  The important thing to
    .map(({ id }) => id);                              │  remember here is that we
}                                                      │  read our values from the data
                                                       │  slice of the store; thus, we
                                                       │  need to access store.data.
```

USETHING.JS

Here, we need to access data from the store and dispatch actions to the store.

Listing 8.21   `src/data/useThing.js`

```
import { useData } from "./useData";
import { actions } from "./store";
import { useDispatch } from "react-redux";
export function useThing(id) {
  const thing = useData((store) =>
    store.data.things.find((t) => t.id === id)
  );
  const dispatch = useDispatch();          ◁─┐
  return {
    thing,
    seeThing: () => dispatch(actions.seeThing(id)),
    removeThing: () => dispatch(actions.removeThing(id)),
    doThing: () => dispatch(actions.doThing(id)),
    seeAllThings: () => dispatch(actions.seeAllThings()),
    undoThing: (index) => dispatch(actions.undoThing({ id, index })),
    undoLastThing: () =>
      dispatch(actions.undoThing({ id, index: thing.done.length - 1 })),
  };
}
```

The only thing new here is that to dispatch an action, we need the dispatch function from Redux, which needs access to the provider, so it has to be retrieved from a hook.

USEADDTHING.JS

We need the dispatch method to create the correct action.

Listing 8.22   `src/data/useAddThing.js`

```
import { actions } from "./store";
import { useDispatch } from "react-redux";
export function useAddThing() {
  const dispatch = useDispatch();
  return (name) => dispatch(actions.addThing(name));
}
```

USECURRENTTHING.JS

This file retrieves a single value from the store.

```
Listing 8.23   src/data/useCurrentThing.js
```

```
import { useData } from "./useData";
export function useCurrentThing() {
  return useData((store) => store.data.currentThing);
}
```

INDEX.JS

This file is identical to the last version.

```
Listing 8.24   src/data/index.js
```

```
export { DataProvider } from "./DataProvider";
export { useAddThing } from "./useAddThing";
export { useAllThings } from "./useAllThings";
export { useThing } from "./useThing";
export { useCurrentThing } from "./useCurrentThing";
```

8.6 *Simplifying data management with zustand*

To make the reducer-based variant in section 8.4 work, we needed five things:

- The reducer functions
- A hook to generate new state when actions are dispatched to the reducer (`useReducer` or `useReduction`)
- A context to hold the state and actions
- A context provider to distribute the data
- A context consumer hook to read the state and retrieve the actions from (`use-Context` or `useContextSelector`)

Suppose that we take away the last three items in the preceding list, leaving only the reducer functions and the main reducer hook. That list would be zustand in a nutshell.

8.6.1 *Zustand*

Zustand comes with a single function, `create()`, which returns a hook that we can use wherever we want. No matter where we use the hook, it works on the same state and contains the same actions reducing said state. If we take away all the context bits and have only a single hook, `useData`, that we create with the zustand API, what we have left is the super-simplified data layer in figure 8.17.

Zustand even comes bundled with Immer, but you don't have to use it. Using Immer in zustand, we apply it as middleware, which means that we don't need to curry each function with `produce()`. We say that the entire reducer object is using Immer-style reducers, and they will be wrapped correctly.

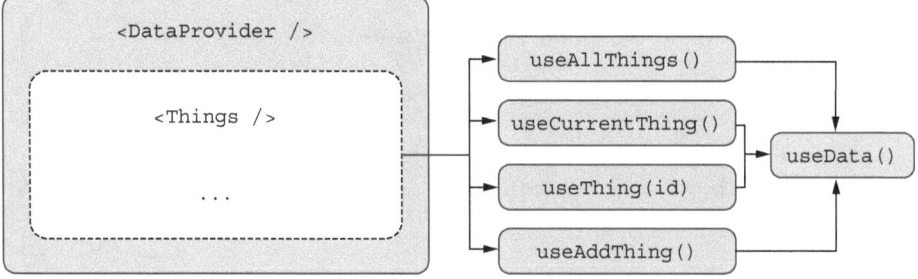

Figure 8.17   With zustand, the data layer becomes extra simple. We have only a single hook that all our hooks go through. There's no context to provide or consume; the state lives inside the hook no matter where we use it. I've displayed the data provider with a dashed outline because it doesn't do anything anymore. I keep it there only because it makes this variant comparable to the others.

8.6.2   Source code

We have only seven files this time, but we still have four public hooks and an index file. The provider does nothing (but we include it so that the data layer API is identical to the other examples), and everything happens in the `useData` hook.

Finally, we need to tackle how to persist the data to local storage. But zustand has even that capability built in, so we can use the `persist()` function from the zustand middleware library and pass our reducer into that function with the relevant storage key.

> **Example: zustand**
>
> This example is in the `zustand` folder. You can use that example by running this command in the source folder:
>
> ```
> $ npm run dev -w ch08/zustand
> ```
>
> Alternatively, you can go to this website to browse the code, see the example in action in your browser, or download the source code as a zip file: https://reactlikea.pro/ch08-zustand.

USEDATA.JS

This file is where all the magic happens in this implementation. In this file, we create a hook by calling zustand, which returns the hook we need. We pass in both the state values and the callbacks we need. All the callbacks use Immer for easier state manipulation.

Listing 8.25   `src/data/useData.js`

```
import { create } from "zustand";
import { v4 as uuid } from "uuid";
import { persist } from "zustand/middleware";
import { immer } from "zustand/middleware/immer";
export const useData = create(          ◁———
```

We create a hook by calling a function that returns a hook. We haven't seen this type of structure before, and it is fairly advanced, but hook generators are apparently a thing.

```
persist(
  immer((set) => ({
    things: [],
    currentThing: null,
    seeThing: (newThing) =>
      set((draft) => {
        draft.currentThing = newThing;
      }),
    seeAllThings: () =>
      set((draft) => {
        draft.currentThing = null;
      }),
    addThing: (name) =>
      set((draft) => {
        draft.things.push({ id: uuid(), name, done: [] });
      }),
    removeThing: (id) =>
      set((draft) => {
        const index = draft.things.findIndex((thing) => thing.id === id);
        if (index !== -1) {
          draft.things.splice(index, 1);
          if (id === draft.currentThing) {
            draft.currentThing = null;
          }
        }
      }),
    doThing: (id) =>
      set((draft) => {
        const thing = draft.things.find((thing) => thing.id === id);
        thing.done.push(Date.now());
      }),
    undoThing: (id, index) =>
      set((draft) => {
        const thing = draft.things.find((thing) => thing.id === id);
        thing.done.splice(index, 1);
      }),
  })),
  { name: "100-things-zustand" }
)
);
```

> We use two pieces of middleware, one to persist the data to local storage and another to curry the reducers with Immer. We could have applied this middleware in any order.

DATAPROVIDER.JSX

The data provider doesn't do anything in this version; it's here only so that this iteration has the same interface as the other ones. The only interesting bit is that we import the useData hook without using it. Importing the hook makes React initialize the hook with the initial data, as this file will be the first one to include this import.

Listing 8.26   `src/data/DataProvider.jsx`

```
import "./useData";
export function DataProvider({ children }) {
  return children;
}
```

> We import the data hook to make sure that it has been initialized—not strictly necessary, only a precaution.

> The provider does nothing but return the children.

USEALLTHINGS.JS

Accessing data from the stateful hook is easy.

> **Listing 8.27   `src/data/useAllThings.js`**

```
import useData from "./useData";
export function useAllThings() {
  return useData((state) => state.things).map(({ id }) => id);
}
```

USETHING.JS

This hook accesses data and callbacks from the context.

> **Listing 8.28   `src/data/useThing.js`**

```
import { useData } from "./useData";
export function useThing(id) {
  const thing =
    useData(
      (state) =>
        state.things.find((t) => t.id === id)
    );
  const seeThing =
    useData((state) => state.seeThing);
  const seeAllThings =
    useData((state) => state.seeAllThings);
  const doThing =
    useData((state) => state.doThing);
  const undoThing =
    useData((state) => state.undoThing);
  const removeThing =
    useData((state) => state.removeThing);
  return {
    thing,
    seeThing: () => seeThing(id),
    removeThing: () => removeThing(id),
    doThing: () => doThing(id),
    seeAllThings,
    undoThing: (index) => undoThing(id, index),
    undoLastThing: () => undoThing(id, thing.done.length - 1),
  };
}
```

By default, zustand lets you select only one thing from the store, but we need six things. We can modify our store to allow the selection of multiple bits, but the effort isn't worthwhile, as we'd need this feature only once. So we make six separate selections, and we're good.

USEADDTHING.JS

This file accesses a single callback from the hook.

> **Listing 8.29   `src/data/useAddThing.js`**

```
import { useData } from "./useData";
export function useAddThing() {
  return useData((state) => state.addThing);
}
```

USECURRENTTHING.JS

This file retrieves data from the hook.

Listing 8.30 `src/data/useCurrentThing.js`

```
import { useData } from "./useData";
export function useCurrentThing() {
  return useData((state) => state.currentThing);
}
```

INDEX.JS

This file is identical to the last iteration.

Listing 8.31 `src/data/index.js`

```
export { DataProvider } from "./DataProvider";
export { useAddThing } from "./useAddThing";
export { useAllThings } from "./useAllThings";
export { useThing } from "./useThing";
export { useCurrentThing } from "./useCurrentThing";
```

8.7 *Rethinking flow and data with XState*

State machines enable us to define the flow of a (complex) operation. Suppose that you are creating the signup section for a website. For this particular website, the user has to input first their email and password. On the next screen, they can enter more information, such as name and birth date, but they can skip this screen. At the end, they have to accept the website terms. Also, they can go backward through the flow. The state can flow in many ways, and creating a state diagram with associated actions can help us visualize what can happen when (figure 8.18).

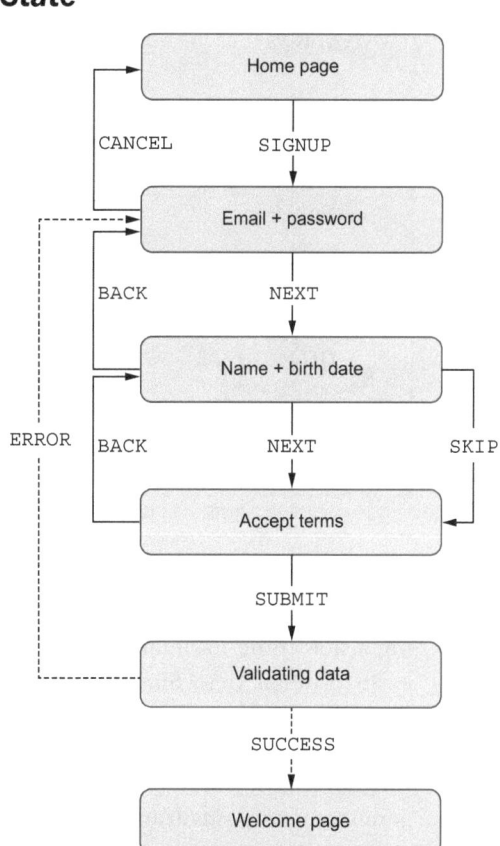

Figure 8.18 As the visitor must have a user to proceed on a given website, they can navigate the different states of the diagram, and in the end, they will be given access to the full website. States are boxes, and transitions are arrows. Only the arrows leading out from a given state are allowed transitions from that state. Fully drawn arrows are user-initiated transitions, and dashed arrows are automatic transitions based on various criteria.

This arrangement seems great for state and flow management, but how can we use it for data management? Well, we can have contextual data that exists outside any particular state, belongs to the overall flow, and is manipulated as transitions occur. Maybe a user logging in can type their password wrong only three times, after which no more retries are allowed. That data would be contextual data that lives above the state diagram, not inside any single state or transition. We can use this feature of a state machine to our advantage so we can keep our business data in the machine context.

8.7.1 A state machine for doing things

Let's see how we would use a state machine for our application. First, we want to create a state diagram for this application. We have two different states: list view and detail view. We also have different transitions, but most of them don't change the state (in state-machine terms). When we add a new thing, for example, we manipulate data, but we don't change the state; we stay in list view. The only times we change the state are when we want to see a thing (change from list view to detail view) and when we want to see all the things or remove a thing (move from detail view to list view). You can see the first iteration in figure 8.19.

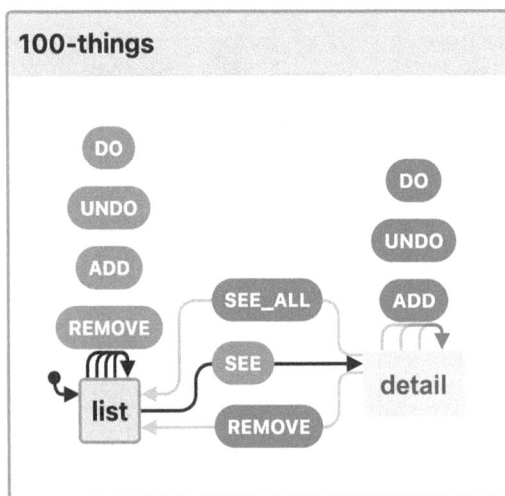

Figure 8.19   In the first iteration of our state flowchart, we are in list view, and we can do five different transitions, only one of which leads to detail view.

Looking at this state diagram more closely, we notice some transitions that don't exist. We can add things only in list view, not in detail view. We don't have a button for adding a new thing in detail view, so the dark-gray ADD transition on the right shouldn't exist in detail view. Similarly, we cannot remove a thing from list view—only from detail view. Figure 8.20 cleans up these extra transitions.

You may wonder where this visualization comes from because it's not like others in this book. The source is an online tool called Stately (https://stately.ai), which can generate these visualizations directly from the code of a state machine.

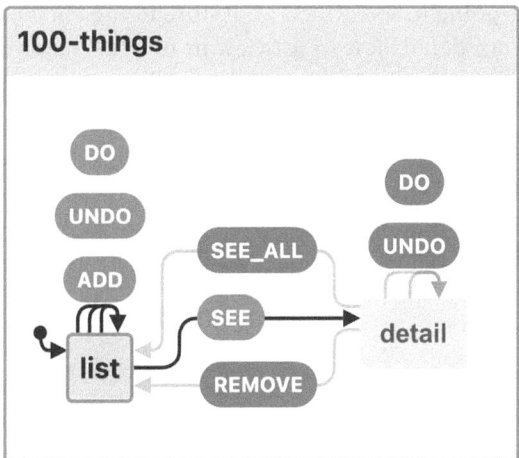

Figure 8.20 We've reduced the number of options a bit because we know how the application works. We can no longer add things in detail view or remove things in list view. This figure more closely represents the transitions in our application.

There's still something a bit weird about this machine, however. The DO action in list view is obviously different from the DO action in detail view. In detail view, we can do only that single thing, but in list view, we can do any of the things in the list. Let's differentiate these transitions as DO_THIS (detail view) and DO_THAT (list view), with the latter transition taking the id of the thing we're doing and vice versa for the UNDO transition to UNDO_THAT and UNDO_THIS. Figure 8.21 shows the result.

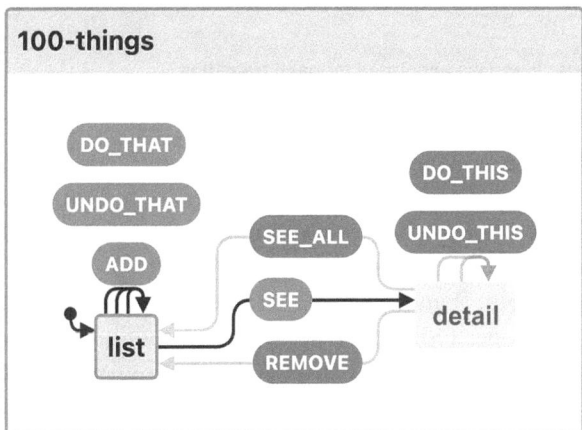

Figure 8.21 The new iteration of the state machine has different transitions for doing things in list view versus detail view.

The next step is defining the context data that exists above this state machine. This data consists of the same two values as earlier: the list of things and the current thing. When we do a transition, we can specify an action that is triggered when the transition occurs. When we want to see a thing and move from list view to detail view, we also need to specify which thing we're going to see, which we'll store in the current thing's context value. When we move from detail view to list view in the SEE_ALL transition, we must reset the current thing. Let's associate an action with each transition, as shown in figure 8.22; later, we'll define what these actions do.

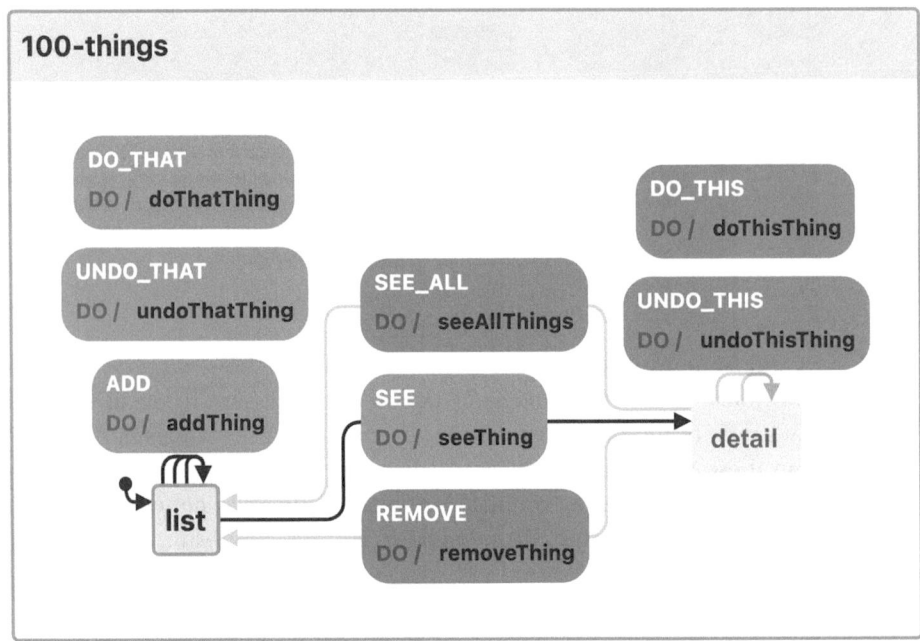

Figure 8.22   The state machine with actions annotated for each transition

We've implemented this final state machine along with the context and all actions in the application, but we've also implemented it in the stately.ai application to create the visualization in figure 8.22 (though the graphics might change over time). You can see this state machine and visualization at https://mng.bz/aEOY.

We're left with a slight problem. Remember that we used the same useThing hook in the Thing component in list view and the SingleThing component in detail view? Now we know that these two states are different and need different functions, so we're going to split the useThing hook into two different hooks instead. These hooks will be helpfully named useThisThing (used in SingleThing in single view) and useThat- Thing (used in Thing in list view).

How do we create this state machine? We'll discuss that topic when we get to the source code of the machine in section 8.7.2. Then we'll discuss how the actions are created in the source code for actions.js.

First, let's see how we can hook this machine up to our React codebase. We're still going to use a context, but this time, we're adding only a single static reference to our state machine. This value never changes, so the context never updates or causes re-renders. But the `useSelector` hook from the XState library does cause updates when the machine changes, so this hook will fuel our application. We're also going to need to send transitions, which we'll do through our custom hook `useSend`. Now the application is structured as shown in figure 8.23.

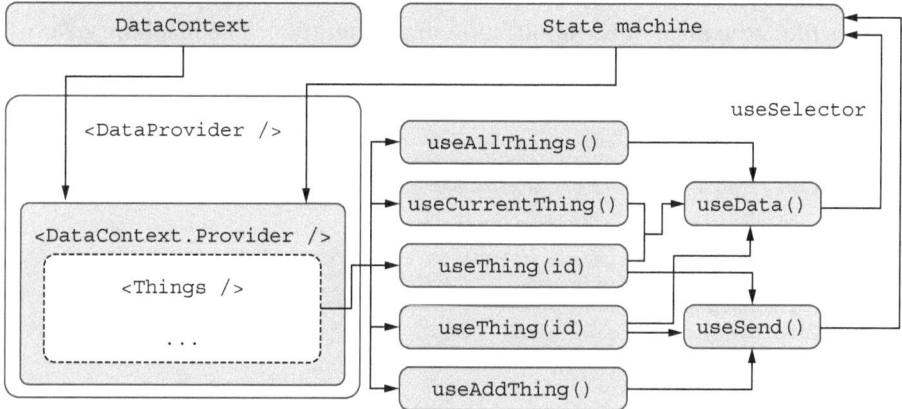

Figure 8.23 **The architecture of our state machine–fueled application. Notice which custom hooks use data and send data. Four hooks use data, three hooks send data, and two hooks do both things.**

8.7.2 Source code

For simplicity's sake, I split the machine into the definition of the machine itself and then the definition of the actions. I could have put everything in the same file, but my chosen approach makes the code look less daunting.

Persisting the data to local storage and reading it again happen in the data provider. We can conveniently override the initial state when we pass a machine to the `useInterpret` hook, and we can listen for any machine changes in a `useEffect` by using `service.subscribe`. Note that we store the whole state (which includes the context) in local storage, not the context alone. This approach is the correct way to restore a state machine in XState. It does mean that we'll put a lot more than the context in local storage, but that's not relevant for our focus.

Note that we're not using Immer-style reducers in this variant. We could, but we don't need to, as the reducers are fairly simple.

Example: xstate

This example is in the `xstate` folder. You can use that example by running this command in the source folder:

```
$ npm run dev -w ch08/xstate
```

(continued)

Alternatively, you can go to this website to browse the code, see the example in action in your browser, or download the source code as a zip file: https://reactlikea .pro/ch08-xstate.

MACHINE.JS

This file is the meat of the application in this iteration. The machine governs how the application state advances, which transitions are allowed at any given state, and what happens when a translation occurs.

Listing 8.32   `src/data/machine.js`

```
import { createMachine } from "xstate";
import {
  doThatThing,
  undoThatThing,
  doThisThing,
  undoThisThing,
  removeThing,
  seeThing,
  seeAllThings,
  addThing,
} from "./actions";
export const machine = createMachine(     ⟵───┐
  {
    predictableActionArguments: true,
    id: "100-things",      ⟵──────────────
    context: { things: [], currentThing: null },
    initial: "list",
    states: {
      list: {
        on: {
          DO_THAT: { target: "list", actions: "doThatThing" },
          UNDO_THAT: { target: "list", actions: "undoThatThing" },
          ADD: { target: "list", actions: "addThing" },
          SEE: { target: "single", actions: "seeThing" },
        },
      },
      single: {
        on: {
          DO_THIS: { target: "single", actions: "doThisThing" },
          UNDO_THIS: { target: "single", actions: "undoThisThing" },
          REMOVE: { target: "list", actions: "removeThing" },
          SEE_ALL: { target: "list", actions: "seeAllThings" },
        },
      },
    },
  },
  {
    actions: {
      addThing,
```

To create a new machine, we have to pass in configuration options.

First, we have to provide a unique name. The name doesn't matter and can make debugging easier.

We pass in an initial context and state, but we're going to overwrite the initial context later, so it doesn't matter here.

Finally, we pass in all the states. For each state, we list which possible transitions can occur to which other state and with which accompanying action.

```
        doThatThing,
        undoThatThing,
        doThisThing,
        undoThisThing,
        seeThing,
        seeAllThings,
        removeThing,
      },
   }
);
```

ACTIONS.JS

This file defines all the action creators that manipulate the state without using Immer, so we write them as immutable code and create minor utility functions to help. I could have used Immer, but this example reminds you that Immer is not mandatory and that our brains are still capable of doing things the old way. All the functions are straightforward, doing a single small thing each.

Listing 8.33 `src/data/actions.js`

```
import { assign } from "xstate";
import { v4 as uuid } from "uuid";
export const addThing = assign({
  things: (context, { name }) =>
    context.things.concat([{ id: uuid(), name, done: [] }]),
});
export const seeThing = assign({
  currentThing: (context, { id }) => id,
});
export const seeAllThings = assign({
  currentThing: null,
});
export const removeThing = assign({
  things: (context) =>
    context.things.filter((t) => t.id !== context.currentThing),
  currentThing: null,
});
function editThing(things, id, cb) {
  return things.map((t) =>
    t.id === id ? { ...t, done: cb(t.done) } : t
  );
}
function doSomeThing(things, id) {
  return editThing(things, id, (done) => done.concat(Date.now()));
}
export const doThatThing = assign({
  things: (context, { id }) => doSomeThing(context.things, id),
});
export const doThisThing = assign({
  things: (context) =>
    doSomeThing(context.things, context.currentThing),
});
function undoSomeThing(things, id, index) {
```

```
  return editThing(things, id, (done) =>
    done.slice(0, index).concat(done.slice(index + 1))
  );
}
export const undoThatThing = assign({
  things: (context, { id, index }) =>
    undoSomeThing(context.things, id, index),
});
export const undoThisThing = assign({
  things: (context, { index }) =>
    undoSomeThing(context.things, context.currentThing, index),
});
```

DATAPROVIDER.JSX

In this iteration, the data provider is merely a wrapper for the underlying state machine that does all the hard work, so the data provider is slim this time around.

Listing 8.34   `src/data/DataProvider.jsx`

```
import { useEffect } from "react";
import { useInterpret } from "@xstate/react";
import { machine } from "./machine";
import { DataContext } from "./DataContext";
const STORAGE_KEY = "100-things-xstate";
export function DataProvider({ children }) {
  const state =
    JSON.parse(
      localStorage.getItem(STORAGE_KEY)
    ) || machine.initialState;
  const service = useInterpret(machine, { state });
  useEffect(() => {
    const subscription =
     service.subscribe((state) =>
        localStorage.setItem(
          STORAGE_KEY,
          JSON.stringify(state),
        )
    );
    return subscription.unsubscribe;
  }, [service]);
  return (
    <DataContext.Provider value={service}>
      {children}
    </DataContext.Provider>
  );
}
```

The two primary responsibilities of the provider in this instance are to make sure that the initial state is set from local storage (or default to the initial state stored in the machine itself) . . .

. . . and to store the current state in local storage when something changes in the machine.

We stuff the machine inside a context only to get a reference to the machine later. The machine is a stable variable and will never change.

USEDATA.JS

When we need to display some data, we have to retrieve it from the machine context by using a selector function. But first, we have to get a reference to the machine from the data context.

Listing 8.35 `src/data/useData.js`

```
import { useContext } from "react";
import { DataContext } from "./DataContext";
import { useSelector } from "@xstate/react";
export function useData(selector) {
  const service = useContext(DataContext);
  return useSelector(service, selector);
}
```

To retrieve values from the machine (be it state or context values), we use a selector function from the library and apply that function to the machine from the context.

USESEND.JS

To manipulate the machine, we need to call the `send` method from the machine, as retrieved from the data context.

Listing 8.36 `src/data/useSend.js`

```
import { useContext } from "react";
import { DataContext } from "./DataContext";
export function useSend() {
  return useContext(DataContext).send;
}
```

To trigger transitions in the machine, we use the send method of the machine.

USEALLTHINGS.JS

This file retrieves data from the machine context by using the `useData` hook.

Listing 8.37 `src/data/useAllThings.js`

```
import { useData } from "./useData";
export function useAllThings() {
  return useData((state) => state.context.things)
    .map(({ id }) => id);
}
```

When we want to read data from the context, we go through the state.context property.

USETHATTHING.JS

This file is the first of the more complex hooks that both access data inside the state machine and allow you to manipulate the machine state by triggering various transitions.

Listing 8.38 `src/data/useThatThing.js`

```
import { useData } from "./useData";
import { useSend } from "./useSend";
export function useThatThing(id) {
  const send = useSend();
  const thing = useData(({ context }) =>
    context.things.find((t) => t.id === id)
  );
  return {
    thing,
```

The hook for a thing item in the list of all the things. It takes an id to identify which thing it works on.

```
      seeThing: () => send({ type: "SEE", id }),
      doThing: () => send({ type: "DO_THAT", id }),
      undoLastThing: () =>
        send({ type: "UNDO_THAT", id, index: thing.done.length - 1 }),
    };
}
```

USETHISTHING.JS

This hook also allows you to trigger various transitions, like the previous hook, but not the same transitions.

Listing 8.39 `src/data/useThisThing.js`

```
import { useData } from "./useData";              This hook is used for a single thing,
import { useSend } from "./useSend";              which is stored in currentThing, so
export function useThisThing() {          ⟵——     we don't need to pass an id to it.
  const send = useSend();
  const thing = useData((({ context }) =>
    context.things.find((t) => t.id === context.currentThing)
  );
  return {
    thing,                                        Note that we can send a transition without
    removeThing: () => send("REMOVE"),            properties as send("TYPE") rather than the
    doThing: () => send("DO_THIS"),               more elaborate send({type:"TYPE"}).
    seeAllThings: () => send("SEE_ALL"),
    undoThing: (index) => send({ type: "UNDO_THIS", index }),
    undoLastThing: () =>
      send({ type: "UNDO_THIS", index: thing.done.length - 1 }),
  };
}
```

USEADDTHING.JS

This hook allows you to create a single specific transition in the machine.

Listing 8.40 `src/data/useAddThing.js`

```
import { useSend } from "./useSend";
export function useAddThing() {
  const send = useSend();
  return (name) => send({ type: "ADD", name });
}
```

USECURRENTTHING.JS

This file is another trivial hook for accessing data from the machine context.

Listing 8.41 `src/data/useCurrentThing.js`

```
import { useData } from "./useData";
export function useCurrentThing() {
  return useData((({ context }) => context.currentThing);
}
```

INDEX.JS

We expose one more hook in this version.

```
Listing 8.42  src/data/index.js
```

```
export { DataProvider } from "./DataProvider";
export { useAddThing } from "./useAddThing";
export { useAllThings } from "./useAllThings";
export { useThatThing } from "./useThatThing";
export { useThisThing } from "./useThisThing";
export { useCurrentThing } from "./useCurrentThing";
```

> We have two hooks here, so we need to export both, and we also need to update both components using the old useThing hook, to use the relevant variant.

8.8 Data management recap

We've seen five ways to implement data management in this chapter, and we've hardly scratched the surface of what's available. We've implemented data management by using only pure React in section 8.3, and we've implemented it by using a few utility libraries, keeping pure React as the main data management library in section 8.4. The three external libraries we tried are Redux (Toolkit), zustand, and XState. Other notable alternatives include Jotai, Recoil, and Valtio. Refer back to chapter 1, figure 1.4, for an overview.

Although all these methods are different, they're all great. I would never fault anyone for using any of these tools. Some shine better in some circumstances than others, but they're all capable.

Often, you'll find yourself working on a project that uses one of these approaches, and it will probably be good enough. If you need to start a new project and have to choose, go with whatever is most comfortable for you. If you're in the rare situation of being able to choose *and* having the time and energy to learn something new, play with a few alternatives while mocking up the central parts of your application. You'll probably find a good candidate for your use case.

Finally, as demonstrated in this chapter, remember that your decision can always be reversed. With little effort, we were able to change the underlying data management library to something similar to or even far from the original while leaving almost all the presentation code intact. Don't be afraid to try something new.

Summary

- An application without data is meaningless. When we have a lot of data, especially if we need to manipulate it in complex ways, we need to think carefully about how to manage that data.
- Many excellent libraries for data management are available, but you don't need one unless you have a special circumstance. React's built-in functionality with context + `useReducer` will take you far, especially if you combine it with `useContextSelector` to minimize rendering.
- Redux is one of the most used data management libraries, mostly because it existed before React had good built-in capabilities itself, but also because it has

been battle tested for ages and simply works. It has a bit of legacy boilerplate, however, even if you use RTK.

- Zustand is one of the newest and most popular kids on the data management block. It's so simple to use that you can't screw it up. It's a bit trickier to use at scale, however, because it doesn't come with any built-in tools or patterns for organizing multiple unrelated data stores.

- State machines have been all the rage for many years in many aspects of computer science, and you'll see them used in all sorts of programming languages, probably more so than in JavaScript. XState is a good library for JavaScript, though, and combined with React, it can improve your understanding of a given complex flow and reduce bugs because it forces you to think more deeply about what can happen when.

- When it comes to choosing the right tool for the right job, go with what you feel most comfortable with. All these tools and many more are essentially interchangeable with only minor changes to the code (as you can see in the implementations in this chapter), so even if you choose wrong at first, you can always change your mind later.

Remote data and
reactive caching

This chapter covers

- Adding remote data to a React application
- Introducing the reactive cache
- Exploring remote data management libraries

All the applications we've built so far are local applications. By that, I mean applications that show data local to your computer. If you spin up one of the applications (such as the goal-tracking application from chapter 8), add some things to do, and then go to another computer, you cannot see the same data in any way. Even if you deploy the application to a website and go to the same website but on a different device (perhaps your phone), you will not be able to work on the same data that you do on your computer. You will also experience this situation if you use a different browser on the same computer.

The reason is that we store the data locally in the browser's local storage. Local storage is like a cookie but allows for more data in a more complex structure, and it's never sent to the server (as cookies can be).

That makes our applications far different from most applications you see out in the wild. On X (formerly Twitter), for example, we all see the same posts; you can interact with tweets by other people and they can interact with yours. This process requires sending the data to some remote server and receiving data from there.

> NOTE   The source code for the examples in this chapter is available at https://reactlikea.pro/ch09.

9.1   *Server complexity*

To make an application accessible to multiple users, you need to introduce server communication. When your computer is communicating with a server, data is sent from your computer to the server in a request, and data is returned from the server as a response. When data moves from one computer to another, several complications are introduced, with one of the primary ones being latency. When you're using local data, that data is available in milliseconds, but when you're communicating with a server, network latency can cause data requests to take seconds. Compare the differences in figure 9.1.

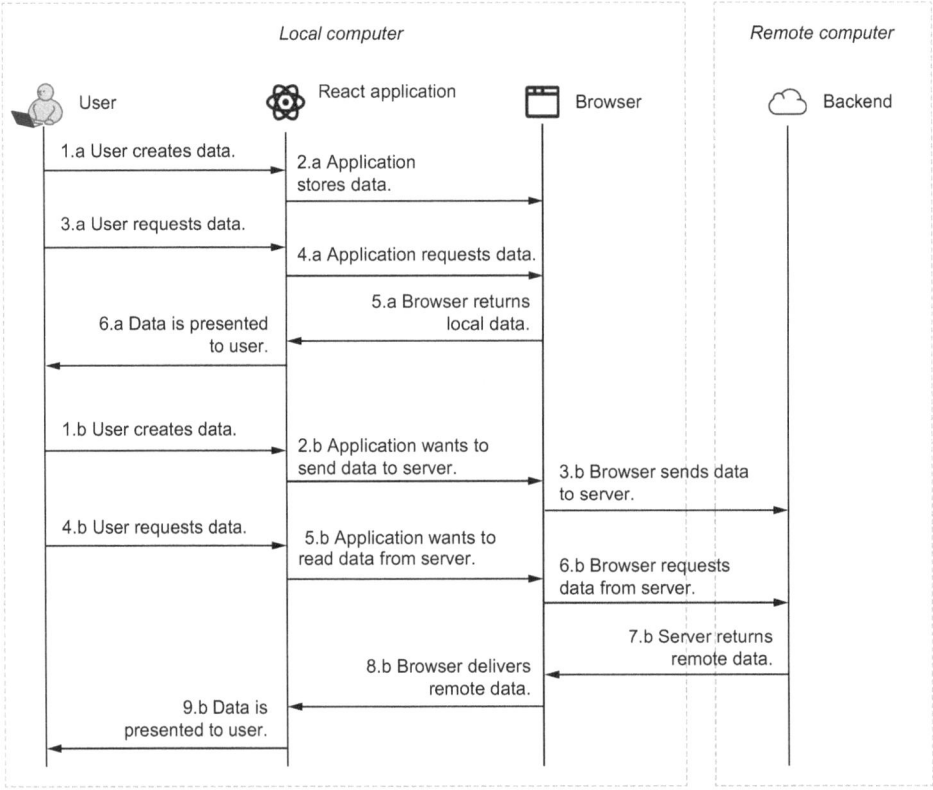

Figure 9.1   In the local-only scenario (1.a through 6.a), we use only data stored on the local computer. In scenario 1.b through 9.b, we go through a remote server, which introduces some extra delay and potential security problems but allows for collaboration between users and devices.

Adding remote data comes with security problems. When you are on X, only you can create and delete *your* tweets, so security is required to make sure that only you have access. This security requires logins, passwords, password recovery, two-factor authentication, social login (single sign-on), and a mess of problems, all of which don't involve React as much as they do the backend. We also need to worry about storing data efficiently in a database, handling multiple clients updating the same data, and so on. All these problems are well-known, nontrivial, backend problems.

Although I would love to introduce a backend framework to you (Express in Node.js and Django in Python are my favorites), that topic is beyond the scope of this book. You can find plenty of great books on those topics. Instead, I'm going to cheat a bit. We'll pretend that we interact with a remote server but the data is still local data. From the perspective of the React application, however, this data will for all intents and purposes work like true remote data. So we can create a local "server" that will never be exposed to the public; thus, we have no need for databases or security. See how this extra option works in figure 9.2.

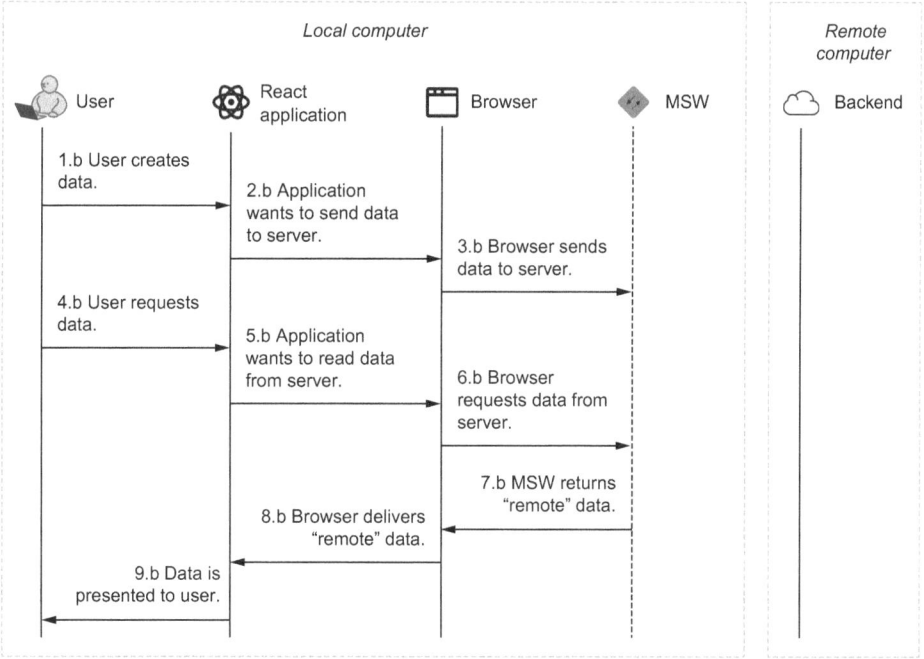

Figure 9.2   With our fake MSW (Mock Service Worker) intercept backend, React (or any other web application) will think that it's interacting with a real, live, web server when it's interacting with our middleware. We can create a React application as though we have a real backend without building said backend; we don't have to worry about databases, security, or anything like that.

Wait—we don't need a server?

No. Creating a server is doable, of course, and we could even run a local server written in Node.js, Python, or some other backend language, but we don't need to. If we did, we would need to introduce a database, security measures, and more, which aren't necessary for React applications. Instead, to make things easy for ourselves, we are going to use a server mocking library called Mock Service Worker (MSW for short).

In this chapter, we will be using MSW for our backends, but the source code for those backends is available only in the online repository, as it is a bit too long and irrelevant to show here.

In this chapter, we will start reexamining the goal-tracking application from chapter 8 using only the context, but this time with a web server handling all the requests. To make the application seem more real, we will add a login/signup screen, but because we use a fake web server, it won't validate the login; it simply allows you in right away regardless of how you log in.

To simulate a real web experience, we will introduce a small but noticeable lag in server responses. The initial simple solution isn't great because of the noticeable delay when nothing happens, but it works. Later, we will discuss how a reactive cache might be a much better solution and eventually reimplement the whole application by using TanStack Query, a reactive cache, data management library for React. We'll start by implementing the tool with the default bare-bones setup. Finally, we'll introduce client-caching principles that make the server-dependent experience much smoother for users.

9.2   *Adding a remote server to do goal tracking*

In this section, we'll add remote data handling to the goal-tracking application. To do so, we'll follow these steps:

1 Add a signup/login flow.
2 Design an API for our requests to go through.
3 Rewrite the data layer to use this new API.
4 Add a loading indicator.
5 Put everything together in the final application.

9.2.1   *Adding signup and login*

We need to add a login/signup screen. This screen is required because when we have a multitenant system (which lets multiple users sign in and work on their own data), we need to add some basic security. Alternatively, we could create a single-tenant system in which all users work on the same data, but that approach seems a bit weird for this type of application. We're not all working on the same goals, are we? Also, some troll would quickly delete all the data and/or add something obnoxious. Figure 9.3 shows the signup/login screen.

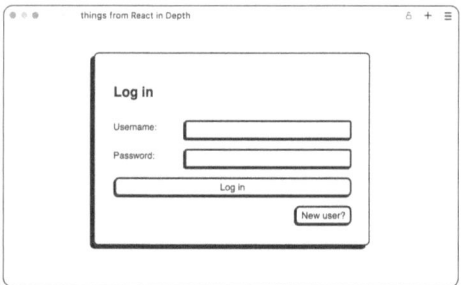 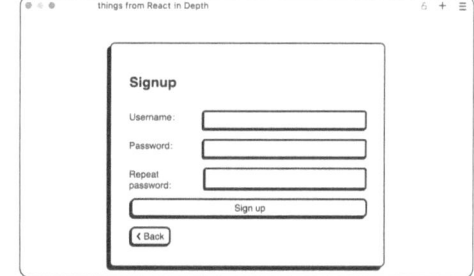

Figure 9.3   When you arrive at the new goal-tracking website for the first time, you have to log in or sign up. Ideally, we'd include a "forgot password" flow, but because we don't have a backend, we don't need that feature for now.

We'll also need to create new data management utilities for this authorization step as well as a new client UI. Finally, we need a logout button for the main list display.

9.2.2   *Designing an API*

In chapter 8, we created our goal-tracking application. This application handles retrieving data by looking inside our locally stored data, and it handles writing data by updating that same locally stored data.

In this section, we are going to use that same architecture but reroute all the requests to a backend server. Well, we'll reroute them to MSW, but that fact is beside the point here. Whenever we want to retrieve data, we ask the server for the data, and whenever we want to write data, we send the new data to the server and receive updated data. Compare these approaches in figure 9.4.

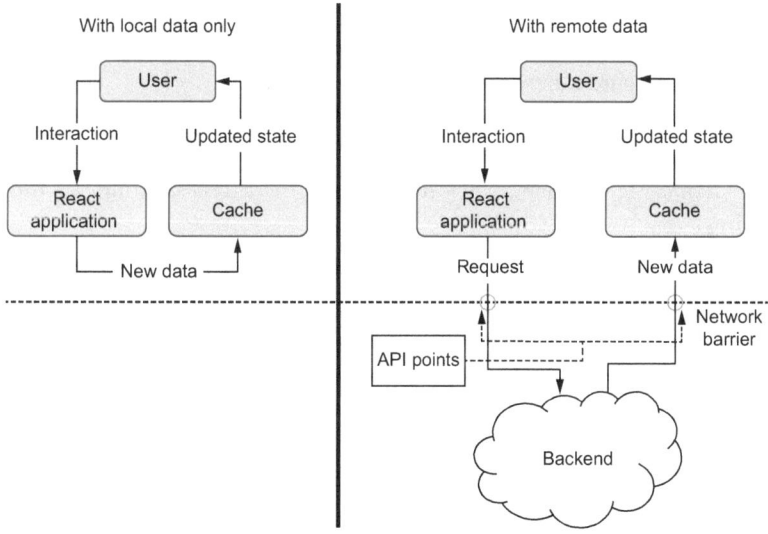

Figure 9.4   When we store data locally, we can dip into the local data when we want to display it, but when we store the data remotely, we have to wait for the server to respond before we can display anything. This process has to occur every time we read or write data. Note also that every time we move from local to remote data, we have to agree on the format between the two parts of the applications; this format agreement is known as the API.

Note the interface between the application and the web server, which is known as an *application programming interface* (API). API design is a category of its own, but for this application, we're going to create a RESTful CRUD interface.

RESTful CRUD?

Both of these terms are related to API design, which is beyond the scope of this book.

REST (Representational State Transfer) can be boiled down to requests being stateless (thus, self-contained) and resource centric. In a RESTful API, you don't have a login method; you have a session resource that you create by sending a username and a password.

CRUD is an acronym for *create*, *read* (or *retrieve*), *update*, and *delete*—the four basic operations that you perform on a resource in a system such as this one. So for every type of resource, you can create a resource, list (read) some or all resources, update a resource, or delete a resource. Not all operations make sense for all types of resources, of course. You can even have nested resources, such as songs on a certain album or books by a certain author.

TIP   If you want to learn more about API design, check out *API Design Patterns*, by JJ Geewax, at https://www.manning.com/books/api-design-patterns.

With these principles in mind, we have the following endpoints in our backend:

- POST /api/session—Log in to the application.
- POST /api/user—Create a new user.
- DELETE /api/session—Log out of the application.
- GET /api/user—Get the current user.
- GET /api/things—List all things by the current user.
- GET /api/things/<id>—Get all information about the thing with the given id.
- DELETE /api/things/<id>—Delete the given thing.
- POST /api/things—Create a new thing.
- DELETE /api/things/<id>/done/<id>—Delete the specific time we did the specific thing.
- DELETE /api/things/<id>/done/last—Delete the most recent time we did the specific thing.
- POST /api/things/<id>/done—Do this specific thing.

With these endpoints, we can replicate all the things we can already do in our application. Note that we haven't defined any API endpoints for updating resources; there isn't anything to update anywhere in the application. We don't even support renaming things. We can only *do* or *undo* things (which in API terms is creating and deleting "done" resources), not *update* the thing itself.

This book doesn't cover the reasoning behind the design and structure of this API. Suppose that a backend coworker tells you that you have to work with this API, and you trust them to have made it correctly. This coworker seems like a nice, competent person, though they do have a weird mania about painting plastic miniatures for board games, but that topic is also beyond the scope of this book.

9.2.3   Rewriting the data layer

Single source of truth is an important concept in computer science, and this principle comes into play here. We store the data in the database on the server, and that server is our single source of truth. Thus, we cannot also store the data elsewhere because that might lead to a conflict if the two sources differ on some data.

Due to this principle, we must hold the data in the backend as the only true source of content. Theoretically, multiple people could be working on the same data, so just because you delete a thing and go back to the list of all things, you cannot assume that only that single change was made. Multiple other changes could have been made. So you have to query the server every time you want to display the list for the data to be considered "live."

Using this principle, we need to query the server every time we update content. We cannot be completely sure what our changes did to the content (the server might reject creating a thing with certain words, for example), and other users might be interacting with the same content. This situation sometimes results in two requests being required for an operation, resulting in double network latency. All these requirements lead to the flow of data shown in figure 9.5.

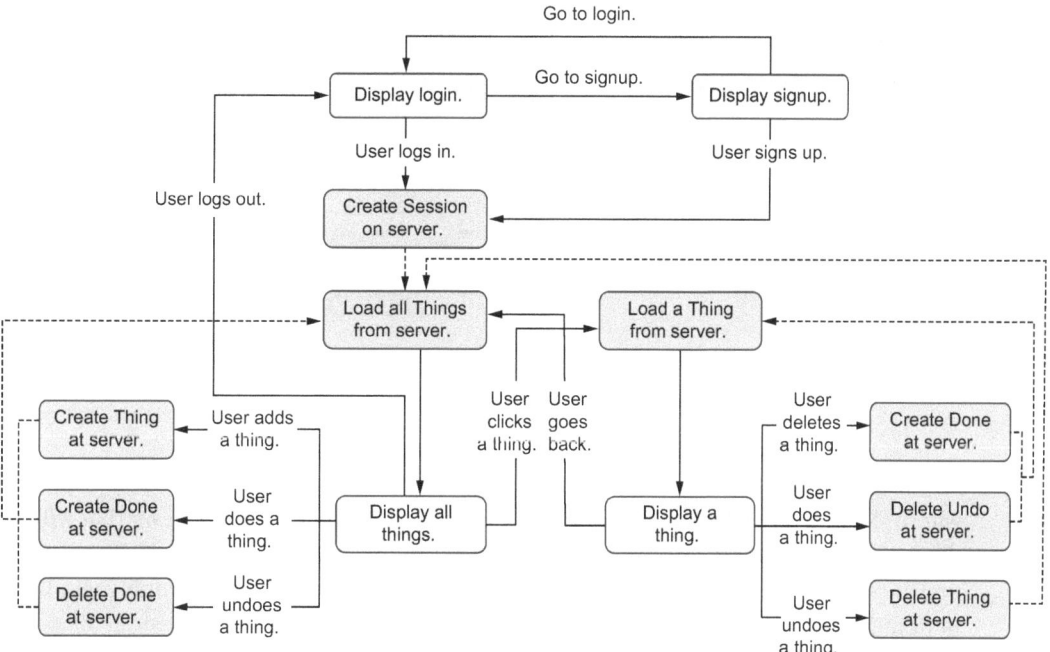

Figure 9.5   We have to request updated data from the server every time we want to display a page to make sure that the data displayed is current. The light-gray boxes are the user screens in the application, and the gray boxes are the server requests. The dashed arrows are the forced updates for new data that must happen after other requests.

Redesigning our entire data layer around this data flow means that we can still use the same structure of the four primary hooks and the global context to access and manipulate data, but behind the scenes, they will do very different things. Before we get too far, we also need to split one of the hooks, useThing, into two different hooks, useThatThing and useThisThing, as we did in the XState example in chapter 8. On top of all that, we need new hooks for the login/signup view and for the logout button. Figure 9.6 shows this rework.

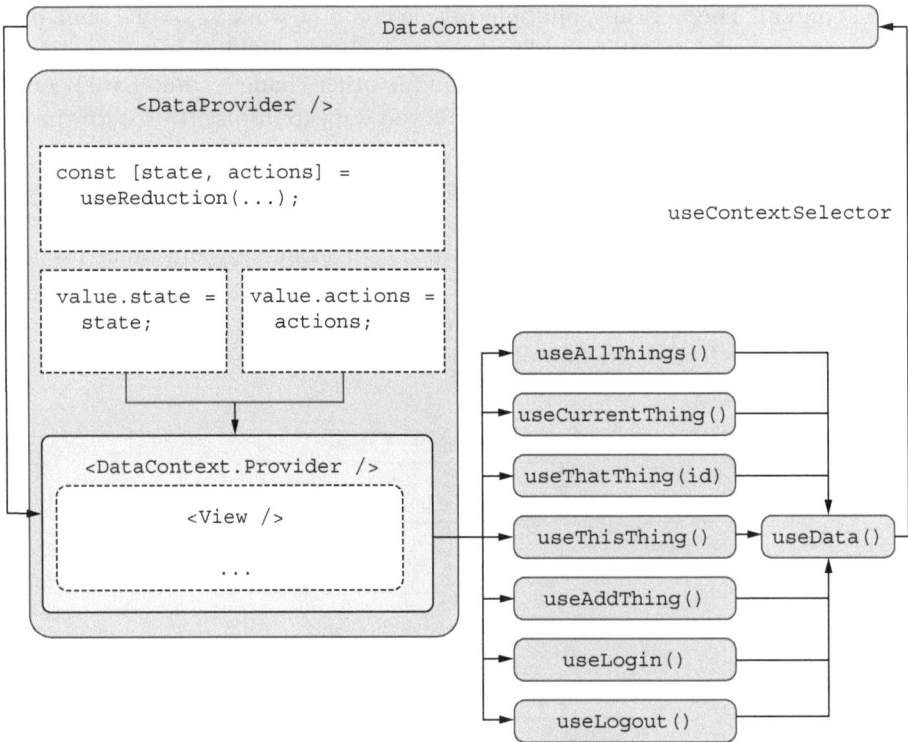

Figure 9.6   Now we require seven primary hooks through which the main application can interact with the data layer.

As a final note on the data layer, we are making some changes to what data is displayed where. Most important, we're adding a new description field to each thing that will be displayed in the thing's detail view but not in the list view. This pattern is fairly common: less information is used in list view (which might be a table of employees) than in detail view (which might be full information about each employee), and it allows us to discuss some important data management topics later.

You can see the updated form for adding a new thing as well as the detail view in figure 9.7. The new description field is displayed right below the thing name.

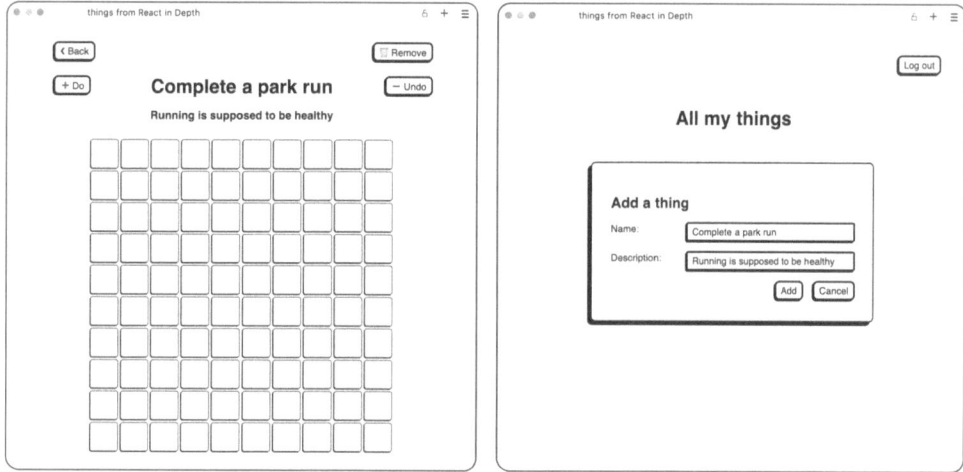

Figure 9.7 Things now have a more detailed description that will be visible only in detail view for a single thing (*Running is supposed to be healthy* on the right side of the figure). The form for adding a thing also looks more like the forms for logging in and signing up, ensuring visual consistency throughout the application. We have a logout button, too!

9.2.4 Adding a loading indicator

Because we now have a server that has to respond to most user actions, we also start to have noticeable lag. We will have double lag in many operations, as I explained in section 9.1.3. User experience (UX) research shows that an application that reacts within 100 milliseconds (ms) is said to react instantly and that no further indication of wait time should be required. Delays longer than 100 ms require some form of loading indicator so the user won't be furious about the lack of feedback and start clicking buttons twice, refreshing the page, or similar actions.

In this section, we will introduce a global loader to the application, overlaying the entire interface whenever some load is happening. This loader will look like figure 9.8—but animated, of course. (Why aren't GIFs supported in print media?)

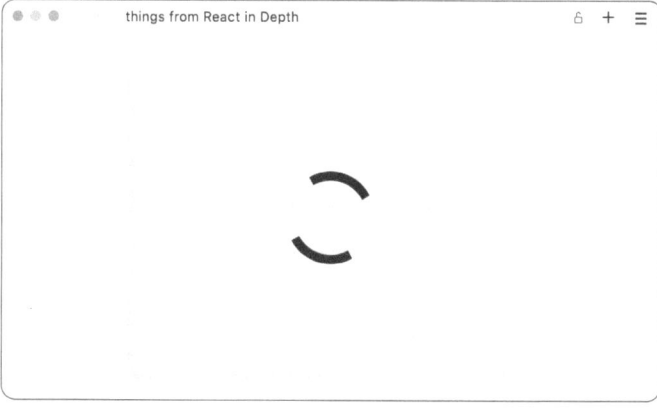

Figure 9.8 A simple loader with two spinning quarter-circles. The background is dimmed 90% while the loader is displayed.

To achieve this effect technically, we'll add a stateful Boolean, `isLoading`, that flips correctly when any server request starts and completes, respectively.

9.2.5   *Putting everything together*

The full application is getting large at this point, so I'm not going to show the entire source code. The application exceeds 1,000 lines of code, which would take up quite a few pages. I will highlight the most important bits of code in listings in the section, however. You can find the full source code in the online repository.

COMPONENT HIERARCHY

Let's start with the full component hierarchy diagram, which contains a lot more than it did earlier due to the new authorization flow (figure 9.9).

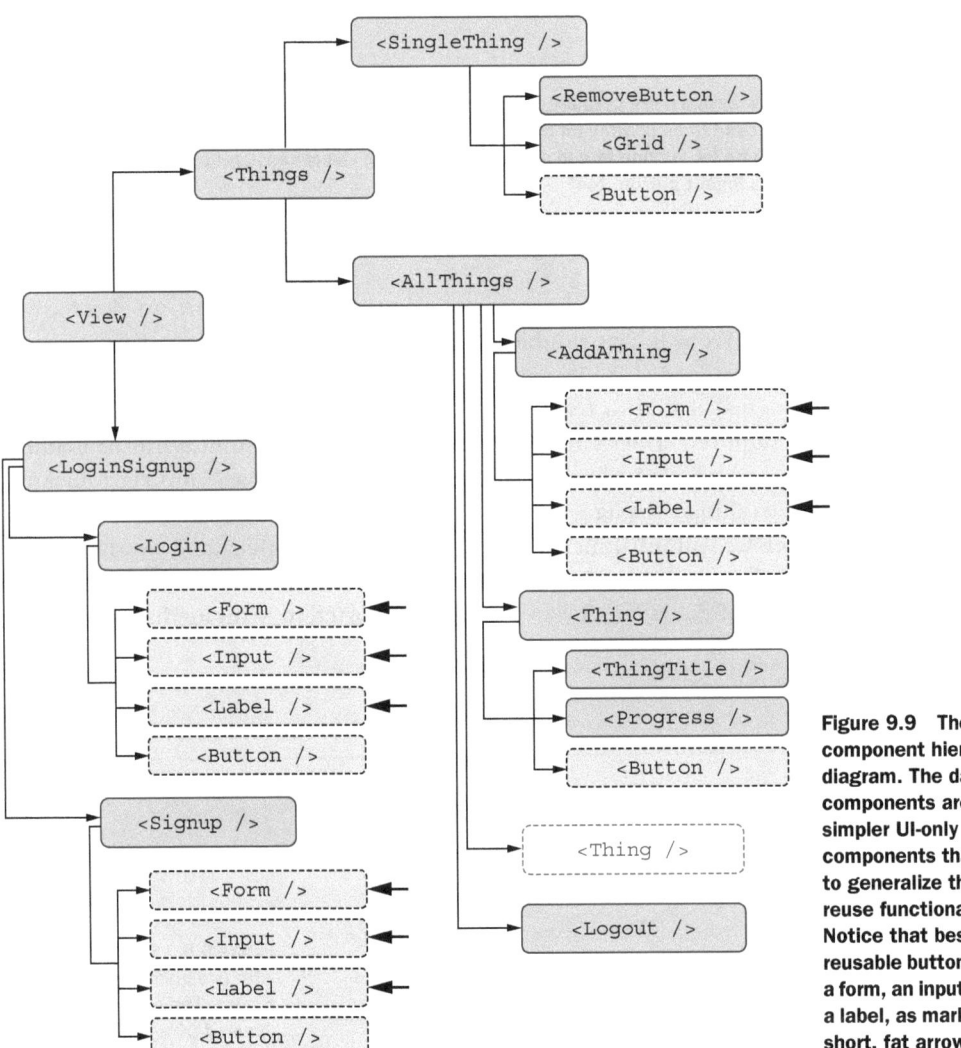

Figure 9.9   The full component hierarchy diagram. The dashed components are the simpler UI-only components that we use to generalize the UI and reuse functionality. Notice that besides a reusable button, we have a form, an input field, and a label, as marked by the short, fat arrows.

FILE STRUCTURE

The complete file structure for this application is a bit comprehensive, with a whopping 38 files and more than 1,000 lines of code, which is why I can't show all the source code in this chapter. This snippet lists the full folder and file structure:

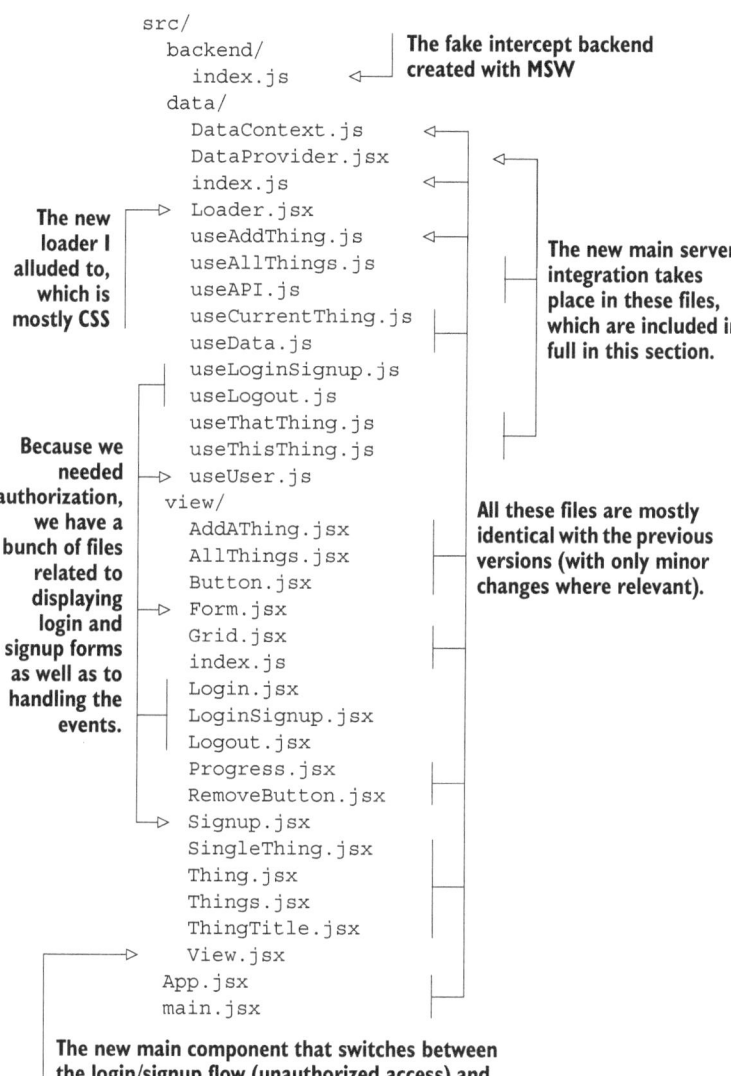

The new loader I alluded to, which is mostly CSS

The fake intercept backend created with MSW

The new main server integration takes place in these files, which are included in full in this section.

Because we needed authorization, we have a bunch of files related to displaying login and signup forms as well as to handling the events.

All these files are mostly identical with the previous versions (with only minor changes where relevant).

The new main component that switches between the login/signup flow (unauthorized access) and the main application (authorized access)

IMPORTANT CODE SNIPPETS

This section discusses the most important code snippets, which are mostly about all the data bits, of course. In particular, we'll discuss the data provider and each individual data hook that feeds data and interaction into the application.

Let's start with a new hook called `useAPI`. This hook exposes several low-level network requests wrapped in a simple function that toggles the loading flag correctly.

The user functions also trigger the authorization flag. Also, both of said flags are exported. The following listing shows this file.

Listing 9.1   `src/data/useAPI.js`

```
import { useState, useMemo } from "react";
const URLS = {
  SESSION: "/api/session",
  USER: "/api/user",
  THINGS: "/api/things",
  THING: (id) => `/api/things/${id}`,
  DONES: (id) => `/api/things/${id}/done`,
  DONE: (id, did) =>
    `/api/things/${id}/done/${did}`,
};
const get = (url) => fetch(url);
const post = (url, data = null) => fetch(
  url,
  { method: "POST", body: JSON.stringify(data) }
);
const remove = (url) =>
  fetch(url, { method: "DELETE" });
export function useAPI() {
  const [isAuthorized, setAuthorized] =
    useState(false);
  const [isLoading, setLoading] =
    useState(false);
  const API = useMemo(() => {
    const auth = () => setAuthorized(true);
    const unauth = () => setAuthorized(false);
    // common wrapper for all network requests
    const wrap = (promise) => {
      setLoading(true);
      return (
        promise
          // This is invoked regardless of result
          .finally(() => setLoading(false))
          // This is invoked for all server responses,
          // but .ok is only true for 20x and 30x responses
          .then((res) => {
            if (!res.ok) {
              throw new Error("Unauthorized");
            }
            return res.json();
          })
          // Finally, this catches both network, auth, and server errors
          .catch((e) => {
            unauth();
            throw e;
          })
      );
    };
    // USER API
```

First is the URL structure used by the API, extracted to make it easier to update.

Second, we have some simple wrappers for the built-in fetch() function to make GET, POST, and DELETE requests.

When the user is logged in (or has recently signed up), the authorization flag is true; otherwise, it's false.

Whenever some request is ongoing, the loading flag is true. As soon as the request completes, whether or not it completes with an error, the flag is toggled to false.

Two small utility functions for toggling the authorization flag

The request wrapper function handles errors as well as toggles the loading flag.

```
    const getUser = () =>
      wrap(get(URLS.USER)).then(auth);
    const login = (data) =>
      wrap(post(URLS.SESSION, data)).then(auth);
    const signup = (data) =>
      wrap(post(URLS.USER, data)).then(auth);
    const logout = () =>
      wrap(remove(URLS.SESSION)).then(unauth);
    // THING API
    const loadThings = () =>
      wrap(get(URLS.THINGS));
    const loadThing = (id) =>
      wrap(get(URLS.THING(id)));
    const addThing = (data) =>
      wrap(post(URLS.THINGS, data));
    const removeThing = (id) =>
      wrap(remove(URLS.THING(id)));
    const doThing = (id) =>
      wrap(post(URLS.DONES(id)));
    const undoThing = (id, did) =>
      wrap(remove(URLS.DONE(id, did)));
    return {
      getUser,
      login,
      signup,
      logout,
      loadThings,
      loadThing,
      addThing,
      removeThing,
      doThing,
      undoThing,
    };
  }, []);
  return { isAuthorized, isLoading, API };
}
```

> The primary part of this hook: the API requests. Note that we don't handle the responses here (except for the authorization functions); we merely make sure that they connect to the right place.

Next up is the data provider in `DataProvider.jsx`. This file is a more business-aware layer built on top of the API exposed in the previous `useAPI` hook.

Listing 9.2 `src/data/DataProvider.jsx`

```
import { useState, useMemo } from "react";
import { DataContext } from "./DataContext";
import { Loader } from "./Loader";
import { useAPI } from "./useAPI";
export function DataProvider({ children }) {
  const { isAuthorized, isLoading, API } =
    useAPI();
  const [things, setThings] = useState([]);
  const [currentId, setCurrentId] =
    useState(null);
```

> We extract the two flags and the API object from the useAPI hook.

> We create some local state values. This one is a temporary store for the list of things retrieved from the server. We never manipulate this value directly; we only store what the server tells us to store.

> The current id is the only part of the state we manipulate directly when we go from list view to detail view, and vice versa.

The current
thing is
similarly
loaded
from the
server only.

```
const [currentThing, setCurrentThing] =
  useState(null);
const actions = useMemo(() => {
  const { getUser, signup, login, logout } =
    API;
  const loadThings = () =>
    API.loadThings().then(setThings);
  const loadThing = (id) =>
    API.loadThing(id).then(setCurrentThing);
  const addThing = (data) =>
    API.addThing(data).then(loadThings);
  const seeThing = (id) =>
    setCurrentId(id);
  const seeAllThings = () =>
    setCurrentId(null);
  const removeThing = (id) =>
    API.removeThing(id).then(seeAllThings);
  const doThisThing = (id) =>
    API.doThing(id).then(loadThings);
  const undoLastThing = (id) =>
    API.undoThing(id, "last").then(loadThings);
  const doThatThing = (id) =>
    API.doThing(id).then(() => loadThing(id));
  const undoThatThing = (id, did) =>
    API.undoThing(id, did)
      .then(() => loadThing(id));
  return {
    addThing,
    doThatThing,
    doThisThing,
    getUser,
    loadThing,
    loadThings,
    login,
    logout,
    removeThing,
    seeAllThings,
    seeThing,
    signup,
    undoThatThing,
    undoThisThing,
  };
}, [API]);
const value = {
  state: { things, currentId, currentThing, isAuthorized },
  actions,
};
return (
  <DataContext.Provider value={value}>
    {isLoading && <Loader />}
    {children}
  </DataContext.Provider>
);
}
```

**Four of the API operations are
used as they are. We don't need
to add any functionality when a
user logs in or signs up.**

**Here, we create our main
interaction functions, mostly
by wrapping the API calls and
either setting state (after data
load) or loading fresh data
(after data mutation).**

**In the returned JSX, we
include the loader only if the
global loading flag is true.**

When we interact with the data provider, we mostly retrieve functions or values directly, so most of the data hooks are super trivial. The hook for listing all the things is a bit more complex because it also initiates loading.

Listing 9.3 `src/data/useAllThings.js`

```
import { useEffect } from "react";
import { useData } from "./useData";
export function useAllThings() {
  const loadThings = useData(({ actions }) => actions.loadThings);
  useEffect(
    () => void loadThings(),
    [loadThings],
  );
  return useData(({ state }) => state.things)
    .map(({ id }) => id);
}
```

When this hook is used, all the things are loaded from the server. void is a JavaScript keyword for throwing away a result and returning nothing. Remember that effect functions cannot return anything except a cleanup function, so using void is a trick to make sure that nothing is returned.

When the results are in, we map it to a list of ids.

When we want to display a single thing inside the list of things, we need access to some of the data-mutation functions as well as to the single thing extracted from the full list.

Listing 9.4 `src/data/useThisThing.js`

```
import { useData } from "./useData";
export function useThisThing(id) {
  const thing = useData(({ state }) =>
    state.things.find((t) => t.id === id)
  );
  const { seeThing, doThisThing, undoLastThing } = useData(
    ({ actions }) => actions
  );
  return {
    thing,
    seeThing: () => seeThing(id),
    doThing: () => doThisThing(id),
    undoLastThing: () => undoLastThing(id),
  };
}
```

A single thing is retrieved from the list of all things by the given id.

Besides the data about the thing, we return some functions curried with the given id.

On the other hand, when we need to display the detail view for a single thing, we can't rely on the existing data in the state. We have to fetch that single thing from the server so that we have all the right information available. (Remember the thing description; we return that information only from the server in detail view, not list view.) This hook is implemented in the following listing.

Listing 9.5   `src/data/useThatThing.js`

```
import { useEffect } from "react";
import { useData } from "./useData";
export function useThatThing() {
  const id = useData((({ state }) =>
    state.currentId);
  const thing = useData((({ state }) =>
    state.currentThing);
  const {
    seeAllThings,
    doThatThing,
    undoThatThing,
    removeThing,
    loadThing
  } = useData((({ actions }) => actions);
  useEffect(
    () => void loadThing(id),
    [id, loadThing],
  );
  return {
    thing,
    removeThing: () => removeThing(id),
    doThing: () => doThatThing(id),
    seeAllThings,
    undoThing: (did) => undoThatThing(id, did),
    undoLastThing: () =>
      undoThatThing(id, "last"),
  };
}
```

> When we load the detail view of a thing, we need access to the thing we're focusing on.

> We have to remember to fetch all the details of the current thing based on the given id.

Finally, to know whether we should display the public login/signup flow or the restricted private data that belongs to the currently authorized user, we need to retrieve the current user. If such a user exists, the authorization flag will update correctly.

Listing 9.6   `src/data/useAddThing.js`

> When this hook is used, the user is loaded from the server, and if that load succeeds, the API sets the authorization flag.

```
import { useEffect } from "react";
import { useData } from "./useData";
export function useAddThing() {
  const getUser = useData((({ actions }) => actions.getUser);
  const isAuthorized = useData((({ state }) => state.isAuthorized);
  useEffect(() => void getUser(), [getUser]);
  return isAuthorized;
}
```

> This hook returns the authorization flag, which is always false on the initial render but might later update to true if the request succeeds.

9.2.6   *Evaluating the solution*

This final application works. We've added a nice, functional login/signup flow, though for a production-grade system, we would probably need to add a password recovery flow as well. You can have a go at it yourself in the repository.

Example: things

This example is in the `things` folder. You can use that example by running this command in the source folder:

```
$ npm run dev -w ch09/things
```

Alternatively, you can go to this website to browse the code, see the example in action in your browser, or download the source code as a zip file: https://reactlikea .pro/ch09-things.

The flow of logic, which requires us to rerun the loaders every time we update something, can get quite complex. We could easily imagine many more ways of updating parts of a system, which would require even more connections between updaters and loaders. That process could become quite a problem. It's also a little confusing that we still have local state variables but must remember not to change them directly, as that would violate the single-source-of-truth principle (and make the server state inconsistent).

To enable us to work better with remote data—including keeping a logical relationship between loading data and updating data and providing better cache management—other libraries have sprung up. One of these libraries is TanStack Query, which we'll look at in section 9.3. TanStack Query is a remote-first state management library that is excellent at doing these things, though it also has some shortcomings. We'll start by using the TanStack Query library with bare-bones capabilities; later, we'll add extra layers of logic for improved UX.

9.3   *Migrating to TanStack Query*

The implementation we created in section 9.1 works. It has some drawbacks, but all in all, it works, and it's a fine solution for many applications as well. You don't need any special libraries to handle an application powered by server data.

That said, we can optimize a few things. Although the application isn't small, it's not big, and many painful problems start to occur only at larger scale. We can see some of those problems starting to creep into even this minor application.

First, we have to store the remote data somewhere locally (that is, *cache* it), and we have to decide whether to read from the cache or fetch fresh information from the server. Furthermore, we have to fetch fresh information from the server manually when we perform various operations, even though we may not need that information currently; we do it only to be safe and make sure that the cache is fresh. Suppose that we increment the number of times we did a thing three times instantly. In the setup from section 9.1, we would be fetching the full list of all the things every time, rather than once at the end of all three increments.

A better way to handle such a cache setup is *cache invalidation*. When we operate on the remote data, it would be better simply to mark the local cached data as invalidated, which means that the next time we need this data, it's prudent to fetch new data from the server.

This is exactly what the TanStack Query library does. Among other things, the library introduces us to a common dichotomy of remote data handling: queries versus mutations. *Queries* fetch data (*retrieve* data, the *R* in *CRUD*), whereas *mutations* change data (*create*, *update*, and *delete*, the remaining letters of *CRUD*).

TanStack Query is not the only library of its kind, of course, but it is the most popular. A rival library is SWR, a name derived from the stale-while-revalidate caching strategy. Stale-while-revalidate partially underlies the design of TanStack Query, as we will discuss. In some sense, SWR is a simpler library to use, but because TanStack Query is much more popular, we will use it in this chapter.

9.3.1 *TanStack Query architecture*

One important thing to understand about TanStack Query and many similar libraries is that it doesn't handle remote communication. It is merely a library for dealing with remote data caching in a sensible way.

To use the library, you have to define the functions that interact with the server yourself. These functions, however, are plain JavaScript functions that return a promise, which eventually resolves to the data requested (or performs the desired mutation). Fortunately, the wonderful built-in browser function `fetch()` can do that work for us.

If you want to use TanStack Query to get remote data from the path `"/api/customers"`, you simply create a function that can do that, and later, you can pass that function to TanStack Query:

```
const getCustomers = () => fetch('/api/customers/')
  .then((res) => res.json());
```

We need this line to read the response as a JSON document.

If you need to create a mutation in TanStack Query that can send data as a POST request to the same path (to create a new customer), you'd create a second function that will take the new data as an argument. Note that for some reason, TanStack Query only allows functions to take a single argument, so make sure to bundle the data in a single object:

```
const createCustomer = (data) =>
  fetch("/api/customers/", {
    method: "POST",
    data: JSON.stringify(data),
  }).then((res) => res.json());
```

A second important bit of TanStack Query architecture is that it works around a single central cache where all the currently cached responses exist—a so-called *query client*. For the central query cache to work in your application, you have to create a new query client at the top level and wrap the entire thing in a `QueryClientProvider` with the given client. This process is reminiscent of how contexts work and essentially the same under the hood. The syntax is familiar:

```
import {
  QueryClient,
  QueryClientProvider,
} from "@tanstack/react-query";
const queryClient = new QueryClient();
function App() {
  return (
    <QueryClientProvider client={queryClient}>
      <TheInnerApplicationGoesHere />
    </QueryClientProvider>
  );
}
export default App;
```

Loads the relevant functions from the library

Creates a query client outside the function, so it's created once as a global variable

To make all hooks work, we provide the query client to the entire application.

We include the main application inside this provider.

With this setup completed, we are ready to start using this library.

9.3.2 *Queries and mutations*

TanStack Query exposes two main hooks, through which you interact with the library on the surface. These hooks are `useQuery` for making queries and `useMutation` for—you guessed it—making mutations.

QUERYING

Queries are made with an existing function, as I explained earlier. You also need an identifier that represents this query: the query key. TanStack Query allows arrays of any combination of values to serve as query keys, but it is common to make the query key an array with a single string (if the query is simple and flat) or an array with a string first and an object second. Let's see some examples. If you make a query for the list of all customers, you would use the array `["customers"]` as the query key:

```
const response = useQuery({
  queryKey: ["customers"],
  queryFn: getCustomers,
});
```

But if you read only a single customer or the first page of customers or maybe search for a specific customer, you would need to include any such parameter as part of the query key:

```
// Get the customer with ID=1
const customerOne = useQuery({
  queryKey: ["customer", { id: 1 }],
  queryFn: () => getCustomer(1),
});
//
// Get page 3 of all customers
const customersP3 = useQuery({
  queryKey: ["customers", { page: 3 }],
  queryFn: () => getCustomersByPage(3),
});
//
// Get customers named "John"
const johns = useQuery({
```

```
  queryKey: ["customers", { name: "John" }],
  queryFn: () => getCustomersByName("John"),
});
```

Note that you would have to create these underlying functions (`getCustomers`, `get-Customer`, `getCustomersByPage`, and `getCustomersByName`) yourself and make sure that they passed the given arguments to the server. The smart thing about these query keys is that we can later reference queries by the exact key or by a partial key. Suppose that we delete a customer. Now any query for any list of customers is potentially invalid, so we can say that all queries with the prefix `"customers"` should be invalidated in the cache; TanStack Query will automatically find those queries and only those queries. We should also invalidate the cache for fetching that particular customer but not the cache for fetching each single customer, which means that we'd still have all the data readily available.

We need to display the data from the server when it arrives, of course, but we might also want to display some kind of loading information. The response returned from the `useQuery` hook is an object with a lot of properties, but we're going to use only a few of them. The most important one is `data`, which is the data returned from the server. But remember that the server responds asynchronously, so the first time around, the data is probably `undefined`.

Suppose that we want to show all the customers, using a `Customer` component for each, but if they haven't loaded yet, we'll show the message `"Loading..."`. We can do that by extracting the `data` property as well as the `isLoading` property from the return value:

```
function Customers() {
  const { data, isLoading } = useQuery({
    queryKey: ["customers"],
    queryFn: getCustomers,
  );
  if (isLoading) return "Loading...";
  return (
    <>
      {data.map((customer) => (
          <Customer key={customer.id} {...customer} />
      ))}
    </>
  );
}
```

> We initiate a fetch for all customers and extract data and isLoading from the return object.

> If isLoading is true, the data hasn't arrived yet.

> We can use the data safely here because we know that it has been loaded from the server.

In a more concrete way, we would want to create a general hook for loading the list of things, `useAllThings()`.

Listing 9.7 A plain query

```
import { useQuery } from "@tanstack/react-query";
import { loadThings } from "./api/api";
export function useAllThings() {
  const { data = [] } = useQuery({
```

```
  queryKey: ["things"]
  queryFn:, loadThings,
 });
 return data.map(({ id }) => id);
}
```

That query is all it takes. We can use this `useAllThings` hook in many places, and Tan-Stack Query will make sure to either serve data from the cache or load fresh data, depending on other factors (which I'll get to soon).

MUTATING

Mutations are surprisingly simple; we pass some data to a function and do "something" when the request succeeds. This time, we don't need to worry about query keys because no cache is automatically created or updated from mutations.

Mutations almost always take an argument but sometimes don't (in the case of a logout mutation, for example). Thus, we can pass in a function that takes an argument, such as for a delete-customer mutation:

```
const deleteMutation = useMutation({
  mutationFn: deleteCustomerById,
});
```

The return value from `useMutation` is an object that has a `.mutate` method, which is what we want to invoke. When the user clicks the delete button, for example, we need to invoke the delete mutation:

```
import { useMutation } from "@tanstack/react-query";
function DeleteCustomer({ id }) {
  const deleteMutation = useMutation({
    mutationFn: deleteCustomerById,
  });
  return <button onClick={() => deleteMutation.mutate(id)}>Delete</button>;
}
```

The second part of a mutation happens when the mutation has completed. You can pass in an `onSuccess` callback as an extra option to the `useMutation` hook that will be invoked when the request succeeds. A common thing to do is invalidate one or more queries, which are now considered invalid based on the mutation. If we delete a customer, we want to invalidate any query with the prefix `["customers"]` as well as any query for the customer with this specific ID.

To invalidate a query, we need access to the query client. We can use the aptly named `useQueryClient` hook, so this delete-customer button becomes

```
import {
  useQueryClient,
  useMutation,
} from "@tanstack/react-query";
function DeleteCustomer({ id }) {
  const queryClient = useQueryClient();
  const onSuccess = () => {
```

```
    queryClient.invalidateQueries({
      queryKey: ["customers"],
    });
    queryClient.invalidateQueries({
      queryKey: ["customer", { id }],
    );
  };
  const deleteMutation = useMutation({
    mutationFn: deleteCustomerById,
    onSuccess,
  });
  return <button onClick={() => deleteMutation.mutate(id)}>Delete</button>;
}
```

> We invalidate any query with the string "customers" as either the full key or a partial key.

> On the second line, we invalidate only queries with both the string key customer and the property id set to this particular customer.

For this concrete case, we want to create hooks for the various mutations required throughout the application, such as a hook for adding a new thing, `useAddThing`. The following listing shows the code.

Listing 9.8   A simple mutation

```
import {
  useQueryClient,
  useMutation,
} from "@tanstack/react-query";
import * as API from "./api";
export function useAddThing() {
  const queryClient = useQueryClient();
  const onSuccess = () =>
    queryClient.invalidateQueries({ queryKey: ["things"] });
  const { mutate: addThing } = useMutation({
    mutationFn: API.addThing,
    onSuccess,
  });
  return addThing;
}
```

The remaining hooks are basically slight variations. The `doThing` and `undoThing` hooks require the query to invalidate as an argument because they're used in both list view and detail view.

Listing 9.9   A slightly more complex mutation

```
import {
  useQueryClient,
  useMutation,
} from "@tanstack/react-query";
import * as API from "./api";
export function useDoThing(queryKey) {
  const queryClient = useQueryClient();
  const onSuccess = () =>
    queryClient.invalidateQueries({ queryKey });
  const { mutate: doThing } = useMutation({
```

> The hook takes an argument, which is a query key.

> We pass the given query key to be invalidated.

```
    mutationFn: API.doThing,
    onSuccess,
  });
  return doThing;
}
```

With this listing, we have all the parts we need to migrate the application to TanStack Query, so let's get to the final implementation.

9.3.3   *Implementation*

Again, we'll study only the key files. The overall structure is similar to the preceding version, with basically the same files, albeit organized a bit differently.

One final bit of functionality is still missing. We need to maintain some UX state: what the current thing is, if any, as the server does not remember the current thing for us. That is, are we in list view or detail view, and if so, what is the `id` of that thing? We will use zustand for this task because it is the easiest library to use for such a tiny application.

FILE STRUCTURE

The new file structure looks like this:

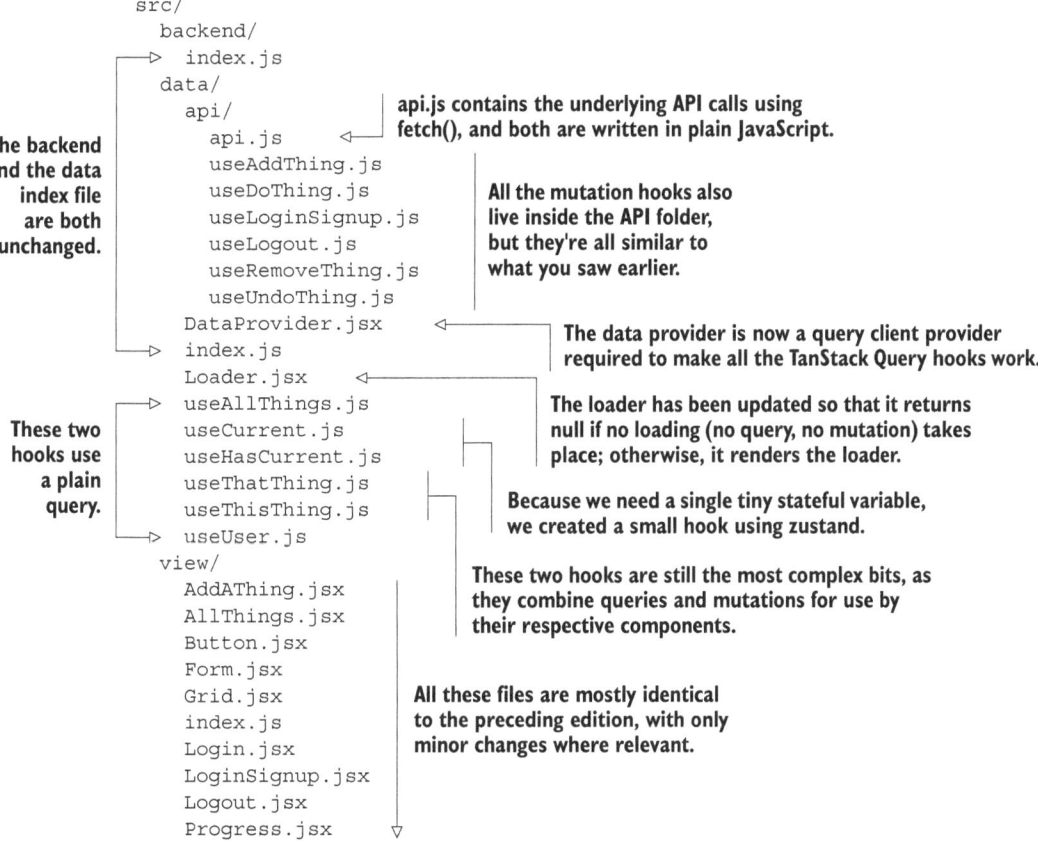

```
      RemoveButton.jsx    ^
      Signup.jsx          |
      SingleThing.jsx     |
      Thing.jsx           |
      Things.jsx          |
      ThingTitle.jsx      |
      View.jsx            |
    App.jsx               |
  main.jsx                |
```

All these files are mostly identical to the preceding edition, with only minor changes where relevant.

SOURCE CODE

We saw how a query works in listing 9.7 and how a mutation works in listings 9.8 and 9.9. In this section, I'll only show the main API file, which contains all the underlying API fetch calls, as well as useThatThing and useThisThing, which are the two most complex hooks in the application.

First is api.js, shown in the following listing. It's structurally similar to the previous version except that it's pure JavaScript, with no stateful variables involved.

Listing 9.10   src/data/api/api.js

```javascript
const URLS = {
  SESSION: "/api/session",
  USER: "/api/user",
  THINGS: "/api/things",
  THING: (id) => `/api/things/${id}`,
  DONES: (id) => `/api/things/${id}/done`,
  DONE: (id, did) => `/api/things/${id}/done/${did}`,
};
const wrappedFetch = async (...args) => {
  const res = await fetch(...args);
  if (!res.ok) {
    throw new Error("Unauthorized");
  }
  return res.json();
};
const get = (url) => wrappedFetch(url);
const post = (url, data) =>
  wrappedFetch(url, {
    method: "POST",
    body: data && JSON.stringify(data),
  });
const remove = (url) => wrappedFetch(url, { method: "DELETE" });
// USER API
const getUser = () =>
  get(URLS.USER).catch(() => false);
const login = (data) =>
  post(URLS.SESSION, data);
const signup = (data) =>
  post(URLS.USER, data);
const logout = () =>
  remove(URLS.SESSION);
// THING API
```

In this file, we simply export the 10 underlying commands required to use the entire API.

```
const loadThings = () =>
  get(URLS.THINGS);
const loadThing = (id) =>
  get(URLS.THING(id));
const addThing = (data) =>
  post(URLS.THINGS, data);
const removeThing = (id) =>
  remove(URLS.THING(id));
const doThing = (id) =>
  post(URLS.DONES(id));
const undoThing = ({ id, did }) =>
  remove(URLS.DONE(id, did));
export {
  getUser,
  login,
  signup,
  logout,
  loadThings,
  loadThing,
  addThing,
  removeThing,
  doThing,
  undoThing,
};
```

> In this file, we simply export the 10 underlying commands required to use the entire API.

Next is the hook rendering a single thing in the list of all things, `useThisThing`.

Listing 9.11 `src/data/useThisThing.js`

```
import { useQuery } from "@tanstack/react-query";
import { loadThings } from "./api/api";
import { useDoThing } from "./api/useDoThing";
import { useUndoThing } from "./api/useUndoThing";
import { useCurrent } from "./useCurrent";
export function useThisThing(id) {
  const { data } = useQuery({
    queryKey: ["things"],
    queryFn: loadThings,
  });
  const thing = data.find((t) => t.id === id);
  const doThing = useDoThing(["things"]);
  const undoThing = useUndoThing(["things"]);
  const seeThing =
    useCurrent((state) => state.seeThing);
  return {
    thing,
    doThing: () => doThing(id),
    undoLastThing: () => undoThing({ id, did: "last" }),
    seeThing: () => seeThing(id),
  };
}
```

> We query for the list of things, but because we know that we have this cached at this point, the library won't query the server for it. TanStack Query retrieves the latest response from the cache instead. Then we extract this particular thing based on the given id.

> The two hooks for getting the callbacks for doing and undoing things need the query key to invalidate postmutation, which is an array with the prefix "things".

To switch to detail view for a single thing, we need an action function from the stateful UI hook, useCurrent, that we made with zustand.

Finally, we have `useThatThing`, which is the API hook that renders the detail view.

Listing 9.12   `src/data/useThatThing.js`

```
import { useQuery } from "@tanstack/react-query";
import { loadThing } from "./api/api";
import { useCurrent } from "./useCurrent";
import { useDoThing } from "./api/useDoThing";
import { useUndoThing } from "./api/useUndoThing";
import { useRemoveThing } from "./api/useRemoveThing";
export function useThatThing() {
  const id =
    useCurrent((state) => state.currentId);
  const seeAllThings =
    useCurrent((state) => state.seeAllThings);
  const doThing = useDoThing(["currentThing"]);
  const undoThing = useUndoThing(["currentThing"]);
  const removeThing =
    useRemoveThing(seeAllThings);
  const { data: thing } = useQuery({
    queryKey: ["currentThing", { id }],
    queryFn: () => loadThing(id),
  });
  return {
    thing,
    doThing: () => doThing(id),
    undoThing: (did) => undoThing({ id, did }),
    undoLastThing: () => undoThing({ id, did: "last" }),
    removeThing: () => removeThing(id),
    seeAllThings,
  };
}
```

First, we have to extract some data and functionality from the stateful UI hook made with zustand in useCurrent.

Next, we include the two mutations to do and undo things. Here, we tell them to invalidate any query with the key prefix "currentThing".

The mutation to remove a thing needs to know what to do next, which is update the stateful UI variable to trigger the application to go back to list view.

Finally, we make the main query: fetching the information about the current thing with the given id.

You can see the full source code and test the application in the repository.

Example: reactive

This example is in the `reactive` folder. You can use that example by running this command in the source folder:

```
$ npm run dev -w ch09/reactive
```

Alternatively, you can go to this website to browse the code, see the example in action in your browser, or download the source code as a zip file: https://reactlikea.pro/ch09-reactive.

9.3.4   *Bonus side effects*

Besides built-in state, easy cache invalidation, more transparent flow, and other benefits that we've already described and used in this chapter, TanStack Query offers several benefits:

- *Network- or window-based automatic refetching*—The first benefit is automatic refetching based on network connection or window focus. TanStack Query automatically detects when your internet connection is cut, and whenever the connection is reestablished, it refetches all live queries. The library does the same for window focus. If you unfocus the browser window (by switching to another program or another tab), TanStack Query automatically refetches all live queries when the window regains focus. Although neither of these benefits would be hard to implement on your own, it's nice to get them for free.
- *Time-based cache invalidation*—The second benefit is cache invalidation based on time. TanStack Query can refetch any stale query that hasn't been updated from the server for a set period of time. Although this feature isn't enabled by default, you can easily enable it. You could set this interval to any value that makes sense for you. Five minutes would be a good start for this project.
- *Response deduping*—The third benefit, response deduping, is a bit more technical: if you have multiple components fetching the same query, TanStack Query pools them automatically, uses the same promise for all the instances, and returns the same data (referentially identical) to all the listeners.
- *Automatic request retries*—Finally, TanStack Query automatically retries any request that fails with a network or server error. This benefit is particularly nice, as you might not think about adding such functionality until you need it, but TanStack Query has it built in.

9.4 Reactive caching with TanStack Query

This section introduces four principles that make working with remote data as a user smoother. All these principles reduce the delay from action to response—or merely the perceived delay:

- Updating the cache directly from a mutation
- Updating the cache optimistically based on expected results
- Preloading partial data where available
- Hiding the loader if partial or old data is available

I'll go over each of these principles in turn. At the end, I'll provide a link to the example for the goal-tracking application rewritten to follow these principles.

9.4.1 Updating cache from a mutation

If you make a mutation toward a single specific resource, and you know (by API specification) that it will update (or add or delete) only that specific resource, you could short-circuit the mutate-then-query flow and return the updated resource directly from the mutation. We can update the API to do that and use the response from the API in the mutation to update the cached query, which in turn will re-render any component using the original query. This process sounds complex but is simple, as you can see in figure 9.10.

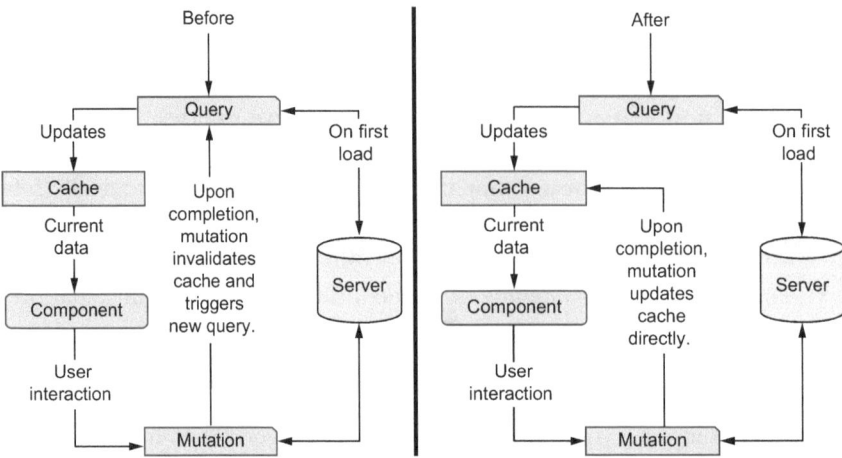

Figure 9.10   The flow when we update the cache query result directly from a mutation reduces server interactions by one for every mutation.

We can update the cache from a mutation in TanStack Query by passing an `onSuccess` callback as an option to `useMutation`. Let's see how this process works when we add a new thing in the `useDoThing` hook in listing 9.9. Note that we have to pass different callbacks in the two instances in which we use the variable because we have to update different queries (the whole list or the single current item), so the callback is a parameter. The following listing includes snippets from the various files to illustrate updating the cache from a mutation.

Listing 9.13   Updating cache directly from a mutation

```
// useDoThing.js (excerpt)
function useDoThing(onSuccess) {
  const { mutate: doThing } = useMutation({
    mutationFn: API.doThing,
    onSuccess,
  });
  return doThing;
}
//
// useThatThing.js (excerpt)
const onSuccess = (newThing) =>
  queryClient.setQueryData(
    ["currentThing", { id }],
    newThing,
  );
const doThing = useDoThing(onSuccess);
//
// useThisThing (excerpt)
const onSuccess = ({ name, done }) =>
  queryClient.setQueryData(
```

We change the useDoThing hook to take an onSuccess callback as an argument so that we can vary what happens when we do a thing in list view compared with detail view.

In detail view, we accept the response from the server (which is the newly updated thing) and replace the cache value. The useQuery in the same file automatically re-renders without querying the server. Note that we have to use the same query key as the original query, including the dynamic id value, to make sure that we update the correct cache value.

```
    ["things"],
    (oldThings) =>
      oldThings.map((oldThing) =>
        oldThing.id !== id
          ? oldThing
          : { id, name, count: done.length }
      )
    );
const doThing = useDoThing(onSuccess);
```

> ⌂ **In the other hook, useThisThing, we need to update the list query but update only the single item we're changing. Remember that in list view, we require the id, name, and count of a thing, so we make sure to include them in the new element.**

This approach seems like a lot of work, but it saves us from making a full network request on every single increment, which saves a lot of round-trip time in the long run. It not only makes the server less stressed but also makes UX a lot faster. Also, we can copy this logic to the undoThing hook as well, saving even more requests and making the experience even faster.

9.4.2 Updating the cache optimistically

A similar optimization is called *optimistic updates.* An optimistic update occurs when we update the cache prematurely as soon as we send the request with the expected result; then we refresh the data after the update as usual. If we did the optimistic update correctly, the user won't notice any difference between the optimistic update and the real update. Figure 9.11 illustrates this concept.

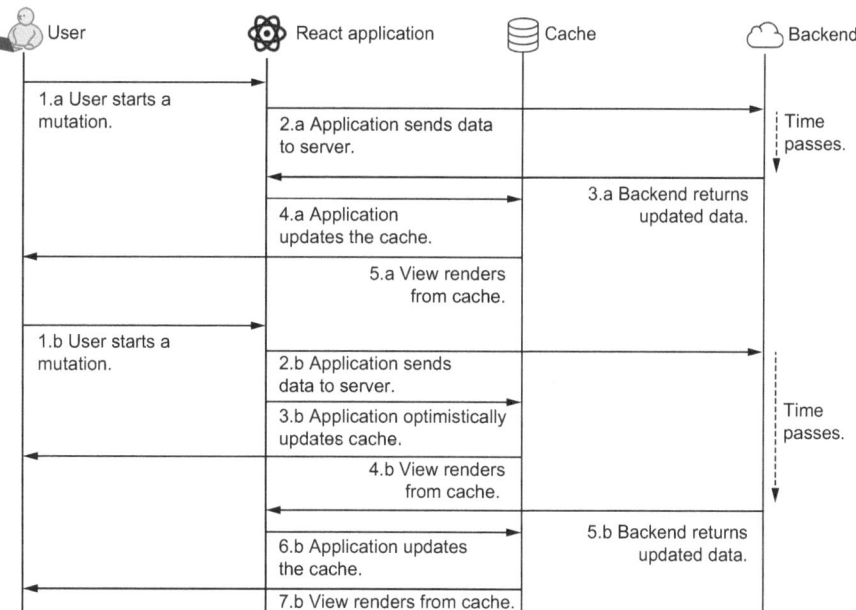

Figure 9.11 With optimistic updates, we update the local cache as soon as we send a mutation, so the application appears to update instantly. But we're ready to roll back the update if a server error occurs. In any case, we always refresh the state from the server after the update, so the optimistic cache value is purely cosmetic—never interacted with.

To accomplish optimistic updates, we have to do three things:

- When we send the mutation to the server, we also update the local cache with what we expect the server to do. If we add something, we can add the same thing locally; if we delete something, we delete the same thing locally, and so on.
- If the server request fails, we immediately roll back any optimistic updates that we performed and revert to whatever the cache state was before we started the request. A failed mutation is the same as status quo: nothing changes.
- If the request succeeds, we use the new data returned by the mutation to update the cache, replacing the optimistic update with the real server side–created data.

That last part—replacing the optimistic data with the real data—is often important. Our optimistic updates are naive, and we can make only the updates for which we have the data. On the server, more things might happen that we can't re-create in the client and wouldn't want to. We want to mimic the server action with as little effort as possible so that the user sees something in the 0.2 to 0.5 second it takes before the real server value comes in. That wait isn't long, so it's okay if the data is partial or not formatted correctly.

When we add a new thing in the goal-tracking application, for example, the server creates a new `thing` object with a random `id`. We can't guess what that `id` will be, and we don't need to. All we need to do is create a temporary item locally; that item will be close enough to the real thing, which will replace it in a very short time.

Achieving the preceding three steps is straightforward in TanStack Query. We pass a callback as an option for each of the three parts of the process:

- We can update the local cache as soon as the mutation is sent by passing an `onMutate` callback. This callback will receive the same data that the mutation function did. If we return something from the `onMutate` callback, it will be remembered internally as the *mutation context*, which will come in handy in the next step.
- We can roll back the optimistic update in an `onError` callback. This callback will receive not only the data passed to the mutation in the first place but also the mutation context returned by the `onMutate` function, if any. We use this context to remember what the cache looked like before we started messing with it, so we're able to roll it back.
- Most likely, the request will succeed, and then the `onSuccess` callback will be invoked. Here, we receive the newly created data from the server and can insert it into the cache instead of the temporary optimistic data. If we did everything correctly, we won't notice the swap. The process is almost like magic.

Figure 9.12 illustrates this more concrete flow. Listing 9.14 shows how this process is implemented for the `useAddThing` hook.

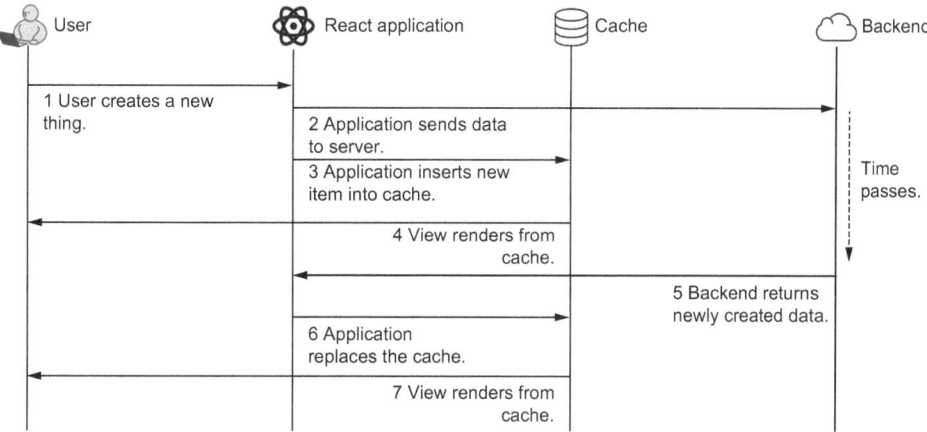

Figure 9.12 When the user adds a new thing to the list of things, we immediately and optimistically add the new thing to the local cache while the mutation is sent to the server. As soon as the real value is available from the server, the optimistic update is thrown out and replaced by the real data. Ideally, the user will not realize that the replacement took place.

Listing 9.14 Optimistic updates as soon as a mutation is sent

```
import {
  useQueryClient,
  useMutation,
} from "@tanstack/react-query";
import * as API from "./api";
export function useAddThing() {
  const queryClient = useQueryClient();
  const { mutate: addThing } = useMutation({
    mutationFn: API.addThing,
    onMutate: async (newData) => {
      await queryClient.cancelQueries({ queryKey: ["things"] });
      const oldValue = queryClient.getQueryData(["things"]);
      const newThing =
        { id: "temp", ...newData, count: 0 };
      queryClient.setQueryData(["things"], (old) => [...old, newThing]);
      return { oldValue };
    },
    onError: (error, data, { oldValue }) => {
      queryClient.setQueryData(["things"], oldValue);
    },
    onSuccess: (data, variables, { oldValue }) => {
      queryClient.setQueryData(["things"], [...oldValue, data]);
    },
  });
  return addThing;
}
```

The onMutate callback is used to update the query cache with the new thing.

Note that we initialize the count value manually to 0, as it is not part of the data we sent to the server, but we can predictably assume it to have a certain value when the real server response comes back.

If an error occurs, the onError callback is invoked. Here, we can restore the original cache from the given context.

Ideally, the request succeeds, and we can replace the optimistic value with the real one returned by the server.

We return the old cache value from the onMutate callback to allow for a smooth rollback later.

For the fun of it, you can try to change the default count value used in the optimistic update of `newThing` in listing 9.14. Try swapping in this line:

```
const newThing = { id: "temp", ...newData, count: 20 };
```

You'll see that a new item is instantly added with the wrong count but is updated to the real value shortly thereafter.

9.4.3 Using partial data where available

When we list all the things, we get only some data about each thing because we need only some of the data that's available. When we want to display all the information about a single thing, we have to query the server for the full trove of data.

Yes, yes, I know—in this case, the difference is minimal. But in a larger application, there could easily be a significant difference in the amount of data loaded. Pretend that it would be too expensive to load all data in list view, okay?

If we're clever, however, we could use the partial data we already have to partially render the detail view while we wait for the full data set to come back from the server. In TanStack Query, this data is called initial data or placeholder data. The difference between initial data and placeholder data is that *initial data* is real data that could be used in place of the original, and *placeholder data* is dummy data that looks like the right thing but most likely isn't.

In other frameworks, this data is sometimes referred to as *skeleton data*. We could use practically anything as placeholder data, such as `Please wait`, `loading`, but because we know something about what we're loading, we can prefill the component with that information as initial data while we wait for the whole lot.

In this case, we need four pieces of information to display a single thing: the ID, the name, the description, and a list of timestamps of every time we did the thing. We already have the ID and the name. We also know how many times we did the thing, though we don't know when we did it each time. The description is missing.

So let's prefill the detail view component with the data we already have, trying to fill in as much as possible while we wait for the server to give us everything. We know that we'll have everything in about 0.2 second, so it doesn't matter if we're a bit off. If we can show something, the user will be happier than they'd be if they were staring at a blank loader. This process involves three steps:

1 Retrieve whatever partial information we have from the local query cache.
2 Augment the partial data as well as possible to simulate the full data set.
3 Use this augmented data as initial data for the query.

In this case, we want to show partial data when we go to detail view and load the thing information in the `useThatThing` hook. Figure 9.13 illustrates the process.

Listing 9.15 shows how this process is implemented in the `useThatThing` hook. Remember that before, we had this query:

```
const { data: thing } = useQuery(["currentThing", { id }], () =>
    loadThing(id));
```

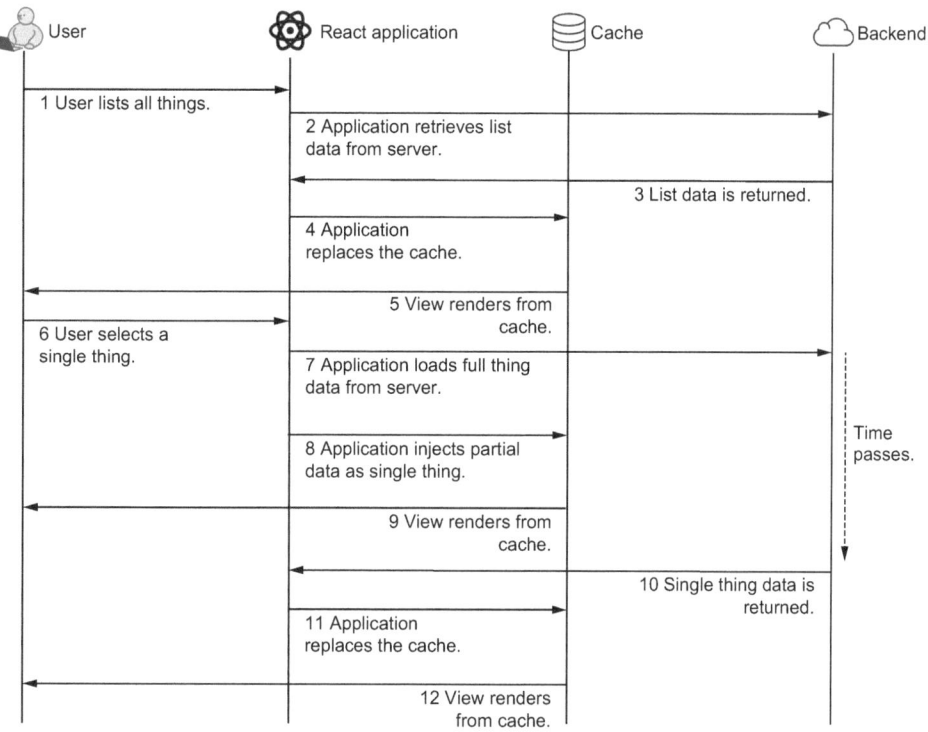

Figure 9.13   As we augment the partial data from the cache, we could put in whatever information we want for any piece of data we don't have. Often, empty data is desirable, but we could use some kind of loading indicator (dashes or dots).

Now, we pass in an extra option to the useQuery hook.

Listing 9.15   A query with placeholder data (excerpt)

```
function useThatThing(id) {
  ...
  // Find what we already know about this thing
  const queryClient = useQueryClient();
  const initialData = useMemo(() => {
    const things =
      queryClient.getQueryData(["things"]);
    const { count, ...partialThing } =
      things.find((t) => t.id === id);
    return {
      ...partialThing,
      description: "...",
      done: Array.from(Array(count))
        .map((k, id) => ({ id })),
    };
  }, [id, queryClient]);
  const { data: thing } = useQuery({
```

We add a dummy description. We can't begin to predict what it will be, so something that indicates missing data is probably best.

We have to find whatever partial information we have for this item in the cache.

Next, we have to go from a count of entries to a list of "done" entries with an id each. We don't have a timestamp for each, so we don't prefill that data, and we make sure that grid view can handle missing timestamps.

```
    queryKey: ["currentThing", { id }],
    queryFn: () => loadThing(id),
    initialData,              We pass this initial data object to the
  });                         useQuery hook as an extra option.
  ...
}
```

The result is that we see a partial detail view for about 0.2 second as soon as we click the detail for a single thing, and when the server data arrives, we see the full result. Compare the two views in figure 9.14.

Figure 9.14   The partial data on the left is missing a description (instead showing some dots), and the timestamps are missing in grid view for all the thing's entries. Because this view is shown so briefly, however, it will suffice.

An added benefit is that we don't need to worry about what to do while we wait for the server data. TanStack Query automatically prefills the data value with the initial data and later re-renders the component with the data value set to the real server data when it arrives. Data is never `undefined` or missing. Our component is unaware of this process and renders whatever it receives.

9.4.4   *Hiding the loader if some data is available*

This last concept is purely cosmetic and doesn't involve anything technical. Remember that now we're doing a bunch of optimizations, and many requests are happening in the background while useful data is displayed onscreen. Sometimes, this data is only partial or optimistic, but it's still useful. For that reason, we can remove the loader in all but the few instances in which we have nothing to display—at this point, data is only completely missing just after login/signup, when we're requesting things from the server for the first time.

TanStack Query allows us to see the difference between what it defines as loading (when you need the data because you have nothing to show) and fetching (when you update the response of a query that you have only old or partial data for). We need to update the loader component, which we display whenever a query or mutation is ongoing. We can amend this component and pass a parameter to the `useIsFetching` hook, checking only for ongoing requests that are `"loading"` rather than merely `"fetching"`:

```
const isFetching = useIsFetching({
  predicate: (query) => query.status === "loading",
});
```

This change is a small one, but it makes a big difference in terms of perception. Not showing a loader makes an application feel faster even if we are still loading data in the background.

9.4.5 *Putting it all together*

I've implemented all four principles in the `better-reactive` example. Check it out to see how much faster it feels than the preceding version.

> **Example: better-reactive**
> This example is in the `better-reactive` folder. You can use that example by running this command in the source folder:
>
> ```
> $ npm run dev -w ch09/better-reactive
> ```
>
> Alternatively, you can go to this website to browse the code, see the example in action in your browser, or download the source code as a zip file: https://reactlikea .pro/ch09-better-reactive.

I feel that this example provides much better UX, though I find the code somewhat cumbersome—especially the optimistic update combined with updating a single array entry in the `useAddThing` hook. The code is lengthy and not pretty, but it's fairly easy to read and improves the experience a great deal.

If you have a lot of optimistic updates in your codebase, you could create your own hook, `useOptimisticMutation`, on top of `useMutation`. This change would make the process smoother and the code easier to maintain.

Finally, I recommend switching to TypeScript for something like this example. The examples in this chapter are implemented in JavaScript to reduce the number of lines of code and details to explain. In the real world, it would be easier to work with in a typesafe environment such as TypeScript, which TanStack Query handles nicely.

Summary

- React applications most often communicate with a server to persist and read remote data.
- React is perfectly capable of dealing with remote data by itself, but as applications get larger, managing data cache gets more complicated.

- Several libraries make working with remote data easier, including TanStack Query. These libraries aren't network request libraries—merely data libraries built for working with remote data.
- TanStack Query takes managing local copies of remote data out of your hands and handles the work, including loading, refreshing, and invalidating.
- TanStack Query allows you to employ more complicated techniques to make remote-dependent applications easier and more pleasant to use:
  - Reactive caching enables your data layer to refresh data only when required and otherwise serve data from cache if it's known to be "fresh enough." Reactive caching is the core principle of many network data management libraries.
  - Another optimization technique is optimistic updates, which allow you to assume that a data mutation will work as intended on the server and temporarily update the cache locally (potentially only partially) while the mutation is sent to the server. When the mutation goes through and the server responds, we can update the cache to the real values resulting from the mutation, which might match what we expected or might be completely different.
  - We can use whatever data we have while we wait for the server to supply the rest. If you go to the details of a book in a list of books, you probably already have the title and author, so you can fill in that much data on the next page while you wait for the server to return the full response for the entire book data object.
  - We show a visual loader more selectively to make the application seem faster. Because we have something lifelike to show as soon as the request is sent, we can stop showing the loader and pretend that the request happened instantaneously. If we did everything correctly, UX is as good as with an instantaneous response.

Unit-testing React

This chapter covers

- Using common testing terminology
- Testing React components correctly
- Adding tests for custom hooks

How do we know that our React applications work as intended? Well, we can click around and see whether everything works the way we want it to work, right? We might forget to click some button or straight up forget some unlikely but possible combination of events. Also, if we're testing our application manually, we have to remember to do all the tests every time we change something to make sure that we didn't break something else.

That approach, of course, is a terrible way to ensure persistent quality in your application. Instead, quality assurance is a prime candidate for automation. With automated tests, you write scripts that emulate how a user would interact with your application (at various scopes) and verify automatically that the application acts the way it is supposed to act.

We'll jump right into testing React components by using React Testing Library (yes, that is the name of the package; it's not all that inventive). This library has many interesting aspects and variations, so we'll discuss a few types of components and how to test them properly. After that, we'll test some custom hooks, setting up some hypothetical situations based on real-world examples.

Note that, in this chapter, we won't create one large application, as we've done in the past few chapters. We don't need a large codebase to discuss proper testing, and the final three project chapters will give us a great chance for testing. All three projects include optional testing homework, if you want an extra challenge.

You can use a ton of tools for testing with different goals and at different levels. In this chapter, we'll discuss how to use Vitest as a test runner and React Testing Library as the component black-box testing framework. Vitest is a new library that's often used with Vite, which we use in our examples. Jest is another testing library that's probably more commonly used in React testing, but Vitest is almost identical in its API and is gaining a lot of traction because of its tie-in with Vite. Both Vitest and Jest can be used on their own without React Testing Library, but React Testing Library has quickly become the standard, as it comes with a better set of tools and utility functions and is built on a better set of principles. We'll get back to those principles in section 10.1.3. So 1-2-3 testing!

> **NOTE**   The source code for the examples in this chapter is available at https://reactlikea.pro/ch10.

10.1 *Testing a static component*

We will start our journey with a simple functional component that could be used in any website's main navigation, `MenuItem`:

```
export function MenuItem({ href, label }) {
  return (
    <li>
      <a href={href} title={label}>
        {label}
      </a>
    </li>
  );
}
```

Before we consider testing this component, let's go up one level and think about what makes this component work. We want to make sure that this component always works, but what does that mean? What does the component do? I'll try to rephrase the responsibility of the component in English rather than in JavaScript:

> *The* `MenuItem` *component renders a list item with a link. The link points to the given* `href` *property and uses the given* `label` *property as both title and link text.*

That text seems like a fair description of what we expect from this component, no? In pseudocode, it would be good if we could test with something like this script:

```
// PSEUDOCODE - DOESN'T WORK
const component =
  <MenuItem href="/blog" label="Blog" />;
```

First, we set up the test with an instance of the component.

```
const listItem =
  findElement(component, "listitem");
const link = findElement(listItem, "link");
expect(link).toHaveProperty("href", "/blog");
expect(link).toHaveProperty("title", "Blog");
expect(link).toHaveTextContent("Blog");
```

We want to find elements with a given role inside some other element.

Then we want to check whether an element has a specific property . . .

. . . as well as specific text content.

Luckily, modern test tools are fairly intuitive. This fictitious pseudocode is close to what we actually do. The following listing shows how we can implement this test correctly with Vitest and React Testing Library.

Listing 10.1 Unit-testing `MenuItem`

```
import {
  render,
  screen,
  getByRole,
} from "@testing-library/react";
import "@testing-library/jest-dom";
import MenuItem from "./MenuItem";
test(
  "MenuItem renders a link in a list item",
  () => {
  // ARRANGE
  render(<MenuItem href="/blog" label="Blog" />);
  // ASSERT
  const listItem = screen.getByRole("listitem");
  const link = getByRole(listItem, "link");
  expect(link).toHaveAttribute("href", "/blog");
  expect(link).toHaveAttribute("title", "Blog");
  expect(link).toHaveTextContent("Blog");
});
```

We import the render() function and two utility functions from React Testing Library.

We need to make sure the jest-dom extension is installed as well; we'll get back to what it does. Also, even though the extension says Jest, it works the same way for Vitest.

We also have to import the component we want to test.

We wrap the test body in the function test() with a descriptive name. This function is provided by Vitest and need not be imported.

We render the component into a JavaScript structure like a document object model (DOM) so we can run tests on it.

The Jest DOM extension allows us to test elements for properties and text content in a meaningful way.

Via screen.getByRole, we can get any element by role in the entire DOM. getByRole as a function allows you to get elements inside other elements by role.

Listing 10.1 contains a lot to unpack because it has some extra content we didn't know we needed—mostly imports of the relevant utilities and some scaffolding that we always need to run tests.

But aren't tests more code?

If you are worried about adding extra code, which means that the whole application will grow larger, (a) you have your head in the right place because reducing bundle size is always a concern, but (b) don't worry about it because tests aren't included in the production bundle.

(continued)

Your test files are run only when you specifically ask to test your project. When you run your project in development mode or build the project for production, the test files are ignored. So don't worry that they'll increase your application's footprint.

If you wonder what `"listitem"` and `"link"` mean in listing 10.1, I hear you; those items are confusing. I'll get to that topic shortly. For now, just know that `<li>` elements have the role `"listitem"` (because that's their role) and `<a>` elements have the role `"link"` (because that's their role).

Where do we put this test, though? Suppose that we have the component defined in `MenuItem.jsx`. We simply put the test in `MenuItem.test.jsx` and place it next to the `MenuItem` component in the same folder, which we've done in the `menuitem` example.

Example: menuitem

This example is in the `menuitem` folder. You can run the tests in that example by running this command in the source folder:

```
$ npm test -w ch10/menuitem
```

Alternatively, you can go to this website to browse the code, see the example in action in your browser, or download the source code as a zip file: https://reactlikea .pro/ch10-menuitem.

The files inside the `src` folder are now

```
src/
  App.jsx
  index.jsx
  MenuItem.jsx
  MenuItem.test.jsx
```

We're now ready to run the test. So let's learn how.

Roles and names

What does the `getByRole` function mean? It refers to ARIA roles. *ARIA* is an acronym for *Accessible Rich Internet Applications*, and *roles* pertain to all elements in a web document. Because there are many types of users of web pages with many wants and needs, web documents must be accessible not only visually but also programmatically.

Users with various disabilities may be using a screen reader to interact with your web page, or a search engine bot or an information service such as Siri or Alexa might try to index your information. Such services can tell you the height of the Eiffel Tower only if they can find that information on some website that is marked up in a way to make that information easily accessible by a computer.

ARIA's *Web Accessibility Initiative* (often called *WAI-ARIA*) is a specification concerning how elements in a web page can be structured, understood, and interacted with in a nonvisual manner that mirrors visual interaction with the same web page.

WAI-ARIA defines the possible roles that elements can take. The specification defines how each role should be understood and, if relevant, how it can be interacted with. Most interesting elements come with an implicit role, but you can override the role of any given element. Some roles are applied only manually, never implicitly.

Most of this discussion is beyond what we need to know here. All we care about is being able to test our components by accessing elements by role rather than by HTML tag name, class name, or other attribute, as roles are similar to how users interact with an application.

Let's get back to practical matters. Links have the role `"link"`. List items have the role `"listitem"`. Headlines (h1–h6) are `"heading"`, buttons are `"button"`, images are `"image"`, and so on. With that information, this line suddenly makes a lot more sense:

```
const listItem = screen.getByRole("listitem");
```

This concept has another important aspect: every element also has an automatically generated *name*. This name is the *accessible name* and has a complicated algorithm behind it, but basically, the name of an element is the text inside it. Consider this snippet:

```
<a href="/blog">Blog</a>
```

This link has the name `"Blog"`. That's obvious. But we also have names for elements with nested nodes, elements with images, Scalable Vector Graphics (SVGs), or other complex HTML elements inside them. We could create another link element with the name `"Blog"` by including an image with the `alt` attribute `"Blog"`:

```
<a href="/blog">
  <img src="/images/blog.png" alt="Blog" />
</a>
```

Both of these links work well visually because the blog image is probably something that a visual user would immediately recognize as a blog icon. A nonvisual user would also know that the link is a link to the blog because its accessible name is `"Blog"` regardless of how it is communicated visually. This example is the core of the concept of an accessible name. You can arrange your document so that your elements have the correct accessible name regardless of how your element appears to sighted users.

We can get an element by role *and* name by passing the name as an option to the `getByRole` function:

```
const listItem = screen.getByRole("listitem", { name: "Blog" });
```

We will be using roles and names throughout our tests.

10.1.1 *Running tests*

Vitest doesn't come bundled with Vite (to reduce the initial download), so we need to do four things to make tests work in a standard Vite setup. I've already done the work for you in the `menuitem` example, but these are the four steps:

1 Install new packages.
2 Update ESLint configuration.
3 Amend Vite configuration with test setup.
4 Add test scripts to `package.json`.

INSTALLING NEW PACKAGES

This step is the easiest one. We simply install four packages and save them in `dev-Dependencies`:

```
$ npm -w ch10/menuitem install --save-dev vitest jsdom
➥@testing-library/react @testing-library/jest-dom
```

These packages are

- `vitest`—The test runner
- `jsdom`—The simulated DOM environment in which we run the tests
- `@testing-library/react`—The testing framework
- `@testing-library/jest-dom`—Some utility methods that make writing tests more elegant

Note the order of the command-line interface (CLI) arguments. If you use `npm install -w <workspace> --save-dev <package>`, that command will *not* save the dependencies to `package.json`. You have to use `npm -w <workspace> install --save-dev <package>` for the installation to work correctly, because we use npm workspaces.

UPDATING ESLINT

ESLint is set up to assume that all your source files are regular React files. But for our tests, we commonly use globally available functions such as `test`, `it`, `describe`, and `expect`. We need to tell ESLint that all files that end with `*.test.js` or `*.test.jsx` are to be run in a Vitest environment. For that purpose, we add this block to `.eslintrc.js`:

```
module.exports = {
  ...
  overrides: [
    {
      files: ["**/*.test.js", "**/*.test.jsx"],
      env: { vitest: true },
    },
  ],
};
```

AMENDING VITE CONFIGURATION

Next, we need to tell Vite that we're using Vitest as the test runner. This process is simple. We add a single line of config to the default:

```
import { defineConfig } from "vite";
import react from "@vitejs/plugin-react";
// https://vitejs.dev/config/
export default defineConfig({
  plugins: [react()],
  test: { globals: true, environment: "jsdom" },
});
```

> **The new line we're adding to set up Vitest** ←⎯

ADDING TEST SCRIPTS

The last step is adding new scripts to `package.json` so we can run them by using the `npm run` command. First, let's add the basic test script:

```
{
  ...
  "scripts": {
    ...
    "test": "vitest",
    ...
  },
  ...
}
```

> **We add an extra script that invokes Vitest with the default parameters.** ←⎯

Now we can run the script by using `npm run test`, and when we do so, we get this output:

```
$ npm test -w ch10/menuitem
> @jrr/ch10-menuitem@0.1.0 test
> vitest
 DEV  v0.34.6 <path>/ch10/menuitem
 ✓ src/MenuItem.test.jsx (1)
   ✓ MenuItem renders a link in a list item
 Test Files  1 passed (1)
      Tests  1 passed (1)
   Start at  23:35:28
   Duration  1.12s (transform 47ms, setup 0ms, collect 218ms,
     tests 63ms, environment 537ms, prepare 101ms)
 PASS  Waiting for file changes...
       press h to show help, press q to quit
```

> **When running, the script prints out every test suite (test file) and test case it comes across and shows it as passing or failing.** ←⎯

> **The script sums up the results.** ⎯|

> **The script doesn't exit after completion but keeps listening for file changes to rerun the tests on any change.** ⎯|

This output looks great. The test passes, which is a good start. As a bonus, `npm` allows us to run the test script by typing `npm test` rather than `npm run test`, so we've already saved a couple of keystrokes.

Notice that in the preceding output, the test runner keeps listening after a full run of all tests. That setting is the default; the test runner monitors your test files continuously. But we can pass a flag to have the test run only once:

```
$ npm test -w ch10/menuitem -- run
```

When we run the command with the `run` flag, the test runs only once, which is nice for this demonstration. For development purposes, it's probably better to run the test without the flag to keep it running as you write your application and observe that all tests always pass.

In the `menuitem` example, I added an extra script called `test:once` that will run the test with the `run` flag. You can run that test by typing `npm run test:once` if is configured like so:

```
{
  ...
  "scripts": {
    ...
    "test": "vitest",
    "test:once": "vitest run",
    ...
  },
  ...
}
```

10.1.2 Test file location

Note that not everybody puts test files next to the components that they're testing, and not everyone follows the same naming patterns. Here are a few other possible patterns:

- Tests go in a separate folder inside each source folder. If you have `/src/MenuItem.jsx` and `/src/library/Button.jsx`, the tests will reside in `/src/test/MenuItem.jsx` and `/src/library/test/Button.jsx`, respectively.
- Tests go in a folder other than the source folder. If you have `/src/MenuItem.jsx` and `/src/library/Button.jsx`, the tests will reside in `/tests/MenuItem.jsx` and `/tests/library/Button.jsx`, respectively.
- Some people use the name fragment `spec` instead of `test`, as in `Button.spec.jsx`.

All these approaches have pros and cons. Make sure that you're consistent, at least.

10.1.3 Test resilience

The menu item test didn't test for several things. For one, it didn't test whether the list item or link had any specific styling. Also, the list item could have content other than the link (maybe an icon), which wouldn't break the functionality of this component. But if you remember the text description of our component, we didn't mention those things, so I argue that those behaviors are not part of what the component *does*.

Is that fact a feature or a bug? The answer probably depends on your application. But many people agree that testing only the important parts and allowing other parts to change makes your application and tests more resilient to change.

Let's see how this process works. Suppose that several months later, some other developer has to update the `MenuItem` component to include a small icon before every element. The following listing shows the new component.

> **Listing 10.2   Unit-testing `MenuItem` with an icon**

```
export function MenuItem({ href, label }) {
  return (
```

```
      <li>
        <a href={href} title={label}>
          <img
            src="/images/link.png"
            width="20"
            alt=""
          />
          {label}
        </a>
      </li>
    );
}
```

We've put a small link icon in every link component.

Example: menuitem-icon

This example is in the `menuitem-icon` folder. You can run the tests in that example by running this command in the source folder:

```
$ npm test -w ch10/menuitem-icon
```

Alternatively, you can go to this website to browse the code, see the example in action in your browser, or download the source code as a zip file: https://reactlikea .pro/ch10-menuitem-icon.

Let's try to run the tests again by using `npm run test:once -w ch10/menuitem-icon`:

```
npm run test:once -w ch10/menuitem-icon
> @jrr/ch10-menuitem-icon@0.0.0 test:once
> vitest run
 RUN  v0.34.6 <path>/ch10/menuitem-icon
 ✓ src/MenuItem.test.jsx (1)
   ✓ MenuItem renders a link in a list item
 Test Files  1 passed (1)
      Tests  1 passed (1)
   Start at  00:20:45
   Duration  1.03s (transform 47ms, setup 0ms, collect 213ms,
     tests 65ms, environment 377ms, prepare 100ms)
```

We run the test:once script in the new example workspace.

The test still passes!

This result is called *test resiliency*. We want our tests to pass when we make nonbreaking changes and fail only when we make significant changes to functionality. Suppose that instead of adding an icon, we added a class name or two to the elements. These things shouldn't cause the test to fail because we're not changing any functionality.

Other test paradigms would break if we made these changes. We could decide to match the exact JSX output of a component to a statically defined one, for example. If we took this approach, the test would break if the JSX changed in even in the slightest way, including changes to class names or other things that may not affect the function-ality of the component.

Different schools of thought exist, but I believe in the former approach: testing func-tionality only at a user-interaction level. This approach is one of the governing principles behind the Testing Library package, which is why I recommend it. Next, let's see what happens when we add stateful components and other interactivity to the mix.

10.2 *Testing interactive components*

In section 10.1, we made a simple test for a simple static component. The component never changes unless the properties change, so we don't have a lot to test. When we start testing more interactive components, however, the tests get a lot more interesting.

If a button activates something, we want our test to simulate a user clicking that button and then verifying that the result occurs. If we have input fields, the interaction sequence can get even more complex, with the input field receiving focus, receiving keyboard inputs, losing focus, and so on.

10.2.1 *Testing a stateful component*

Let's go back to Old Faithful: the click counter. This counter is one of the most basic components to create in React, and you probably made several variants when you were learning how stateful components work. The following listing shows a two-button variant.

Listing 10.3   The click counter

```
import { useState } from "react";          This component has four interesting
export function Counter({ start = 0 }) {   bits. First is the initial value passed
  const [counter, setCounter] = useState(start);   as a property, which defaults to 0.
  const update = (delta) => () =>          Then we have the stateful variable
    setCounter((value) => value + delta);  counter and its update function.
  return (
    <main>
      <h1>Counter: {counter}</h1>          We display the counter
      <button onClick={update(1)}>         in a heading here.
        Increment
      </button>
      <button onClick={update(-1)}>        We update the counter in
        Decrement                          the two buttons for up
      </button>                            and down, respectively.
    </main>
  );
}
```

Before we start testing anything, it might make sense to formulate in plain English what we want to test:

- The counter component should display the current value in a heading.
- The counter component should initialize the counter to the given `start` property.
- The counter component should initialize the counter to `0` if no `start` property is given.

- When you click the increment button, the counter should increment and the heading should update.
- When you click the decrement button, the counter should decrement and the heading should update.
- If you instantiate the counter and later pass a different `start` property to the component, the counter does not change to reflect the value of the `start` property and can be changed only via the buttons.

That list seems to be exhaustive. First, let's start the test runner in the terminal. The test runner will run the tests automatically as we write and save them, checking them live. To enable that feature, execute `npm test -w ch10/click-counter` in the terminal.

We can implement the first three tests quickly (and we'll test only the first one implicitly via the two others). The following listing shows how.

Listing 10.4   Testing the static parts of the click counter

```
import { render, screen } from "@testing-library/react";
import "@testing-library/jest-dom";
import { Counter } from "./Counter";
test(
  "Counter should start at the given value",
  () => {
  // ARRANGE
  render(<Counter start={10} />);
  // ASSERT
    const heading = screen.getByRole(
      "heading",
      { name: "Counter: 10" },
    );
  expect(heading).toBeInTheDocument();
});
test(
  "Counter should start at 0 if no value is given",
  () => {
  // ARRANGE
  render(<Counter />);
  // ASSERT
    const heading = screen.getByRole(
      "heading",
      { name: "Counter: 0" },
    );
  expect(heading).toBeInTheDocument();
});
```

In the first test, we start the counter at 10 and verify that it displays a heading with that value.

In the second test, we start the counter without a start value and verify that it displays a heading with 0.

The test runner should pick up this new test automatically and display the following:

```
✓ src/Counter.test.jsx (2)
   ✓ Counter should start at the given value
   ✓ Counter should start at 0 if no value is given
 Test Files  1 passed (1)
     Tests  2 passed (2)
```

```
Start at   20:33:07
Duration   381ms
```

Great start! Next, we need to test the buttons. How do we click a button? Do we find the button and call its `click()` method? Do we send an event to the button by using `dispatchEvent`? Do we hover the button first (by using an event) because that's what a real user does?

We don't have to worry about any of those things because we will use another library (a package that is also part of Testing Library): `user-event`. This library has great methods for easily interacting with elements as a user would. Do you need to click a button, drag a slider, hover over an image, or type in an input field? All those things and many more are neatly solved by the `user-event` library. Let's add the test for clicking the increment button.

Listing 10.5 Clicking a button

```
import { render, screen } from "@testing-library/react";
import userEvent
  from "@testing-library/user-event";          ◁──  We import the
import "@testing-library/jest-dom";                  userEvent library.
import { Counter } from "./Counter";
test(
  "Counter should start at the given value",
  () => {...},
);                                               We collapsed the old
test(                                            tests to reduce clutter,
  "Counter should start at 0 if no value is given",   but they're still there.
  () => {...},
);
test(
  "Counter should increment when button is clicked",      Notice that we added async
  async () => {                                            to the function definition
  // ARRANGE      To use the user-event library, we start the   because we'll have to wait
  render(<Counter />);   session by calling the setup method   for something to complete
  // ACT               and getting a user session back.        before progressing.
  const user = userEvent.setup();        ◁──
  const increment = screen.getByRole(         We find the button we need to click by
    "button",                                 role and name (because we have two
    { name: "Increment" },                    buttons now, so the name is required).
  );
  await user.click(increment);      ◁──────   We click the button via the
  // ASSERT                                   user session. This line of code
  const heading = screen.getByRole(           is the one we have to wait
    "heading",                                for—hence, the await in
    { name: "Counter: 1" },      Finally, we  front. This line works because
  );                             validate that it returns a promise that
  expect(heading).toBeInTheDocument();  the counter  resolves when everything
});                              has updated.  that happens from the click
                                               has been executed.
```

If you still have the test runner running in the background, check the terminal to see whether the new test also passes. Ideally, you'll see something like this:

```
✓ src/Counter.test.jsx (3)
   ✓ Counter should start at the given value
   ✓ Counter should start at 0 if no value is given
   ✓ Counter should increment when button is clicked
 Test Files  1 passed (1)
      Tests  3 passed (3)
   Start at  20:34:45
   Duration  413ms
```

Woohoo! That's awesome. We can easily copy that last test to test the decrement button. For that final test, what happens if we update the property passed to a component?

I've hidden one thing from you (probably a ton of things, but this one is relevant now). The `render()` function from React Testing Library returns something useful: an object with some convenient properties. One of those properties is the `rerender` function, which does exactly what it says on the tin: it allows you to render the component with potentially different properties but in the same instance, so it will update the existing component. The test for the last item in our plain-English wish list becomes what you see in the following listing.

Listing 10.6 Re-rendering a component

```
import { render, screen } from "@testing-library/react";
import userEvent from "@testing-library/user-event";
import "@testing-library/jest-dom";
import { Counter } from "./Counter";
test("Counter should start at the given value", () => {...});
test("Counter should start at 0 if no value is given", () => {...});
test("Counter should increment when button is pressed", async () => {...});
test("Counter should decrement when button is pressed", async () => {...});
test(
  "Counter should not update value if passed start property changes",
  () => {
  // ARRANGE
    const { rerender } =
      render(<Counter start={10} />);
  // ACT
  rerender(<Counter start={20} />);
  // ASSERT
  const heading = screen.getByRole(
    "heading",
    { name: "Counter: 10" },
  );
  expect(heading).toBeInTheDocument();
});
```

> We destructure the rerender function from the return value of the render call.

> We rerender the component with a new property passed in. Note that this happens synchronously, so there's no need for await here (or for async in the test in general).

> We test the heading as usual.

Again, you can check the test runner terminal window and see that all five tests are passing.

ARRANGE, ACT, ASSERT

You may have noticed the `ARRANGE`, `ACT`, `ASSERT` comments in the tests. (Sometimes, the `ACT` part is skipped if it's not relevant.) What are those comments about?

These comments are homages to the classic pattern of organizing your tests this way for a more structured approach. That pattern is unsurprisingly called *Arrange-Act-Assert*. (Programmers are terrible at creative writing, though they do get a few points for alliteration!)

It is not uncommon to see people adding these comments to indicate clearly what happens on which line. Note that, sometimes, multiple rounds of `ACT` and `ASSERT` take place, as we will see in listing 10.11.

While we're here, let's make the tests a bit nicer to look at. We are often looking for the heading to check the current value, so why not make that check a bit easier? We also need a reference to the buttons, which we could make easier to access.

It is common practice to create a custom setup function at the top of a test file that initializes the test case for use throughout the component. I included this final test file in the following listing.

Listing 10.7 The full test file with a convenient setup function

```
import { render, screen } from "@testing-library/react";
import userEvent from "@testing-library/user-event";
import "@testing-library/jest-dom";
import { Counter } from "./Counter";          We define the setup function
function setup(start) {                        outside the test cases.
  const { rerender } = render(<Counter start={start} />);
  const getCounter = (val) => screen.getByRole(      This setup function defines a getCounter
    "heading",                                       function that allows us to query for the
    { name: `Counter: ${val}` },                     heading with a given counter value.
  );
  const increment = screen.getByRole("button", { name: "Increment" });
  const decrement = screen.getByRole("button", { name: "Decrement" });
  const user = userEvent.setup();
  return {              We return an object with
    getCounter,         all the things we're going
    increment,          to need for all the tests.
    decrement,
    user,
    rerender: (newStart) => rerender(<Counter start={newStart} />),
  };
}                                                    Here, we set up a counter
test("Counter should start at the given value", () => {   with an initial value of 10
  // ARRANGE                                               and have easy access to the
  const { getCounter } = setup(10);                        getCounter function as a result.
  // ASSERT
  expect(getCounter(10)).toBeInTheDocument();    We invoke the getCounter function
});                                              with the expected counter value.
```

```
test("Counter should start at 0 if no value is given", () => {
  // ARRANGE
  const { getCounter } = setup();
  // ASSERT
  expect(getCounter(0)).toBeInTheDocument();
});
test("Counter should increment when button is pressed", async () => {
  // ARRANGE
  const { getCounter, increment, user } = setup();
  // ACT
  await user.click(increment);        ◄─────────────
  // ASSERT
  expect(getCounter(1)).toBeInTheDocument();
});
test("Counter should decrement when button is clicked", async () => {
  // ARRANGE
  const { getCounter, decrement, user } = setup();
  // ACT
  await user.click(decrement);
  // ASSERT
  expect(getCounter(-1)).toBeInTheDocument();
});
test("Counter should not update value if passed start property changes", ()
    => {
  // ARRANGE
  const { getCounter, rerender } = setup(10);
  // ACT
  rerender(20);       ◄─┤
  // ASSERT
  expect(getCounter(10)).toBeInTheDocument();
});
```

We can click the increment button in a single line because we get both the button reference and the user session instance from the setup function.

We can even re-render the component with a new start value via the rerender property.

Example: click-counter

This example is in the `click-counter` folder. You can run the tests in that example by running this command in the source folder:

```
$ npm test -w ch10/click-counter
```

Alternatively, you can go to this website to browse the code, see the example in action in your browser, or download the source code as a zip file: https://reactlikea .pro/ch10-click-counter.

Now, that's a clean-looking test suite (*chef's kiss*)! All the tests have one line of arrangement, optionally one line of acting, and, finally, one line of assertion. It's immediately clear what every test does both from the description and from reading the code. This result almost brings a tear to one's eye. Almost.

10.2.2 Testing callbacks

How do we test a component when part of its function is invoking a callback passed as a parameter? This may not seem like a big deal, but this pattern is common, so it's very important to test such a component properly so that it doesn't break down due to a typo and end up being pushed to production while broken.

Consider another standard application that every React developer created *ad infinitum* in their early days: the to-do application. For our example application, we have a component that shows all the items and a delete button next to each item. When the delete button is clicked, the `onDelete` callback property is invoked with the to-do item in question. The following listing shows the source code for the `Items` component.

Listing 10.8   The items component from a to-do app

```
export function Items({ items, onDelete }) {
  return (
    <>
      <h2>Todo items</h2>
      <ul>
        {items.map((todo) => (
          <li key={todo}>
            {todo}
            <button
              title={`Delete '${todo}'`}
              onClick={() => onDelete(todo)}
            >
              <span aria-hidden>×</span>
            </button>
          </li>
        ))}
      </ul>
    </>
  );
}
```

The component accepts a property that is a function to be invoked when the user interacts with the component.

We add a descriptive title to the button to serve as its accessible name for various textual interfaces.

The title is used as the accessible name only if the button does not have text content, so we hide the X icon inside the button from screen readers by using aria-hidden.

Let's see how we test this component. We want to pass in some callback that we can test if it's invoked later, and Vitest has a built-in method for that purpose: `vi.fn()`. The following listing shows how to use this method.

Listing 10.9   Testing the items component from a `Todo` app

```
import { render, screen } from "@testing-library/react";
import userEvent from "@testing-library/user-event";
import "@testing-library/jest-dom";
import { vi } from "vitest";
import { Items } from "./Items";
test("Items should call onDelete callback
when item is deleted", async () => {
  // ARRANGE
  const items = ["Item A", "Item B"];
  const mockDelete = vi.fn();
  render(
    <Items items={items} onDelete={mockDelete} />,
  );
  // ACT
  const user = userEvent.setup();
```

We create a variable with vi.fn. This method returns a mock function, which we can later ask whether it has been called, how many times, with which arguments, and so on.

We pass in this mock function like any other property.

```
const secondItemDelete = screen.getByRole("button", {
  name: "Delete 'Item B'",
});
await user.click(secondItemDelete);
```

We click the button as we now know how to do (but remember to await the click).

```
// ASSERT
expect(mockDelete)
  .toHaveBeenCalledWith("Item B");
});
```

Finally, we expect the mock function to have been called with the string "Item B" because we clicked the button next to the second item.

Example: todo

This example is in the `todo` folder. You can run the tests in that example by running this command in the source folder:

```
$ npm test -w ch10/todo
```

Alternatively, you can go to this website to browse the code, see the example in action in your browser, or download the source code as a zip file: https://reactlikea .pro/ch10-todo.

That code is fairly easy to read (except for the slightly cryptic `vi.fn` call). A mock function is versatile and can be used every time you have to pass in a function and control what it does or what it returns, or to validate its invocation. Please check the documentation at https://vitest.dev/guide/mocking.html#functions to find out what mocking functions can do for you.

10.2.3 Testing a form

Now we get to one of the more complex types of interactive components: the form. As you will see, it's not too complex to test when we apply what we know.

For this example, I'm using a slightly more complex application to fully illustrate how to integrate a test into a somewhat larger project. The application is a timer; the user can define multiple timers and start and stop each one individually. When you want to add a timer, you input the minutes and seconds in a simple form rendered by the `AddTimer` component.

Listing 10.10   A form to add a new timer

```
import { useState } from "react";
import { Button } from "./Button";
import { Input } from "./Input";
const EMPTY = { minutes: 0, seconds: 0 };
export function AddTimer({ onAdd }) {
  const [data, setData] = useState(EMPTY);
  const onChange = (evt) => {
    setData((oldData) => ({
      ...oldData,
      [evt.target.name]:
        evt.target.valueAsNumber,
    }));
  };
```

The only property is a callback.

When anything in the form changes, we update local state data.

```
const onSubmit = (evt) => {
  evt.preventDefault();
  onAdd(data.minutes * 60 + data.seconds);
  setData(EMPTY);
};
return (
  <form onSubmit={onSubmit} className="timer timer-new">
    <ul className="parts">
      <Input
        name="minutes"
        value={data.minutes}
        onChange={onChange}
      />
      <li className="colon">:</li>
      <Input
        name="seconds"
        value={data.seconds}
        onChange={onChange}
      />
    </ul>
    <Button icon="play" label="Start" />
  </form>
);
}
```

> When the form is submitted, we invoke the callback with the form data and reset it.

> The two inputs have labels—"minutes" and "seconds"—that also serve as their accessible names.

> We also have a submit button in the form labeled "Start".

We don't do any error handling here. Also, we don't handle the case in which the user submits the form but the time is zero, so we don't want to bother testing for that. We want to test whether the callback is invoked correctly when the user inputs values and clicks the submit button. To do this test, we need to be able to find the relevant elements and interact with them appropriately.

We already know how to find the button (`getByRole("button", { name: "Start" })`) and interact with it (`user.click(button)`), but how do we find the inputs? The default role for a regular input field is `textbox`, but for a number input field, the implicit role is `spinbutton` because you can use the arrow keys to update the value as well as type it. We interact with it through the user event method `.type()`, simply passing in what we want to type in the input field. Then the `user-event` library correctly submits all the events involved in typing: focusing the fields, inputting the characters, triggering the change handler after each character, and so on. Putting everything together, we can test this component by using the test suite you see in the following listing.

> ### Listing 10.11   Testing a form

```
import { render, screen } from "@testing-library/react";
import userEvent from "@testing-library/user-event";
import "@testing-library/jest-dom";
import { vi } from "vitest";
import { AddTimer } from "./AddTimer";
function setup() {
```

> We start with a setup function to make things a bit easier even though we have only a single test case (so far). If we add some error handling later, this function will make adding a second test case much quicker.

```
  const onAdd = vi.fn();
  render(<AddTimer onAdd={onAdd} />);
  const minutes = screen.getByRole(
    "spinbutton",
    {name: "minutes"},
  );
  const seconds = screen.getByRole(
    "spinbutton",
    {name: "seconds"},
  );
  const start = screen.getByRole(
    "button",
    { name: "Start" },
  );
  const user = userEvent.setup();
  return { onAdd, minutes, seconds, start, user };
}
test("AddTimer should invoke callback when submitted", async () => {
  // ARRANGE
  const { onAdd, user, minutes, seconds, start } = setup();
  // ASSERT
  expect(minutes).toHaveValue(0);
  expect(seconds).toHaveValue(0);
  // ACT
  await user.type(minutes, "5");
  await user.type(seconds, "30");
  // ASSERT
  expect(minutes).toHaveValue(5);
  expect(seconds).toHaveValue(30);
  // ACT
  await user.click(start);
  // ASSERT
  const expectedNumber = 5 * 60 + 30;
  expect(onAdd)
    .toHaveBeenCalledWith(expectedNumber);
  expect(minutes).toHaveValue(0);
  expect(seconds).toHaveValue(0);
});
```

The submit callback is a Vitest mock function.

We get references to all the elements we care about.

First, we validate that the form inputs are initially empty.

Then, we type in both fields and validate that the fields contain what we typed.

After we click the start button (which submits the form), we validate that the callback has been invoked with the correct number and that the form inputs have reset to 0.

Example: timer

This example is in the `timer` folder. You can run the tests in that example by running this command in the source folder:

```
$ npm test -w ch10/timer
```

Alternatively, you can go to this website to browse the code, see the example in action in your browser, or download the source code as a zip file: https://reactlikea .pro/ch10-timer.

That's it. In general, if you need to interact with a component in any way, the user-event library almost always has you covered. In a few specialized cases, that library won't cover your needs, but you can use the more low-level `fireEvent` from the React Testing Library itself.

> ### Don't test implementation details
>
> Note that we specifically *don't* test several things. When we enter data in input fields, for example, we don't test whether the internal state variable data is updated correctly because we don't care. If someone changes the component to store the data in some other way, but the component works otherwise, our tests should happily carry on passing and not report anything as being broken (because nothing broke). We call such a thing an *implementation detail*, which you should never test. We test the component as though it is a black box. We can give it some inputs (properties and events) and see what it outputs (callbacks and DOM), but we can and should never look inside it to see how it works (effects, stateful variables, and so on). Those internals are implementation details that may change.
>
> You can implement a specific piece of functionality in hundreds of ways, and your tests should accept all of them, not just the one that you happened to have used.

10.2.4 Testing a hook

Custom hooks in React are used only inside components, so if you thoroughly test all your components, by inference you invariably also test all your custom hooks. Sometimes, however, it's hard to test every combination of inputs for every hook in a big, complicated component that uses many custom hooks. If you have a general hook that's used in multiple places, you want to make sure it works correctly. In such a case, it can be helpful to set up a test case for the custom hook itself. But because hooks are special functions, you can't call a hook like a regular function, so you can't test it like any other function.

For that purpose, React Testing Library comes with a utility for testing hooks specifically. In this example, which involves a game, we need to tell whether keys are pressed to move the correct elements around. We'll create a small hook, `useIsKeyPressed`, that takes the name of a keyboard key and returns `true` or `false` depending on whether the key is pressed. Most important, the hook causes the component to rerender, as the key is pressed and released throughout the application lifetime. You can see the hook in the following listing.

Listing 10.12   A custom hook

```
import { useState, useEffect } from "react";
export function useIsKeyPressed(target) {
  const [pressed, setPressed] = useState(false);
  useEffect(() => {
    const getHandler =
      (isPressed) =>
      ({ key }) =>
        key === target && setPressed(isPressed);
    const downHandler = getHandler(true);
```

The hook accepts the name of a key, such as "ArrowDown" or "g".

When the particular key is pressed anywhere inside the window, the Boolean state flag is set to the appropriate state.

```
    const upHandler = getHandler(false);
    window                                        ⌖ When the particular key is
      .addEventListener("keydown", downHandler);    pressed anywhere inside the
    window.addEventListener("keyup", upHandler);    window, the Boolean state flag is
    return () => {                                   set to the appropriate state.
      window.removeEventListener("keydown", downHandler);
      window.removeEventListener("keyup", upHandler);
    };
  }, [target]);
  return pressed;
}
```

We can test this hook with the `renderHook` function from the React Testing Library. This function returns (among other things) a reference with the current return value from the hook, which we need to check at various times to see whether it has the right value. This test is implemented in the following listing. Beware—the syntax for pressing and releasing a key using the `user-event` library is a bit weird.

> **TIP**   For help with the syntax for pressing, holding, and releasing keys, check the full documentation on the React Testing Library website at https://mng.bz/gv9n.

Listing 10.13   Testing a custom hook

```
import { renderHook } from "@testing-library/react";
import userEvent from "@testing-library/user-event";
import { useIsKeyPressed } from "./useIsKeyPressed";
test(
  "useIsKeyPressed should react to the target key and only that key",
  async () => {
  // ARRANGE
    const { result } =                        We render the hook and destruct the
      renderHook(() => useIsKeyPressed("h"));  result reference from the response. We
  const user = userEvent.setup();              set the hook up to look for the "h" key.
  // ASSERT
  expect(result.current).toBe(false);      ◀── First, we verify that the key is
  // ACT                                        not pressed at the beginning.
  await user.keyboard("{f>}");
  // ASSERT                                 Then we press and hold the "f" key,
  expect(result.current).toBe(false);       which should not change anything.
  // ACT
  await user.keyboard("{h>}");
  // ASSERT                                 We press and hold the "h" key, which should
  expect(result.current).toBe(true);        do something. Now the hook returns true.
  // ACT
  await user.keyboard("{/f}");
  // ASSERT                                 We release the "f" key. The
  expect(result.current).toBe(true);        hook still returns true.
  // ACT
  await user.keyboard("{/h}");
  // ASSERT                                 Finally, we release the "h" key. Now
  expect(result.current).toBe(false);       the hook correctly returns false.
});
```

> **Example: keypress**
>
> This example is in the `keypress` folder. You can run the tests in that example by running this command in the source folder:
>
> ```
> $ npm test -w ch10/keypress
> ```
>
> Alternatively, you can go to this website to browse the code, see the example in action in your browser, or download the source code as a zip file: https://reactlikea .pro/ch10-keypress.

TIP `renderHook` has a bunch of other capabilities for testing more complex hooks, but this example demonstrates the basic way it works and how and when it can be used. If you need to test a hook for some application, it's always a good idea to check the documentation, located at https://mng.bz/ eo0Z.

10.3   *Testing a component with dependencies*

Sometimes, you have a component that depends on some external or even some complex internal functionality for your component to work, but that functionality is undesirable or improbable to include in the test of said component. You might have a component that displays the user's current coordinates as reported by the browser's geolocation API. You want to test what your component does when the geolocation functionality is turned off or when the user refuses to give you the data, as well as whether you receive the data. How would you go about automating this test? Moving your computer around to test it from different locations seems to be counterproductive.

Similarly, you might have a component that depends on an external library and the functionality it provides. Let's say that your component loads data from a web server by using Axios, which is a popular data-fetching library—an alternative to the built-in `fetch()` method. We don't want to query our server every time, and we also want to control whether the server responds with an error message or the correct data. Again, we need to figure out how to automate this test.

Finally, we might have some complex internal functionality, such as an app-wide context, that is updated in many ways, but we want to test our component in isolation for various configurations. We need to figure out how we can use our context in a controlled fashion so it can deliver the right inputs to the component we want to test.

All these examples involve mocking. When you *mock* something, you replace it with a tiny bit of pseudocode that doesn't do what the thing normally does; it's a drop-in replacement that you fully control. Let's see how to go about this process.

10.3.1   *Mocking the browser API*

Suppose that you have a simple component that, at the click of a button, asks the user for their current position, using the browser geolocation API. If the user chooses to divulge this information, their coordinates are displayed; if not, an error message is displayed. Figure 10.1 shows this simple component flow.

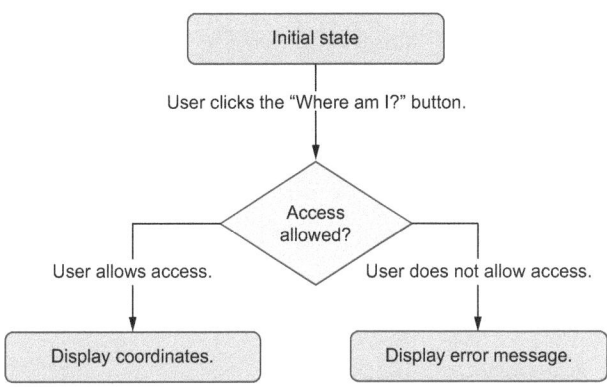

Figure 10.1 When the user clicks the "Where Am I?" button, we ask the browser for the geolocation, using the `navigator.geolocation` API. If we're allowed to, we show the coordinates; otherwise, we show an error.

We will implement this component with a simple `useState` hook because it's so small. The following listing shows the implementation.

Listing 10.14 Where am I? No, really, I'm not sure!

```
import { useState } from "react";
const initialState = { status: "initial" };
export function WhereAmI() {
  const [state, setState] = useState(initialState);
  if (state.status === "initial") {
    const onSuccess = ({ coords }) =>
      setState({ status: "success", coords });
    const onError = ({ message }) =>
      setState({ status: "error", message });
    const onClick = () =>
      navigator.geolocation
        .getCurrentPosition(onSuccess, onError);
    return <button onClick={onClick}>Where am I?</button>;
  }
  if (state.status === "error") {
    return <h1>Error: {state.message}</h1>;
  }
  const { latitude, longitude } = state.coords;
  return (
    <h1>
      Coordinates: {latitude}, {longitude}
    </h1>
  );
}
```

> We invoke the geolocation API, and depending on which callback is invoked, we transition the state to the success or the error state.

To test this component, we need to control what the geolocation API returns, but we can't. We can replace the API with one that we do control, however. We mock the global `navigator.geolocation` object and replace the `getCurrentPosition` function with a mock function over which we have full control.

Listing 10.15 Mocking the browser API for test purposes

```
import { render, screen } from "@testing-library/react";
import userEvent from "@testing-library/user-event";
import "@testing-library/jest-dom";
import { vi } from "vitest";
import { WhereAmI } from "./WhereAmI";
function setup() {
  const mockAPI = vi.fn();
  global.navigator.geolocation =
    { getCurrentPosition: mockAPI };
  render(<WhereAmI />);
  const button = () => screen.getByRole("button");
  const heading = () => screen.getByRole("heading");
  const user = userEvent.setup();
  return { mockAPI, button, heading, user };
}
describe("WhereAmI component", () => {
  test("should show the coordinates if the user allows it", async () => {
    // ARRANGE
    const { mockAPI, button, heading, user } = setup();
    mockAPI.mockImplementationOnce(
      (success, error) =>
        success({
          coords: { latitude: 55, longitude: 12 }
        })
    );
    // ACT
    await user.click(button());
    // ASSERT
    expect(heading()).toHaveTextContent("Coordinates: 55, 12");
  });
  test(
    "should show an error if the user does not allow access",
    async () => {
    // ARRANGE
    const { mockAPI, button, heading, user } = setup();
      mockAPI.mockImplementationOnce(
        (success, error) =>
        error({ message: "User denied access" })
    );
    // ACT
    await user.click(button());
    // ASSERT
    expect(heading()).toHaveTextContent("Error: User denied access");
  });
});
```

In the setup function, we mock the global navigator geolocation object with our mock function.

This time, we group the test cases in a describe block, which is a way to group related tests. You'll see it in the output.

When we want the API lookup to succeed, we set the implementation of the mock function to call the success callback with a properly formatted response.

When we want the API lookup to fail, we call the error callback in the mock function implementation.

> **Example: geo**
>
> This example is in the `geo` folder. You can run the tests in that example by running this command in the source folder:
>
> `$ npm test -w ch10/geo`
>
> Alternatively, you can go to this website to browse the code, see the example in action in your browser, or download the source code as a zip file: https://reactlikea .pro/ch10-geo.

If we run this code, we get the following output:

```
✓ src/WhereAmI.test.jsx (2)
  ✓ WhereAmI component (2)           ◀——————  The describe block is used to group
    ✓ should show the coordinates if the user        related tests. Describe blocks can
      allows it                                       be nested as much as necessary.
    ✓ should show an error if the user does
      not allow access                        Each test inside a describe
 Test Files  1 passed (1)                     block is indented a bit further
      Tests  2 passed (2)                      to show the hierarchy.
   Start at  21:16:51
   Duration  400ms
```

Using this method, you can mock any API that your components might be using from the browser, including local storage, network requests (`fetch`), battery status, and screen capture.

10.3.2 Mocking a library

In this example, we want to make a list of the first 10 starships in some famous movie series about starships from a galaxy far, far away. We will use the convenient `swapi.dev` resource; feel free to guess what the `sw` part of that URL stands for. That web service has a (paginated) list of starships available at this URL: https://swapi.dev/api/ starships/. We'll request only the first page of results for this exercise, but you can add pagination if you're so inclined.

To make this network request, we could use the built-in `fetch()` function, but for this exercise, we will use the Axios library, which is a popular library for making network requests. When we use Axios, we can implement this `StarshipList` component as in the following listing.

Listing 10.16 A component with a network request using Axios

```
import { useState, useEffect } from "react";
import axios from "axios";
const URL = "https://swapi.dev/api/starships/";
export function StarshipList() {
  const [state, setState] = useState({ status: "initial" });
```

```
useEffect(() => {
  setState({ status: "loading" });
  axios
    .get(URL)
    .then(({ data }) =>
      setState({
        status: "success",
        list: data.results },
      )
    )
    .catch(({ message }) =>
      setState({
        status: "error",
        error: message },
      )
    );
}, []);
if (["loading", "initial"].includes(state.status)) {
  return <h1>Loading...</h1>;
}
if (state.status === "error") {
  return <h1>Error: {state.error}</h1>;
}
return (
  <>
    <h1>List of Starships:</h1>
    <table border="1">
      <thead>
        <tr>
          <th>Name</th>
          <th>Model</th>
          <th>Class</th>
        </tr>
      </thead>
      <tbody>
        {state.list.map(({ url, name, model, starship_class }) => (
          <tr key={url}>
            <td>{name}</td>
            <td>{model}</td>
            <td>{starship_class}</td>
          </tr>
        ))}
      </tbody>
    </table>
  </>
);
}
```

Using Axios, we make a request for the given URL.

If the request succeeds, we update the state accordingly.

If the request fails, we also update the state, but to a slightly different status.

This component requests that URL every time it is loaded because that's what we want it to do. We don't want our tests to do the same thing, however. For one thing, network requests are slow; more important, this URL is an external service, and we don't want to bombard it with requests or hit any rate limits on requests from the same IP address. Finally, we would have a hard time testing the request failure state because how can we ensure that the request fails when we don't control the backend?

To avoid making the request to the server but still test the component, we can mock out the entire Axios library and replace it with a mock function that we can control within our tests. We can set that function to return either a positive or negative result, and we can validate that the component works correctly. The following listing implements this test suite.

Listing 10.17 Mocking a library when testing a component

We import the Axios library here, but because we mock it (later), the mock implementation is imported, not the real library.

```
import { render, screen } from "@testing-library/react";
import "@testing-library/jest-dom";
import axios from "axios";
import { vi } from "vitest";
import { StarshipList } from "./StarshipList";
vi.mock("axios", () => ({
  default: { get: vi.fn() },
}));
describe("StarshipList component", () => {
  test("should initially be in a loading state while fetching", () => {
    // ARRANGE
    axios.get.mockImplementationOnce(
      () => new Promise(() => {})
    );
    render(<StarshipList />);
    // ASSERT
    const heading = screen.getByRole("heading", { name: "Loading..." });
    expect(heading).toBeInTheDocument();
  });
  test("should show an error message on failure", async () => {
    // ARRANGE
    axios.get.mockImplementationOnce(() =>
      Promise
        .reject({ message: "Request failed" })
    );
    render(<StarshipList />);
    // ASSERT
    const title =
      await screen.findByRole("heading",
      { name: "Error: Request failed" },
    );
    expect(title).toBeInTheDocument();
  });
  test("should show a list of ships when all goes well", async () => {
    // ARRANGE
    axios.get.mockImplementationOnce(() =>
      Promise.resolve({
        data: {results: [
          { name: "Tardis", url: "/tardis" },
        ] },
      })
    );
    render(<StarshipList />);
```

The library mock is created here, and even though it occurs after all the imports, Vitest runs all mocks before any imports are resolved, so the library will be mocked everywhere it is used.

When we want to test the loading state, we make sure that the promise returned from the Axios get method never settles.

To test the error state, we return a rejected promise with an appropriate error message.

Because the promise is resolved inside an effect inside the component, the error message won't be visible on first render of the component. If we wait a while, however, that message will appear. We can use the findByRole method for that purpose, as it waits for the given node to be in the document and throws an error if that doesn't happen within a reasonable time (default timeout: 5 seconds).

To test the successful case, we return a resolved promise, and we must be careful to format the response as the real response would be formatted.

```
    // ASSERT
    const heading = await screen.findByRole("heading", {
      name: "List of Starships:",
    });
    expect(heading).toBeInTheDocument();
    const firstName = screen.getByRole(
      "cell",
      { name: "Tardis" },
    );
    expect(firstName).toBeInTheDocument();
  });
});
```

> We test not only the headline but also the rendered table rows to check whether they match the mock data.

Example: axios

This example is in the `axios` folder. You can run the tests in that example by running this command in the source folder:

```
$ npm test -w ch10/axios
```

Alternatively, you can go to this website to browse the code, see the example in action in your browser, or download the source code as a zip file: https://reactlikea .pro/ch10-axios.

Although this component is extremely simple (and a bit naive), it does show the power of mocking a whole library. You can use the same method to mock internal files by using a relative mock path such as `vi.mock("../someLibrary", () => { ... })`. This approach is a handy way to test only the component in question—not all sorts of dependencies, which might have weird side effects that you don't want to trigger.

> **NOTE** For networking libraries, I recommend using Mock Service Worker (MSW) instead to mock out the entire backend rather than the network library itself, which is a much more reliable and future-proof method of mocking the API layer. Feel free to go back to chapter 9, which discusses how MSW works. The method described in this section is still valid and useful, however.

10.3.3 *Mocking a context*

We're going to go back to an application that we've already implemented in many iterations through the book: the dark mode application. We first implemented it in chapter 2 but have since amended it in several iterations. This application has several components, several of which require access to different parts of a context provided by an app-wide provider.

We use a selectable context from the `use-context-selector` library rather than the built-in context from React itself in this application. The principles used in this section are identical to using a React context, however. Nothing changes except that we would import `createContext` and `useContext` from the React package rather than from the `use-context-selector` package (and we couldn't use selectors, of course).

In this application, components are not individually wrapped by a provider (which would serve no purpose), so if we test a component in isolation, it can't access that context and will have access only to the default context defined in the call to `create-Context()`. The following listing shows one of those components—the button—from the dark mode application.

Listing 10.18   A context-dependent button component

```
import { useContextSelector }
  from "use-context-selector";          We import the relevant parts
import { DarkModeContext }              from outside this component.
  from "./DarkModeContext";
function Button({ children, ...rest }) {
  const isDarkMode = useContextSelector(
    DarkModeContext,                         Then we select the isDarkMode
    (contextValue) => contextValue.isDarkMode    flag from the context.
  );
  const style = {
    backgroundColor:
      isDarkMode ? "#333" : "#CCC",   ◁───┐  Finally, we style the button based
    border: "1px solid",                  │  on the flag, using inline styles.
    color: "inherit",                        (How naive we were back then).
  };
  return (
    <button style={style} {...rest}>
      {children}
    </button>
  );
}
```

This component works well in the context of the full application, but when we test it in isolation, we need to surround the button with the relevant values in the proper context.

Listing 10.19   Wrapping the button in a mock context for testing

```
import { render, screen } from "@testing-library/react";
import "@testing-library/jest-dom";
import { Button } from "./Button";
import { DarkModeContext }              We have to import the raw context
  from "./DarkModeContext";            because we need to provide it.
function setup(text, isDarkMode = false) {    We create the context
  const value = { isDarkMode };               value dynamically.
  render(
    <DarkModeContext.Provider value={value}>  We render the button
      <Button>{text}</Button>                 wrapped in a context provider
    </DarkModeContext.Provider>               with the dynamic value.
  );
  return screen.getByRole("button");
}
describe("Button component", () => {
```

```
test("should render in light mode", () => {
  // ARRANGE
  const button = setup("Click me");          ←  When we want to test light mode,
  // ASSERT                                       we use the default value (false).
  expect(button).toHaveTextContent("Click me");
  expect(button.style.backgroundColor)
    .toBe("rgb(204, 204, 204)");              ┐   We have to validate the
});                                           │   style this way, which we
test("should render in dark mode if enabled", () => {  │  can do via button.style
  // ARRANGE                                            │  because we used inline
  const button = setup("Click me", true);    ←          │  styles. Had we used some
  // ASSERT                                   │          │  CSS rule, we would have to
  expect(button.style.backgroundColor)       │          │  use getComputedStyle.
    .toBe("rgb(51, 51, 51)");                 ┐
});                                           │   When we test the dark mode
});                    We test the button    │   variant of the button, we
                      color in the same way. │   make sure to set the flag.
```

That code is relatively straightforward. Let's see how we test using a function from the context. In the toggle button component, we use the `toggleDarkMode` function from the context.

Listing 10.20   The toggle button using a context function

```
import { useContextSelector } from "use-context-selector";
import { Button } from "./Button";
import { DarkModeContext } from "./DarkModeContext";
export function ToggleButton() {
  const toggleDarkMode = useContextSelector(
    DarkModeContext,                                    Retrieves the toggleDarkMode
    (contextValue) => contextValue.toggleDarkMode       callback from the context
  );
  return (
    <Button onClick={toggleDarkMode}>     ←   Assigns the callback to the onClick
      Toggle mode                             event handler on the button
    </Button>
  );
}
```

We already know how to test this component. We know how to mock a context (from listing 10.19), and we know how to test a callback (from listing 10.9), so we need to put these two things together, as I've done in the following listing.

Listing 10.21   Wrapping the button in a mock context for testing

```
import { render, screen } from "@testing-library/react";
import userEvent from "@testing-library/user-event";
import "@testing-library/jest-dom";
import { vi } from "vitest";
import { ToggleButton } from "./ToggleButton";
```

```
import { DarkModeContext } from "./DarkModeContext";
function setup() {
  const toggleDarkMode = vi.fn();
  const value = { toggleDarkMode };
  render(
    <DarkModeContext.Provider value={value}>
      <ToggleButton />
    </DarkModeContext.Provider>
  );
  return { button: screen.getByRole("button"), toggleDarkMode };
}
describe("ToggleButton component", () => {
  test("should invoke the toggle on click", async () => {
    // ARRANGE
    const { button, toggleDarkMode } = setup();
    // ACT
    const user = userEvent.setup();
    await user.click(button);
    // ASSERT
    expect(toggleDarkMode)
      .toHaveBeenCalledTimes(1);
  });
});
```

> Again, we set up the button wrapped in a context provider with a custom value containing a mock function.

> We check whether the mock function is invoked once when we click the button.

Example: dark-mode

This example is in the `dark-mode` folder. You can run the tests in that example by running this command in the source folder:

```
$ npm test -w ch10/dark-mode
```

Alternatively, you can go to this website to browse the code, see the example in action in your browser, or download the source code as a zip file: https://reactlikea .pro/ch10-dark-mode.

Running this code gives us slightly different output because now our project has multiple test files. The output from the example with the two tests looks like this:

```
✓ src/Button.test.jsx (2)
 ✓ src/ToggleButton.test.jsx (1)
 Test Files  2 passed (2)
      Tests  3 passed (3)
   Start at  21:41:44
   Duration  1.09s (transform 67ms, setup 1ms, collect 565ms, tests 168ms,
     environment 775ms, prepare 186ms)
```

> Both files, both suites, and all three tests pass. Looking good!

Again, this context is simple. Testing a more complex context requires doing these same tricks with more variables. If you have multiple contexts, you can wrap your component in all of them.

Summary

- Testing your components is a great way to future-proof your application against bugs and regressions when you add new functionality or change existing functionality down the line.
- An application created with Vite comes without testing infrastructure, but we can easily add it in with Vitest. You may want to extend the testing infrastructure with some additional packages from Testing Library, including (most importantly) the React package.
- You can test both static and interactive components in a fairly straightforward and easy-to-understand manner if you follow the Arrange-Act-Assert pattern of test writing.
- If your component has external or complex internal dependencies, it can be a great help to mock them. You can mock dependencies in several ways that depending on where the dependencies are located.
- You can mock browser APIs, files, folders, and whole libraries. You can also mock a context, which is going to be a useful skill going forward, as you will most likely encounter a lot of contexts in your career.

React website frameworks

This chapter covers

- Rendering React on the server
- Developing a fullstack application in Next.js and Remix

React website frameworks allow us to run React on the server. You may wonder why you would want to, and both the short and the long answers are *speed* and *performance*. Your page renders a lot faster and your website becomes a lot more performant. These results are good for visitor retention, search engine optimization, and overall user experience—and most likely will also be good for your (or your employer's) bottom line.

So how does rendering React on the server make the application faster? It seems to involve simply moving the work from one computer (yours) to another (the server). Well, the reasons are many and fairly technical, so I'll dive into them in section 11.1. For now, let's summarize the reason: short-circuiting a lot of data transfer round-trips and even bypassing JavaScript to render the page to the visitor in as few milliseconds as possible.

The difference can be huge. Almost any website will be faster if it uses a React website framework (correctly!) rather than a client side–only React application, and some websites get orders of magnitude faster. It's not uncommon for a page to go from being ready in more than 5 seconds to being ready in less than 1 second. Now, that's good news!

In this chapter, I'll go over these technical details and discuss what makes server-side rendering (SSR) of React faster in general. Then I'll show how we can make a server side–rendered React application for a weather app in two popular React website frameworks: *Next.js* (https://nextjs.org) and *Remix* (https://remix.run).

I could have dedicated this entire book to either framework, but as I'm going to cover both frameworks in a single chapter, I'll have to skip some details. Both frameworks have excellent documentation, though, so please follow the preceding links to learn more if you need more context.

> **NOTE**   The source code for the examples in this chapter is available at https://reactlikea.pro/ch11.

11.1   *What's a website framework?*

React is a JavaScript framework, and browsers run JavaScript, so browsers can run React. But environments other than browsers also run JavaScript, so other environments, such as Node on a web server, can run React.

The fact that you can run React anywhere that supports JavaScript is the cornerstone of a React website framework. You run React on the server, so you can generate HTML on the server by using React as a templating language. Running React on the server gives you several benefits, including the following:

- *Fullstack development*—This type of development enables you to build your entire website in a single application with frontend and backend merging. You don't have to have two different projects or codebases or even two different teams that need to coordinate. Everything is built together, so you have optimal colocation. You can directly change what is loaded from the database and where it goes in the final HTML in a single file, even though those things happen in the backend and frontend, respectively.
- *SSR*—With SSR, HTML is served instantly from the server, improving page-load times, which might in turn improve both visitor retention and search engine ranking.
- *Dynamic content*—You can integrate any content into your website seamlessly because you control the whole stack. You can load content from a database or from an external API, even with some secrets that you normally wouldn't put in your frontend application. The framework will make sure that your content is passed correctly from backend to frontend; you don't have to do anything.
- *URL routing*—URL routing allows you to use the URL as a source of navigation. Complex routing rules are built into most frameworks, making it easy to create pages.

But the benefits come with one particular requirement: hydration. When the client renders the React output for the first time, every single byte of output has to match that of the server rendering.

The rest of this section touches on these concepts in general. When we understand what makes a React website framework tick, we'll discuss the two candidate frameworks in section 11.2.

11.1.1   Fullstack React as a concept

Normally, React is a frontend-only technology, limited by the normal restrictions by which frontends abide. These restrictions include the following:

- You need a separate backend developed next to or even separate from the frontend to be able to talk to a database or any similar form of shared storage.
- Everything in the codebase is public knowledge, so you cannot use secret API keys or similar content that you don't want strangers to access (because they might be able to extract private data from your application).
- You need an agreed-upon API to communicate between the React application and the backend. If you update some view in the frontend, you may need new data from the backend, so you have to update the API and update the backend to accommodate this change.
- Deep linking (with HTML rendered on the server) is next to impossible.

When you introduce fullstack React, however, you eliminate all of these problems because you run React on both the frontend *and* the backend. These problems suddenly vanish:

- You develop the frontend and the backend as one single application, so you don't have to spend much time thinking about accessing a database or saving files to permanent storage.
- You can easily annotate which parts of the code are compartmentalized to run only on the client or only on the server, so you can hide your API keys on the server with little effort.
- API worries go away because you literally write the frontend using the data and the backend providing the data in the same file.
- Deep linking is trivial and built into the platform.

Compare what happens underneath the UI when you visit the page for a specific movie on a movie-database website in two different setups. In setup A, we run React as frontend only, and we have a separate backend written in another language (which could .NET, Python, or COBOL for all we care). In setup B, we run React as part of a fullstack React framework such as Next.js or Remix. We are going to visit a detail page somewhere deeper on the website (so, not the front page). Figure 11.1 illustrates what happens in each setup.

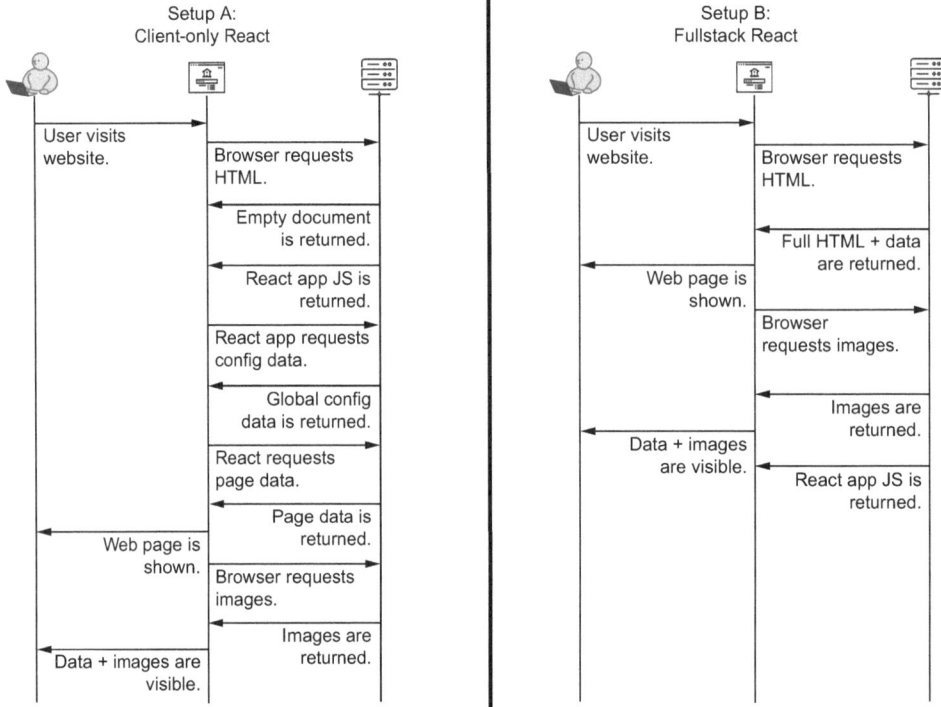

Figure 11.1 In setup A, which has a classic backend, we need a lot of communication and setup between the two parts of the application before the page can render. In setup B, we return everything in one go, and the client is ready to serve the proper content instantly.

One of the coolest things about fullstack React is that, because the HTML comes pre-rendered and fully ready to display the entire page from the server, JavaScript isn't required to display that page. As you see in the last step of setup B in figure 11.1, the JavaScript for the React application can be loaded after the page is shown to the user. Yes, the React application is required to make the page fully interactive, but that behavior isn't required for the first display, making the website even faster.

11.1.2 *Rendering HTML on the server*

We've been using Vite for all our applications so far, and it's great for playing around with React, but it's bad at doing one thing: serving relevant HTML from the server. You may remember that we have a file called `index.html` in all our Vite-based applications. This file is the same one (with some scripts and stylesheets inserted) that will be served from the server and loaded in the browser. You may also remember that this file is empty for all intents and purposes. When we ignore nonvisual elements (such as scripts and meta tags), the file is

```
<!doctype html>
<html lang="en">
```

```
  <body>
    <div id="root"></div>
  </body>
</html>
```

That's it. The file contains an empty `<div>`. If you use an old phone, have JavaScript disabled, are on a slow connection, or if the scripts fail to load for some reason, you will see a blank web page.

With SSR, we render the full HTML on the server, which means that we run the entire React application with all the correct data put in all the correct components, take a snapshot of the resulting HTML, and return that HTML to the browser. Compare the new approach with the classic one in figure 11.2.

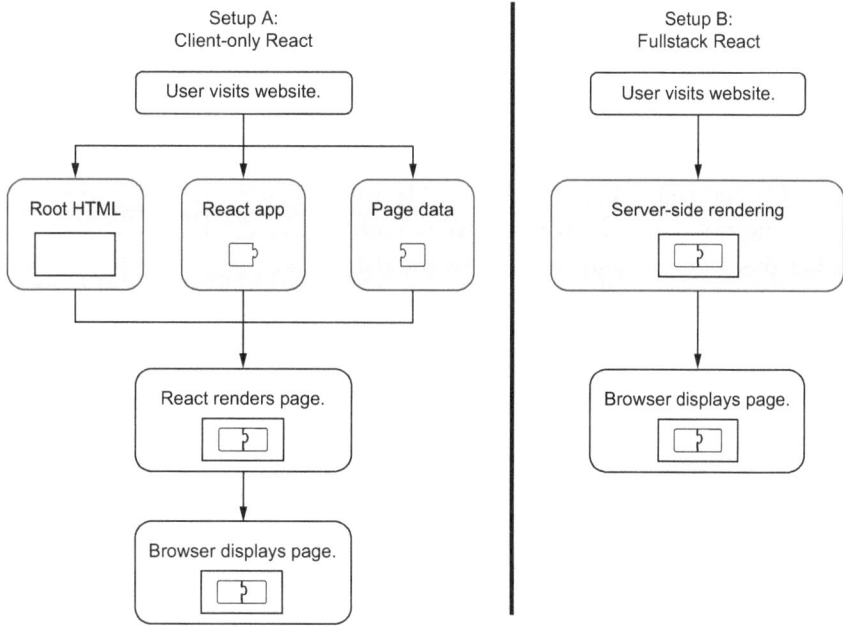

Figure 11.2 **Imagine a page to display as the simplest puzzle ever. It has only two pieces: a component defined in React that defines the template and a data package that contains the data required to turn the template into HTML. In a classic React setup, we retrieve those two pieces in two separate requests and put them together in the browser when everything is loaded. In the framework setup, we get both pieces at the same time instantly.**

One question about figure 11.2 may arise: what happens if we start on one page and then move to a different page that requires data from the server—do we have to wait for the server to render the full HTML for that page as well?

The answer, luckily, is no. The server render takes place for the first page. After that, only the data is loaded from the server. That's why, when we write components for SSR, we write them as two separate items: a component and a data package. For the first page in a visit, the two are combined on the server and returned along with the JavaScript application. But for subsequent page visits, only the data package is requested for each page, as we already have the React application (including the component) available in the browser, so all we need is the data for each page. Figure 11.3 illustrates a visit to a website.

This concept of every page having two pieces—data and a React component—is central to the way React website frameworks function. That data piece can contain all sorts of dynamic content, as we will discuss next.

11.1.3 *Dynamic content*

Because we generate the data package for every page on the server, we can load whatever we want—information from a database, a file, or a third-party API—or generate new content. We can even combine any number of sources of data and collect the data into a single package that we use in rendering the page. The framework takes care of using that package on the server or on the client depending on how the page will render (as in section 11.1.2), so all we have to worry about is gathering that data.

We're not going to spend much time discussing various Node.js frameworks for working with data, but we will discuss a single library—a very popular database wrapper library named Prisma. Prisma is an object-relational mapping (ORM) library. Essentially, such a library is an abstraction library built on top of SQL (or even NoSQL), abstracting away the complexities of writing SQL queries and instead using simple object notation for writing data to and retrieving data from a database.

Remix comes with Prisma as the strongly recommended database engine, already installed in many of

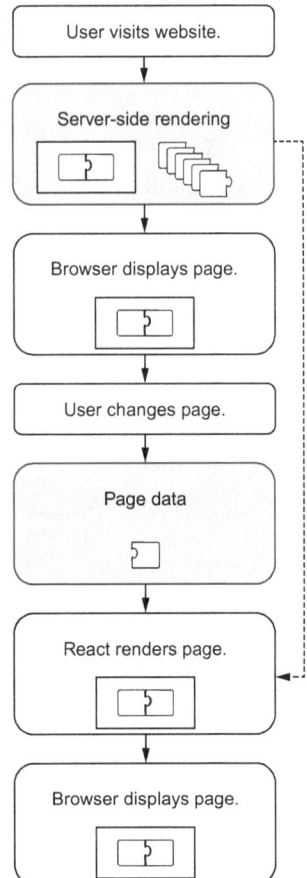

Figure 11.3 On the first page during a visit, the full HTML is rendered on the server, but for subsequent page visits, only the data package is returned. In puzzle lingo, we get the full puzzle for the first page on the first render and the template piece for every other page puzzle instantly. Then we have to retrieve only the data piece for each new page we have to render.

the example applications available for Remix. Next.js is a bit more open minded, having example applications that use other frameworks as well, but Prisma is still a strong recommendation, so we're going to use Prisma in this chapter and in chapter 12 too.

Prisma thrives in TypeScript because it elegantly makes your code typesafe even for complex queries, with the types being extracted from your database schema automatically. In this chapter, we'll use JavaScript instead of TypeScript, but for the project in chapter 12, we'll dive into typed database queries.

> **TIP**   Prisma is fairly complex but also well documented, so please check the documentation on their website (https://www.prisma.io) to learn more.

11.1.4 Hydration is necessary

I have to confess that one very important aspect is missing from figure 11.3. Let's amend that situation in figure 11.4 before we discuss why it's so important.

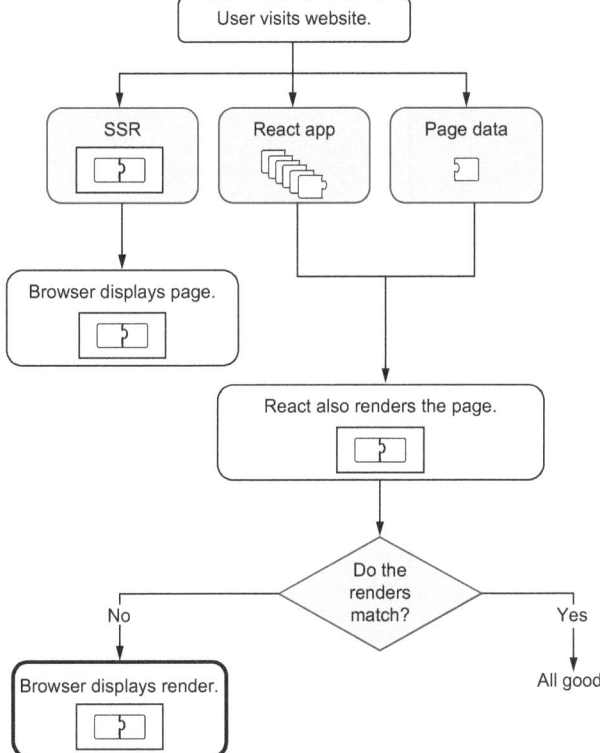

Figure 11.4   React also renders the HTML page and compares the React-rendered version with the server-rendered version. This process is called *hydration*, and only when the two HTML versions are identical is React happy. If they aren't, React forces the browser to render the React-created HTML instead, displayed in the box with the thick border at bottom left.

The step of figure 11.4 in which React also renders the page and compares the rendered HTML with the server-generated HTML, is called *hydration*. This step is important for gaining the performance boost that SSR offers. We'll discuss these implications in the next few sections.

ONLY PERFECT HYDRATION IS ALLOWED
For hydration to work correctly, you must have the same output down to the last byte. Nothing can differ; otherwise, React will complain. This situation results in several

consequences, the most obvious one being that you cannot have anything random generated inside your application because it would affect the output.

If you want to display a random quote in a hero banner (or random ads on your blog), for example, you cannot make that random choice in React. This random choice has to happen on the server outside React and be sent into React in a deterministic fashion. You need to include the random choice in the data package and not let React choose (figure 11.5).

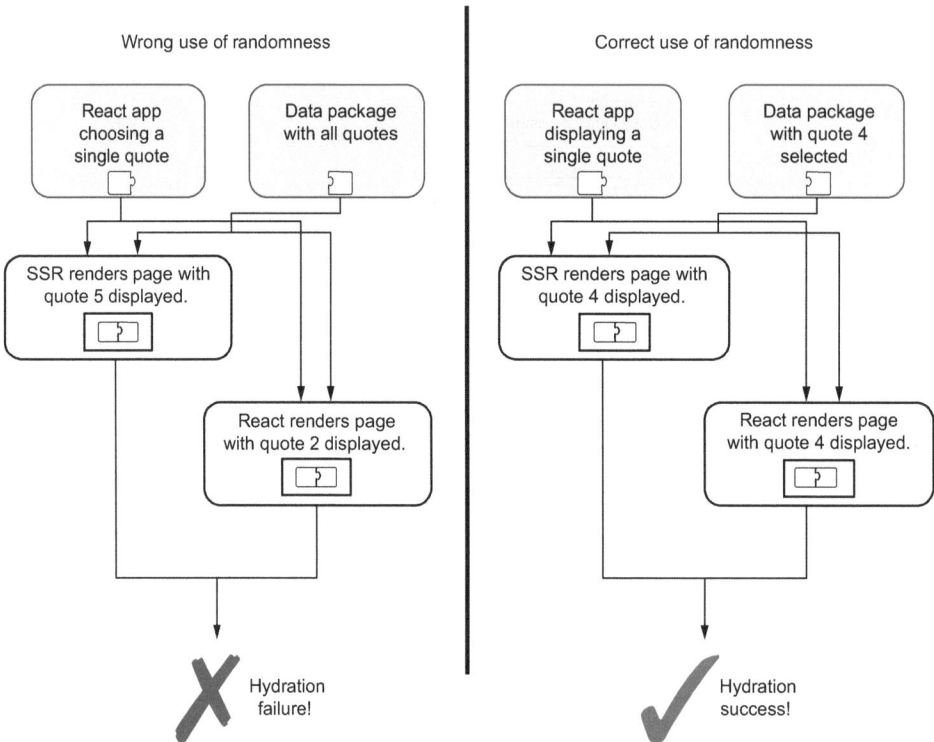

Figure 11.5   To display a random quote, we need to place the random source of information in the data package and then use that data on both the server and the client to ensure proper hydration.

WHAT'S THE PROBLEM WITH NONPERFECT HYDRATION?

You may wonder why hydration has to be pixel perfect—why it can't work if some parts differ slightly. That's just how React is built; it's an all-or-nothing concept.

What happens if you do break this principle? Will the application break? No, nothing of the sort happens. Hydration will work, but with a performance penalty. Let me explain why that penalty occurs.

If hydration succeeds, React starts up faster than normal because it doesn't have to render to the document object model (DOM)—only check for any differences (which is faster than rendering). But if hydration fails, React clears the document and re-renders the whole page from an empty page, but only after checking for differences, which makes it slower—not by a lot, but still slower. Another factor is HTML file size. In a classic setup, the HTML file is tiny because it's empty. But when it's server rendered, the HTML file can be quite big if the page is complex. So only if hydration works correctly does server-generated React gain a performance boost. Compare the differences in figure 11.6.

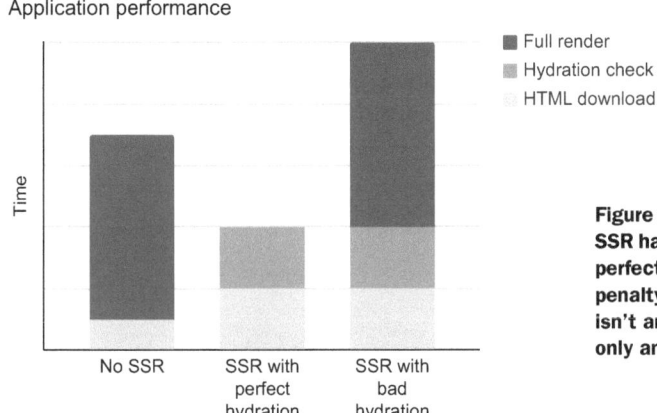

Figure 11.6   The performance boost of SSR happens only when hydration works perfectly. Otherwise, a significant penalty occurs. Note that this figure isn't an actual graph in milliseconds, only an illustration of the concept.

WHAT ABOUT PARTIAL HYDRATION?

Partial hydration is fairly new; it involves splitting content into smaller bits that can be hydrated or not individually. This topic is fairly complex and well beyond the scope of this book, but I want to mention it in case you want to dive deeper.

A lot of modern React development happens in this arena, but it's quite complicated and requires more introduction that I can provide in this chapter. Topics such as React Server Components, streaming content delivery, server actions, tainted objects, and so on are part of bleeding-edge React frameworks, and most of these new features boil down to the benefits of partial hydration.

> **NOTE**   Several of the new features in React 19 are also related to server actions, and we will see big improvements in the performance of React website frameworks with the adoption of React 19. I won't be discussing these new features in this book but stick to full hydration only.

11.2   *Implementations*

With our newfound understanding of the challenges and benefits of React website frameworks in general, let's take a closer look at our two contestants to see what makes them special, how to get started, and how to get your hands on my implementations.

11.2.1 *Next.js*

First, we have Next.js, the *grand old man* in the React website framework category. Besides being a great product, with all the bells and whistles you want from a React website framework, Next.js is popular because of its primary sponsor. It's created and supported by Vercel, an online hosting service for (among other things) fullstack React websites. So their incentive is obvious: Next.js is optimized for hosting, speed, and performance all around. If you want to read more about the framework and its benefits, please check https://nextjs.org.

Next.js recently came out with support for partial hydration and React Server Components, but it still supports the old model, which we'll use exclusively in this book. In the Next.js documentation, these two approaches are known as App Router using React Server Components and Pages Router using only regular components. We'll stick to Pages Router, so make sure that when you're using the Next.js documentation, you're on the Pages Router section of the website: https://nextjs.org/docs/pages. See figure 11.7 for additional hints.

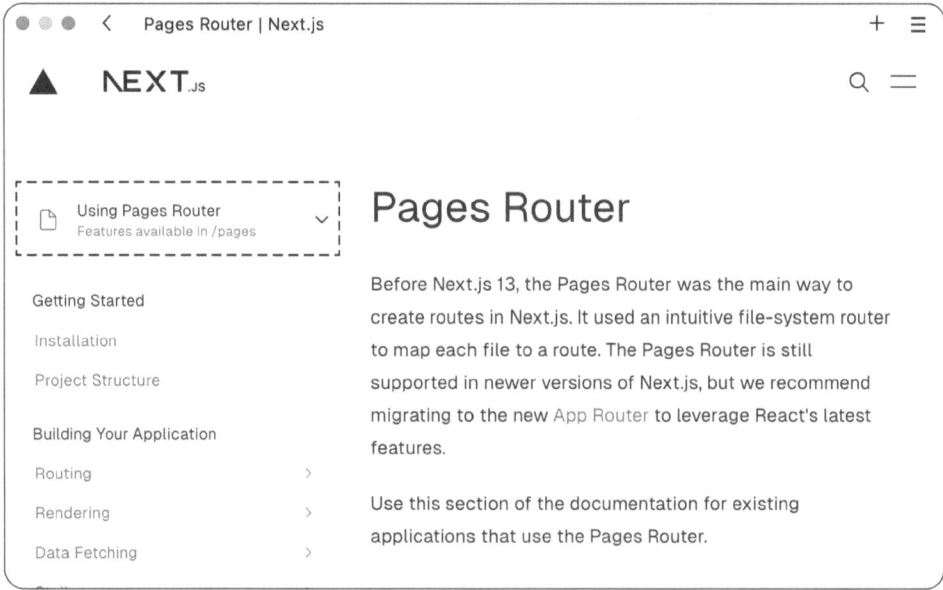

Figure 11.7   The Pages Router part of the documentation. If the menu heading is Using App Router, you can't use whatever information you read in a Pages Router–based application.

A CLEAN NEXT.JS PROJECT

To start a new, blank Next.js project, initialize it with the following command-line script, which is similar to how we create projects with Vite:

```
$ npx create-next-app@latest
```

This script asks you a couple of questions, including whether you want to use Type-Script. For this project, we're not going to use TypeScript, but I recommend it in general; Next.js is well typed, and using TypeScript is a great experience. The script will also ask whether you want to use the new App Router or the classic Pages Router. Choose Pages Router, which is the version we're using in this chapter. The result is a clean, empty Next.js application with a single default route (figure 11.8).

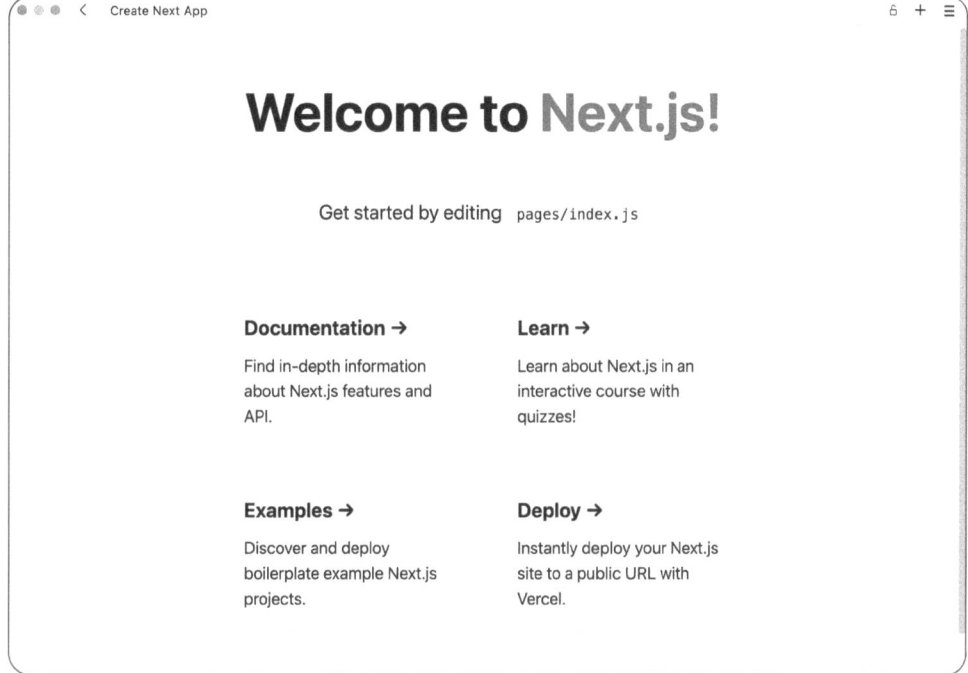

Figure 11.8 The default Next.js application comes with a single route and some helpful links.

MY SOLUTION

Rather than start with a clean slate, you may want to look at my example implementation of the weather app that we're building in this chapter. You can get it by checking out the `ch11/nextjs` example.

> **Example: nextjs**
>
> This example is in the `ch11/nextjs` folder. Note that this example is nonstandard and doesn't use the regular Vite setup; it's a custom Next.js setup. Before you run this example locally, make sure to run the setup first (only once for this example):
>
> ```
> $ npm run setup -w ch11/nextjs
> ```

> **(continued)**
>
> Then you can run the example by running this command:
>
> ```
> $ npm run dev -w ch11/nextjs
> ```
>
> Alternatively, you can go to this website to browse the code or download the source code as a zip file: https://reactlikea.pro/ch11-nextjs.

11.2.2 Remix

Remix, also known as Remix.run, is a rather new tool for building React websites, but it has taken the community by storm and is quickly gaining traction. Remix was created by Ryan Florence, known as the creator of React Router, a popular routing library that sits at the core of Remix. Remix has since been acquired by Shopify, which chose to fully open source the project, so it comes with a lot of professional support and experience.

One of the main features of this library is its surprising underreliance on JavaScript. Yes, a correctly produced Remix web application will work even without enabling JavaScript in the browser. This JavaScript independence, of course, doesn't extend to interactive client side–only features such as dialog boxes and menus, but basic form handling and navigation work perfectly fine without JavaScript. In that sense, building Remix websites feels akin to building websites back in the old days before all the modern features came along, but using React as the wonderfully powerful templating engine.

There's a lot more to this framework, but the concept of making websites that work even without JavaScript enabled permeates the architecture and influences many of its features, which we'll see a lot more of later.

A CLEAN REMIX PROJECT

To start a new Remix project, as you do in Vite and Next.js, you call a command-line script:

```
$ npx create-remix@latest
```

This script asks you some questions about the install, and then you're good to go. When the project is up and running, you'll see something like figure 11.9.

Remix comes with some starter templates called *stacks.* Stacks are collections of tools and principles that are commonly used in React development projects, so these tools can be all the things I've introduced in the past many

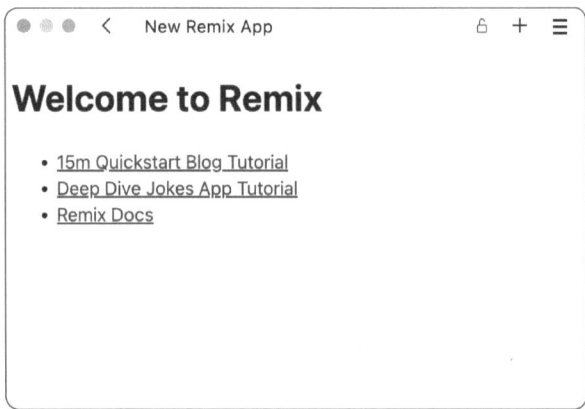

Figure 11.9   The default Remix application is a lot more bare-bones than the Next.js one but still contains a few useful links.

chapters: styling frameworks, testing tools, caching libraries, data handling, and so on. You can check out the default stacks in the Remix documentation at https://mng.bz/ pp50.

MY SOLUTION

Rather than start with a blank slate or a premade stack, you probably want to see my application, which implements the chapter 11 weather app. It's available in the `ch11/ remix` example.

> ### Example: remix
>
> This example is in the `ch11/remix` folder. Note that this example is nonstandard and doesn't use the regular Vite setup, but a custom Remix setup. Before you run this example locally, make sure to run the setup (only once for this example):
>
> ```
> $ npm run setup -w ch11/remix
> ```
>
> Then you can run the example by running this command:
>
> ```
> $ npm run dev -w ch11/remix
> ```
>
> Alternatively, you can go to this website to browse the code or download the source code as a zip file: https://reactlikea.pro/ch11-remix.

11.2.3 Environment values and API keys

Before I dive into the details of the app, you may notice that when you check out one of the preceding two examples, they don't work straight away. The folders are missing a few environment variables. These variables are supposed to be defined in a file named .env (for Remix) or .env.local (for Next.js), but this file is not included per convention because it includes local secrets you shouldn't share with others. Instead, I've provided an example file named .env.example. You should copy this file to .env(.local) and edit it to your liking.

The only value you need to change in this file is OPENWEATHER_API_KEY. The value is set to "<YOUR_API_KEY>" in the example file, which doesn't work. You need to go to the OpenWeather website, get your own API key, and insert it into your own .env(.local) file. Follow these steps:

1 Go to https://home.openweathermap.org/users/sign_up to sign up.
2 Click the confirmation link that you receive via email.
3 After confirmation, go to this page to see your API key: https://home.open-weathermap.org/api_keys.
4 Copy the 32-character alphanumeric string and insert it between quotes in your .env(.local) file like so:

```
OPENWEATHER_API_KEY="ABC123...ABC123"
```

You need to change the other value, DATABASE_URL, in the .env(.local) file only if you want to use a different database from a simple SQLite file–based one. Otherwise, ignore the database setting. The Remix example also has a secret key used for cookie encryption. This key is not important to edit in this example, but you should edit it if you want to store private information in cookies.

The setup scripts for both examples also copy the example environment file for you, but you'll still have to enter a real key acquired from the OpenWeather website.

11.3   Let's create a weather app!

In this section, we'll implement a weather app that can load the weather for any location in the world. The final result will look like figure 11.10.

 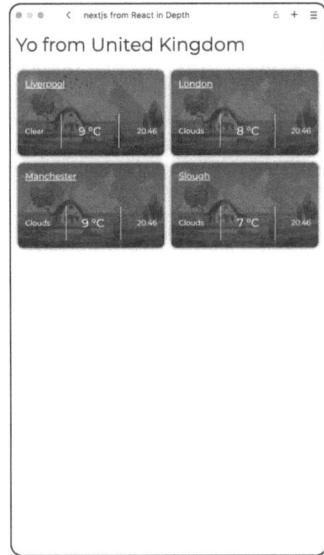 

Figure 11.10   The final product, our weather application, as it will be implemented with Next.js and Remix. Notice that the application displays weather conditions around the world and has a front page, a country page, and a city page.

In this section, we'll go through the key parts of this application and discuss why this particular website will be a challenge. Then we're going to solve this challenge in both Next.js and Remix to compare and evaluate. These key parts are

- Using the URL to display different pages
- Loading data on the server and reusing that data on the client
- Persisting local state data in a cookie
- Creating an API that allows React to interact directly with the server

11.3.1 *Using the URL*

One crucial thing that the screenshots in figure 11.10 don't show is the URL. I've been taking screenshots in the extremely minimalist browser named Min, which hides the URL. This approach has been perfect so far, as the URL has always been `http://localhost:3000/`. For every app, every state, every view so far, we've always been at this URL. In this application, however, we need to see the URL as we navigate around. So let's repeat the screenshots in a slightly less minimalist browser, Brave (figure 11.11).

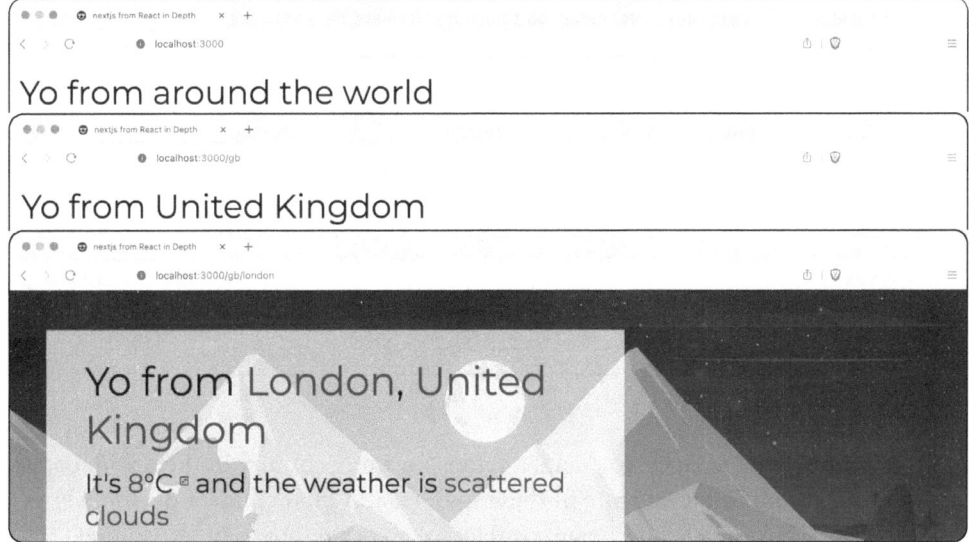

Figure 11.11   **The same three views as in figure 11.10 with the URL visible. The root (`/`) is the front page, a country code (such as `/gb`) leads to the country page, and if we append the city name (such as `/gb/london`), we get the city page.**

Easy URL mapping is one of the core features of most React website frameworks. Although normal React applications using Vite or Create React App are built solely with components, most React website frameworks use both components and pages as their building blocks.

Pages in this context are still React components, but they're organized slightly differently. Their names are related directly to the URL, and they can be extended with some additional functionality.

Suppose that you want to have a page on your website named `/about`, where people can read about your website. In both Next.js and Remix (and in most other frameworks), this task requires simply placing a file named `about.jsx` in the `routes/` or `app/pages/` folder. (The folder structure varies a bit with the frameworks.) Then this file simply has to export a React component, which becomes the contents of the about page. If you want to put the page at `/about/team`, you create a component in a file named `team.jsx` inside the `about/` folder inside the `routes/` folder (in the case of Remix) or the `app/pages/` folder (in the case of Next.js).

Remix v2 came out in September 2023 and included a new flat routing scheme. Whereas Remix v1 used the same folder structure in the `routes` folder that was used in the URL, Remix v2 uses a flat structure with periods (`.`) as folder separators. The Remix v2 page component for the route `/about/team` becomes `/app/routes/about.team.jsx`. One curious detail in Remix v2 routing is that the root index page is called `_index.jsx` rather than `index.jsx`. Table 11.1 summarizes the route system.

Table 11.1 Basic routes are resolved to straightforward files with file and folder naming.

URL	Component location		
	Next.js	Remix v1	Remix v2
`http://localhost:3000`	`/pages`	`/app/routes`	`/app/routes`
`/`	`/index.jsx`	`/index.jsx`	`/_index.jsx`
`/about`	`/about.jsx`	`/about.jsx`	`/about.jsx`
`/about/team`	`/about` `- /team.jsx`	`/about` `- /team.jsx`	`/about.team.jsx`

ROUTING DYNAMICALLY

But wait—do we have to create a folder for every country in the world, copy the same component into every one of these folders, and then create a file for every city in the world? That task would be impossible, so, no, we're not going to do that.

Instead, we're going to use dynamic routing, which both of our frameworks handle well though differently. The idea is to use parameterized URLs. You indicate, through naming, that a given file or folder should match any string of letters, and you can resolve it later.

Suppose that you have a team-member page for every person in your company, which has more than 200 employees, and you have all those employees listed in a database. You want this URL structure:

- `/about/team/jack-johnson`
- `/about/team/john-jackson`

But you want all those pages to be resolved by the same component. Instead of creating a file for every employee name, you create a single file with a parameterized name. Next.js uses `[employee].js`, whereas Remix uses `$employee.js`. Then you'd be able to extract the name of the employee from the file by using the parameter in the filename. You can do the same thing with folders too, so you can have a `[country]/` or `$country/` folder. Table 11.2 shows some examples.

Table 11.2 Dynamic routing in a website framework includes parameterized URLs inside the regular location.

URL	Component location		
	Next.js	Remix v1	Remix v2
`http://localhost`	`/pages`	`/app/routes`	`/app/routes`

`/user/1`
`/user/2`
`/user/...`
	`/user`
	`  /[id].jsx`
		`/user`
		`  /$id.jsx`
			`/user.$id.jsx`

`/shop/chairs/page/1`
`/shop/tables/page/1`
`/show/tables/page/2`
`/shop/.../page/...`
	`/shop`
	`- /[cat]`
	`  - /page`
	`    - /[page].jsx`
		`/shop`
		`- /$cat`
		`  - /page`
		`    - /$page.jsx`
			`/shop.$cat.page.`
			`➥$page.jsx`

In the last example in table 11.2, the folder structure gets quite complex in both Next.js and Remix v1, whereas in Remix v2, the folder structure is still flat, which is the main reason why Remix changed its routing mechanism. If your website has 30 pages, it can be difficult to get an overview if the files are spread across many folders, often containing only one or two files. With a flat file structure, development is much easier.

There are many more aspects of dynamic and nested routing to consider for complex applications, but for our simple application, we have all we need. When we get to the frameworks, we'll see that both solve our needs elegantly.

ROUTING IN OUR WEATHER APP

In our weather app, we need a root route for the front page, a route for the country page, and a route for the city page. All in all, these requirements result in the component locations in table 11.3. Note that we will be using Remix v2 routing for our application.

Table 11.3 The three routes required in our weather application and their file locations inside Next.js, Remix v1, and Remix v2

URL	Component location		
	Next.js	Remix v1	Remix v2
`http://localhost`	`/pages`	`/app/routes`	`/app/routes`
`/`	`/index.jsx`	`/index.jsx`	`/_index.jsx`
`/{country}`	`/[cc]/index.jsx`	`/$cc/index.jsx`	`/$cc.jsx`
`/{country}/{city}`	`/[cc]/[city].jsx`	`/$cc/$city.jsx`	`/$cc.$city.jsx`

11.3.2 Using data in a route

Now we know where to place our components, but what do we put in them? How do we load data from the database and from external services and put that data in our React components?

This next part is one of the main purposes of using a React website framework: you want to be able to preload your HTML from the server, already filled with all the relevant data required to display the page even before React starts doing its magic in the browser.

Earlier, I described the full page as two pieces of a simple puzzle. Each framework creates this puzzle slightly differently, but it will be obvious that these puzzles are both simple and easy to modify.

DEFINING ROUTE DATA IN NEXT.JS

Routes in Next.js are React components defined in route files. Route files are files inside the pages folder, and each page must export a default React component to be a route that can be rendered in the browser.

If you also want a data package to go with that route, define it in a function named `getServerSideProps` and plunk it next to the component. First, let's sketch it in a diagram (figure 11.12).

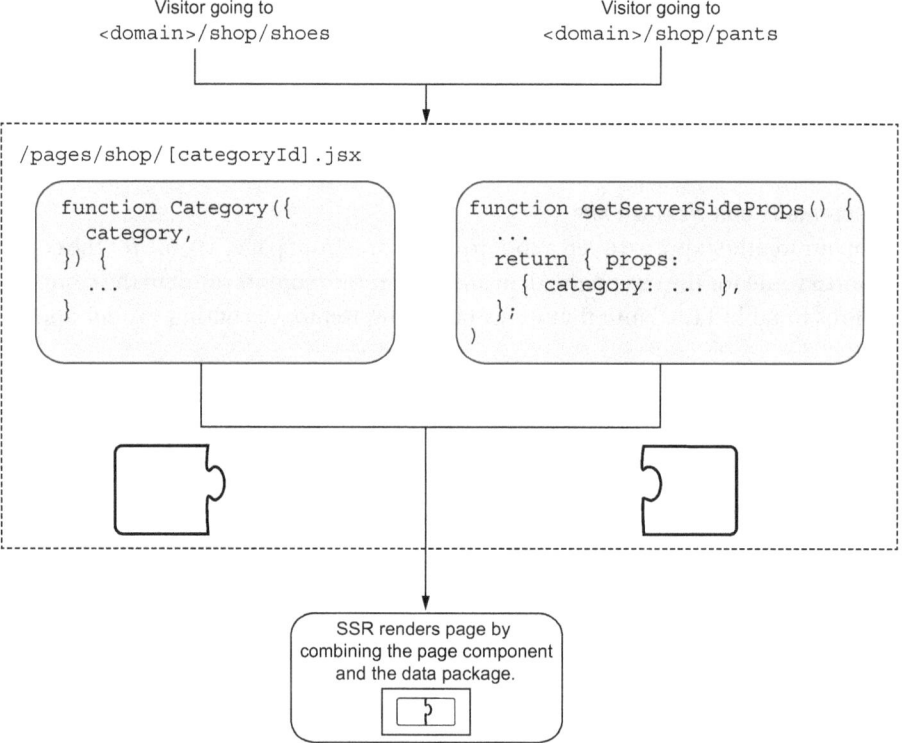

Figure 11.12 For a fictional website, we have shop categories with the URLs /shop/shoes and /shop/pants. We dynamically load the category information from the categoryId in the URL, and pass that information into the React component. We have to match the same variable name in the return of the former and the property of the latter.

Let's see how this code would implement figure 11.12:

```
// This is the code in the file
// /pages/shop/[categoryId].jsx
export async function
getServerSideProps(context) {
  const { categoryId } = context.query;
  const category =
    await getCategoryData(categoryId);
  if (!category) {
    return {
      redirect: {
        destination: "/",
        permanent: false,
      },
    };
  }
  return { props: { category } };
}
function Category({ category }) {
  return (
    <h1>This is the page for the {category.name} category</h1>
  );
}
export default Category;
```

Our two functions go in the same route file.

The data package is defined by this function, which takes a context parameter and must return the props for the component to render. It is often asynchronous because of network tasks.

We can get parameters from the URL through the context.

If something fails (such as a bad categoryId), we can return a redirect.

We invoke whatever function we need to retrieve the data from storage or database.

When things go well, we return an object with a props property.

We have to make sure to accept the same props in our component that the data package returns.

Note that the component is a default export, whereas the data package function is a named export.

For our specific application, we're going to need to put some extra things in the data package before we can implement it. We have to load cookies too.

DEFINING ROUTE DATA IN REMIX

Let's do the same thing in Remix that we did in Next.js. First, let's illustrate it in an updated diagram (figure 11.13).

If we implement this same example in code, we'll see many of the same ideas and concepts but with slightly different names:

```
// This is the code in the file
// /app/routes/shop.$categoryId.jsx
export async function loader(context) {
  const { categoryId } = context.params;
  const category = await getCategoryData(categoryId);
  if (!category) {
    redirect("/");
  }
  return json({ category });
}
function Category() {
  const { category } = useLoaderData();
  return (
    <h1>This is the page for the {category.name} category</h1>
  );
}
export default Category;
```

Remember the different naming for parameterized URLs.

The data package is defined in a loader function.

The URL parameters are retrieved from the params property on the context.

Redirects are a bit simpler.

We return JSON using the json() function.

Finally, we read the data package by using a hook inside the component rather than direct props.

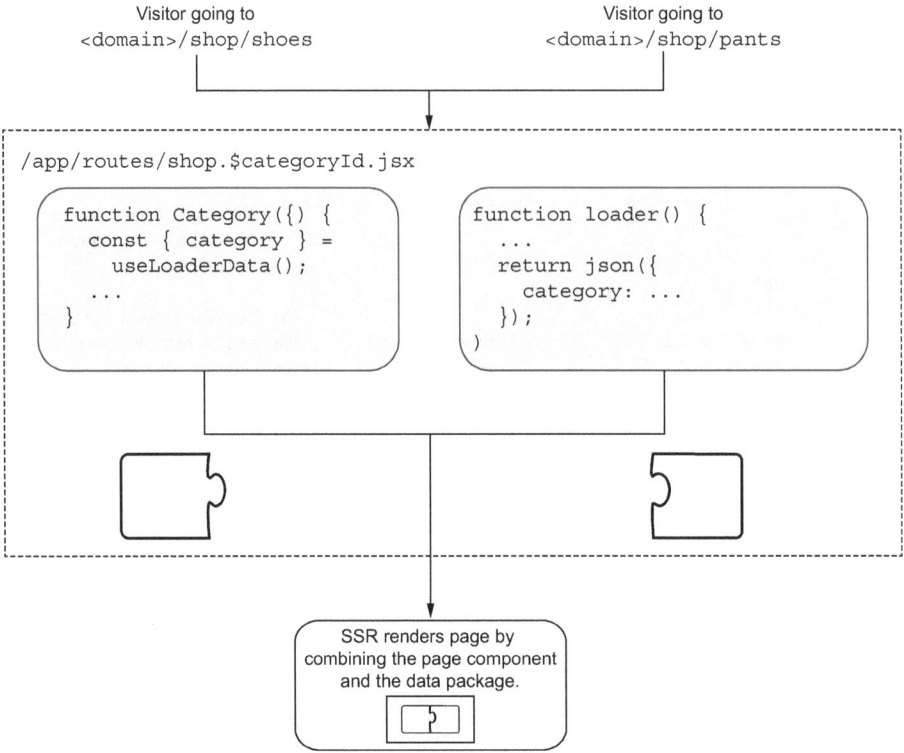

Figure 11.13 In Remix, we name the file slightly differently, define the data package slightly differently, and retrieve the data package values slightly differently. Otherwise, the concept is much like what we did Next.js. There are only so many ways to skin a cat, after all.

Again, we need to understand cookies before we see how to implement data fetching for our particular application.

11.3.3 Storing local data

Everyone in the world can agree on one thing: nobody agrees on everything. Thus, a weather app will always have the problem of displaying temperatures in the wrong scale, so users need a way to toggle between degrees Celsius and degrees Fahrenheit. Yes, I know that there are other scales, but I'll stick to those two. Feel free to implement additional scales in your own implementation.

Which scale you prefer is something you need to store locally, but it would be a bit much to require you to create a user and select a password just to store this tiny bit of info. Instead, we store it locally in your browser so that you can access it when you visit the website again. For this purpose, we've been using `localStorage` throughout this book, but `localStorage` works only in the browser, not on the server.

What's the problem? Well, perfect hydration stops us again. Our server has to render the temperature in one of the two scales, and if the client detects a local browser setting indicating a different scale, hydration fails (figure 11.14).

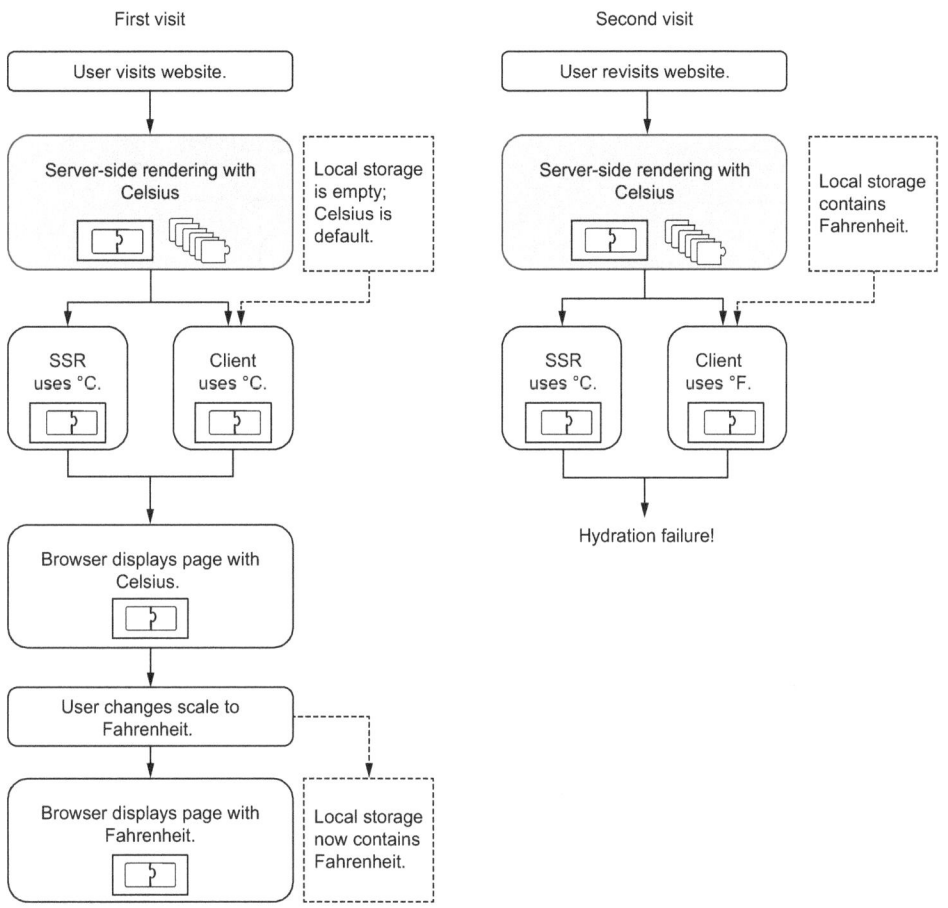

Figure 11.14   The server renders the temperature in Celsius, but local storage in the browser causes the client to render the temperature in Fahrenheit, and perfect hydration fails.

Instead, we can use cookies. Cookies work on both the client and the server, as they are sent to and from the server in every request. Sending data in every request does seem a bit wasteful, which is why you're limited to fewer bytes than you can store in `localStorage`. Our examples that store to-do data in `localStorage` could probably not have been implemented with cookies, as we would have run out of room quickly. With cookies, you get the flow you see in figure 11.15.

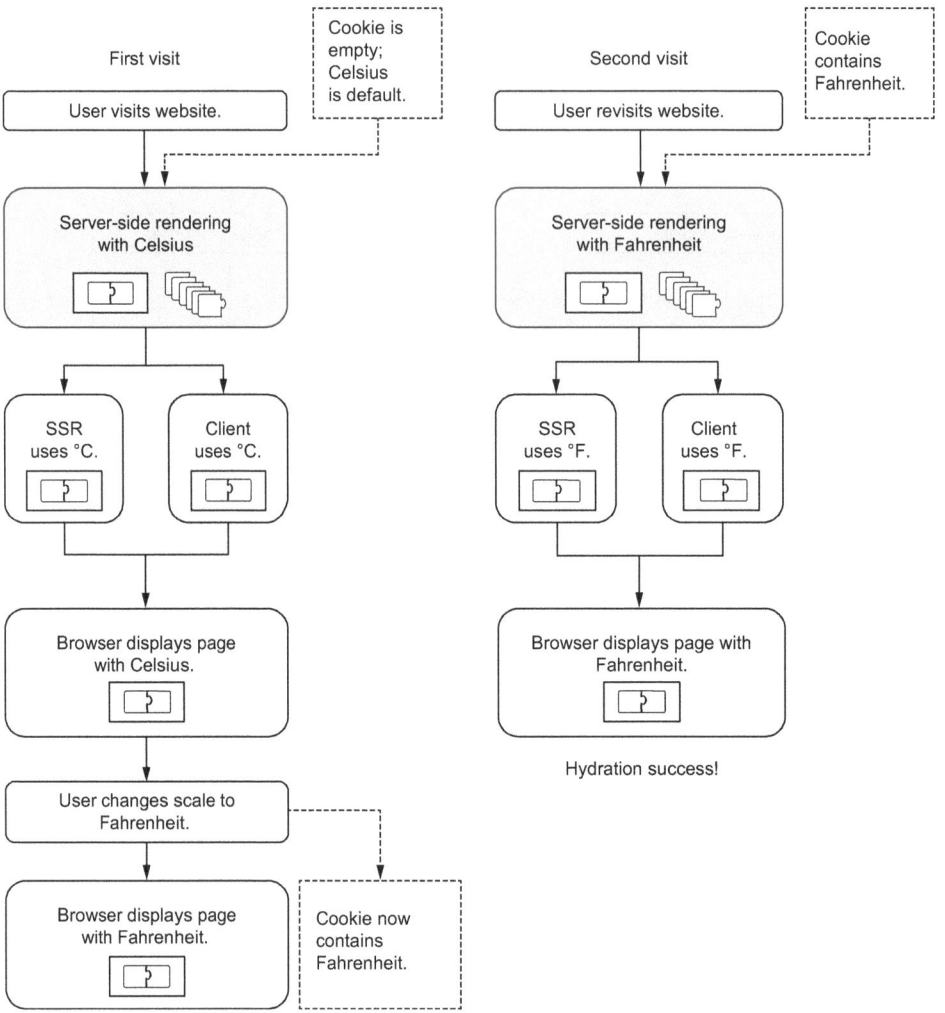

Figure 11.15 **With cookies, we can update the local setting on the client and make sure that when the page reloads, the server will also know the correct scale to use, so hydration will happen perfectly.**

Cookies can be set, read, edited, and deleted on both the client and the server, so they're perfect for our example. Setting cookies manually in either setting is a bit cumbersome, but fortunately, both of the frameworks we're using come with great tools for manipulating cookies. In Remix, this feature is built into the core, whereas in Next.js, a utility library called `cookies-next` does the job perfectly.

I should mention that we are going to use cookies for another thing: we need to store the user's local position to make it easy for them to find their local weather from the front page. I won't detail how we implement this feature, so check the source code for details.

COOKIES IN NEXT.JS

In Next.js, cookies are implemented by a small third-party module called `cookies-next`. With that module installed (using npm or Yarn as usual), we can read and write cookies on both the client and the server by using a similar (but not identical) API. On the server, you need access to the request object to read cookies, and you need to return the correct header to set a cookie, but on the client, you can read and set a cookie from anywhere, and the browser API will allow the function to work correctly. In our application, we will set cookies only in the browser and read cookies only on the server, which makes things a bit easier. Let's put the proper API calls inside the flow described in figure 11.15, which becomes figure 11.16.

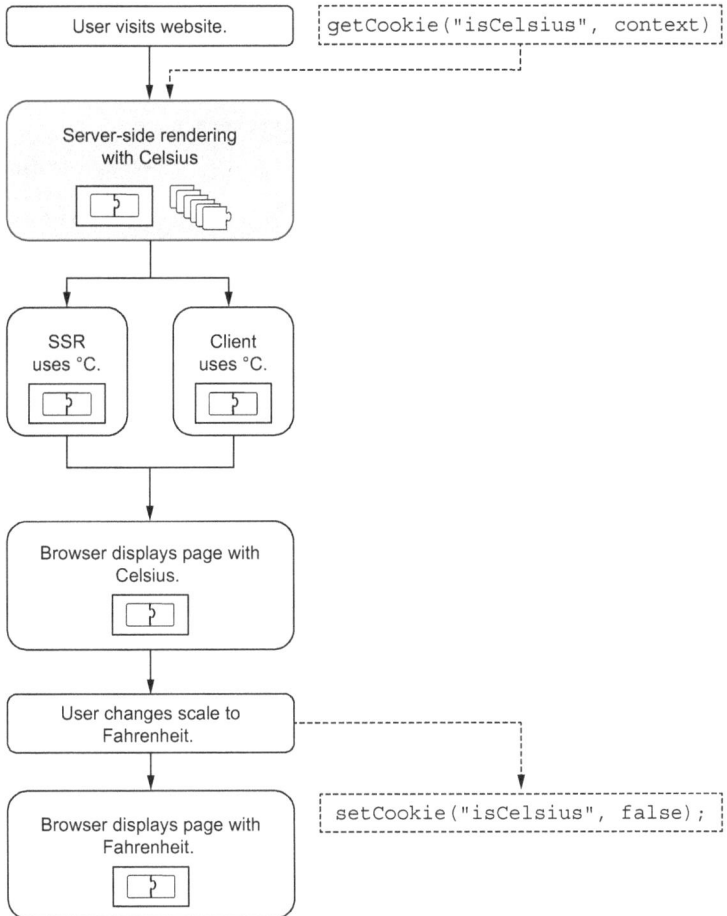

Figure 11.16   We set a cookie by calling `setCookie`**, and we read a cookie by calling** `getCookie`**. (Big-brained stuff here.) Because we want to read the cookie on the server, however, we also pass the context to it.**

We use cookies as shown in figure 11.16 for both the temperature (toggling `isCelsius`) and the time format (toggling `hour12`). Putting everything together with the general data loading explained in section 11.3.2, the full city route file, `/pages/[cc]/[city].js`, becomes listing 11.1.

Listing 11.1 City route in Next.js

```
import { getCityData } from "../../services/data";
import { getDefaultFormats } from "../../services/cookies";
import { FormatProvider } from "../../format";
import { CityDisplay } from "../../components";
export async function getServerSideProps(context) {
  const { cc, city } = context.query;
  const data =
    await getCityData(cc.toUpperCase(), city);
  const defaultFormats =
    getDefaultFormats(context);
  if (data.slug !== city) {
    // Redirect, as city was resolved under a different name
    return {
      redirect: {
        destination: `/${cc}/${data.slug}/`,
        permanent: false,
      },
    };

  }
  return { props: { data, defaultFormats } };
}

function City({ data, defaultFormats }) {
  return (
    <FormatProvider
      defaultFormats={defaultFormats}
    >
      <CityDisplay data={data} />
    </FormatProvider>
  );
}
export default City;
```

First, we load the relevant data from the server.

Next, we load more data from cookies by using a utility function because we need to do the same thing in multiple routes.

We have to handle some error cases for the city database result here.

The data package concludes by returning the two relevant bits of information: the city data and the format configuration.

The component starts with those same two pieces of info that the data package contains.

The page is wrapped in a format provider with the relevant configuration.

The main display component uses the city data to render the page.

The `getDefaultFormats` function is moved to a separate file because we need the functionality in multiple routes. This function is defined in the file `/services/cookies.js`, which you see in listing 11.2.

Listing 11.2 Cookie utils

```
import { getCookie } from "cookies-next";
export function getDefaultFormats(context) {
  const isCelsius = getCookie("nextjs-isCelsius", context);
```

```
  const hour12 = getCookie("nextjs-hour12", context);
  return {
    isCelsius: isCelsius !== "false",
    hour12: hour12 === "true",
  };
}
```

The temperature defaults to Celsius.

The time defaults to 24-hour format.

The two other routes, front page and country page, use similar logic and components to render their contents. Check them out in the example.

COOKIES IN REMIX

Cookies in Remix are slightly more complex, and we need a bit of extra context to fully understand why we have to do things differently. In Remix, cookies are encrypted, which sounds good but has consequences. To set or read the cookie, we need a special secret key. If we put that key in the browser, anyone can see it, so the encryption is null and void. Thus, we can read and set cookies only on the server.

> **Encrypted server-only cookies**
>
> Using encrypted cookies might seem weird but is a common choice in web development. A cookie can be read by any script on a page. It's not uncommon for a web page to include external scripts, such as analytics tools or various trackers, and you don't want them to access possibly private data. You could store the preferred shipping address or the saved login email in a cookie, and you don't want others to be able to spy on this data. That's why Remix uses encrypted cookies, which become server-only cookies.
>
> We could circumvent this built-in functionality and interact with the cookies as normal by using the HTTP headers, because we don't need the protection of encryption in this case, but we will stick to the framework and its best practices for now.

If we can read and set cookies only on the server, we need to send the information we want to store to the server before it will be stored in a cookie. This approach aligns perfectly with Remix's stated goal of being less dependent on JavaScript. We can create the application in such a way that we can use cookies without JavaScript because we round-trip to the server every time. If the user has JavaScript, however, we'll make the round trip a lot faster courtesy of Remix magic (figure 11.17).

But sending cookie data to the server means that we need to handle this incoming data in Remix. When the form submits and the data is sent to the route by either the browser or Remix, we need to handle that data. For that purpose, we need a third item in the route besides the component and the data package. We also need a data handler. Data handlers, which are integral to Remix, are the opposite of the data package function, `loader()`. The data handler function is called `action()`.

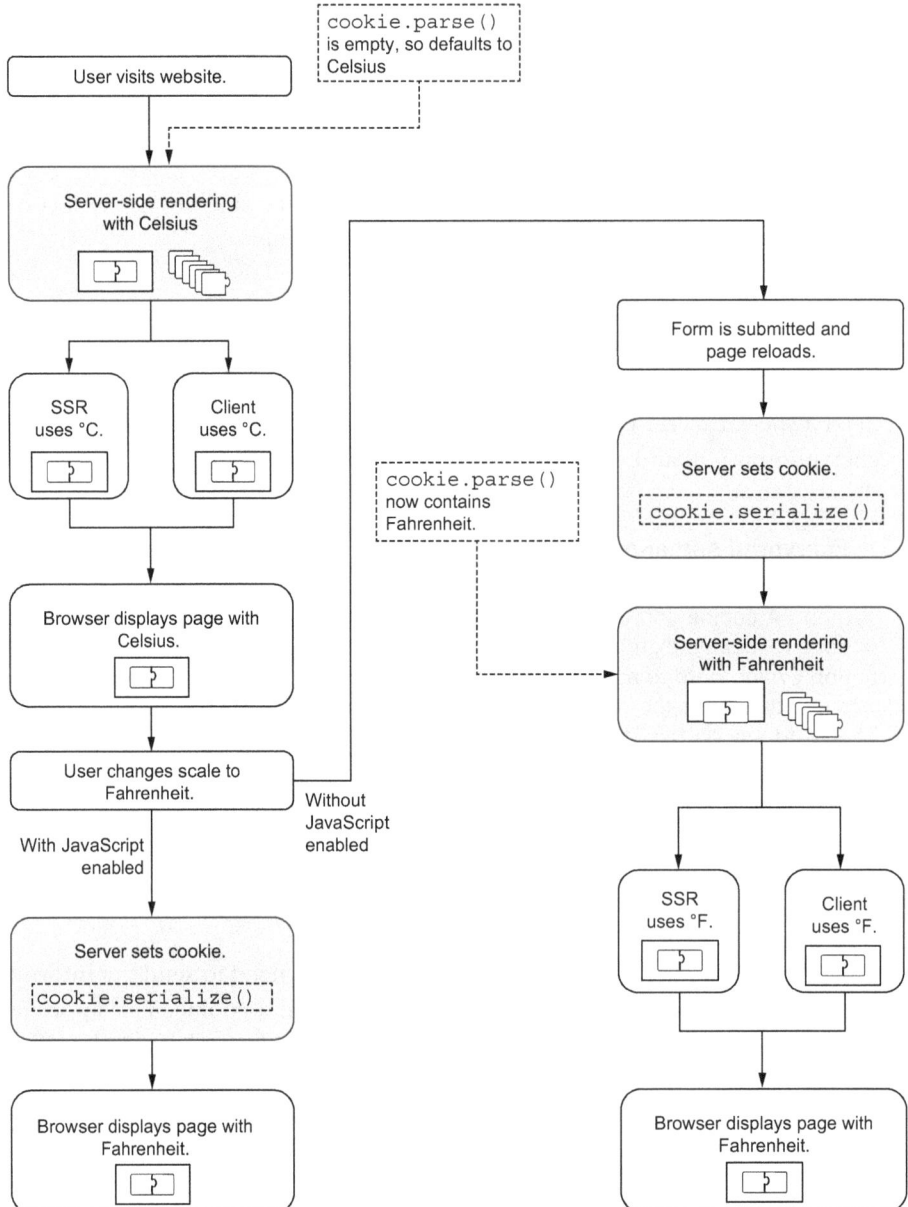

Figure 11.17   The API for setting and reading cookies is a little bit less obvious in Remix, using `parse()` **to read and** `serialize()` **to set. The button to change scale is a submit button in a form. If JavaScript is enabled, Remix kicks in and hijacks the form, sending only data back and forth to the server. If not, the format change still works after the whole page reloads.**

All in all, the structure of the Remix route for a city page looks like figure 11.18.

```
/app/routes/$cc.$city.jsx

  function loader({ request, params }) {
    const data = await getCityData(params.cc, params.city);
    ...
    const defaultFormats = await getDefaultFormats(request);    ◄────── Data package
    ...
    return json({ data, defaultFormats });
  )

  function action({ request }) {
    const bodyParams = await request.formData();
    ...                                                          ◄────── Data handler
  }

  function City() {
    const { data, defaultFormats } = useLoaderData();
    ...                                                          ◄────── Main component
  }
```

Figure 11.18   The overall structure of the Remix city route contains three parts. Besides the data package and component, which I've covered extensively, we also have a data handler that's capable of handling form submissions.

The following listing shows how we implement the city route.

Listing 11.3   The Remix city route

```
import { useLoaderData } from "@remix-run/react";
import { json, redirect } from "@remix-run/node";
import { getCityData } from "~/services/data";
import { FormatProvider } from "~/format";
import { CityDisplay } from "~/components/cityDisplay";
import {
  getDefaultFormats,
  toggleTemperature,
  toggleTime,
} from "~/services/cookies";
export async function loader({
  request,
  params,
}) {
```

> **The loader function in Remix is fairly identical to the loader function in Next.js but with a Remix-specific API.**

```
    const data = await getCityData(params.cc.toUpperCase(), params.city);
    if (!data) {
      redirect("/");
    }
    if (data.slug !== params.city) {
      return redirect(`/${params.cc}/${data.slug}/`);
    }
    const defaultFormats =
      await getDefaultFormats(request);
    return json({ data, defaultFormats });
  }
  export async function action({ request }) {
    const bodyParams = await request.formData();
    if (bodyParams.has("toggle-temperature")) {
      return toggleTemperature(request);
    }
    if (bodyParams.has("toggle-time")) {
      return toggleTime(request);
    }
  }
  export default function City() {
    const { data, defaultFormats } =
      useLoaderData();
    return (
      <FormatProvider defaultFormats={defaultFormats}>
        <CityDisplay data={data} />
      </FormatProvider>
    );
  }
```

We load the default formats by using a utility function as before. Note that we have to await it, as parsing cookies is an asynchronous operation in Remix (unlike Next.js).

The data package contains city data and format information.

Next is the data handler function.

We check to see whether this request is an attempt to toggle the temperature, and if so, we do that.

If it is an attempt to toggle the time format, we do that. Note that we return whatever the toggle util returns.

The component works as normal. We load the data package by using the Remix-provided hook for that purpose.

We have moved some cookie utils to a helper function in `/app/services/cookies`, and you can see an excerpt in the following listing (with some parts that aren't relevant to the city route hidden).

> **Listing 11.4   Remix cookie utils (excerpt)**

```
import { redirect } from "@remix-run/node";
import { temperatureCookie, timeCookie } from "~/cookies.server";
function setCookie(request, value) {
  return redirect(
    request.headers.get("Referer"),
    { headers: { "Set-Cookie": value } },
  );
}
export async function getDefaultFormats(request) {
  const cookieHeader =
    request.headers.get("Cookie") || "";
  const isCelsius = (
    await temperatureCookie.parse(cookieHeader)
  ) !== false;
  const hour12 = (
    await timeCookie.parse(cookieHeader)
  ) !== false;
  return { isCelsius, hour12 };
```

We need a little helper function to return a response that updates a cookie. This function, unfortunately, is not built into Remix.

When reading cookies, we first have to extract the cookie header from the request.

Then we parse the cookie header for each cookie and check the result. Note that we can have nonstring values in the parsed cookie.

```
}
export async function toggleTemperature(request) {
  const { isCelsius } =
    await getDefaultFormats(request);
  return setCookie(
    request,
    await temperatureCookie.serialize(!isCelsius),
  );
}
export async function toggleTime(request) {
  const { hour12 } =
    await getDefaultFormats(request);
  return setCookie(
    request,
    await timeCookie.serialize(!hour12)
  );
}
```

When we toggle one of these format cookies, we first retrieve the current value and then return a response updating the cookie to the opposite value.

Finally, we have the cookie definitions, which are located in `/app/cookies.server.js` per Remix conventions. This file is a very simple, as you see in the following listing.

Listing 11.5 Remix cookie definitions

```
import { createCookie } from "@remix-run/node";
const maxAge = 86_400 * 365; // one year
export const temperatureCookie =
  createCookie("temperature", { maxAge });
export const timeCookie =
  createCookie("time", { maxAge });
export const myCityCookie =
  createCookie("myCity", { maxAge });
```

We define three cookies in the same way but with different names. They're all set to expire after a year.

TIP The Remix cookie is a bit more complex to use and has a slightly unexpected API. Please refer to the Remix documentation for full details on how to use it: https://remix.run/docs/en/main/utils/cookies.

11.3.4 Creating an API

Lastly, I want to demonstrate how to create an API in the framework. Although you can create regular data update flows as described in section 11.3.3, which is perfect for forms and similar interactive data, sometimes you need an API that you can invoke from JavaScript and resolve in the client. You may want to manipulate the data by using some client side–only functionality or some external library. If you want to display things in an interactive Google Map instance, you can do so only in a client side setting.

Creating an API is easy in both frameworks, as you'll see when we get to implementations. We need an API to convert coordinates to city names because when we ask the browser for the current location of the visitor, we get only coordinates back. We want to redirect the user to the correct page, but we don't know the names of the city or country from the two numbers, so we use a third-party API to look them up. This functionality is built into the weather service that we're using. The process of converting coordinates to their real-name counterparts is known as *geocoding*. We place this API route in /api/geocode.

API ROUTES IN NEXT.JS

In Next.js, an API route is configured differently from a normal component route. Rather than return a component from the route file, you return a handler function, which is similar to a handler function in Express.js (the underlying server library that powers the Next.js HTTP functionality).

A handler function takes a request and a response as arguments and returns via the response object by setting the status code and response body directly on that object. Following is an example for an API route that returns the string `"Hello world!"`:

```
export default function handler(req, res) {
  res.status(200).json("Hello world!");
}
```

Note that we set the response code and the response JSON object directly rather than return something. This function can be asynchronous as well if we need to wait for data to load. Our API requires us to do three things:

- Read coordinates (latitude and longitude) from the request query.
- Geocode the coordinates via a third-party API.
- Return the response to the client or an error if nothing is found.

We can implement the geocoding API in Next.js.

Listing 11.6   Geocoding API in Next.js

```
import slugify from "slugify";
import { getCityForCoordinate } from "../../services/api";
import { getCountryName } from "../../services/data";        First, we retrieve
export default async function handler(req, res) {            the coordinates
  const { lat, lng } = req.query;          ◄──────────       from the query
  const { cityName, countryCode } =                  Then, we use the OpenWeather
    await getCityForCoordinate(lat, lng);            API to look up the location name.
  if (!cityName || !countryCode) {
    res.status(404).json({ result: "error" });       If it fails, we return an error. (The
    return;                                           coordinate is probably lost at sea.)
  }
  const country = await getCountryName(countryCode);
  const path = `/${slugify(countryCode)}/${slugify(cityName)}`;
  res.status(200)                                   If all goes well, we return
    .json({ path, country, city: cityName });       a successful response.
}
```

API ROUTES IN REMIX

In Remix, API routes aren't special. They're the same as regular component-based routes; they just don't have a component. So if you define only a data package in a route file, it is automatically an API route, which is convenient because we already know how to define a Remix data package. That same example with a route returning the string `"Hello world!"` becomes

```
import { json } from "@remix-run/node";
export function loader({ request }) {
  return json("Hello world!");
}
```

The implementation of our application API route is located in `/app/routes/api.geocode.js`.

Listing 11.7   Geocoding API in Remix

```
import { json, Response } from "@remix-run/node";
import slugify from "slugify";
import { getCityForCoordinate } from "../../services/api";
import { getCountryName } from "../../services/data";
export async function loader({ request }) {
  const url = new URL(request.url);
  const lat = url.searchParams.get("lat");         First, we retrieve the coordinates
  const lng = url.searchParams.get("lng");         from the query string.
  const { cityName, countryCode } =                  Then, we use the OpenWeather
    await getCityForCoordinate(lat, lng);            API to look up the location name.
  if (!cityName || !countryCode) {
    throw new Response(
      "Not Found",                                 If it fails, we return an
      { status: 404 },                             error. (Maybe the
    );                                             coordinates are in space.)
  }
  const country = await getCountryName(countryCode);
  const path = `/${slugify(countryCode)}/${slugify(cityName)}`;
  return json({ path, country, city: cityName });     ◁─┐ If all goes well, we return
}                                                          a successful response.
```

11.4   Alternative React-based website frameworks

Next.js and Remix aren't the only choices, of course; they're the most popular and the most hyped, respectively. Remix is fairly new, so if you read this book a couple of years down the line, it may have been scrapped, for all I know. Next.js is much more likely to still be around, as it has been around for quite a while.

Other libraries try to market themselves within a niche of the web application market rather than tackle all web applications, like the frameworks I've detailed in this chapter. Some noteworthy alternatives include

- *Gatsby* (https://www.gatsbyjs.com)—This framework is best for small websites and can even compile your React components down to a pure HTML-and-CSS-only website with no JavaScript in sight.
- *Astro* (https://astro.build)—Astro is another fairly new project that's ideal for content-heavy websites rather than complex web applications. It's ideal for marketing websites, documentation, blogs, news sites, and the like. Astro is not React specific and can work with other libraries.

- *RedwoodJS* (https://redwoodjs.com)—This framework is good for fast prototyping if you're building a new startup and want to get going quickly without worrying much about customization and tailoring. With a few lines of script, you have a basic website and content management system (CMS) up and running. This CMS includes forms and tables to list, display, create, and edit your objects in the database, and it comes with many great tools built in.
- *Qwik* (https://qwik.builder.io)—This framework is hyperfocused on performance and speed, so if delivering your website in milliseconds is most important, such as for a web shop or a campaign landing page, Qwik may be your best choice. By default, Qwik uses its own simpler, scaled-down variant of React, but you can use regular React within it.

Note that all these alternatives have found a niche, whereas Next.js targets any type of website. The reason is mostly that Next.js has been king of React website frameworks for a long time, and most direct competitors have drowned in its wake.

Only Remix dared take the reigning champion on directly, and we've yet to see who will emerge as the victor. Remix and Next.js may end up splitting the market, but for now, these two are the main contenders for the general React website framework throne. Next.js and Remix are far from alone, however, so always check around to see whether some other framework fits your use case better.

Summary

- React website frameworks are powerful ways to build React websites or even regular HTML websites.
- React website frameworks allow you to use React as a natural part of a JavaScript- or TypeScript-based fullstack development environment, in which React serves as both the templating engine for server-side rendered HTML and the front end UI when the data has been delivered to the browser.
- Many React website frameworks are optimized for extremely fast performance, and this optimization alone is reason enough to consider using them.
- The performance gain from React website frameworks comes primarily from SSR. By pregenerating the HTML on the server, the browser can show the resulting page in milliseconds after the visitor arrives rather than after React loads and kicks in. To get this performance gain in a React website framework with SSR, however, you need perfect hydration. When React hydrates your page, React expects the browser-rendered HTML to be identical to the server-rendered HTML. If hydration fails, a significant performance penalty overshadows the initial performance gain.
- Next.js and Remix are two of the most popular frameworks for rendering React on the server. Both frameworks come with a slew of other web development libraries as recommendations: styling, data management, database access, and so on.

- Using external APIs in a React website framework is a breeze because we can use the full functionality of JavaScript in Node.js as it runs on the server and render the resulting output only in the browser, using the less-capable browser JavaScript engine.
- Routes are essential in both Next.js and Remix. When defining routes, you can use tools to define more or less complex routes, including dynamic data loading, data handlers, and parameterized URLs.
- Local storage is a no-go for SSR because it is not available on the server. Using cookies is often a reasonable alternative as long as the data items are relatively small. Using cookies in either framework is fairly easy, but Remix has a significant amount of extra overhead due to the slightly more complicated implementation.
- Remix and Next.js aren't the only libraries available, so do some research for your particular project. You might find some other framework that's tailored perfectly to your use case.

Project: Build an expense tracker with Remix

This chapter covers

- Defining the desired goal for a project
- Figuring out how to use Remix to get to that goal

Congratulations. You've learned all I have to teach you. From here on out, you're ready to dive deeper and expand your knowledge at an impressive pace.

You're probably still early in your React developer career. The state of modern web development is such that you'll experience continual new development, better libraries, new tools, changing paradigms, and general chaos. You have to keep adapting; you can't rest on your laurels.

In these last three chapters, I'm going to give you some tougher challenges, all of which are going to involve a lot of self-study. You need to be good at reading online documentation and finding out how different bits go together. You'll not only be using tools in ways I haven't described in this book; you may use new tools that you haven't even heard about.

That experience is what your career is going to look like from now on. You'll rarely join a new project and instantly be familiar with every tool used in the stack.

You'll almost always have something new to learn (or maybe even something old), so you might as well start getting used to this situation. Over the years, you might use hundreds of frontend libraries across dozens of frameworks, mastering the skill of learning new things quickly so that you can use them in a new setting.

In this first project, we're going to use Remix to create an expense tracker. The first section covers all the details about how the project is going to work and what it's going to look like. Then I'll explain what you will have to do. I've created three challenges in this project:

- *Starting from scratch*—First, if you want a big challenge, you can start from scratch with a minimal application that contains only basic user management. You can log in and sign up, and that's it. You have to build the rest.
- *Taking the backend challenge*—If you're a little less ambitious, or if you feel that you've created more than enough simple React components, you can try the backend challenge. In this challenge, you start with the basic framework of the entire application, and you get all the visual frontend components premade. You "only" have to extend the database and hook up all the forms, data loaders, and action handlers required to convert the application from dummy data to real, database-persisted data.
- *Taking the frontend challenge*—Finally, if you're a bit insecure about the whole backend thing, you can stick with the frontend challenge. You get a backend-only application with all the pages, data managers, loaders, and actions set up for you. But all the pages are missing the visual components that will make them look nice, so you have to create React components to display beautiful forms, visually pleasing UI components, and complex page layouts.

Oh, there's one other thing I haven't mentioned: when you use Remix, you almost always use TypeScript. Therefore, all these challenges have to be completed in TypeScript with all the types and interfaces required. Luckily, you get a lot for free because Prisma autogenerates a lot of relevant types based on the schema and because Remix itself is so well typed. See, there's your first curveball. Let's get to it!

> **NOTE** The source code for the examples in this chapter is available at https://reactlikea.pro/ch12.

12.1 Creating the expense tracker

Figuring out how much you have left to spend on delicious cookies after all your regular expenses have been paid is a struggle for many people. In this project, you'll build a small simple expense tracker, in which you can enter your monthly income and all your regular expenses grouped by category. The application displays several pages before you log in, as you see in figure 12.1.

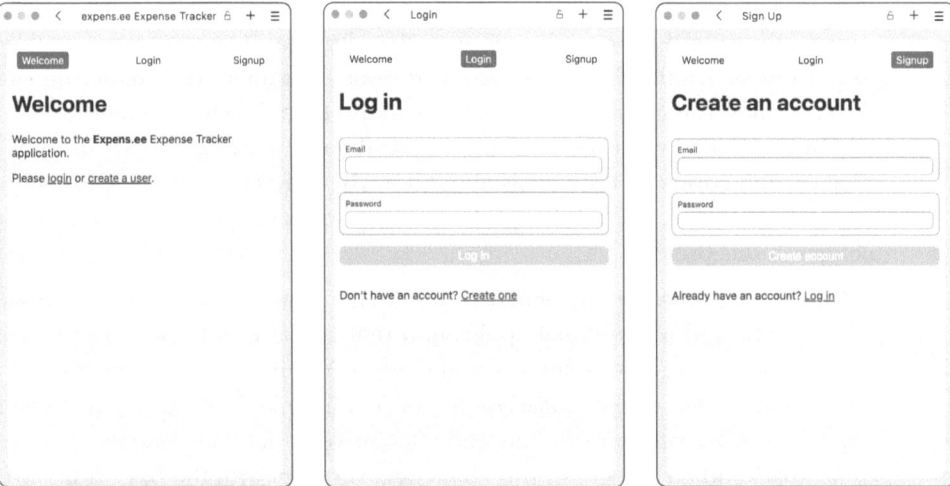

Figure 12.1   **The three pages before you log in are a simple welcome page and the login and signup forms.**

When you're logged in, you see a different set of pages (figure 12.2).

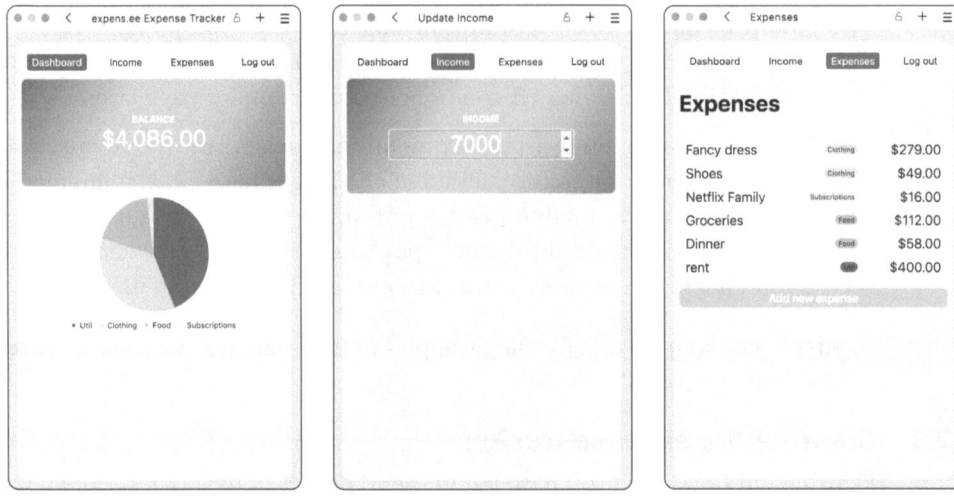

Figure 12.2   **When you're logged in, you can view your dashboard, edit your monthly income, or see the list of expenses, to which you can add new expenses. This figure may not look like much in grayscale on a printed page, but believe me, it looks marvelous in full color!**

The form for adding an expense has two different states, depending on whether you want to add a new category or pick an existing one (figure 12.3).

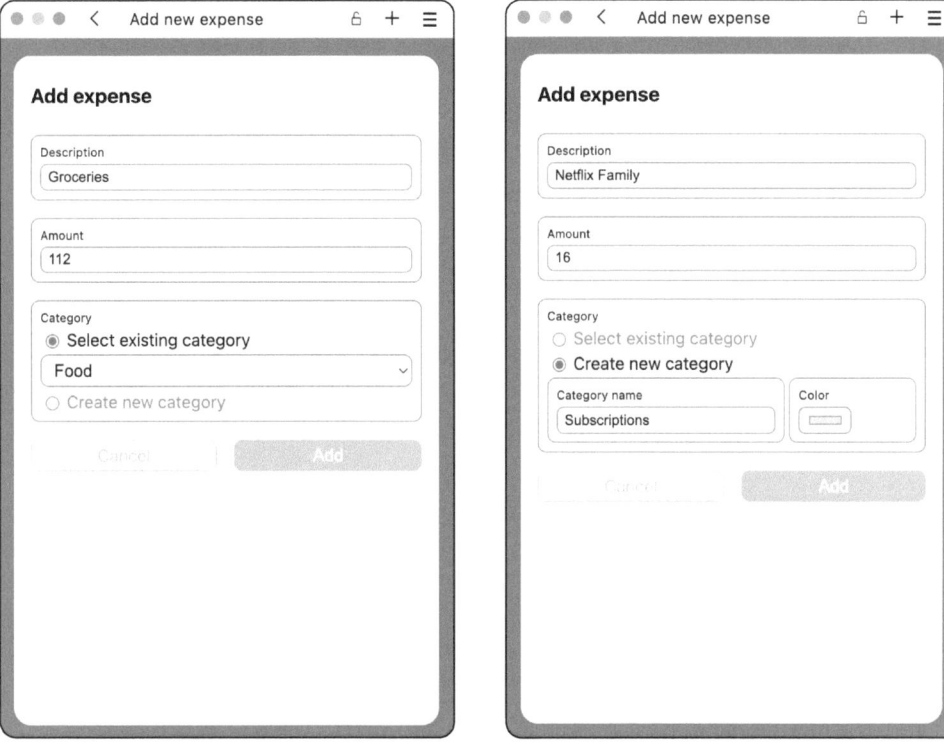

Figure 12.3 **When you're adding a new expense, you can pick an existing category or add a new one with a specific color.**

When you use the application yourself, you may notice that the URL changes as you navigate between pages, which is possible through the built-in routing system in Remix (discussed in chapter 11). Routing is actually central to the way Remix defines an application.

But that's enough talking and presenting screenshots. Why don't you try this application right now? Go to https://www.expens.ee and check it out. At that domain, you can try the exact expense-tracker application that you're going to build in this chapter. I've set up a database, deployed it to a real host, and pointed a domain at it. That's all it takes for a Remix project to go live!

12.1.1 Choosing your own adventure

As I mentioned in the start of this chapter, you get to choose your challenge based on complexity level. There are three levels, with the first being the hardest:

1 Build the entire application from scratch.
2 Start with all the frontend bits premade and build only the backend.
3 Start with all the backend bits premade and build only the frontend.

The rest of this chapter consists of a bunch of hints and a lot of links to show you how to go about completing this project. Please read on to see how to tackle the adventure of your choice.

Whichever challenge you choose, you should follow up by reading section 12.5, which rounds off the chapter and the project in general.

LEVEL 1: BUILD THE WHOLE APPLICATION

If you choose level 1, please open the project located in the `skeleton` folder.

> ### Example: skeleton
>
> This example is in the `skeleton` folder. Note that this example is nonstandard and doesn't use the regular Vite setup, but a custom Remix setup. Before you run this example locally, make sure to run the setup (only once for this example):
>
> ```
> $ npm run setup -w ch12/skeleton
> ```
>
> Then you can run the example by running this command:
>
> ```
> $ npm run dev -w ch12/skeleton
> ```
>
> Alternatively, you can go to this website to browse the code or download the source code as a zip file: https://reactlikea.pro/ch12-skeleton.

This project contains only the user model and the pages related to the user (welcome, login, and signup)—nothing else. The app looks like figure 12.4. You have to take it from there to achieve the full functionality displayed in figures 12.1 through 12.3 earlier in this chapter.

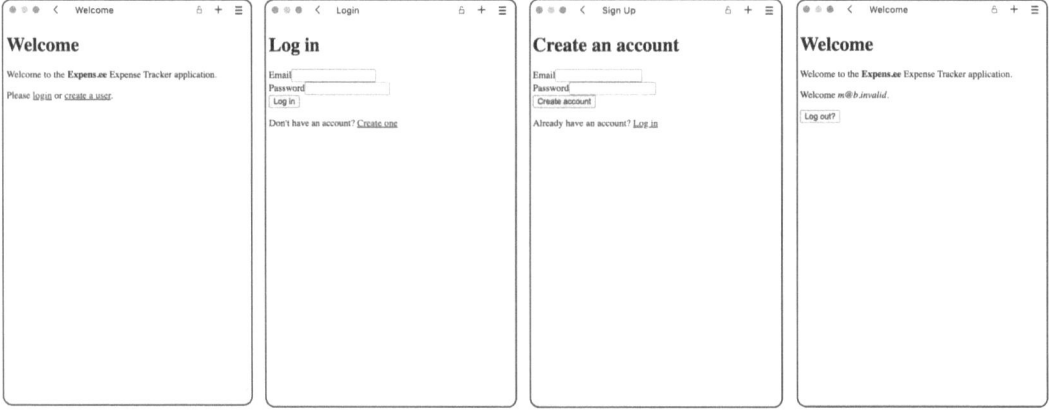

Figure 12.4   In the skeleton project, you have only a welcome screen (which varies a bit depending on whether you're logged in, as you can see in the first and last screens), as well as basic login and signup forms. There are no menus or fancy components, and the whole data layer for expenses and categories is missing.

Then go through sections 12.2, 12.3, and 12.4 in order, slowly building up the required structure, functionality, and the visual UI library to make the application pop and make it pleasant to use.

LEVEL 2: BUILD ONLY THE DATA LAYER

If you choose level 2, please go to the project located in the `frontend-only` folder.

Example: frontend-only

This example is in the `frontend-only` folder. Note that this example is nonstandard and doesn't use the regular Vite setup, but a custom Remix setup. Before you run this example locally, make sure to run the setup (only once for this example):

```
$ npm run setup -w ch12/frontend-only
```

Then you can run the example by running this command:

```
$ npm run dev -w ch12/frontend-only
```

Alternatively, you can go to this website to browse the code or download the source code as a zip file: https://reactlikea.pro/ch12-frontend-only.

As the name indicates, this project includes all the frontend bits required to complete the project. But the data structure and object-relational mapping (ORM) wrappers are missing, as well as all loaders and actions.

This project looks like figure 12.5. It seems to be complete, but all the data is dummy data, and you can't update or change anything.

Then go straight to section 12.3, which contains all the guidance you need to complete the project. You can ignore section 12.4, as it is irrelevant to this challenge.

Figure 12.5   All the pages are there, and all the right UI components are displayed, but the data is static and noninteractive. It's your job to add the data layer to make this application fully functional. You can see that the data isn't real because the information on the various pages doesn't add up.

LEVEL 3: BUILD ONLY THE UI LAYER

Finally, if you choose level 3, please look at the project located in the `backend-only` folder.

> ## Example: backend-only
>
> This example is in the `backend-only` folder. Note that this example is nonstandard and doesn't use the regular Vite setup, but a custom Remix setup. Before you run this example locally, make sure to run the setup (only once for this example):
>
> ```
> $ npm run setup -w ch12/backend-only
> ```
>
> Then you can run the example by running this command:
>
> ```
> $ npm run dev -w ch12/backend-only
> ```
>
> Alternatively, you can go to this website to browse the code or download the source code as a zip file: https://reactlikea.pro/ch12-backend-only.

As the name indicates, this project includes all the bits related to the database and to reading and writing data, but the presentation layer leaves a lot to be desired. In this project, all the pages are there, and all the data is present, but you can't see it too well. The login/signup forms are very basic, as you see in figure 12.6.

Figure 12.6 Albeit fully functional, these forms leave a bit to be desired UI-wise. The menus are there, though, so that's a start.

When you do log in, all the data pages contain only raw JSON data. No lovely data visualization or usable forms are in sight, as you see in figure 12.7.

Figure 12.7   The backend-only project needs some visual UI components to make the application look great and be functional. The last screenshot doesn't even contain a dialog box—only more code. I mean, what is this, the Matrix?

Then go straight to section 12.4 and complete that section to get to the desired result.

SOLUTIONS

Whatever complexity level you choose, feel free to compare your solution with mine in the `complete` folder when you're done. You can also use my solution as a reference if you get stuck.

> **Example: complete**
>
> This example is in the `complete` folder. Note that this example is nonstandard and doesn't use the regular Vite setup, but a custom Remix setup. Before you run this example locally, make sure to run the setup (only once for this example):
>
> ```
> $ npm run setup -w ch12/complete
> ```
>
> Then you can run the example by running this command:
>
> ```
> $ npm run dev -w ch12/complete
> ```
>
> Alternatively, you can go to this website to browse the code or download the source code as a zip file: https://reactlikea.pro/ch12-complete.

12.2   Starting from scratch

If you start from scratch, please open the `ch12/skeleton` example in your editor. Then I recommend that you complete these steps before tackling anything else:

1 Create the basic visual framework for all the pages.

2 Extend the route system.

After completing these two tasks, you will be at the stage where you can add the data layer for the new types (described in section 12.3) and then add the visual layer (as described in section 12.4).

12.2.1 Creating the basic visual framework

As you saw in figure 12.4 earlier in this chapter, the application is completely unstyled and even missing the base styles for the entire application, as well as the menu. Adding these two bits is a good effort at this stage, allowing you to shape the architecture around them.

The root styles are in `app/root.tsx`. Here, you see the main HTML structure for the entire web page, including the application. (Unlike in a Vite application, React also renders the `<html>` and `<body>` elements in Remix!) You can add styles directly in this file or import them from another file, as always. I suggest that you put the styles in a file such as `components/Root.tsx`, but anything is valid.

To add the menu, you can create a component for the menu itself and another for the individual menu items. The menu items should extend the `Link` component from Remix. You probably need to create two different menus, depending on the user's authorization status, but that task should be fairly straightforward. Remember that you need to know which menu item is the current one because it is highlighted differently.

One final bit of advice: when you add the logout button (to the menu for authorized users), you have to make that button a submit button inside a form, not a link. See the current `app/routes/_index.tsx` to see how this form should be defined. You can use the same styles as for the regular menu item; simply render the item as a button rather than a link and then wrap it in a Remix `Form` component with the expected properties.

12.2.2 Extending routes

Next, we need to add all the routes we're going to need to make this application serve our needs. We currently have routes for the front page, login page, signup page, and logout page. But we also need routes for the dashboard page (which is at the same route as the front page!), the income page, the expenses page, and the add-expense page. The extra pages should reside at these URLs, so the file structure should resemble the following:

- *Dashboard page*
  - *URL*: /
  - *File*: `app/routes/_index.tsx`
- *Income page*
  - *URL*: `/income`
  - *File*: `app/routes/income.tsx`

- *Expenses page*
  - *URL*: `/expenses`
  - *File*: `app/routes/expenses.tsx`
- *Add-expense page*
  - *URL*: `/expenses/add`
  - *File*: `app/routes/expenses.add.tsx`

Because the dashboard page has to reside inside the same file as the front page, extend that route to handle the two different scenarios (using the `useOptionalUser` hook) and render the appropriate version of this page.

You can include some dummy content on each page. It would make sense to include the proper menu from the preceding step and make sure that it renders the correct menu item as the current one.

With this work done, we're ready to add the data types and migrations and then add actions and loaders to the routes so we can start reading and manipulating data.

12.3 Adding the backend

To add the backend, you need to complete these steps:

1 Extend the database.
2 Add new server-side wrapper functions for the ORM.
3 Update components to use Prisma-generated types.
4 Update the four new pages to use real database data rather than dummy data.

12.3.1 Extending the database

Next, update the schema with the extra attributes for the user and add the new types. The schema is defined in the file `prisma/schema.prisma`. The user has to be extended with an income property as well as lists of categories and expenses. The two new types are

- Categories that have an autogenerated ID, a name, and a color belong to a user and have a list of expenses.
- Expenses that have an autogenerated ID, an item field, and a value field belong to both a user and a category.

It is customary to add `createdAt` and `updatedAt` fields if for no other purpose than sorting. Please see how these same fields are defined for the user.

Next, you can add some default categories and expenses to the default user created in the seed file in `prisma/seed.ts`.

Finally, add and apply a migration to the database, and make sure to regenerate all types. To do all this, run these two commands:

```
$ npx prisma migrate dev
$ npx prisma generate
```

If you added new fixtures to the seed file, you can reset the database and run the seed by running this command:

```
$ npx prisma migrate reset
```

Note that this command clears the database.

With all that done, you should be ready to import the database and start working with the new types directly. If you're ever in doubt, remember to check the relevant documentation pages:

- *Prisma schema*— https://www.prisma.io/docs/orm/prisma-schema
- *Prisma seed*—https://mng.bz/GZ0N

> **TIP**   It can also be helpful to compare your types with the types from the simple blogging app in the Remix introductory tutorial: https://remix.run/docs/en/main/tutorials/blog.

12.3.2 *Defining ORM wrappers*

It is a general best practice in Remix to add model files in the `app/models/` folder for each type in your system to create higher-level utility functions around your ORM rather than access the ORM directly in your loaders and actions. First, you want to add a new function to the user model in `models/user.server.ts` to allow the updating of the income attribute. Then you want to create new files (probably based on the user model) named `models/category.server.ts` and `models/expense.server.ts` with all the functions required to read and write to these model types. Remember that the interactions are as follows:

- *Category*
  - You need to create a category for a given user with a given name and color.
  - You need to read all categories by a given user.
- *Expense*
  - You need to create an expense for a given user with a given item, value, and category ID.
  - You need to read all expenses and for each expense also read the name and color of its category (required for the expense list).
  - You need to get the sum of expenses grouped by category (required for the pie chart).

Again, refer to the Prisma documentation to see how to achieve the more complex bits:

- *Nested queries (for the category of an expense)*—https://mng.bz/rVwx
- *Aggregations and group by*—https://mng.bz/VxeN

These two files may be tricky to create, and you probably won't create them correctly the first time around. But as you develop the application further, you'll figure out the mistakes and make sure to add all the right arguments and return properties.

12.3.3 Updating components

> **NOTE** This subsection does not apply if you are starting from scratch. If so, simply skip this section and go straight to section 12.3.4.

Update the types for the `Expense` and `PieChart` components to be based on the actual object types generated by Prisma rather than inline unconnected types. Remember that you can import these generated types directly from the Prisma client or from your own model ORM wrappers.

12.3.4 Adding server-side data to routes

The last bit required to make the routes fully data powered is to connect the data and models to the routes. You use loaders to load data and actions to manipulate data. The four pages need the following connections:

- *Dashboard*—On the dashboard page, add a loader for the categories (preferably with expenses summarized in an aggregation), and read income from the user object.
- *Income*—On the income page, add an action to update the income in the user object, and read the income from the same object.
- *Expenses*—On the expenses page, add a loader to read all the expenses with category information.
- *Add-expense*—On the add-expense page, add a loader to read the list of categories, and add an action to create the new expense with an existing category or a new category.

If you're in doubt, here are the relevant pages in the Remix documentation:

- *Loaders*—https://remix.run/docs/en/main/guides/data-loading
- *Actions*—https://remix.run/docs/en/main/guides/data-writes

12.4 Adding the frontend

To add the frontend, you need to complete these steps:

- Create a form component library.
- Create components for the dashboard page.
- Create components for the income page.
- Create components for the expenses list page.
- Create components for the add-expense form page.

12.4.1 Form library

First, let's make the login and signup forms look like they're supposed to. One way is to create a new form component library, perhaps in `app/components/Form.tsx`, where you can create the necessary elements. You can structure and name your components however you like, but the following list is common nomenclature:

- `Form`—The form itself, which probably wraps the `Form` from Remix
- `Group`—A wrapper for an input with a label
- `Label`—The label text that goes above the input (which doesn't have to be a `<label>` element; the `Group` might be the `<label>` element to allow you to skip the `htmlFor` attribute)
- `Input`—The input itself
- `Submit`—The submit button

Using these five components in the right structure should allow you to reuse the components perfectly and create lovely forms on both the login and signup pages.

12.4.2 Dashboard components

The dashboard page needs two components: the balance and a pie chart with a legend. The balance is fairly simple; the most complex part is crafting the lovely gradient behind it. You can go to a website such as CSS Gradient (https//cssgradient.io) to generate a suitable gradient.

The pie chart is a bit more complex. You can render a pie chart manually by crafting a Scalable Vector Graphics (SVG) image, using an existing charting library, or (if you don't mind the chart's being completely static and noninteractive) using a conic gradient. You can find a great codepen for creating pie charts with conic gradients at https://codepen.io/chriscoyier/pen/RPLqMg. The legend is "only" a properly styled ordered list with a small colored bullet for each category.

Make sure to use the proper types for the inputs of these components. The balance component takes a number, and the pie chart component take a list of categories, with the sum of expenses being a property of each category. You can define the types for the pie chart component in TypeScript by combining the type of a `Category` with a `Pick` of the `value` property from the `Expense` type:

```
type CategoryWithValue = Category & Pick<Expense, "value">;
type Props = { items: CategoryWithValue[] };
function PieChart({ items }: Props) {
  ...
```

That example should be enough to get you started. But creating that pie chart is probably going to be tricky!

12.4.3 Income component

The income page needs an income-display component, which is similar to the balance-display component from the dashboard page, but here, the value will be displayed in an input. You probably don't want to include the form itself inside the income component; you can create that on the income page.

Remember that you have two ways to render forms: controlled and uncontrolled. For this component, it makes sense to use an uncontrolled form because we probably don't need to edit the input value from the script if we make it a `type="number"` input. So, passing in a `defaultValue` (and a `name`, of course) may be the easiest way to go.

12.4.4 Expenses component

You need to style two things on the expenses page: a list of expenses and a styled link to the add form. The latter is easier; you can reuse the submit button style from the form library that you created but apply the CSS class name to a Remix `<Link />` component instead of a regular `<button>`.

You can make the expenses list in either of two ways:

- Create a single `ExpenseList` component that takes a list of expenses as an argument. (Remember that for the types, each expense has a category with a title and color.)
- Map the expenses directly on the expenses page to individual `Expense` components.

12.4.5 Add-expense component

On the add-expense page, extend the form element library with the required elements to add the extra input configurations, including radio groups and drop-down menus. Also, make sure the whole page renders with a dialog box on top of the page by positioning it absolutely and adding a semitransparent scrim behind it. (I used a 50% black background to make it stand out.)

12.5   Future work

Congratulations on building your first React + Remix application, regardless of which approach you took. Although the resulting application is decent, incorporating a lot of great features of Remix and showing how you can use the platform, it may not be the most feature-complete application. If you haven't done so already, feel free to compare your solution with mine, located in the `complete` folder.

This section contains ideas for expanding the application to be more useful. I've provided some relevant hints but haven't completed any of the steps, so you're on your own!

12.5.1 Showing error messages

You may have noticed that we return JSON error messages in the actions on various pages—particularly on the login and signup pages but also on the add-expense form. But currently, we don't use those error messages for anything.

It would be helpful to display these error messages so that users know why their request failed. Perhaps their new password is too short, or they forgot to enter the amount for a new expense item.

To add this functionality, use the `useActionData` hook, which allows you to dip into the return values from a (failed) action. The documentation even describes this hook as being ideal for form-validation error messages and includes examples of how to use it; see https://remix.run/docs/en/main/guides/form-validation.

12.5.2   *Editing and deleting objects*

Allowing the user to create expenses is necessary to make the app functional, but you might make an error, and in the current state of the application, you can't do anything about it. You can't edit an expense; you can't even delete it. The same thing goes for categories. So, adding editing/deleting functionality would be useful.

There's nothing mysterious about adding this functionality, but remember that you have to go through the server. The Remix way is to use a form for that purpose, so you can't have a delete link; you must have a submit button inside a form. Hidden fields are a common way to inform the form handler of the user's intent. It is commonplace to use a field like this one inside the form:

```
<Form method="post">
  <input type="hidden" name="intent" value="delete" />
  <input type="hidden" name="expenseId" value={expenseId} />
  <button>Delete expense</button>
</Form>
```

Then, in your action, you can switch on the value of the `intent` parameter and handle the situation appropriately. This way, you can have many actions on the same route, such as update expense, delete expense, and delete category.

12.5.3   *Making the pie chart interactive*

The current pie chart is a graphic that shows the sizes of different slices, but it is static and not all that useful. Using SVG, you can draw a proper pie chart and annotate each slice to show what it represents, and you can allow the user to click a slice for more information.

You can do this job on your own, of course, but it's going to be complex. Using a library would probably be easier. You have many libraries to choose from, so feel free to search the internet for your favorite charting solution.

12.5.4   *Filtering, ordering, and paginating the expense list*

If you have many expenses—say, hundreds—the expense list becomes a bit unwieldy, as it lists all expenses in reverse order of creation (newest first). Adding filtering, sorting, and perhaps even pagination would make it much more useful.

You can easily do all these things by using the ORM. Please check the documentation on Prisma's `findMany` method (https://mng.bz/x2w7 to see how to add `where` clauses for filtering, `orderBy` clauses for sorting, and `take/skip` properties for pagination.

Project:
Create a React UI library

This chapter covers

- Creating UI components from a product brief
- Composing a UI library by using Storybook
- Testing UI components exhaustively

"Hi, and welcome. It's great to see a new face in the office. Before we show you around, let's get right to the task we hired you for. We need a common UI library across all our React projects to make our brand look great and uniform and make it a lot easier to prototype new features across all our products quickly. We've started a library with some tools we'd like you to use, but it's all on you to expand it to all the components we need.

"Our design team has created some visualizations for you, with all the pixels and hex codes you desire, and the product team has written up some specifications for each component so you know exactly what they're supposed to do and how they interface with the world and the user. Let me introduce you to the team. Come along!"

375

With this fictional intro, pretend that you're a new hire at a company. Your job is to extend a budding new UI library using whatever tech stack this company happens to use.

Before we get to the tech stack, let's talk about UI libraries. There are already a ton of them out there, so why would you create your own? Why does every middle-size and larger company always create its own rather than repurpose something that's already available? The scenario in the chapter introduction is more common than you might think. It seems so wasteful to spend resources creating a huge component library from scratch when you can use an existing library. Teams do so anyway for several reasons. The two most important ones are

- *Ownership*—You want to own your stack, especially the most important bits of it. If you need a special variant of a component that's not supported by the external library you're using, you want to be able to fix it yourself, not depend on someone else to add it. Also, if you ever find a bug, you want to be able to fix it quickly without going through a third party.
- *Freedom*—When you build your own thing, you have complete freedom to do what you need. You may need a particular combination of components that no library currently supports, but when you roll your own, you can include what you need—nothing else.

A third, less important reason may be more personal. Not Invented Here syndrome is common mostly among junior developers who don't like to use an existing framework or library; they'd rather build one on their own. As you mature as a developer, however, you quickly realize that building a framework such as React or a library such as date-fns is immensely complex, and these projects have already seen and dealt with edge cases that you haven't even considered relevant.

Similar things happen to designers who want to create a unique style and make it their own. This wish is often at odds with how inflexible existing libraries are, so you end up having to create your own library. Luckily, this scenario is not one of the primary reasons for creating a custom UI library, but it's probably a common minor one, regardless.

That said, your job is to extend the UI library that your new employer created and follow the instructions you're given. In this chapter, I'll give you three challenges of increasing complexity. Your job is to create these components as designed and described, as well as follow the conventions and patterns of the existing stack. Before I get to what we're going to build, I'll show how I built the base library and, more importantly, how I'm testing it (exhaustively!).

With all that work ahead of us, let's hope that this new employer at least has a great Friday bar. I hear that they have karaoke!

NOTE   The source code for the examples in this chapter is available at https://reactlikea.pro/ch13.

13.1 The existing stack

The current stack is built on React. Phew! That's a load off your shoulders already because you already know how to use React. Right? You can check out the stack and the base library by using the following example in one of the usual ways.

Example: base

This example is in the `base` folder. You can use that example by running this command in the source folder:

```
$ npm run dev -w ch13/base
```

Alternatively, you can go to this website to browse the code, see the example in action in your browser, or download the source code as a zip file: https://reactlikea .pro/ch13-base.

Here are all the technologies in the stack other than React itself:

- *Build tool*—esbuild
- *Bundler*—Vite
- *Icon library*—react-icons
- *Test runner*—Vitest
- *Test library*—Testing Library
- *Linter*—ESLint
- *Formatter*—Prettier
- *Visual test tool*—Storybook
- *Coverage reporter*—Istanbul

You should be very familiar with most of the components in this stack at this point. The first line is what every Vite setup is built on behind the scenes. You don't notice that esbuild is doing the work, but it has been working behind the scenes up until this point, so it shouldn't put you off.

The icon library is simply an icon library. It's a collection of collections of icons and easy to use, so I'm not going to cover it much more.

But what are the last two things? What's a *visual test tool*, and what does *coverage* mean in this context? I'll get to those topics in the next two sections.

13.1.1 Storybook: Visual testing

Suppose that you already have a UI library, and you need to use it to implement a new feature. You are given a design that features different types of buttons and different inputs. You know that all these components already exist in your library, but how would you go about finding them? How do you know which setting in which component gives you the result you see in the design?

This scenario is where a visual test tool comes in. Storybook is probably the only tool of its kind, and many teams have adopted it. It is perfect for this kind of UI library visualization.

In short, Storybook is a visual way to browse your codebase. You can see what every component looks like in every possible combination of properties and inputs that you might configure. If you set things up correctly, you can even play with the components live to see how they interact. Also, you see the code behind the given component visualization. For the custom UI library that we're going to work with in this chapter, the output of Storybook is what you see in figure 13.1.

Figure 13.1 Storybook has a menu with all your components (currently, only the button) and the variants for each to the left, with the main canvas and component display on the right. Below the component display are various knobs and controls that you can manipulate to interact with the displayed component. Here, you can change the button label, for example.

Storybook is already set up in the base UI library, and you can run it by running the command

```
$ npm run storybook -w ch13/base
```

Storybook starts running in the terminal and opens a browser window to the URL localhost:6006, which is the default URL. You can configure the port in package.json if you so desire. In fact, I recommend that you run Storybook now so you can see how it works.

Above the main component display in figure 13.1 are buttons that allow you to see the component in various configurations. You can do a lot with Storybook, so I recommend that you test it.

So, how do you add a component to Storybook? Does Storybook pick up the component automatically? Unfortunately, it's not that clever. You create a file named `*.stories.js` (or `.jsx`, `.ts`, or `.tsx`, depending on your setup), and it will be included if it's formatted correctly. For the button, I created `Button.stories.jsx`, which you see in the following listing.

Listing 13.1   Storybook configuration for a button

```
import { Button } from "./Button";
import {
  FaPaperPlane,
  FaUserCircle,
} from "react-icons/fa";
export default {
  title: "Library/Button",
  component: Button,
  argTypes: {
    children: {
      control: "text",
      name: "Button label",
    },
    variant: {
      control: "select",
      options: ["regular", "outline", "ghost"],
      name: "Variant",
    },
    disabled: {
      control: "boolean",
      name: "Is it disabled?",
    },
    isIconFirst: {
      control: "boolean",
      name: "Is the icon first?",
    },
    icon: {
      control: "none",
    },
  },
};
export const Default = {
  args: { children: "Regular button" }
};
export const Outline = {
  args: {
    variant: "outline",
    children: "Fancy",
  },
};
export const Ghost = {
```

We import some icons to test some variations

The default export contains a title that matches the folder structure you see in the Storybook output.

The default metadata export also contains a link to the component itself.

Defines the control knobs that you see below the component in figure 13.1

For each variant of the component we want to display as a separate page in Storybook, we pass in the args required to render that specific variant of the main component.

```
    args: {
      variant: "ghost",
      children: "Ghost-like!",
    },
};
export const Disabled = {
  args: {
    disabled: true,
    children: "I'm disabled",
  },
};
export const WithIcon = {
  args: {
    children: "Send",
    icon: <FaPaperPlane />,
  },
};
export const WithStartIcon = {
  args: {
    children: "Profile",
    isIconFirst: true,
    icon: <FaUserCircle />,
  },
};
```

For each variant of the component we want to display as a separate page in Storybook, we pass in the args required to render that specific variant of the main component.

The best way to understand Storybook is to play with `Button.stories.jsx` and see how the output in Storybook matches the code in the source file. Notice, for example, that the folder structure in the Storybook menu matches the titles and names of the named exports in the code file, and the controls below each component on the canvas match the definitions in `argTypes`.

As you see, I also created a Storybook file for the button-group component, which is a companion component to the button component. This new component stacks multiple buttons horizontally or vertically, as you can see in Storybook if you expand the Button Group folder. If you click the last story in the Button Group folder, you see a grid of various buttons in a single display (figure 13.2).

Such a grid is a great way to communicate easily to other developers (and even designers) that your components can be used in different ways. Storybook provides one extra benefit: you can use the stories and variants that you've already created in Storybook as the setup in your unit tests. Storybook comes with a coupler for most test libraries, including both Vitest and Testing Library, so you can use the various definitions of component variants to run tests.

The following listing shows a snippet of the current `Button.test.jsx`. In this code, I reuse the component variants from Storybook as the basis of the unit tests.

Listing 13.2   Unit test of button based on Storybook (excerpt)

```
import { render } from "@testing-library/react";
import { composeStories } from "@storybook/react";
import userEvent from "@testing-library/user-event";
```

Uses a Storybook utility to set up components for use with Testing Library

```
import "@testing-library/jest-dom";
import { vi } from "vitest";
import * as stories from "./Button.stories";    ◄──── Imports all the variants of the
const {                                                component we want to test
  Default,                                             directly from the story file
  Outline,
  Ghost,                      Converts the story components
  WithIcon,                   to testable components through
  WithStartIcon,              the composeStories utility
  Disabled,
} = composeStories(stories);         Uses the composed components
describe("Button", () => {           like any other component, but
  test("should be clickable", async () => {    we have already configured it
    // ARRANGE                                  with various properties as
    const mockOnClick = vi.fn();                required. We can still add more
    const { getByRole } =                       properties, of course, like this
      render(<Default onClick={mockOnClick} />);  onClick handler here.
    // ACT
    const user = userEvent.setup();
    await user.click(getByRole("button", { name: "Regular button" }));
    // ASSERT
    expect(mockOnClick).toHaveBeenCalledTimes(1);
  });
  ...
});
```

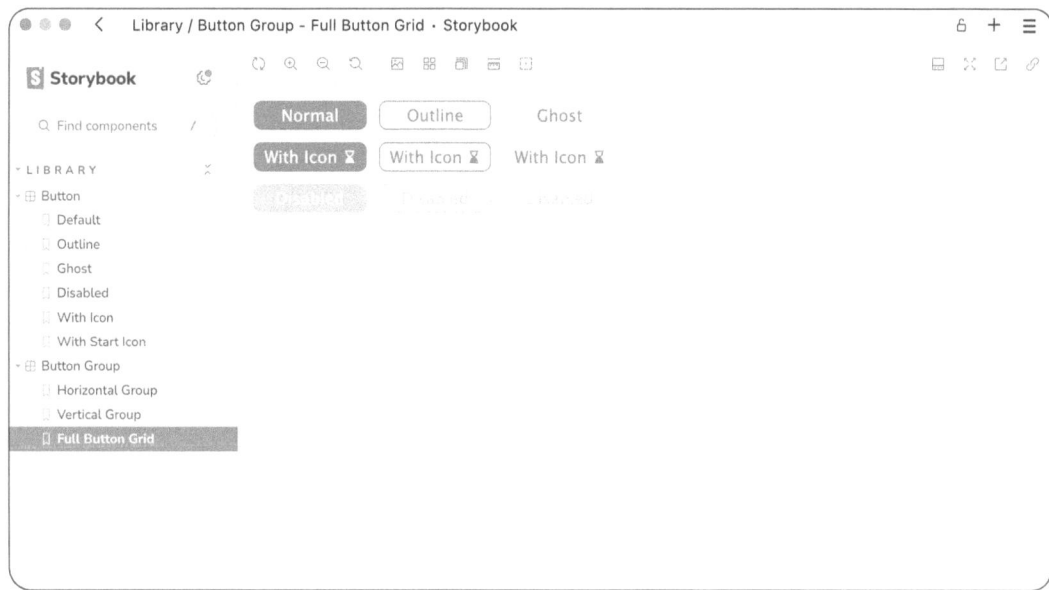

Figure 13.2 A grid of various button combinations for easy overview. I should note that the button's main color is purple, which you can't see in a grayscale print book, but you are free to use any other primary color you see fit. The color is defined in the storybook config file .storybook/preview.jsx.

For this particular button component, there isn't a lot of setup in the story file, so it would be easy to re-create all the variants by using the "raw" button component in the test file. But for more complex components, reusing Storybook definitions can save a lot of time, and it's a nice way of making sure that all the variants you're displaying in Storybook work correctly.

13.1.2 *Istanbul: Code coverage reporting*

The big question about unit tests is how much testing is enough testing. This question has many answers, including this simple one: when every bit of the code has been tested. How can you tell which lines and parts of lines have been covered by a test? The key term here is *code coverage*. A code coverage reporting tool can tell (through the magic of computer science) which bits of code have been executed how many times while the whole test is running. Istanbul is one such tool; it's one of the most popular tools for code coverage in JavaScript and TypeScript. Suppose that we have this function, which returns the display name for a person with some extra optional information:

```
function getName(person, prefix = "") {
  if (person.title) {
    return `${prefix}${person.title} ${person.name}`;
  }
  return `${prefix}${person.name}`;
}
```

We create this test for the function:

```
test("getName returns the name", () => {
  const untitledPerson = { name: "John" };
  expect(getName(untitledPerson, "Sir ")).toBe("Sir John");
});
```

How much of the code have we covered? We haven't tested what happens if the `if` statement is `true` or what happens if the prefix is missing. If we run this test with code coverage enabled, Istanbul highlights those missing bits of code execution (figure 13.3).

At the top of the screenshot in figure 13.3, we see a summary of the report. Istanbul reports that only two out of three statements are executed, only one out of three branches is followed, and only two out of three lines are evaluated. All functions are run, however, so that's a small win. If we change the test to look like this,

```
test("getName returns the name", () => {
 const titledPerson = { title: "Dr.", name: "Jane" };
 expect(getName(titledPerson)).toBe("Dr. Jane");
});
```

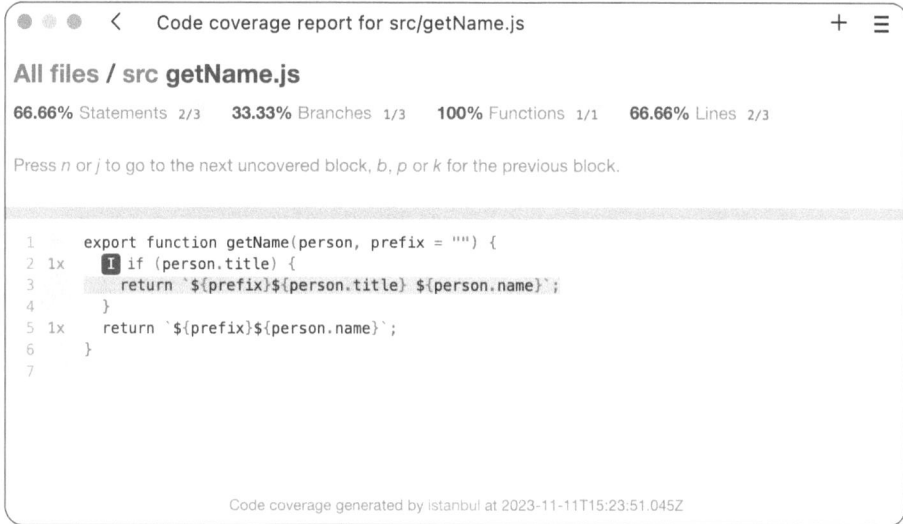

Figure 13.3   The Istanbul coverage report for our `getName` function contains three highlights: the `if` statement is never tested for being `true`, line 3 is never executed, and the prefix default value is never used.

we get a little closer to the goal but not all the way there, as you see in figure 13.4.

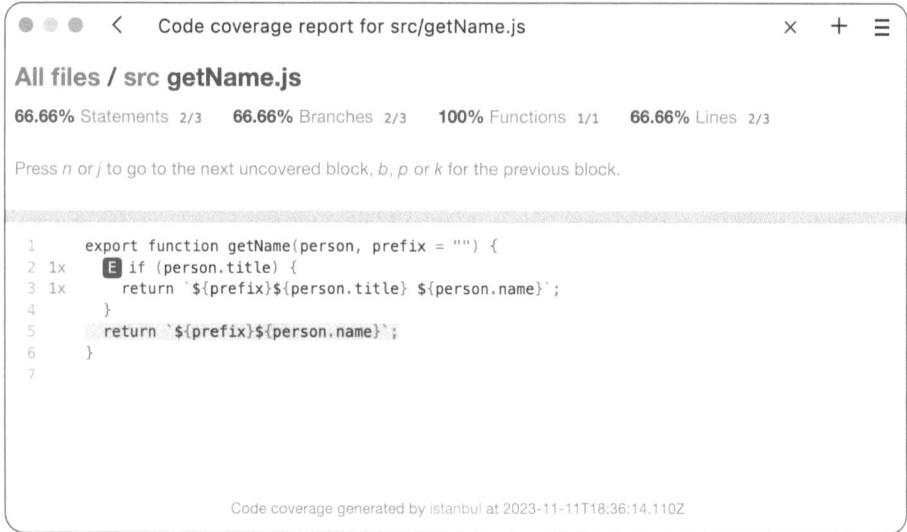

Figure 13.4   Coverage is a little better but still a way off. The `else` branch of the `if` statement is not traversed, and the last return is never executed.

If, however, we run both tests in unison, like so,

```
test("getName returns the name for an untitled prefixed person", () => {
  const untitledPerson = { name: "John" };
  expect(getName(untitledPerson, "Sir ")).toBe("Sir John");
});
test("getName returns the name for a titled unprefixed person", () => {
  const titledPerson = { title: "Dr.", name: "Jane" };
  expect(getName(titledPerson)).toBe("Dr. Jane");
});
```

we have full coverage of this function, with all statements and lines executed and all branches followed (figure 13.5).

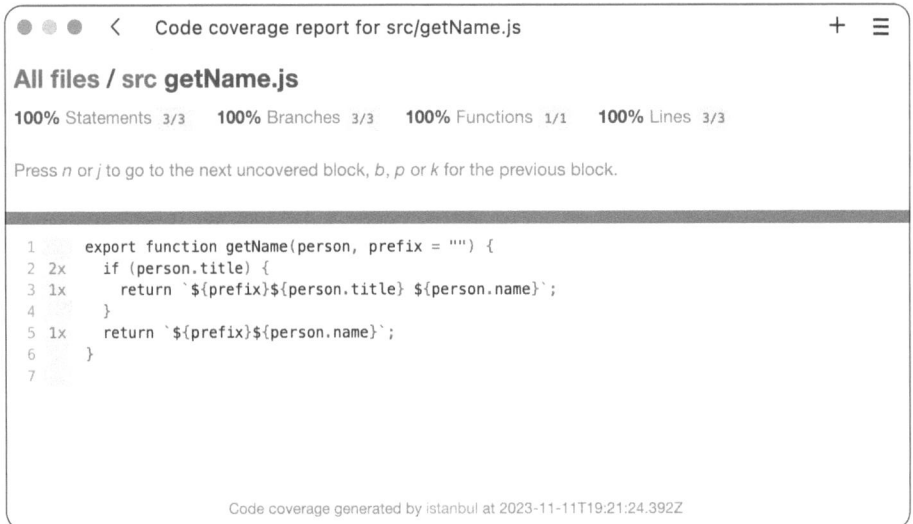

Figure 13.5   We finally have full coverage. We can even see that the line with the `if` statement is executed twice (`2x` in the margin), but each return is executed only once (`1x` in the margin).

How Istanbul works is beyond me. I consider it pure magic. Somehow, Istanbul is able to hook into the compiler, and we can watch what it does in files. We don't need to know how it works. We only have to trust that it works. Where does the coverage report show up, and how is it generated? If it's enabled, Vitest does the work. Vitest supports Istanbul but doesn't bundle it directly, so setup is quick. We can add some configuration options, and we're good to go.

In the base-library example (section 13.1, in the sidebar "Example: base"), I added some configuration options for Vitest in `package.json`, as well as a new script called `test:coverage`. You can run that script in the terminal by running

```
$ npm run test:coverage -w ch13/base
```

If you do, you see the following output:

```
PASS  src/library/button/ButtonGroup.test.jsx
PASS  src/library/button/Button.test.jsx


============================= Coverage summary =============================
Statements   : 100% ( 15/15 )
Branches     : 100% ( 15/15 )        Now the test output
Functions    : 100% ( 4/4 )          also contains a
Lines        : 100% ( 15/15 )        coverage summary.
============================================================================


Test Suites: 2 passed, 2 total
Tests:       8 passed, 8 total
Snapshots:   0 total
Time:        2.173 s
```

You get the coverage summary directly in the output and also generate the full HTML report in a library named `coverage/`, so you can open the file `coverage/index.html` like so:

```
$ open ch13/base/coverage/index.html
```

Then you see the report shown in figure 13.6.

Chasing that magic 100% coverage is often futile, especially if you try to do it for the entire project. But getting 100% coverage on select files, folders, or packages might be worthwhile, especially if they contain generalized functions or utilities used throughout the application or are especially intensive or complex mathwise.

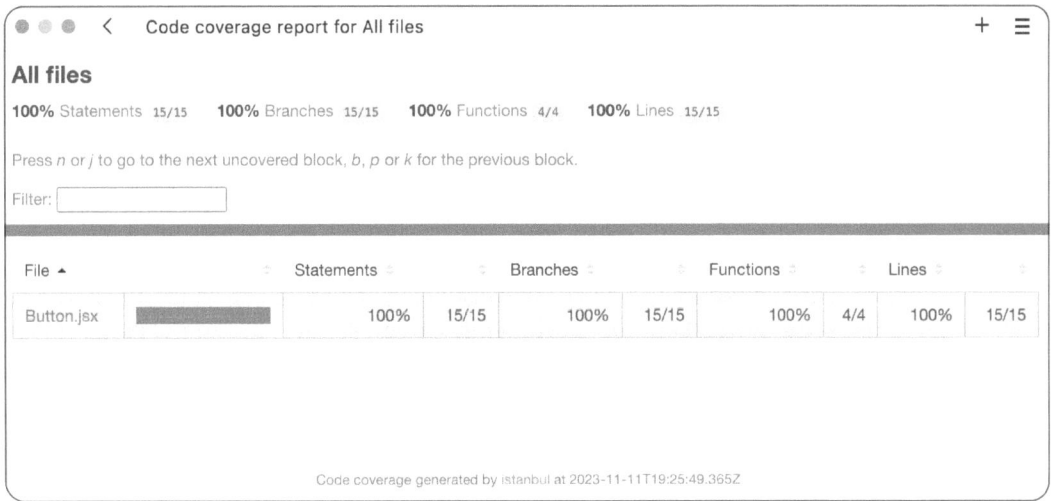

Figure 13.6   The coverage report for the initial base library shows 100% coverage across all components (one, in this case).

I achieved 100% test coverage for the initial button, as you see in figure 13.6. Similarly, I can reveal that in the final solution for all the components we'll build in this chapter, I achieved 100% coverage (figure 13.7).

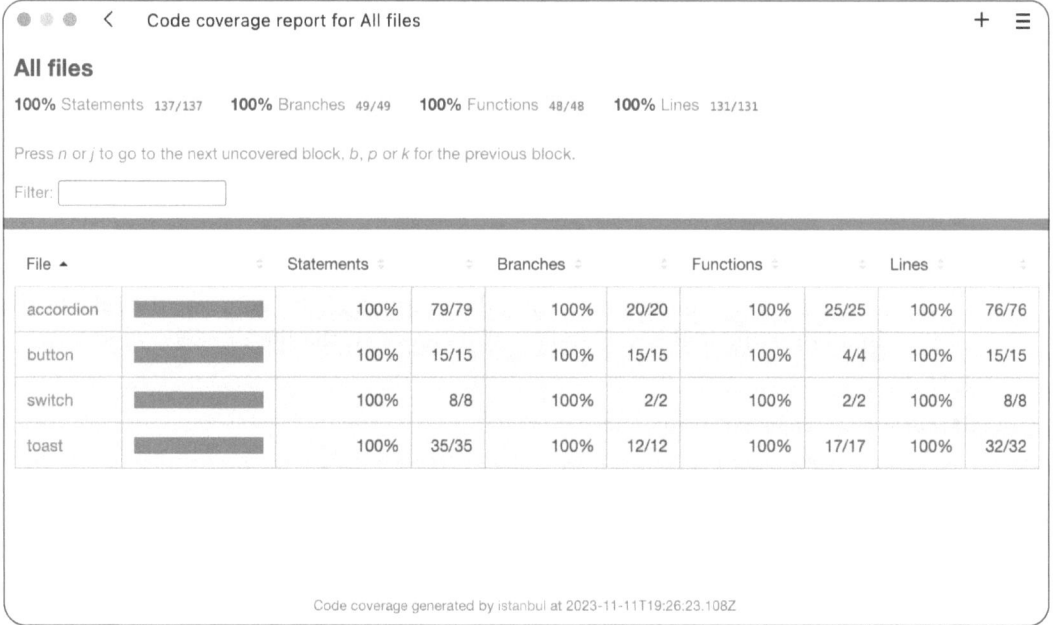

Figure 13.7   In the example with the completed library for reference, I achieved full coverage across all four components. You can see by the pure numbers that the accordion and toast components are a lot more complex than the button and switch.

You are not obliged to chase 100% coverage, but it would be a good idea to keep an eye on the coverage as you test your components. Think about whether it makes sense to cover a particular line or branch.

13.2   *Your new job: Extending the library*

You have three components to complete:

1   First is the switch component, which is easy to set up but requires some fancy CSS to make it pretty. Functionally, it doesn't do a lot, so there isn't that much for you to do, and you should get a quick win. Just setting up the stories and adding the tests will prove to be a good challenge.

2   Next is the accordion component, which is easy to get going, but you have to take a lot of extra concerns into consideration to complete the task. Writing tests for this component is going to be extra tricky because you have to test some fairly complex keyboard-based interactions.

3   Finally, you have a toast component. This component isn't about making break-
fast; it creates floating messages atop the application that can be dismissed or
that go away by themselves. Such messages are used for asynchronous feedback,
such as "Account created successfully" and "The message could not be delivered." Toasts are tricky to implement and involve a bit of React API that I
haven't discussed: *portals*. Portals are a lot more boring than they sound,
though—no interstellar travel or parallel universes. Sorry!

As I set you up for the tasks ahead, I'm going to cover three areas for each component
that will guide you in your solution:

- *Design*—What will the component look like, and what will it look like during
certain interactions? If something can be focused, for example, the design
should include both a hover style and a focus style for that particular element.
(The hover and the focus styles might be the same, though.)
- *List of acceptance criteria*—"Acceptance criteria" (AC) is the formal term for "What
does this thing do?" Stakeholders use AC when evaluating whether a thing does
what they expect it to do. If a button is expected to invoke its callback when it's
clicked except when it's disabled, that expectation is an explicit AC.
- *Relevant standards to follow and/or reference implementations*—For some types of
components, users often already have a well-defined expectation of how the
component is supposed to work. If you have a range slider, people expect to
manipulate the slider thumb by pressing the arrow keys on the keyboard. For
the components built in this chapter, I'll provide links to relevant standards for
how these components are generally supposed to be built. Sometimes I will also
provide relevant reference implementations either by standardizing bodies or
by other UI libraries. I might even add some links to clever ways to implement a
specific snippet or style.

13.2.1 A Switch component

We need a switch component. You may not recognize it by the name, but it's a modern
version of a check box used in mobile UIs. Figure 13.8 shows what such a component
looks like in various mobile operating systems.

iOS   Android

**Figure 13.8   A switch is a popular mobile UI component that's
making its way into nonmobile web interfaces.**

The following sections go over the requirements for the component you're about to
build, starting with the design.

DESIGN GUIDELINE

The switch component needs to look like figure 13.9. You may be reading this chapter in a grayscale paper book; in that case, imagine any color for the active state. In the original here, we use the same purple as in the button component, but in your implementation, you can use any other reasonably dark color.

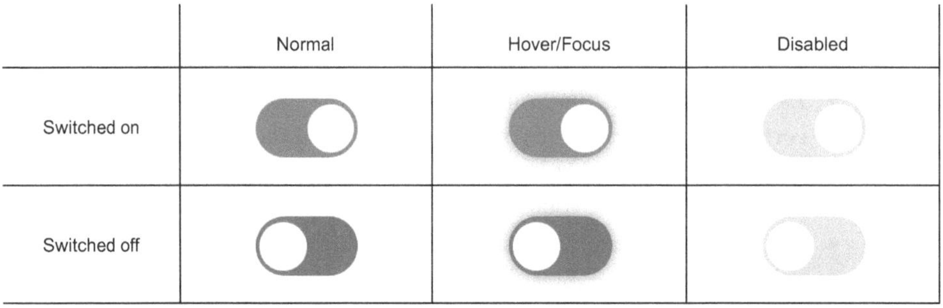

	Normal	Hover/Focus	Disabled
Switched on			
Switched off			

Figure 13.9 The switch component in various states. Note that the hover and focus states are identical and that no hover or focus states apply to the disabled component. Regarding the colors, both hover and normal on states should have a nongray color, and the focus/hover outline should be a shade of the active color.

ACCEPTANCE CRITERIA

The switch is correctly implemented if these criteria are true for your implementation:

- The component should semantically be a check box, as in an `<input type="checkbox" />` element.
- Users should be able to toggle the component by clicking any part of the component itself, clicking the associated label, or focusing the component and pressing the Enter key, the spacebar, or the left- or right-arrow key on the keyboard.

  Most of these interactions are automatically supported if you use a proper semantic check box. But you have to add some interactions (hint: three of the keyboard interactions) manually.
- The component signature must be

```
function Switch({ label, ...props }) {
   ...
}
```

  This signature means that the component must take a label as an argument and that any other properties passed to it will be forwarded to the check box `<input />` element.

- The component must work in your daily browser of choice. Cross-browser support is not required.
- The component should follow best practices for accessible check boxes.

REFERENCE IMPLEMENTATIONS AND BEST PRACTICES

Feel free to look at the following resources for specifications and inspiration:

- *Web Accessibility Initiative-Accessible Rich Internet Applications (WAI-ARIA) standards for a two-state check box*—https://www.w3.org/WAI/ARIA/apg/patterns/checkbox
- *CSS inspiration*—https://mng.bz/AdEe (more comprehensive than necessary)
- *Reference implementations*
  - *MUI*—https://mui.com/material-ui/react-switch
  - *Ant Design*—https://ant.design/components/switch
  - *Chakra UI*—https://chakra-ui.com/docs/components/switch

13.2.2 An accordion component

The second UI element is an accordion component. These components are ubiquitous across the web in many forms. Figure 13.10 shows a few examples.

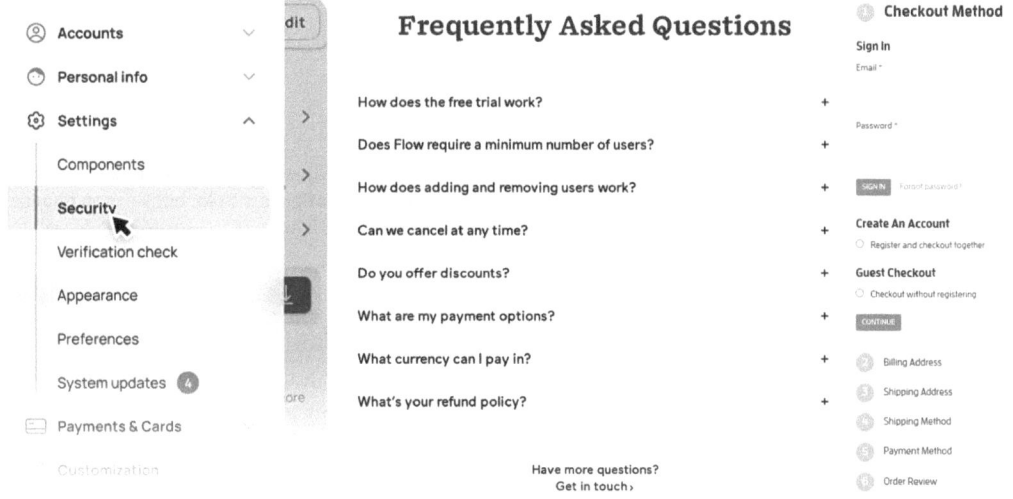

Figure 13.10   Three examples of an accordion component: a menu, an FAQ section, and a checkout flow

DESIGN GUIDELINE

The accordion component can have many appearances, depending on how you want to use it. For our use case, we'll go for a simple, clean component. Figure 13.11 shows various combinations of states, including focus and hover.

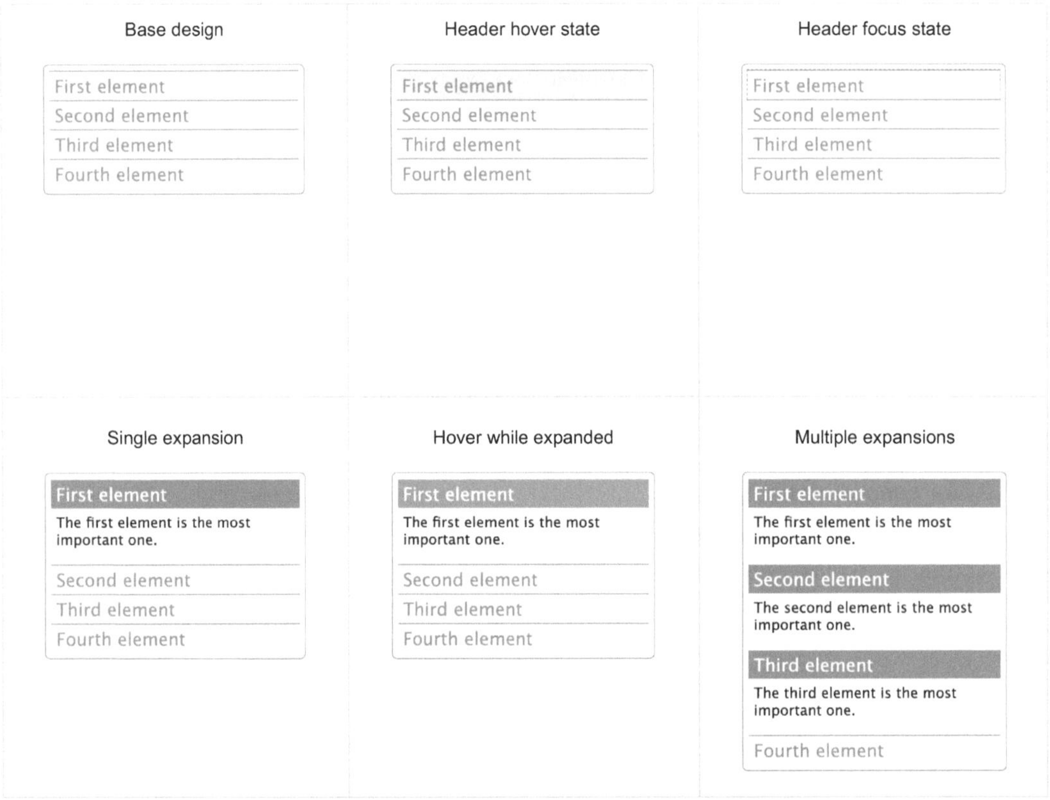

Base design	Header hover state	Header focus state
First element	First element	First element
Second element	Second element	Second element
Third element	Third element	Third element
Fourth element	Fourth element	Fourth element

Single expansion	Hover while expanded	Multiple expansions
First element	**First element**	**First element**
The first element is the most important one.	The first element is the most important one.	The first element is the most important one.
Second element	Second element	**Second element**
Third element	Third element	The second element is the most important one.
Fourth element	Fourth element	**Third element**
		The third element is the most important one.
		Fourth element

Figure 13.11 **The accordion component in various states. It's important to pay attention to all the variants in your implementation. Again, the active color (used for the headline) in my implementation is purple, but you can choose any appropriate color. Refer to the component signature to see the different options.**

ACCEPTANCE CRITERIA

- The accordion is correctly implemented if these criteria are true for your implementation: the component should semantically be a section with an article for each item, each consisting of a button for the header and an article for the item content.

- The component should follow WAI-ARIA guidelines for keyboard interaction. (Note that arrow-key interaction is optional but recommended.)

- The component should follow WAI-ARIA guidelines for `aria-*` properties. In particular, item headers should point to their associated content through `aria-controls`, and item content should point to their headers through `aria-labelledby`.

- The component signature must be

```
<Accordion
  activeIndex={0}
```

The component accepts three arguments. The first argument is the index of the initially active item, which defaults to 0. Set it to –1 to have all the arguments collapsed initially.

Per default, an expanded accordion item cannot be collapsed unless another is expanded. If you want to allow collapsing an item again, set isCollapsed to true.

```
isCollapsible={false}
allowsMultiple={false}
>
<Accordion.Item>
  <Accordion.Header>
    First element
  </Accordion.Header>
  <Accordion.Content>
    The first element is the most important one.
  </Accordion.Content>
</Accordion.Item>
...
</Accordion>
```

If multiple items can be expanded at the same time, set allowsMultiple to true, which automatically allows items to be collapsible.

Each item in the accordion must be wrapped in this component.

The item consists of a header, which is always visible, and content, which is visible only when expanded.

Add multiple items by adding more items inside the accordion component.

- It must be possible for the developer to put any content inside each accordion item.
- The component must work in your daily browser of choice. Cross-browser support is not required.

REFERENCE IMPLEMENTATIONS AND BEST PRACTICES

Feel free to look at the following resources for specifications and inspiration:

- *WAI-ARIA standards for an accordion*—https://www.w3.org/WAI/ARIA/apg/patterns/accordion
- *Reference implementations*
  - *MUI*—https://mui.com/material-ui/react-accordion
  - *Ant Design*—https://ant.design/components/collapse
  - *Semantic UI*—https://react.semantic-ui.com/modules/accordion
  - *Chakra UI*—https://chakra-ui.com/docs/components/accordion/usage

13.2.3 *A toast component*

The third UI element we need is a toast component. This component is known by many names, including notification, snack bar, alert, and message. The component informs a user about something happening in the application with a potentially dismissible notification. Figure 13.12 shows some real-world examples of toast messages.

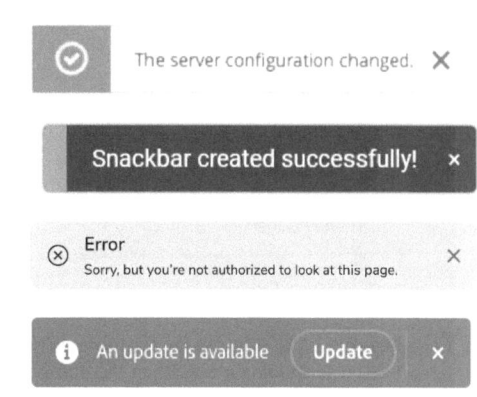

Figure 13.12   Variants of toast messages used on the web. Note that these examples use different combinations of icons, buttons, and headlines.

DESIGN GUIDELINE

We use a simple toast message but with an alternate (inverted) UI option. The dismiss button is configurable (default: off). See figure 13.13 for details.

Figure 13.13   The design for the toasts in our UI with the two variants and their states displayed. The button to dismiss a toast has the same style for both hover and focus, as shown in the bottom rows.

ACCEPTANCE CRITERIA

The toast is correctly implemented if these criteria are true for your implementation.

- To use toast messages in an application, two things must be added:
  - A toast provider wrapping the entire application.
  - Invocation of a `useToast` hook that displays toast messages.
- Toast messages must be displayed globally in the browser window at the bottom-center position, regardless of the position of the toast provider in the document object model (DOM) structure. (Hint: use a React portal.)
- Toast messages are displayed by using either the primary or the alternate (inverted) style, with the latter triggered by setting the `isOutline` property to `true`.
- Toast messages normally don't include a dismiss button but will if the `canDismiss` property is set to `true`.
- Toast messages disappear automatically after 3 seconds (even if they're dismissible) unless the `isPersistent` property is set to `true`. Note that if this property is `true`, the toast message is dismissible automatically, regardless of the `canDismiss` flag.
- The toast provider does not take any properties and is used as a wrapper around the relevant section of the application:

```
<ToastProvider>
  <App />
</ToastProvider>
```

- The `useToast` hook is used as follows with the relevant properties:

```
const addToast = useToast();     The hook returns a function
addToast({                       to display the toast.          The only required parameter
  message: "This is the toast message",    ◁─────────          is the toast message.
  canDismiss: false,
  isPersistent: false,           The other three options toggle the other
  isOutline: false,              variants, which default to false and can
});                              be combined freely except as noted.
```

- Toast messages should follow WAI-ARIA best practices for a polite live region.
- The component must work in your daily browser of choice. Cross-browser support is not required.

REFERENCE IMPLEMENTATIONS AND BEST PRACTICES

Feel free to look at the following resources for specifications and inspiration:

- *WAI-ARIA standards for live regions*—https://mng.bz/0GpE
- *React documentation on portals*—https://react.dev/reference/react-dom/create-Portal
- *A concrete React portal example*—https://mng.bz/KZQg
- *Reference implementations*
  - *MUI (Snackbar)*—https://mui.com/material-ui/react-snackbar

- *Ant Design (Message)*—https://ant.design/components/message
- *Chakra UI (Toast)*—https://chakra-ui.com/docs/components/toast

13.2.4 *My solution*

I made my own implementation of this project. My solution is one possible solution but far from the only one, and it might not even be the best one. You can see my solution in the following example.

> **Example: complete**
>
> This example is in the `complete` folder. You can use that example by running this command in the source folder:
>
> ```
> $ npm run dev -w ch13/complete
> ```
>
> Alternatively, you can go to this website to browse the code, see the example in action in your browser, or download the source code as a zip file: https://reactlikea .pro/ch13-complete.

13.3 *Future work*

This UI library could be expanded in many ways. The most obvious way is to add other component types. More form elements are especially common in UI libraries, such as drop-down menus and input variants. I don't need to tell you what should go in this library; it's yours now, so feel free to expand it as you see fit.

I still need to address another issue with the existing library: accessibility. You may think that we've already looked at the WAI-ARIA recommendations for each of these types of components, followed the best practices, and addressed `aria-*` properties, screen readers, and keyboard accessibility. How much more can there be to do? There are quite a few accessibility concerns that we haven't considered:

- These components only support English and cannot be translated.
- If you could translate them, the components do not necessarily work correctly in right-to-left writing mode (as in Hebrew or Arabic writing).
- These components don't support dark mode because they don't respect the `prefers-color-scheme` browser setting.
- The components don't respect the `prefers-reduced-motion` browser setting, which allows people with vestibular motion disorders to ask pages to avoid unnecessary animations and motion.
- Some Microsoft devices use a high-contrast setting for Surface laptops. Imagine a Kindle reader with an all-black-and-white screen so that it's readable in direct sunlight. Microsoft Surface laptops use similar high contrast in flip mode to be readable in direct sunlight, but this feature only works if the visited websites support it.

- The components do not scale with the browser font size, so people with reduced eyesight (or using a screen further away) are not able to increase their browser font size, which all UI elements should respect.

These and many other concerns are some of the features that the best UI libraries take into consideration (in addition to the features we've already implemented).

Project: Develop a word game in React

This chapter covers

- Solving a complex challenge by breaking it down
- Choosing your own stack

This chapter is the end of the line, the big finale, the grand exam. It has been quite a journey, and we've covered a lot of ground. In this last challenge, you'll be mostly on your own. I will help with some of the meta decisions on tackling the project, but I won't discuss any code. But I have a lot of faith in you. You can do it! Go, team!

> **NOTE** The source code for the example in this chapter is available at https://reactlikea.pro/ch14.

14.1 Building a game

You'll be building a certain five-letter word-guessing game. You've probably heard of it. This game could end up looking like figure 14.1.

396

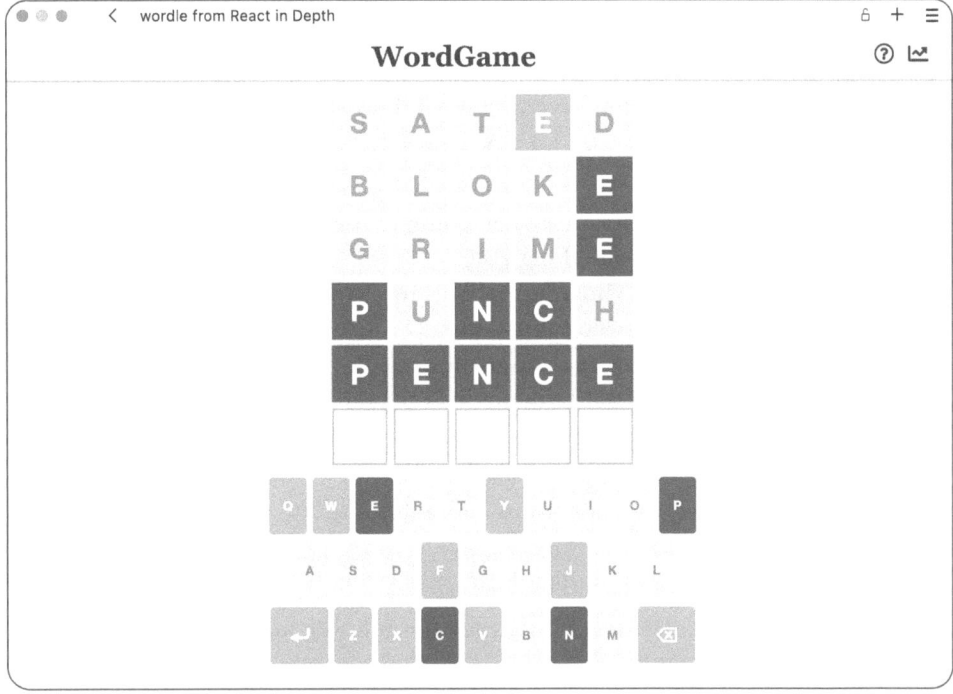

Figure 14.1   My implementation of the word game ended up looking something like this (but only in dark mode, this figure is an approximate conversion to light mode for print purposes). I didn't fare too well in this round and barely managed to get the answer in five words.

14.2   Choose your ambition

Before you start, it's a good idea to choose your ambition level. The application consists of two equally complex parts:

- The game engine, with a keyboard and a grid, allows you to guess a specified word.
- The web application around the game engine picks a daily word, remembers whether you've already played today (and if so, what happened), remembers past results, and provides statistics. It also welcomes new players.

That second part may look innocent or trivial, but the game engine of itself is lacking several things in order to become a good web application, which is what that second part does.

The first part is integral to the word game, but you could skip the second part to make the project a bit easier. The first part is more fun, in my experience, so I recommend that if you feel a bit daunted by this challenge, ignore storage, persistence, and the welcome screen. Make a game component that takes a word and allows you to guess it.

Regardless of whether you implement only the game or the application envelope as well, the challenge is still not set in stone. Many facets of the game and the application are optional, allowing you to fine-tune the challenge based on your ambition level. In the game engine, you have the following things to consider:

- Do you want to support hard mode? Check the original game if you don't know what it does.
- Which word database are you going to use? Do you want to use the same one as the original or something else?
- The grid and keyboard have a distinct style and color scheme. Do you want to copy them or develop your own?
- Do you want to include animations and transitions to make the game look a bit nicer, or do you want to skip them for simplicity?
- Do you want to support light mode only, light and dark mode, or dark mode only?
- Do you want to support color-blind mode with increased contrast?
- Do you want to add translations for various messages to make them more accessible?
- How do you want to handle errors—similarly to the original or differently?

If you're building the second part for the full web application experience, you have the following things to consider:

- You probably have to implement both a welcome/help dialog box and a result dialog box. Do you want to do the same thing as the existing game or something different? You can skip the welcome/help dialog box to make the project easier.
- Do you want to build a menu at the top, and if so, what should go in the menu?
- Do you want to track and display statistics on the results screen or only display the result of a single game?
- How will the game pick a daily word, and how will it make sure that the word is the same for everyone on a given day (if that's important)?

My choice

I chose to implement the following features of the word game:

- One new word per day based on the local time zone
- The same word database but a different word-selection algorithm
- Statistics saved in a similar fashion as the original
- Slightly different welcome and results dialog boxes
- No share button
- Keyboard and grid display similar to the original, including reveal and win animations
- Errors displayed with a wiggle and alert messages in the same style as the original
- No hard mode, no color-blind mode, dark mode only, no translations, and no settings

14.3 *Choose your stack*

After you figure out what you want to build, figure out how you want to build it. If you want to build it as a static website with URL routing and search engine optimization (SEO) performance, you probably want to use Next or Remix. If you want to work fast and not worry much about design, you might pull in an existing design library to make prototyping go faster. Although no design library is capable of facilitating a word game–like onscreen keyboard or word game–like letterwise reveals, you may be able to find smaller libraries that do those things. You need to make choices in the following categories:

- *Base framework*—Which base framework will you build this project on? You can use Vite, which we've done many times in this book, but you're also free to choose a different base, such as Next or Remix.
- *Developer experience (DX)*—Do you want to use tools to assist in the development experience, such as TypeScript, formatters, and linters?
- *Styling*—Do you want to use an existing UI library, a styling library, or plain CSS? Do you want to use transitions and animations? React has some nice libraries for handling those elements.
- *State and flow management*—How do you want to store and manipulate data in your application: with `useState`, with reducers, or with some external library (or combination of libraries)?
- *Testing*—Do you want to write any tests? If so, what type of tests and using which libraries?

My choice

I chose the following stack:

- *Main build tool*—Vite
- *DX*
  - *TypeScript* for improving code clarity and robustness
  - *Prettier* for uniform formatting
  - *ESLint* for maintaining proper React style
- *Styling*
  - *@emotion/styled* for CSS-in-JS. (This library is similar to styled-components, but it's a bit newer and thus a bit faster.)
  - *react-icons/fa* for icons for the menu
  - *Plain CSS* for the transitions and animations
- *State and flow management*
  - *XState* for elegant flow management through the different stages of the various components and overall game
  - *Immer* inside *XState* for simplified state updates
  - *React Context* for distributing global state and providing overlay utility
- *Testing*
  - *Storybook* for visual testing

(continued)
    – React Testing Library for component testing
    – *Vitest* as the main test runner

You are by no means required to use the same tools, but I like the ones in this stack. Feel free to pick your own tools or to copy some or all of what I did.

14.4 My implementation

You can see what I did in the repository.

Example: wordle

This example is in the `wordle` folder. You can use that example by running this command in the source folder:

```
$ npm run dev -w ch14/wordle
```

Alternatively, you can go to this website to browse the code, see the example in action in your browser, or download the source code as a zip file: https://reactlikea .pro/ch14-wordle.

I'll also show you a few previews to get you curious. First, I developed all the base components and hooked them up with Storybook so you can see and explore how everything works. Figure 14.2 shows some screenshots from Storybook.

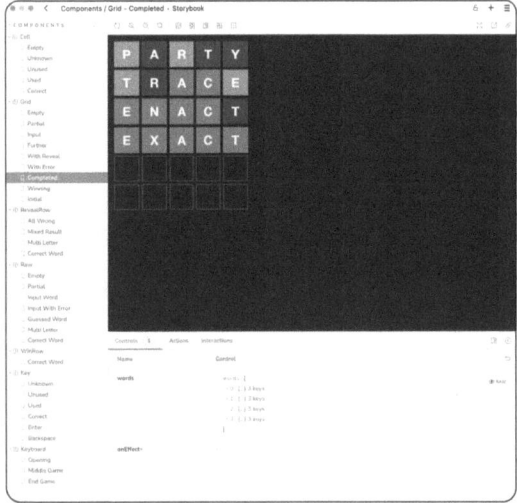
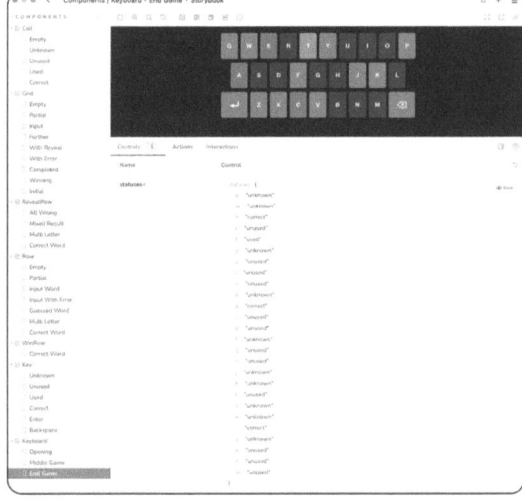

Figure 14.2   On the left is the grid display with rows of various states passed in. On the right is the keyboard with some custom state passed in. Notice all the components and variants on the left menu.

I built the main game logic in XState. Figure 14.3 shows the flow diagram.

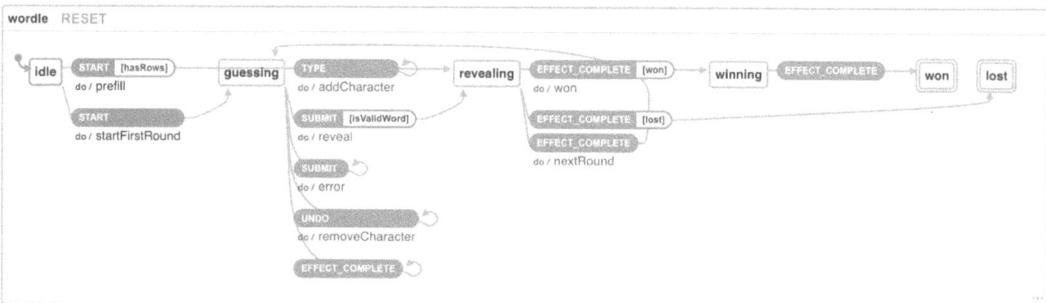

Figure 14.3   The XState flow diagram is surprisingly simple and is this complex only because of the reveal and win animations. Without those animations, it's even simpler. Guards and actions associated with the arrows make the game work as intended.

14.5   *Share your result*

I'm dying to see how you approach this challenge, and I want to see your results! Feel free to share your wins, frustrations, and any other experiences with me in the live-Book forums on Manning.com or on LinkedIn; feel free to @tag me at https://linkedin.com/in/barklund.

index